StatView ®

*The ultimate
integrated data
analysis and
presentation
system*

The proper citation for this software and manual is:
Abacus Concepts, StatView. (Abacus Concepts, Inc., Berkeley, CA, 1992)

This manual is printed on recycled paper.

RECYCLED
PAPER

Abacus Concepts, Inc.
1984 Bonita Avenue
Berkeley, CA 94704
(510) 540-1949
Fax (510) 540-0260

ISBN: 0-944800-03-3

Credits

StatView® was written and developed by:

> Keith A. Haycock, Ph.D.
>
> Jay Roth
>
> Jim Gagnon
>
> William F. Finzer
>
> Charles Soper

The StatView manual was written by Samantha Sager, with assistance from Tony Rocco

Statistical consulting was provided by Phil Spector, Ph.D., Department of Statistics, University of California at Berkeley

The graphics in the manual were designed by Laura Bauer

StatView was tested by Sibley Bacon, Clifford Baron, Ph.D., Joe Fendel, Patrick Lee, Anne Lipp, Carl Smith, and Rachel Scheibe

The StatView project was managed by Daniel S. Feldman. Jr.

Acknowledgements.

This software would not be in your hands without the dedicated efforts of the entire Abacus staff, in particular: Jim Beatty, Dale Bengston, Donna Beretta, Shannon Dailey, Sarah Gandt, Robin Kallman, and Will Scoggin. Their good humor and support create a healthy and enthusiastic atmosphere in which to work. We are grateful to the thousands of you who use our software, and particularly appreciative of your comments, criticism, suggestions and praise. A special note of recognition is due the users who volunteered their time to beta test the software. Their observant comments spurred a final burst of improvements and corrections to the software. Special thanks to Austin Shelton for his generous work on the dataset we did not use, Emily B. Roberson for her technical advice, testing, and assistance in all aspects of program design and manual preparation, Joe Simpson for his help in validating program results, and Al Best for his comments on the analysis chapters. A hearty welcome to Devin Patrick Finzer and Sam Michael Kallman, born in the midst of our labor.

Table of Contents

Table of Contents

Chapter 4   Importing and Exporting Data

Chapter 5   Managing Your Data

Chapter 6   Exploring Subsets of Your Data

Chapter 7   Templates

Chapter 8   Building Analyses

Table of Contents

Chapter 9 Customizing Graphs and Tables

Chapter 10   Drawing and Graphics

Chapter 11   Descriptive Statistics

Table of Contents

Chapter 17   Regression

Chapter 18   Analysis of Variance (ANOVA)

Chapter 19   Contingency Tables

Chapter 20   Nonparametrics

Chapter 23   Troubleshooting

Appendices

1

Overview and Requirements

Welcome to StatView, an advanced statistical analysis program for the entire Macintosh® line of computers.

StatView highlights

StatView is the first software package that offers in a single application all the tools that scientists and researchers need to analyze and present their data. In the past, you first entered data into a spreadsheet program where you performed transformations or mathematical manipulations; the transformed data was then imported into a second application for statistical analysis; a third program was used to create graphs; and finally a drawing program was required to prepare tables and graphs for presentation. Each of these transfers added time to your project, introduced the possibility of error, and forced you to learn separate applications. By allowing you to perform all these tasks inside one application, StatView can significantly decrease the time you spend on data analysis and presentation.

Unlike some integrated software, StatView is not four applications roughly spliced together. There are no modules that you have to move between in order to use the program. StatView is a seamlessly integrated data analysis environment, designed so that all its features are at your fingertips at all times. And StatView's innovative templates offer a graphical way to record the steps you use to analyze and present data so you do not have to repeat steps as you do your work.

The sections below offer an introduction to many of StatView's features.

Spreadsheet-like data management

StatView's data management give you full control over your data. Data is stored in a column/row format, like a spreadsheet. You have many options for customizing the appearance of the dataset: font, size, number of decimal places, etc. The dataset offers a wide variety of data types including real, integer, date/time, string, currencies, and more. And the variable attribute pane allows you to view descriptive statistics for all your variables at any time and change the type and format of any column with a single click of the mouse.

StatView's formula generator contains over 150 functions which can be used to create new variables using simple or complex mathematical, statistical, Boolean, and other expressions. If your original data columns change, formula-generated columns change accordingly. The formula generator also generates numerous series, distributions, and random numbers. You can also easily explore your data by restricting an analyses to any user-defined subset of a dataset using the Criteria feature.

Fully customizable graphs and tables

Graphs offered by the program include interaction bar, line, and point charts, pie charts, univariate and bivariate scattergrams and line charts, frequency distribution histograms, percentile plots, regression plots, box plots and more. You can add error bars to your graphs, using any error type you wish. Simple and polynomial regression lines and equations can be added to scattergrams.

Every component of a graph is individually customizable, including the font and size of axis labels, point type, size, and color, bar or pie slice fills and color, the location and size of tick marks, graph frame style, and axis bounds. The exact dimensions of each graph can be specified to meet the requirements of any journal or report format. StatView also offers ten table formats and allows you to create your own table format as well.

A complete drawing environment

All output appears in our view window which has all the features of a drawing document and can cover as many pages as you wish. You can move drawn objects, text, graphs and tables to anywhere in this document. You can align objects to a grid or use rulers to precisely position your output. You can group objects together and position them in different layers.

The Draw menu offers sophisticated tools for adding embellishments to your output, such as arrows, rectangles, lines, splines, and more. You have complete control over color. Text of any font, size, or style can be added anywhere in the view.

Broad-based statistics

Of course, StatView offers a comprehensive range of statistical analyses. From basic descriptive statistics to ANOVA and factor analysis, to a wide range of nonparametric tests. Each statistic offers you many options for specifying to exact detail the parameters of your analysis. And best of all there are no intimidating commands you have to learn to use a statistic. StatView's expertly designed dialog boxes allow you to quickly and easily choose your statistical tests. This statistical breadth and ease of use has made StatView the most popular statistics package on the Macintosh.

Reduce your data analysis time

StatView contains additional features designed to minimize the time that you spend on the repetitive aspects of data analysis and presentation.

Templates

Templates are similar to batch programs or spreadsheet macros. They store complex series of instructions, which the program executes all at once in response to a single command. Unlike macros or batch programs however, templates are incredibly easy to create using StatView's graphic interface. Templates retain every detail of an analysis, from the null hypothesis to the size of the tick marks on a graph. All these details are reproduced when you use a template to analyze new data.

There are many ways to use templates to streamline your work. A supervisor or statistical consultant may set up a template tailored to a particular task. The work is done only once. After that, anyone can use the template - simply by specifying a new dataset and variables. Templates can also be used to speed the production of reports or journal articles that must meet standard requirements for figure size and appearance, font size and type, etc.

To use a template, you simply select it from the Analyze menu. All your specifications are reproduced with one click of the mouse. In addition, if you do not want to create your own templates, StatView comes with many ready-made templates which generate a wide variety of analyses and graphs.

Action objects

All results, both tables and graphs, generated by StatView are action objects. This means they retain information about the steps that were required to generate them: the analysis and variable specifications. This information can be used to generate subsequent analyses without you having to specify the same information over again. Action objects significantly reduce the amount of time it takes to generate a series of related analyses.

Interactivity

All Abacus Concepts software is completely interactive. Results are dynamically linked to datasets so that any changes to your data are automatically reflected in results. Simply make the change to your dataset, and StatView automatically recalculates your results.This feature makes it easy to perform "what-ifs" on data. It also means that once you have generated your graphs and tables, there is no need to repeat the whole process if you find a data error or want to eliminate a possible outlier.

Hints

Help is available for most facets of the program. If you are running System 7, you can turn on balloon help and get information on each menu item, control, dialog box button and more. If you are running System 6, the same information is available in a floating hints window (which you can also use under System 7). If you are ever unclear about a program operation, you can simply open the hints window or turn on balloon help to discover how the program works.

Extensibility

Finally, StatView has been developed using the latest object-oriented technology allowing Abacus Concepts to deliver new program features to you as modular extensions. Instead of releasing an entirely new version, we can deliver a single extension to the program which, once placed in the Tools folder, will appear in the program. These extensions can be anything from new graphs and statistics to additional data management functions. We would like to here from you about the extensions to StatView that you would like to see.

Compatibility

You can import delimited text files from any Macintosh application (such as Excel) into StatView. Similarly, data from a StatView dataset can be saved as text for use in other applications or transferred to other applications via the Clipboard. StatView can open data files from any other StatView package and write a data file that is compatible with StatView 512+, StatView SE+Graphics and StatView II. StatView can read and write SuperANOVA datasets as well. Data exchanged with MacSpin must be in delimited text format.

Preferences

You can set preferences that govern the behavior of many different parts of StatView, using the Preferences command in the Manage menu. You can set the following preferences:

Application	Graph
Color Palette	Hints
Dataset	Table
Formula	View

Application preferences affect the overall application and are discussed here. The other preferences are discussed in appropriate chapters throughout the manual.

Application preferences determine: whether windows take up the full screen or allow room to display Finder icons (useful when running under MultiFinder in System 6.0.x or under System 7); the font and size of text that appears in the analysis, variable and results browsers; and whether browsers appear automatically or have to be chosen. To change any of these preferences:

- Choose Preferences from the Manage menu. The Choose Preferences dialog box appears.

- Select Application from the scrolling list and click Modify. You see the Application Preferences dialog box:

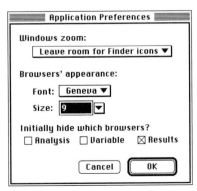

- In the "Windows zoom" pop-up menu, "Leave room for Finder icons" is the default preference. This determines how much of your screen is occupied by StatView windows when you click their zoom boxes. Choose "Occupy full screen" to have the windows zoom to the full size of the monitor. This affects the next window you open.

- From the "Browser's appearance" pop-up menus, choose new font and size settings. 9 point Geneva is the default. You can type in sizes not on the menu. New settings take effect the next time you open StatView.

- Under "Initially hide which browsers?" Results is checked by default. This means the results browser will be hidden and must be deliberately chosen to appear. If you want the analysis and variable browsers to also remain hidden until you open them, click in their respective checkboxes. The analysis browser setting changes for the next view opened; the variable browser setting takes effect the next time you open the application.

- Click OK when you are finished setting preferences. You return to the Choose Preferences dialog box.

- Click Done to execute the new preferences.

System requirements

To use StatView you need a Macintosh with the following:

- a minimum of 2 megabytes of main memory (RAM)
- Macintosh Operating System version 6.0.4 or later
- a hard disk

If you are running MultiFinder or Apple System 7, you may need additional main memory depending on your system settings. StatView is completely compatible with MultiFinder and System 7.

The StatView diskettes contain two versions of the program: one which requires a floating-point math coprocessor (FPU) and one which is designed to run without the FPU. The installation software determines which type of machine you have and installs the correct version for your Macintosh. You may also customize the installation to install a specific version.

If you plan to use StatView on two Macintoshes which require different versions of the StatView software, you can purchase a license to run StatView on both machines. Please contact Abacus Concepts at (510) 540-1949 for more information.

Memory recommendations

By default, StatView sets aside a minimum of 1536K and a maximum of 2048K memory for its use. If you have large datasets, run complex calculations or generate a large number of results, you should consider increasing the amount of memory available to StatView. This will increase the performance of the application. Please see Chapter 23, the section entitled "Running out of memory," for information on increasing the amount of memory available to the application.

Small screen monitors

StatView does not require a large screen display. However, if you are running StatView on a Macintosh that has a built-in 9" screen, we recommend the following:

- Set the Application Preferences so the analysis and variable browsers are initially hidden. This gives you more screen space to work with when performing analyses and customizing results.

- Create and use templates that generate the statistical tables and graphs you use most often. This allows you to keep the analysis and variable browsers hidden until you need them for additional work.

Application Preferences are described earlier in the chapter.

Color

StatView operates on color and non-color systems. Non-color systems include black and white Macintosh computers, as well as color Macintoshes with monitors set to less than sixteen colors or grays. With a monochrome monitor, StatView can display gray scales. If you do not have color on your Macintosh, you can still print the eight QuickDraw colors (black, red, green, yellow, blue, magenta, cyan and white) on a color output device.

With a color monitor, you can use the Macintosh's color capabilities to their fullest. StatView takes advantage of whatever color capabilities your system has. If your monitor can display 16 colors, the color palette displays 16 colors; if it displays 256 or more colors, the color palette displays 64 colors. StatView can recognize and display any of the sixteen million colors in each palette slot.

Printers

StatView prints from any printer, color plotter or slide maker that is compatible with the Macintosh and exploits the full capabilities of the ImageWriter, ImageWriter II, ImageWriter LQ, StyleWriter and entire LaserWriter family. Print quality depends on the type of printer and driver software. Tables, text and graphs are constructed in a resolution-independent manner, so printouts are generated to the full resolution of your printer.

You can obtain color hard copy of your StatView output on an ImageWriter II or ImageWriter LQ with a color ribbon or on any Macintosh-compatible color printers, plotters and slide-making hardware.

Installing StatView

Before installing, make a back-up of the disks and place the originals in a safe place. Write-protect the StatView disks by exposing the hole in the upper right corner of each disk.

The Installer program copies the StatView application and related files to your hard disk. The files will be placed in a folder titled "StatView 4.0 (FPU)" or "StatView 4.0 (Non-FPU)" depending on which version of StatView is installed. The installer provides two options — Easy Install and Customize. With the Easy Install option the installer software determines which model of the Macintosh you are using and installs the correct version of StatView for your model. With the Customize option you can choose which version of StatView you wish to install. You should use the Easy Install option unless you have a specific reason for installing a different version.

To install StatView:

- Put "Disk 1-Installer" into the internal floppy disk drive of your computer.

- Double-click on the Installer icon.

- Click OK after you have read the welcome screen. The Install dialog box appears.

- If necessary, click the Switch Drive button to select the drive on which you want to put the application and files.

- You have two installation options now:

    Click Install to automatically install the version appropriate for your Macintosh.

    Click Customize to choose which version to install, regardless of the type of Macintosh you have. (You can select both versions by holding down the Shift key.)

- Once you click Install, the Installer begins to install StatView on your hard disk.

- When "Disk 1-Installer" is ejected, the Installer will prompt you to insert a different disk. Follow these instructions, inserting each disk as requested by the Installer. You may not need to use all of the disks shipped with the program, unless you install both the FPU and non-FPU versions simultaneously.

A decompression process is the second phase of installation. A dialog box advises you of progress.

• When you see a message that the installation was successful, click Quit.

• Eject "Disk 1-Installer".

You will find a folder titled either "StatView 4.0 (FPU)" or "StatView 4.0 (Non-FPU)" on your hard disk. This folder contains:

Document/Folder name	Description
StatView 4.0	The StatView program
StatView Tools	A folder that holds the analyses available in StatView.
StatView Templates	A folder that contains the templates shipped with StatView and into which you can place templates you create
Additional Templates	A folder containing additional sample templates
Sample Data	A folder containing the sample datasets used in this manual.
StatView Library	A document that contains reference information that StatView uses.
TeachText	An application that allows you to read the release notes document.
Release notes	A TeachText document that contains information about StatView that is not included in the manual.

You can move this folder to other hard disks if you wish. You are now ready to run StatView.

Use of the manual

This manual explains and illustrates everything you need to know to use StatView effectively. It assumes that you have a basic familiarity with the use of the Apple Macintosh® computer. You should know how to open, close and save files; choose commands from menus; use dialog boxes; navigate folder hierarchies; click and drag the mouse; and so forth. For instructions on Macintosh basics, please read the *Macintosh Reference* that came with your computer.

Although this manual is not intended as a textbook on statistics, it does include in-depth discussions of important statistical concepts, some of which vary in their interpretation and usage. Chapters 11 through 22 discuss the analyses StatView is capable of performing. Examples demonstrate how these analyses are applied to real-world data.

Icons as guides

The icons below are used in this manual to mark important information, point you to related information elsewhere, cross-reference information, and guide you to the exercises presented in each chapter.

 Gem of wisdom, helpful hint or tidbit

 Tutorial using sample data provided with StatView

 Important information, sometimes a caution or a warning

 Cross-reference pointer to related information

Chapters 11 through 22 describe all the analyses StatView performs. The following icons appear in those chapters to indicate the graphic output of each analysis:

 Pie chart   Scattergram

 Line chart   Bar chart

 Box plot   Table

Where to find information

This manual is organized to provide information on specific tasks in separate chapters. The sequence of chapters follows the flow of the analysis process: data entry, data management, statistical analysis, and customizing results. Eleven chapters are devoted to the theory and application of each analysis. Exercises are included throughout the manual to illustrate each tool, concept and process. The table below can guide you to the chapter containing the information you need. You may also want to look at a similar table at the end of the following chapter, and make use of the Table of Contents and Index to find topics of interest.

1 Overview and Requirements — A brief survey of StatView's features and abilities, including installation instructions, and application preferences

2 Quick Start Tutorial — A hands-on introduction to the concepts of the program, in a series of five tutorials that teach you how to use StatView

3 Datasets — Explanation of each part of a dataset, how to enter, arrange and edit your data

4 Importing and Exporting Data — How to get data into StatView from another application, and transfer it out again

5 Managing Your Data — Techniques to transform existing data and create new columns of series or random numbers

6 Exploring Subsets of Your Data — Several methods for limiting analyses to portions of your data

7 Templates — How to use the ready-made templates shipped on your StatView disk to perform analyses

8 Building Analyses — How to create analyses from scratch, using the analysis and variable browsers in the view, along with an explanation of the parts of a view, and instructions for creating your own templates

9 Customizing Graphs and Tables — Formatting tools and techniques to alter the structure and appearance of graphs and tables

10 Drawing and Graphics — Use of the drawing tools, how to add color, patterns, shapes and text to your results

11 Descriptive Statistics
12 Frequency Distribution
13 One Sample Analyses
14 Paired Comparisons
15 Unpaired Comparisons
16 Correlation and Covariance
17 Regression
18 Analysis of Variance (ANOVA)
19 Contingency Tables
20 Nonparametrics
21 Factor Analysis
22 Plots

Each analysis chapter explains the theory and application of the analysis. In addition, each chapter also explains how to generate each analysis, including what variable browser buttons to use, the class of variables to assign, how the dialog box works, and the tables and graphs that the analysis produces. There are exercises in each chapter to illustrate the process of creating each analysis.

23 Troubleshooting	Tips on solving some common problems, an explanation of the on-line help system, and how to contact Abacus Concepts for technical support
Appendix A, B, and C	Lists of mouse and keyboard shortcuts, formulae and algorithms used in calculation, functions found in StatView, and references
Glossary	Definitions of terms that are not described elsewhere in the manual

SuperANOVA and MacSpin from Abacus Concepts

Abacus Concepts develops and publishes award-winning data analysis software exclusively for the Macintosh. In addition to the StatView® line, we also offer SuperANOVA™ and MacSpin™.

SuperANOVA — Full-featured general linear modeling

"SuperANOVA demonstrates that power nearly equivalent to that of SAS Proc GLM can be had with far less effort on the part of the user."— *American Statistician*, November 1991

Winner of the 1989 *MacUser* Editors' Choice Award for Best New Data Analysis Program, SuperANOVA analyzes virtually any general linear model, including ANOVA, ANCOVA, MANOVA, MANCOVA, repeated measures, and more. With SuperANOVA you can create, modify and save model designs, as well as annotate them with a complete set of presentation drawing tools. Once created, these models may be saved and applied to any data.

SuperANOVA handles balanced, unbalanced, and missing cell designs, and solves repeated measures using univariate or multivariate models. Additional analyses include a dozen post-hoc tests, contrasts, interaction plots, residual plots, and means tables.

MacSpin — Three-dimensional exploratory data analysis and visualization

"MacSpin is still the best and most complete Mac program for 3D visualization of data."
    — *Macworld*, March 1992

Winner of the 1988 *MacUser* Editors' Choice Award for Best Scientific/Engineering Product, MacSpin helps you understand your data by allowing you to visualize it.

Choose X, Y, and Z variables and instantly see a 3D scattergram. Rotate this scattergram in any direction with any of several rotation tools. Rotating data can reveal trends and patterns which may not come to light using traditional 2D analysis techniques. In giving you a qualitative feel for your data, MacSpin helps you determine what further analyses are appropriate.

In addition to 3D plots, MacSpin also displays two-dimensional plots: scattergrams, line charts, bar charts, histograms, and pie charts. All charts and data are linked — clicking on a single point or a group of points in one plot highlights the same points in all other visible 2D and 3D plots, as well as in the data window.

MacSpin has many more great features. Click on a point and instantly see its label. Or connect a series of points with lines. MacSpin also lets you customize plots with a full set of presentation drawing tools.

Call for more information

As a registered StatView user, you may qualify for discounts on SuperANOVA and MacSpin. Please call Abacus Concepts 510-540-1949. Ask us about our student version of StatView — StatView Student — as well.

2

Quick Start Tutorial

The five exercises in this tutorial provide an introduction to the tools and concepts of StatView. It is a worthwhile investment of your time to go through these exercises to learn how StatView can help you analyze your data and present your results. Once you are familiar with the range of capabilities available with this program, the detailed sections later in the manual can serve as a guide for putting StatView's power to your own use. The exercises are as follows:

1. Use a ready-made template and save results

2. Create a dataset and analysis from scratch and save your work as a template

3. Work with the template you created and customize graphs

4. Customize your results for presentation and publication

5. Manipulate your data using formula and criteria

Overview

StatView is an integrated data analysis system, combining powerful graphing, drawing, spreadsheet-like data management tools and comprehensive statistical capabilities, all in a single application. All this functionality is accessible through StatView's innovative, fast and easy-to-use analysis process.

Data management

StatView holds its data in a dataset, a spreadsheet format in which columns represent variables (such as gender, weight, height) and rows represent cases (such as patients in a medical study or plots in a field study). You can enter data by hand, or easily import it as a text file from another application. The Formula generator allows you to create variables using simple or complex arithmetic functions and generate various series or distributions. The dataset includes an attribute pane, in which descriptive statistics for each variable can be accessed by a click of the mouse. You will also find it easy to look at subsets of your data using criteria or splitting by different grouping variables.

View window

After entering or importing data, you are ready to perform analyses. All the results of your analyses are placed in a view. A single view can display tables and graphs from an unlimited number of analyses. A view can also simultaneously display results from different datasets. You can even combine variables from different datasets in a single analysis. You can save a view, with all its contents, and reopen it later for review or modification. The figure below shows the important features of a view.

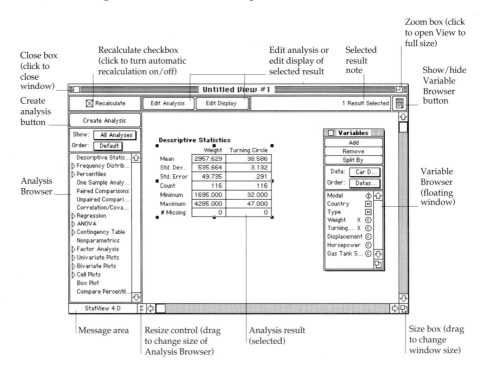

Analysis process

There are two ways to generate graphical and statistical analyses in StatView: choose a template (shipped with the program or created by you) using the Analyze menu, or create an analysis from scratch using the analysis browser and the variable browser.

Templates

Templates are similar to batch programs or spreadsheet macros in that they record your actions and store them as a series of instructions, which the program executes all at once in response to a single command. You can customize a template to include frequently-used analyses along with extensive format specifications for graphs and tables. Templates are easy to create using StatView's innovative graphic interface, but you may also use StatView's ready-made templates to perform analyses without learning any other features of the program. In order to take full advantage of StatView's potential, however, we recommend that you learn to create your own templates.

Analysis and variable browsers

The analysis and variable browsers are the tools you use to create analyses from scratch and to create templates. The analysis browser lists all analyses, both statistical and graphical, so you can create any analysis with two clicks of the mouse. Most analyses present a dialog box in which you set the parameters of the analysis (specify the null hypothesis, significance levels, etc.).

The variable browser allows you to assign variables to your analyses. This browser lists all the variables in any open datasets; you can use it to open additional datasets as well. Variables are assigned, just as analyses are created, with two clicks of the mouse. The variable browser also offers several options for the order in which variables appear in the browser and displays information about how variables are used in analyses. These features will help you to use StatView effortlessly and efficiently.

Action objects

Another important StatView concept is "action objects." All results generated by StatView are action objects, they retain information about the analysis parameters and variable specifications that were required to generate them. This information can be used to generate subsequent analyses without repeating those steps. Action objects can significantly reduce the amount of time it takes to generate a series of related analyses.

Graphing and drawing

Once you have created results you can customize and embellish them for presentation or publication. A wide spectrum of plots is available to support your conclusions graphically. StatView also contains powerful formatting tools that give you extensive control over the style, position, size, pattern and color of every object in the view and of every component of graphs and tables. The view is a complete drawing environment. The tools in the Draw menu can be used to add drawn objects such as arrows and circles to emphasize important points in your results. You can also add text anywhere in the view.

The following exercises provide an introduction to all these features of StatView. Detailed information for all program features and each analysis can be found in other chapters of the manual.

Exercise 1: Use a template and save results

StatView is designed to be easy and quick to use. Templates are central to this goal. Templates can be created to perform any combination of statistical or graphical analyses you wish, and they can contain detailed format specifications for the position, font, size, and other characteristics of the results. You do not have to make your own templates to use in StatView. There are many ready-made templates that generate a wide variety of analyses and graphs. Before you learn to create your own templates, you will first learn to use these ready-made templates to analyze data.

 Note that only a selection of the ready-made templates is initially installed in the Analyze menu. The remaining templates are in the StatView templates folder, which can be reached by choosing Templates from the Analyze menu. You can customize this menu yourself, as explained below.

In this first exercise, you use a ready-made template to generate descriptive statistics and save your results. You will analyze four variables from the sample dataset Car Data. The dataset has information about weight, gas tank size, turning circle, horsepower and engine displacement for 116 cars from different countries. You will generate descriptive statistics that will allow you to make comparisons among the cars from different countries.

• Open Car Data in the Sample Data folder. The dataset appears on the screen.

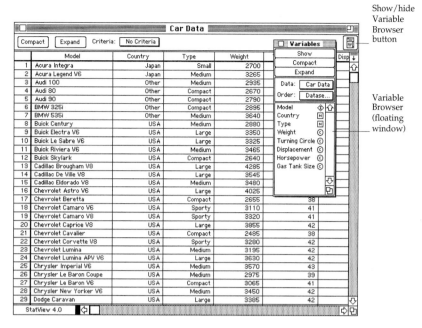

Show/hide
Variable
Browser
button

Variable
Browser
(floating
window)

- Notice the smaller window floating above the dataset. It is the variable browser, a floating window that shows a list of all variables in the dataset. When you select a variable from the variable browser and double-click on it (or click the Show button), that variable is selected in the dataset, which automatically scrolls so the variable's column is visible in the window.

- Click the show/hide variable browser button in the upper right corner of the dataset. The variable browser is now hidden, and you can see more of the dataset. This button allows you to easily show or hide the variable browser at any time.

- Choose New View from the Analyze menu. An empty view appears on the screen.

19

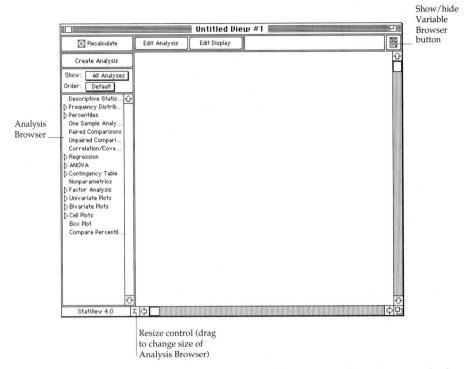

Show/hide Variable Browser button

Analysis Browser

Resize control (drag
to change size of
Analysis Browser)

The analysis browser at the left of the view lists the statistical analyses and plots available in StatView. (Notice that the view also has a show/hide variable browser button in the upper right corner.) Since you will use a template to generate the analysis in this exercise, you will not use the analysis browser.

- Close the analysis browser by double-clicking on the Σ symbol. This maximizes the amount of space in which you can view your results.

Hide analysis and variable browsers

If you are operating StatView on a Macintosh with a small screen (Plus, SE, Classic, SE/30), you may want to use the program with the analysis and variable browsers initially hidden.This will give you more space in which to work. You can set the Application preferences by choosing Preferences from the Manage menu to show or hide these browsers on program startup.

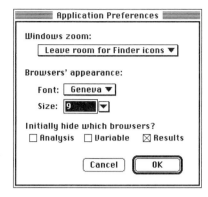

The default, as you have just seen, is to show both browsers. If you choose to hide them, the variable browser will remain hidden until you choose to show it by clicking the show/hide variable browser button. The analysis browser will remain closed until you drag on the resize symbol ⊞ to show it.

Use a template

- From the Analyze menu, choose Descriptive Statistics.

  If Descriptive Statistics does not appear in the menu, choose Templates instead. In the resulting dialog box, you can add any template to the Analyze menu by clicking in the check box to the right of the template's name and clicking Change Menu. You can use the Descriptive Statistics template directly from this dialog box by selecting it and clicking Use Template.

- After you select a template, the Assign Variables dialog box appears.

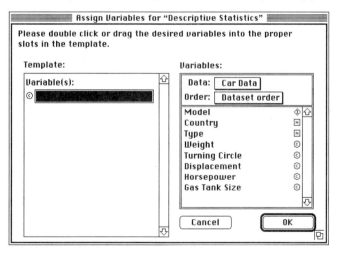

- Click on the variable Horsepower in the list on the right. Drag to the "Variable(s)" slot on the left until the gray rectangle outline of the Horsepower variable appears in the slot.

Variable(s):

Release the mouse. The horsepower variable is placed in the template slot.

- Double-click on the variable Weight. It is also added to the slot, directly below Horsepower. Notice that the slot grows to contain multiple variables.

Variable(s):

- Click the OK button and the results of the template appear in the view:

Descriptive Statistics

	Horsepower	Weight
Mean	130.198	2957.629
Std. Dev.	39.822	535.664
Std. Error	3.697	49.735
Count	116	116
Minimum	55.000	1695.000
Maximum	278.000	4285.000
# Missing	0	0

You have just created your first analysis using StatView. Notice how little time it took and how easy it is to use a template to generate results.

Saving results

You can save your work at any time by saving the view. Remember that when you save a view in StatView, you are not simply saving the text or pictures of the output — you are saving all aspects of the work you have done. When you reopen the document, your work is as you left it, ready for you to pick up where you left off.

- Choose Save from the File menu. The directory dialog box appears.

- Name the view "Car Analysis" in the text box. Place the file in the Sample Data folder, and click Save.

- Close "Car Analysis" by choosing Close from the File menu.

- To re-open your work, choose Open from the File menu.

- Locate the file "Car Analysis" and click Open. This dialog box appears:

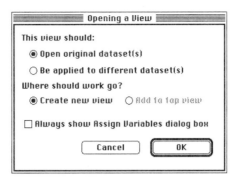

The most common use of this dialog box is to leave the default settings and click OK. The default settings tell StatView to use the original variables, from the original dataset(s) and place the output in a new view. Using these defaults will open a view with everything as you left it when the view was saved.

- Click OK.

The view reappears exactly as you left it. In fact, the program did not even have to recalculate your results. By default, all results are saved with a view. If your data has not changed, you can re-open a view and get back to your analysis immediately. For detailed information on using templates, saving your work, and re-opening views, see Chapter 7, Templates, and Chapter 8, Building Analyses.

Before continuing on to the next example, close both Car Analysis and Car Data by choosing Close from the File menu. Note that you will want to close the view (Car Analysis) before closing the dataset. Do not save any changes to these documents.

Exercise 2: Create a dataset and analysis from scratch

In this exercise you create a dataset that contains two variables: a continuous variable and a nominal variable. You then use the analysis and variable browsers (rather than a template) to analyze your data by performing an unpaired t-test. Once the analysis is complete, you will save your work as a template for future use.

As you complete this exercise, you learn that the steps you take to generate results are the same ones you follow to create a template. With this knowledge you can decide how you would like to use StatView to analyze your data. You can use the analysis and variable browsers exclusively or templates exclusively, or a mixture of both. The choice is yours. We recommend that you create custom templates to take full advantage of StatView and meet your specific needs. As this exercise shows, StatView makes this easy to do.

The attribute pane

- Choose New from the File menu. An empty dataset appears on the screen.

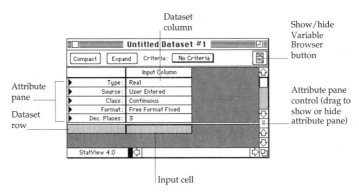

The rows above the body of the dataset contain attribute and summary information about the variable in the column below. Together, these rows are called the attribute pane, and you can show or hide as many of the rows as you desire. In a new dataset, the first five rows of the attribute pane are visible. These contain pop-up menus for each of the five attributes of a variable: its data type (string, real, integer, date/time, etc.), its source (whether it was user entered or created using a formula), its class (nominal, continuous, or informative), and the number of decimal places displayed (StatView carries 18 significant digits through all calculations and analyses; this attribute applies only to the way real numbers appear in the column). For more information on the attribute pane and data attributes, see Chapter 3, Datasets.

Create a dataset

First you will create a column (variable) containing continuous real data. The attribute pane shows the Type and Class for each variable. The default Type and Class for input columns are Real and Continuous. These defaults are appropriate for this variable so you do not need to make any changes before you enter data into the column. An empty cell appears below the attribute pane. This is called the input cell.

- Click the mouse in the input cell to select it, and enter the number 3.2. Press Return.

When you enter a value in the input cell, a new input cell appears directly beneath it and a new input column appears to the right. In this way the dataset grows to include as many rows and columns as are necessary to accommodate your data.

- Enter the numbers 4, 5.8, 6, 12, 8.5, 5.5 and 10.3 in the column. Move down the column using the Return key (or the Enter key if you are using a numeric keypad to enter data).

Now create the column containing the nominal grouping variable for the analysis.

- Use the Type pop-up menu in the attribute pane of the Input Column (the column to the right of Column 1) to change the variable's Type to String. To do so, click on Real and when the pop-up menu appears, drag to String. Notice that the Class automatically changes to Nominal.

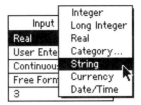

- Click in the top cell of the input column. Enter the values of the grouping variable as follows: Low, Low, High, Low, High, High, Low, High

Next you will name the two columns you have created and save the dataset.

- Select the name "Column 1" and type "Variable 1". Use the Tab key to move to "Column 2" and type "Variable 2". Press Return to enter the new variable names.

- Choose Save As from the File menu. Find and open the Sample Data folder in the directory list. Name this file "Quick Start Data" and click Save.

- Click on the ⊠ symbol between the two scroll bars on the right and drag down to expose the remaining rows in the attribute pane. You can examine descriptive information about the two columns you created.

	Variable 1	Variable 2	Input Column
Type:	Real	String	Real
Source:	User Entered	User Entered	User Entered
Class:	Continuous	Nominal	Continuous
Format:	Free Format Fi...	•	Free Format Fixed
Dec. Places:	3	•	3
Mean:	6.912	•	•
Std. Deviation:	3.075	•	•
Std. Error:	1.087	•	•
Variance:	9.458	•	•
Coeff. of Variation:	.445	•	•
Minimum:	3.200	High	•
Maximum:	12.000	Low	•
Range:	8.800	1.000	•
Count:	8	8	•
Missing Cells:	0	0	•
Sum:	55.300	•	•
Sum of Squares:	448.470	•	•

1	3.200	Low
2	4.000	Low
3	5.800	High
4	6.000	Low
5	12.000	High
6	8.500	High
7	5.500	Low
8	10.300	High

Quick Start Data — Compact / Expand / Criteria: No Criteria — StatView 4.0

- Double-click on the ⊠ symbol to hide all but the first five rows of the attribute pane. (Double-clicking a second time closes the entire attribute pane.)

Create your own analysis using the analysis and variable browsers

Now you will use the variable and analysis browsers to analyze the data and create a template.

- Choose New View from the Analyze menu. An empty view appears on the screen.

- In the analysis browser, select Unpaired Comparisons and click the Create Analysis button above the list.

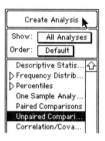

A dialog box appears, allowing you to set the parameters for this analysis.

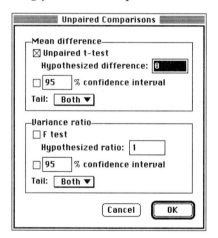

- The default dialog box settings, an unpaired t-test with an hypothesized difference of 0 between group means, are appropriate, so click OK. Empty placeholder tables will appear in the view with the variable requirements for the analysis noted beneath them.

- If the variable browser is hidden, show it by clicking the show/hide variable browser button at the upper right of the view.

- In the variable browser, select Variable 1 and click the Add button. An X appears to the right of it, indicating that it is assigned to the analysis.

- Select Variable 2 and click the Add button. An G appears to the right of it, showing that it is assigned as a grouping variable in the analysis.

- An unpaired t-test table and a group information table appear in the view.

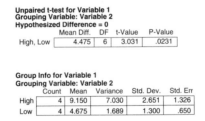

Unpaired t-test for Variable 1
Grouping Variable: Variable 2
Hypothesized Difference = 0

	Mean Diff.	DF	t-Value	P-Value
High, Low	4.475	6	3.031	.0231

Group Info for Variable 1
Grouping Variable: Variable 2

	Count	Mean	Variance	Std. Dev.	Std. Err
High	4	9.150	7.030	2.651	1.326
Low	4	4.675	1.689	1.300	.650

You have just seen how easy it is to use the analysis and variable browser to perform analyses in StatView.

StatView is completely interactive

One of the unique features of StatView is that it is completely interactive. Any changes you make to the dataset, including the use of criteria (see Exercise 5), cause your results to recalculate automatically so the information in your results is always up-to-date. You do not have to start an analysis over from the beginning if you make a mistake or change a data value.

- Choose Quick Start Data from the Window (or Σ) menu. Change the value in row 3 from 5.8 to 7.8. Press Return or Enter. The rotating yin-yang symbol 🌓 indicates that the results are recalculating. In fact, whenever this symbol appears, you can cancel the current program operation by pressing Command (🍎) -period.

- Choose Untitled View #1 from the Window menu to see the effect of this change on the results.

If you want to make many changes to your dataset, you may want to turn automatic recalculation off, by clicking in the Recalculate check box (or directly on the word "Recalculate") in the upper left corner of the view.

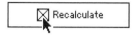

Recheck the box after you have completed your changes, and results in the view will recalculate.

Save your analysis as a template

In a few steps, you created a template that performs an unpaired t-test on any set of data. You will now add this template to the Analyze menu for easy access.

- Choose Save from the File menu.

- Find and open the StatView Templates folder in the directory list. Name this file "Exercise Template" and click Save.

- From the Analyze menu, choose Templates. Select Exercise Template in the scrolling list and click in the checkbox to its right.

Exercise Template

- Click the Change Menu button. The template you created is now available for easy use through the Analyze menu.

- Close the Exercise Template and the Quick Start Data. Do not save any changes that you have made.

Exercise 3: Work with templates and action objects

One common use of templates is for a supervisor or statistical consultant to set up a template tailored to a particular task. The work is done only once. After that, anyone can use the template, simply by specifying a new dataset and variables. You can also create a template to speed the production of reports or journal articles that must be meet standard requirements for figure size and appearance, font size and type, etc.

In this exercise, you will use the template you created in the last exercise and the analysis and variable browsers to generate tables and graphs. Finally, you will customize a graph.

Apply a template to new variables

First, make sure that all datasets and views from previous examples are closed.

- From the Analyze menu, choose Exercise Template. The directory dialog box appears for you to locate the dataset you wish to analyze.

- Locate Lipid Data in the Sample Data folder and click Open.

The Assign Variables dialog box appears for you to assign variables to the template.

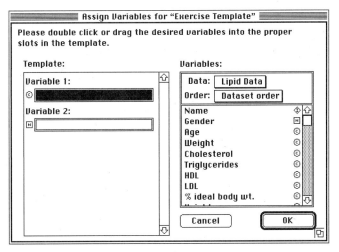

 Note that the order of template slots is not fixed. Either Variable 1 may appear on top (as pictured above) or Variable 2 may appear on top. Make sure that as you continue the exercise below you assign the variables to the correct slot.

Hints

On-line help, in the form of a Hints window, is available for almost every feature of the program. Hints explain everything from the function of dialog box buttons to the buttons in the analysis and variable browsers. The Hints window is a valuable tool to help you understand how to use StatView. You will use Hints here to familiarize yourself with the use of the Assign Variables dialog box.

- Choose Hints from the Window menu. The Hints window appears on the screen. It is a floating window that floats above all other StatView windows, including the browsers and dialog boxes.

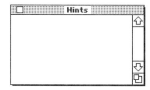

- Click in the slot labelled "Variable 1" in the list on the left of the Assign Variables dialog box. The Hints window describes how the variable you drag into this slot will be used in the view generated by this template. Select "Variable 2" to read a hint about its function in the template. Close the Hints window to get it out of the way. You may choose it from the Window menu any time to learn about the program.

You will now assign variables to the slots in the template. These variables contain data on the percent of ideal body weight of students before and after three years of medical school.

- Drag the variable "% ideal body wt." into the Variable 1 slot.

- Use the scrolling variable list to locate "% ideal body weight-3 yr". Drag it into the Variable 1 slot as well. (You can also double-click on a variable to assign it to a slot. In addition, holding down the Command key and double-clicking allows you to control which slot variables go into. Chapter 7, Templates, contains detailed information on using the Assign Variables dialog box)

Since you assigned both variables to the same slot, they will be used identically in the analysis. When a template contains several variable slots, each slot represents one variable in the original view. As you assign a variable to a slot, it is used in all the places the original variable appeared. If you assign two variables to one slot, then, everywhere the original variable was used there will now be two.

- Select the Variable 2 slot by clicking on it. Double-click on Gender in the variables list to assign it to the Variable 2 slot (the grouping variable in the analysis). Click OK.

A new view opens containing the results of the template. As you can see, four tables are generated, one pair for each continuous variable assigned.

Unpaired t-test for % ideal body wt.
Grouping Variable: Gender
Hypothesized Difference = 0

	Mean Diff.	DF	t-Value	P-Value
male, female	.626	93	.195	.8460

Group Info for % ideal body wt.
Grouping Variable: Gender

	Count	Mean	Variance	Std. Dev.	Std. Err
male	71	100.808	179.108	13.383	1.588
female	24	100.182	205.700	14.342	2.928

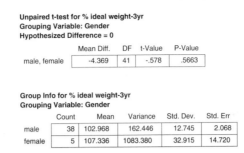

Unpaired t-test for % ideal weight-3yr
Grouping Variable: Gender
Hypothesized Difference = 0

	Mean Diff.	DF	t-Value	P-Value
male, female	-4.369	41	-.578	.5663

Group Info for % ideal weight-3yr
Grouping Variable: Gender

	Count	Mean	Variance	Std. Dev.	Std. Err
male	38	102.968	162.446	12.745	2.068
female	5	107.336	1083.380	32.915	14.720

Action objects and additional output

Now you will be introduced to another central feature of StatView: action objects. All output generated by the program, whether tables or graphs, are "action objects," because they retain information about the variables and analysis parameters that define them, and contribute this information to subsequent analyses. When you click the Create Analysis button or assign a variable with the variable browser, StatView uses the attributes of the *selected* action object to determine what to do next, so you do not have to respecify all the information. An understanding of how action objects work is important for taking full advantage of the speed and ease with which you can analyze data. See Chapter 8, Building Analyses, for more information about action objects.

To use action objects, you must be aware of which variables and results are currently selected. StatView provides several ways to monitor selection: (1)You can see the selection handles around selected results; (2) the Results Selected note in the upper right corner of the view reports the number of results selected; and (3) usage markers to the right of variables in the variable browser reflect usage in the currently selected result.

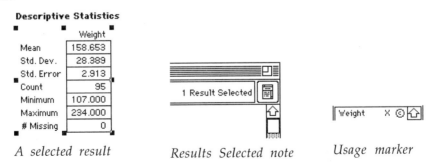

A selected result	Results Selected note	Usage marker

In the view that you just generated, notice that the second set of tables is selected.

- Deselect the tables by clicking in any white (empty) space in the view. Select the first unpaired t-test table (Unpaired t-test for % ideal body wt.) by clicking on it so that only one action object is selected. Notice how the variable browser usage markers and the Results Selected note change as selection changes.

- In the analysis browser, click on the triangle next to Cell Plots. In the indented list that appears beneath it, double-click on Bar Chart (this has the same effect as clicking the Create Analysis button). The Cell Plot dialog box appears.

- The default settings are appropriate, so click OK. A graph appears with two bars, one for the mean of male body weight and one for the mean of female body weight.

The bar chart that appears in the view contains the same variables as the unpaired t-test table, yet you did not have to assign variables for the second analysis. You can see that the bar chart visually confirms the results of the unpaired t-test which indicate no significant difference between the means of male and female body weights.

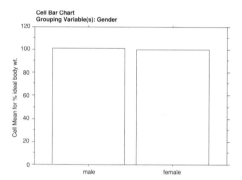

- Follow the same procedure to create a second bar chart for % ideal body weight - 3yr.

Next you will see how to use the information in action objects to quickly generate additional analyses for new variables.

Adding a variable to a selected table

You can assign additional variables to an analysis by selecting the result (table or graph) and using the variable browser again.

- Deselect all output by clicking on any empty space in the view. You can confirm that nothing is selected by looking at the Results Selected note. It should be blank.

- Select the unpaired t-test or group info table for % ideal body wt. in order to access the information on the variables, analysis and parameters of these action objects.

Notice the usage markers in the variable browser next to the grouping variable (Gender) and the dependent variable (% ideal body wt.). You can see this information more conveniently if you change the display order for the variable browser to "by Usage."

- Click on the Order pop-up menu and select "by Usage." Notice that the variables currently being used by the selected analysis appear at the top of the browser.

- Select Cholesterol in the variable browser and click the Add button.

A new unpaired t-test is created combining the new continuous dependent variable Cholesterol with the original grouping variable Gender. You did not have to respecify either the analysis, its parameters, or the grouping variable.

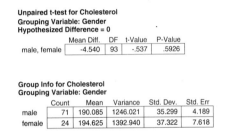

Unpaired t-test for Cholesterol
Grouping Variable: Gender
Hypothesized Difference = 0

	Mean Diff.	DF	t-Value	P-Value
male, female	-4.540	93	-.537	.5926

Group Info for Cholesterol
Grouping Variable: Gender

	Count	Mean	Variance	Std. Dev.	Std. Err
male	71	190.085	1246.021	35.299	4.189
female	24	194.625	1392.940	37.322	7.618

Notice that these two new tables are selected when they are created. The Results Selected note and the variable browser have updated to reflect this.

Split by

There are two ways you can easily examine results for subsets of your data. One is to use the Criteria feature, which is demonstrated in Exercise 5. Another is to use the Split By button in the variable browser. When you assign a nominal variable as a split-by variable, the results are generated for each group of the nominal variable. You will now use the Split By button to examine the effects of alcohol use on the body weight of male and female students in this study. For more information about split-by variables, see Chapter 8, Building Analyses.

- Select the % ideal body weight-3yr bar chart by clicking on it.

- In the variable browser, select "Alcohol use" and click the Split By button. The bar chart changes to display bars for each level of alcohol use in the study group. The legend to the right of the graph identifies the levels of alcohol use by fill pattern in each bar. There are two missing bars (male >6 and females none), indicating that no subjects fall in those cells.

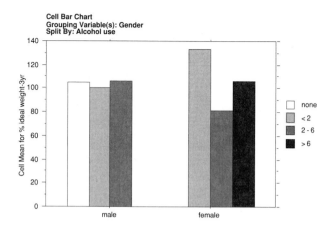

While this example shows how to use the Split By button with graphs, you can just as easily use it with tables in order to see statistical tables broken down by the groups of a nominal variable. You can do all of this without having to re-order your dataset. You can apply a split-by variable to all the analyses generated in StatView.

Customizing bar charts

You access StatView's many options for graph customization through the Edit Display button and the Draw menu. The graph above has several components that you can customize: axis intervals and labels, presence or absence of the legend and title, the frame, and the fill patterns for each of the bars. Customizing graphs is covered in detail in Chapter 9, Customizing Graphs and Tables.

You have to select an item in order to customize it. When a graph is first created, selection handles appear around the border, indicating the whole graph is selected. You have access to the analysis parameters through the Edit Analysis button, and to the graph format through the Edit Display button.

The pattern in the bars can be changed by selecting the symbols in the legend (to the right of the graph) that show the fill patterns for each bar. A dotted line surrounds the one you select. The Draw menu has a pop-up menu of fill patterns to choose from.

Graph preferences

The default order in which fills are used for bars is one of the many global graph preferences you can set through the Preferences command in the Manage menu.

- Choose Preferences from the Manage menu.

- In the Preferences dialog box, select Graph and click the Modify button. The Graph Preferences dialog box appears.

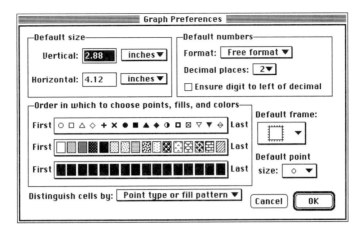

This dialog box governs the default settings for all graphs. Any changes you make here affect every subsequent graph you create, but existing graphs will not change to conform to the new settings. The options are discussed in detail in Chapter 9, Customizing Graphs and Tables.

Points, fills and colors for graphs are used in the order displayed in the dialog box. The bar fills of the graph you created match the order in the dialog box. The bar for the first variable uses the first fill, the bar for the second variable used the second fill, etc. You can change this default order as follows:

- Place the cursor over the sixth fill ▓. When you click, a palette of all fills appears as a pop-up menu. The current sixth fill is highlighted.

- Drag to the rectangle above the highlighted one ▦ and release the mouse. The sixth fill in the dialog box is now ▦ instead of ▓. This order applies to all graphs you create from now on. The existing bar chart has not changed.

- Click OK in this dialog box, then click Done in the Choose Preferences dialog box to execute the new preferences.

You can change the fills in the existing chart directly through the Draw menu.

- With the plot selected, tear the Draw menu off the menu bar as follows:

    Select the Draw menu, drag the cursor downwards. As you move the cursor off the border of the menu, a dotted outline of the Draw menu moves with the cursor. This outline indicates where the menu will appear when you release the mouse. Position the dotted outline so it does not block your view of the plot, and release the mouse.

    The rectangle next to Fill says None, because no filled object is selected.

- Click in the legend on the filled square labelled "none". The rectangle next to Fill displays the current fill for the selected variable.

- Click on the fill in the Draw menu to display the same palette of fills you saw in the Graph Preferences dialog box. This pop-up menu works the same way.

- Drag to the fill you selected earlier ▦ and release the mouse. The rectangle next to fill changes, and the bar in the chart contains the new fill, as does the symbol in the legend.

This simple process for specifying fills applies to any area filled with a pattern. Fill patterns in graph backgrounds, plots (bars, pies, boxes), the legend and objects you draw in the view can all be customized in this way. Drawn objects have other aspects you can modify as well, as you will see in the next exercise.

You will now save the customizations you made to the analysis. You can save a view at any time. Remember that when you save a view in StatView, you are not simply saving the text or pictures of the output — you are saving all aspects of the work you have done. When you reopen the document, your work is as you left it, and your document is still completely interactive.

- Choose Save from the File menu.

The dialog box that appears prompts you to name your document.

- Name this file Exercise 3 and place it in the Sample Data folder.

You may now continue to the next exercise to learn about further options for customizing the output using the Draw menu.

Exercise 4: Drawing and page layout for presentation.

StatView is designed to allow you to work through a project completely, from raw data to presentation, all in the same application. StatView's drawing tools allow you to add those crucial finishing touches that can change a collection of tables and graphs into an informative (even entertaining) slide, poster, or report.

In this exercise, you will use the Draw menu to add drawn objects to the analysis you created in Exercise 3. Make sure that the view created in Exercise 3 is open and is the topmost window.

Drawing and text tools

- In the Draw menu, which should still be open, select the ellipse tool ⬭ by clicking on it.

- Position the cursor above and to the left of the left bar in the male bar group (males, 0 drinks/week). Click and drag down and to the right, creating an ellipse that encircles all the bars for males. Release the mouse when the ellipse is the desired size.

- In the Draw menu, select the line tool ▱ by clicking on it. Position the cursor at the upper right edge of the ellipse and click and drag to draw a diagonal line up and to the right, where you will add a text explanation. If you have trouble positioning the line, you may want to turn off the grid using the Turn Grid Off command located in the ruler portion of the Draw menu (or type Command-Y).

- In the Draw menu, select the text tool [A] by clicking on it. Position the cursor near the end of the line you drew, and click once. A text box containing a flashing cursor appears, indicating where the text you type will appear.

- Type "No obvious relationship between", press Return and type "drinking and body weight."

- In the Draw menu, select the arrow ▸ to return to a regular cursor, and click the close box of the menu.

- Select the text you added by clicking on it.

- In the Text menu, select Size and drag over and down in the pop-up menu to select 12. The text changes to 12 point type. You can change the font of the text in the same way, and move the text around or change the shape of the text box just as you repositioned the ellipse.

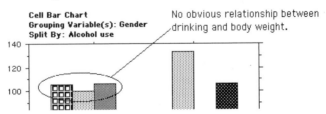

Clean up and printing

Since you can easily create so many different kinds of output, the number of objects in a view can be very large. StatView offers tools that you can use to find objects and organize their position and alignment in the view. You may have generated multiple tables and graphs from different analyses, and perhaps have experimented with placing them in different positions on the page. Before printing, you want to arrange the output neatly.

If you were to print the Exercise 3 view now, the second graph would be split between two pages. Scroll through the view to see that the graph is bisected by a page break, which looks like this: · · · · · · · · · · · · · · · ·

You will want to use the Clean Up command to automatically reposition the analysis results away from page breaks. First, however, you must make sure that the drawing you added to the first graph will move with it when the objects in the view are moved.

- Select the drawing, the line, the text, and the graph by clicking and dragging the finger cursor 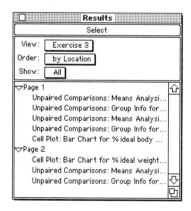 to surround them with a dotted line. When you release the mouse, check that each of the four items is surrounded by selection handles. Choose Group from the Layout menu. Observe that the grouped objects are now surrounded by a single set of selection handles.

- From the Layout menu, choose Clean Up Items. The default settings in the dialog box are appropriate so click OK. The objects in the view are moved so that they do not overlap page breaks or each other.

Another tool used to manage multiple analyses in a view is the results browser, an index of the tables and graphs in all open views. If a view contains a great deal of output or you are working with several views at once, it is easy to lose track of what you have done, what is currently selected and where particular results are located. Using this index, you can select a result from the scrolling list, click the Select button, and the view scrolls to and selects the result.

The results browser presents several options for viewing results. If you order results by Location in the browser, you can see how many pages are in a document and which results are located on each page. You can then choose to print some or all pages, or to rearrange the output.

- Choose Results from the Window menu. The results browser appears.

- Use the Order pop-up menu to order the results by Location. You can see which results are on each page.

- Close the results browser using the close box in the upper left corner.

Hairlines

When printing to certain printers, you may wish to consider the use of hairline-width lines in tables and graphs. These can give your document a more professional look.

- From the Manage menu, choose Preferences. In the resulting dialog box, select View, and click Modify.

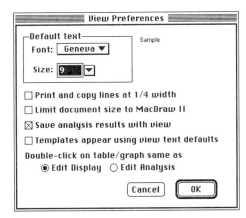

- Click the checkbox to "Print and copy results at 1/4 width." You can also change the font and size of the type in tables and graphs here, but those changes will apply to future tables and graphs you create, not the existing ones. Click OK, then click Done in the next dialog box.

Once you set this 1/4 width preference, it applies to all documents you copy or print, regardless of whether you created them before or after you set the preference. No difference is visible on the screen. For more information on view preferences, see Chapter 8, Building Analyses.

Now you can print the analysis you have created and customized.

- Choose Print from the File menu. The standard Print dialog box appears for the printer currently selected in the Chooser. Accept the default settings by clicking OK, or press Return to start printing. While printing, StatView displays a dialog box that allows you to cancel printing or suspend printing on non-LaserWriter printers. For further details on printing, refer to Chapter 8, Building Analyses, or to your Macintosh Reference Guide.

You will now save the customizations you made to the analysis.

- Choose Save from the File menu.

- Close the view and the Lipid Data.

Exercise 5: Data management

The exercises so far have shown you how to use StatView's powerful statistical, graphics, and drawing features. This exercise introduces you to the last component of StatView's functionality: data management. A powerful formula generator lets you apply a wide variety of statistical, logical, and mathematical functions to your data. You can create new variables using these functions and simple or complex combinations of existing variables.

StatView also includes functions that allow you to easily explore different portions of your data by defining criteria which restrict analyses to a user-specified subset of a dataset. This example will introduce you to the Formula and Criteria dialog boxes which give you access to these features of the program.

Formula dialog box

• Open Car Data from the Sample Data folder.

Scroll through the dataset to examine its contents. This dataset contains information on 116 cars produced in various countries. You will examine the relationship between the horsepower and weight of these cars, but first you must adjust the units in which car weights are reported. You will use the formula dialog box to change the values for weight from pounds to kilograms.

• Choose Formula from the Manage menu. The Formula dialog box appears.

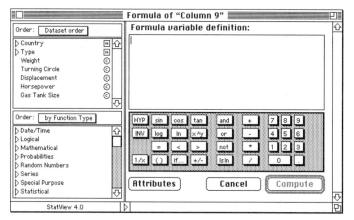

The dialog box contains four main areas: the variables list in the upper left corner, the function list in the lower left corner, the keypad at the lower right containing buttons for frequently used functions as well as a numeric keypad for adding numbers to formulae, and the formula definition area above the keypad where the formula is specified. By default, the function list is grouped by function type. Each function type has a triangle to its left. Click on the triangle in order to display the available functions for each type. You may also display all available functions in alphabetical order using the Order pop-up menu. See Chapter 5, Managing Your Data, for more information about formulas.

- Double-click on Weight in the variable list. It appears in the definition area.

- Click on the " /" symbol in the keypad. A division symbol is added to the formula.

- Use the numeric keypad to enter the value 2.2, the number of pounds in a kilogram. This value is added to the formula. The formula should read "Weight/2.2."

- Name the new variable by clicking on the Attributes button at the bottom of the dialog box. Type "Weight (kg)" into the space following variable name and click OK to accept the default settings for the variable.

- Click Compute in the Formula dialog box. The dataset comes to the front and the values of the new variable are calculated and placed in a new column labelled "Weight (kg)."

The formula definition is saved with the column when you save the dataset. You can check its accuracy or edit the formula at any time.

- Locate and select the column "Weight (kg)" in the dataset by clicking on the column name in the variable browser and clicking Show. (If the variable browser is not showing, click the show variable browser button to bring it to the front.)

- Make sure the attribute pane is open. If it is not, open it by double-clicking on the symbol at the right of the dataset.

Notice that the source entry in the column's attribute pane is Dynamic Formula rather than User Entered. This means that the column was created using the formula dialog box and that its values are dynamically tied to values in other columns, in this case to the column "Weight". If any values are changed in a column that is being used to specify a Dynamic Formula column, the values in the Dynamic Formula column automatically update.

- Click on Dynamic Formula in the attribute pane. The Formula dialog box appears, containing the formula specifications for the variable. You may edit any of the formula specifications in the dialog box.

- Close the Formula dialog box by clicking Cancel or the close box at the upper left.

Using a regression template

You will now use a template to generate a regression analysis, incorporating the formula-generated variable you just created.

- In the Analyze menu, choose Templates. A dialog box appears for you to choose a template.

- In the Templates dialog box, select Regression-Simple and click the Use Template button. The Assign Variables dialog box appears.

- Drag the variable Weight (kg) into the Independent slot. Drag the variable Horsepower into the Dependent slot, and click OK.

You have created a regression analysis consisting of several tables of information and a scattergram. Notice that there is a strong positive linear relationship between the two variables, but the high degree of scatter in the data keeps the R^2 relatively low. This analysis is a good candidate for a log transformation of the dependent variable since the plot of residuals vs the independent variable is cone-shaped. More detail about regression analysis is offered in Chapter 17, Regression.

Customizing tables

Before you go on to use criteria, introduce yourself to some of the options for customizing tables and scattergrams.

- Scroll down to the Regression Coefficients table.

- Place the cursor between the headings Coefficients and Std. Err. until it changes to ✛. Drag to the right to widen the column.

- Deselect the output by clicking in any white (empty) space in the view.

- Select the Regression Summary, ANOVA, and Regression Coefficients tables by holding down the Shift key and clicking on them.

- Click the Edit Display button. The Table dialog box appears.

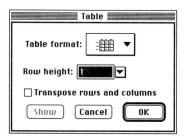

- Click on the triangle in the Table format pop-up menu. Drag down to the fourth option and release the mouse.

- Click the Show button to see what this format looks like applied to the first table. Choose several different formats, clicking Show after each, to see how the various formats look on these tables. When you find one you like, click OK.

The Table dialog box now appears for the second (ANOVA) table. Format it as you did the first, Click OK, and go through the same process for the third table (Regression Coefficients).

Customizing scattergrams

- Click once in the interior of the Regression Plot (but not directly over a point) to select the graph. Small squares appear around the frame and the Results Selected note in the upper right corner of the view tells you one result is selected.

- Click the Edit Display button at the top of the view. The Graph dialog box appears, containing some of the formatting options for this graph.

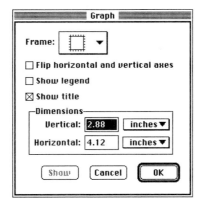

- Click on the triangle in the Frame pop-up menu, drag to the L-shaped frame ⌐ and click OK.

- In the Draw menu, click on the empty circle next to the word "point." A pop-up menu of point types appears.

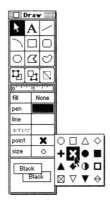

- Drag to the ✖ symbol and release the mouse. The points in the regression plot change from empty circles to x's.

- Close the Draw menu by clicking its close box.

Criteria

The next step is to use the Criteria dialog box to explore your data. You will create a criterion and apply it to this analysis.

- Choose Create Criteria from the Manage menu. The Criteria dialog box appears.

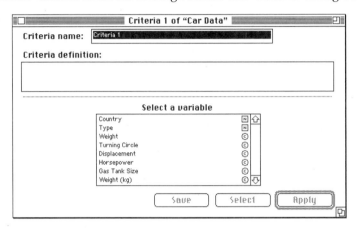

This dialog box contains three regions: the criteria name area (top), criteria definition area (middle), and the choices area (bottom). You will use the criteria name to apply the criterion, as you will see later. You will now create a criterion which restricts all calculations to cars produced in the U.S.

- First name the criterion by typing "United States" into the criteria name box.

- Double-click on Country in the variable list in the choices area. The variable appears in the criterion definition space, and the choices area changes to display a list of comparison operators.

- Double-click on the ? = ? operator in the choices area. An = sign appears to the right of the word Country in the definition area, and the choices area changes to display the available values for the variable Country.

- Double-click on the value USA in the choices area. The definition area should now read "Country = USA". Click Save to save the criterion with the dataset for future use.

Bring the view you are working on to the front. Note the number and pattern of points in the regression plot and the parameters of the regression equation.

- Choose Edit/Apply Criteria from the Manage menu.

- Select the criterion United States from the list of criteria, and click Apply.

The analysis recalculates, now including only information for those cars manufactured in the U.S.

- Choose Car Data from the Window menu to see the effect of the criterion on the dataset.

Model	Country	Type	
1 Acura Integra	Japan	Small	
2 Acura Legend V6	Japan	Medium	
3 Audi 100	Other	Medium	
4 Audi 80	Other	Compact	
5 Audi 90	Other	Compact	
6 BMW 325i	Other	Compact	
7 BMW 535i	Other	Medium	
8 Buick Century	USA	Medium	
9 Buick Electra V6	USA	Large	
10 Buick Le Sabre V6	USA	Large	
11 Buick Riviera V6	USA	Medium	
12 Buick Skylark	USA	Compact	

Car Data — Compact / Expand / Criteria: United States — StatView 4.0

The row numbers (on the far left of the dataset) are dimmed for the rows that contain information on cars not made in the U.S.

The Criteria pop-up menu at the top of the dataset should show the words "United States" to indicate that the criterion is in effect. The pop-up menu lists all the criteria that have been specified for a dataset. You can use the menu to easily and quickly toggle between various alternative criteria to explore their effects on the dataset and on your analysis. You can also use the "New" command in this pop-up menu to get access to the Create Criteria dialog box.

- Click on the ⊡ symbol between the two scroll bars on the right and drag down to expose the attribute pane. You can see descriptive information about each variable in the dataset.

- Choose No Criteria from the pop-up menu. Notice how all row numbers in the dataset become black, showing that all rows are now included in the analysis. The rotating yin-yang symbol ☯ shows that the results are recalculating. The attribute pane updates to display information about all rows in the dataset.

Close the view first and then the dataset without saving changes to either one.

Where to go next

The preceding exercises illustrate the basic steps in using StatView to meet all of your data analysis needs. The rest of the manual covers these and other topics in greater depth. Information on how this manual is organized is located in the preceding chapter. The table below directs you to the appropriate chapter for each task listed.

Create a dataset and edit your data	Chapter 3
Import data from another application	Chapter 4
Export data to another application	Chapter 4
Generate new columns by transforming existing columns	Chapter 5
Create a new column based on a series or distribution	Chapter 5
Create a graph	Chapters 7, 8 and 22
See the graphs you can create in StatView	Chapter 22
Change the appearance of a graph or table	Chapter 9
Perform a statistical analysis	Chapters 7, 8 and 11-22
Learn to use the analysis browser and variable browser	Chapter 8
Apply a ready-made analysis template	Chapter 7
Create your own template to reduce work time	Chapter 8
Use variables from different datasets in a single view	Chapter 8
Update graphs or tables regularly with new data	Chapter 7
Embellish your tables and graphs for presentation	Chapter 10
Work with your data before or after analyzing it	Chapter 5
Work with a subset of your data	Chapter 6
Combine data from different datasets in one analysis	Chapter 8
Work with shapes, text and color	Chapter 10
Learn about a particular analysis, test or graph	Chapters 11 -22
Get help with a problem	Chapter 23
Discover keyboard shortcuts	Appendix A

3

Datasets

In order to do analyses, you need to get your data into a dataset. The dataset is a column-by-row window, with rows comprised of individual cases and columns containing variables (measurements of one kind). If you have ever worked with a spreadsheet or database application, you are familiar with this basic column and row format. If not, you will find it easy to learn.

This chapter is about entering data directly into a dataset and covers the basic concepts and features of the dataset. If you plan to import data rather than enter it directly in StatView, we advise you to read this chapter first to learn about basic data window features. Importing data is covered in the chapter that follows this one, Importing and Exporting Data.

This introduction to datasets and the data window gives you a solid foundation for the other chapters that explore StatView's advanced dataset features: Exploring Subsets of your Data and Managing Your Data.

On the next page is a picture of a sample dataset with all its components labelled. As you use the program and read through the chapter, you may find it helpful to refer to this picture if you are unsure of any terms you encounter.

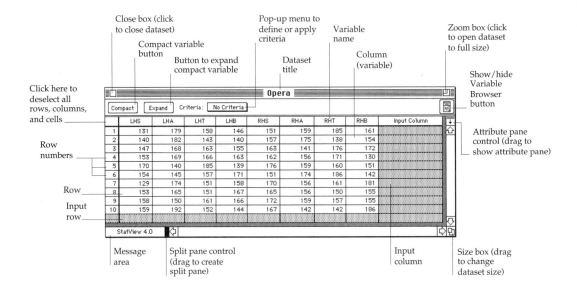

Dataset organization

Visualizing the structure of your data is a very important first step in creating your dataset. The kind of analyses you want to perform determine the appropriate organization of your data. If you set up your data in a manner not conducive to the analysis you want to perform, you may have to completely re-enter the data or cut and paste a lot to get it into a proper format. Be particularly careful when using an analysis that compares different groups (unpaired t-test, ANOVA, unpaired nonparametric tests, contingency table) or using plots that display groups (cell plots, compare percentiles). These analyses require your data organized in a way that identifies which group an observation belongs to. In addition, the repeated measures ANOVA uses a compact variable which requires a particular structuring of your data. A discussion of the theory and use of compact variables comes later in this chapter.

To correctly enter data into a StatView dataset, you must understand two important concepts:

- The structure of a dataset must be consistent with both the information you are entering and how the analysis you are using expects to find the data.

- There are two basic classes of information that are treated very differently by StatView: continuous and nominal. Continuous data can assume any numerical value over a given interval; nominal data identifies the group an observation belongs to. (There is also an informational data class, but it is not used in analyses.)

The standard format for a dataset has each row representing a distinct case (observation) and each column containing a variable. For example, a study on heart disease has a row for each patient in the study and a column for each quantity measured. This layout is shown below:

	Name	Gender	Weight	Cholesterol
1	J. Suds	Male	145	168
2	H. Fitz	Female	123	167
3	R. Blunt	Male	245	265
4	T. Stout	Male	223	187
5	S. Small	Female	142	202

In this dataset, Weight and Cholesterol are continuous variables and contain the weight and cholesterol measurements of each patient. Gender is a nominal variable that labels each row of the dataset with the gender of the patient — male or female.

Comparing groups

In the dataset shown above, you may want to compare cholesterol levels for males and females. To do so you you would assign both the nominal variable Gender and the continuous variable Cholesterol to the appropriate analysis. The nominal variable Gender acts as a grouping variable that identifies the group (male or female) for each Cholesterol measurement. If additional group information was recorded for these patients, such as eye color or occupation, you could enter them as additional columns in the dataset and use them as grouping variables as well.

StatView offers an alternative, called a compact variable, for identifying the group to which each observation belongs. In a compact variable each group is identified by the *column* it belongs to, not the row. As a result, the conventional structure of the dataset may not apply since each row does not have to contain information on distinct cases. The cholesterol measurements for male and female from the above dataset look like this in a compact variable format:

	Cholesterol	
	Male	Female
1	168	167
2	265	202
3	187	●

Notice that the male cholesterol measurements are all placed in one column and the female cholesterol measurements in another. The column identifies which group the cholesterol is from, not the row. You may find that for some work you are more comfortable entering different groups in separate columns and therefore would use a compact variable to identify groups.

Correctly identifying groups

It is necessary to correctly group your data so StatView can identify the group for each measurement. This is important not only for comparing groups, but for performing an analysis on subsets of data. You can perform an analysis broken down by groups at any time using the Split By button in the variable browser. If you plan to graph your data as well, it is important to understand how to define groups since all graphs in StatView allow you to visually compare different groups.

The analyses that compare groups are: unpaired comparisons (unpaired t-test, unpaired variance test), ANOVA, unpaired nonparametric tests (Mann-Whitney, Kolmogorov-Smirnov, Wald-Wolfowitz) and chi-square tests (contingency table). Contingency table analysis is a special case of comparing grouped data and offers three different ways of arranging your data in a dataset (see Special data layouts below).

Dataset organization is discussed in the exercises in later chapters on statistics. To determine how your data should be arranged, review the appropriate analysis chapters.

Before entering data into a dataset:

1. Make sure you understand how a particular analysis expects its data to appear. (See Chapters 11 - 22)

2. If you are using the contingency table analysis, note that there are several different ways of entering data (see the section, Special data layouts, in this chapter).

3. Understand that StatView offers great flexibility in using variables as nominal variables. For a clear understanding of nominal variables, read the following section, Nominal and continuous data class.

4. Read the section on compact variables to see if you prefer to use this feature to identify the groups in your data.

Nominal and continuous data class

The class of a variable is crucial to how it is used in an analysis. StatView interprets a variable differently depending on whether it is continuous or nominal. One of StatView's most powerful features is the flexibility it allows in making any data type nominal.

Continuous data can assume any numerical value over a given interval, such as the weight of a car or the batting average of a baseball player. Nominal data is used to identify the group an observation belongs to, such as the country of origin of a car or whether a baseball player plays in the National League or American League. For many analyses, the chief question of interest is whether there are differences between groups, such as between the batting averages for National League batters and American League batters. If you set the class of a variable to nominal (explained in the Data class section in this chapter), StatView will automatically use the data to describe different groups in the dataset. Changing the class of the data does nothing to the data itself, it only affects how the data is used in an analysis.

Special data layouts

Most analyses expect the variables they are analyzing to be in a standard format with each row representing a distinct case and each column containing a variable. Two analyses can read data entered into different formats:

> Factor analysis can analyze data from a correlation matrix.
>
> Contingency table analysis can analyze two formats of summarized data: coded summary data and a two-way table.

These formats are discussed below.

Correlation matrix

A correlation matrix is a tabular arrangement of data with a correlation coefficient in each cell of the table. StatView offers the option of creating a correlation matrix in the Factor Analysis and Correlation/Covariance analyses. You can also enter a correlation matrix by hand. Data in this arrangement can be used in a Factor analysis and is chosen as "Correlation Matrix" in the Factor Analysis dialog box.

Coded summary data

Coded summary data contains one or more nominal grouping variables in columns and an additional column with a count (total) for each combination of groups. Data in this arrangement can be used in a contingency table analysis and is chosen as "Coded Summary Data" in the Contingency Table dialog box.

Two way table

A two way table allows you to enter a contingency table into a dataset as input for a contingency table analysis. Each column is a column of the contingency table and each row a row. The observed frequencies are entered as individual observations. A two way table can be used in a contingency table analysis and is chosen as "Two Way Table" in the Contingency Table dialog box.

Open a data window

A StatView dataset is simply a specialized Macintosh file window. It can be activated, resized, repositioned and scrolled. Up to 8191 datasets can be open at the same time on your desktop, depending on memory limitations. Your first step in creating a dataset is to open a new data window. Choose New from the File menu, and an empty dataset appears:

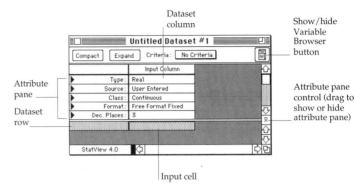

Click in the Zoom-up box at the upper right of the dataset window to enlarge the window. The dimmed cell in the upper left corner of a new dataset represents both an input row and an input column. As soon as you enter a data value into this cell, a new input row appears below it and a new input column appears to the right. You create columns (variables) by entering values into the input column and add rows by entering values in the input row. Each row represents a case and each column contains a variable.

A new column is created (and a new input column appears at the right side of the dataset) when you enter data into the input column (by typing or pasting) or change the name of the input column. You can also use the Add Multiple Columns command in the Manage menu (see Manipulating columns and rows later in this chapter) to add several columns at one time.

When your dataset has many columns, you may find it helpful to split the window vertically, so you can visually compare columns that are far apart in the dataset. To split the dataset, click and drag on the black rectangle just to the right of the message area in the lower left corner. Double-clicking on this control splits the dataset into two panes, double-clicking again returns it to a single pane. When the dataset is split, you can use the scroll bars at the bottom to scroll either half of the dataset.

Terminology: columns and variables

In the dataset, a distinction is made between columns and variables, although for most purposes the two terms are interchangeable. Strictly speaking, a column is the vertical arrangement of cells in a dataset that contains a variable. A variable is the data contained within the column. Therefore, when we refer to a column in this chapter and throughout the manual, we are referring to the structure itself rather than data. For example, you are adding a **column** when adding an empty structure to your dataset which is to contain a variable. You are selecting a **variable** when you click on the name at the top of a column that contains data. Compact variables present an exception to this, since they are comprised of several columns, yet are treated as a single variable.

Dataset preferences

You can set preferences for the dataset that affect decimal formatting, the appearance of text and the way the Enter key moves the cursor. To set these preferences:

• Choose Preferences from the Manage window.

• From the scrolling list of preferences, choose Dataset and click Modify. The Dataset Preferences dialog box appears:

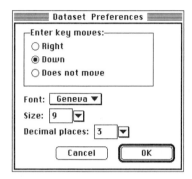

• From the Font and Size pop-up menus select the size and font for text. You can type in a size that is not on the menu. These changes go into effect for the next new untitled or imported dataset.

• From the Decimal places pop-up menu, choose the default number of decimal places to appear after real numbers. This setting goes into effect for the next new column, and can be changed in the attribute pane for individual columns.

• Use the "Enter Key Moves" pop-up menu to specify whether the Enter key (at the lower right corner of your numeric keypad) moves the cursor to the right, downward or not at all. This change goes into effect immediately.

• Click OK to return to the Choose Preferences dialog box. Click Done to execute the new preferences.

Set variable attributes

Each column in the dataset has specific attributes that describe the variable you enter in the column. These attributes are data type, class, format, and number of decimal places. You are advised to specify new column attributes for each column *before* entering data, unless they are same as the default attributes. Doing this ensures that each column is set up appropriately for the data it is to contain. If you enter data that is not compatible with the attributes specified, StatView warns you that the data is incompatible. You may change the attributes at any time, except for columns in a compact variable.

To specify column attributes for the input column:

- Place the pointer over an attribute for the input column (either Type, Source, Class, Format or Decimal Places). The cursor changes to a pop-up menu icon: 🖳.

- Click the mouse to open a pop-up menu for the attribute.

- Drag and release the mouse to make the desired menu selection. The chosen attribute is applied to the column.

Attribute pane

You set variable attributes in a part of the data window called the attribute pane. The first five lines of this area are pop-up menus, controlling the settings for each variable attribute. The remaining lines display summary statistics for each variable. A triangle appears to the left of each of the attributes:

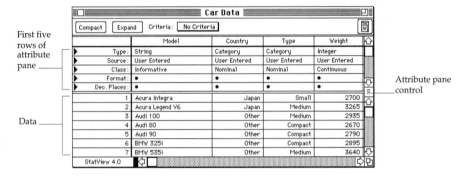

As you move the cursor over the first five rows in the attribute pane, it changes to resemble a pop-up menu: 🖳. The current choice for each attribute is highlighted in the respective pop-up menu. Drag the cursor through the pop-up menu list to select a different attribute for any variable.

The input column appears with these default attributes:

	Input Column
Type:	Real
Source:	User Entered
Class:	Continuous
Format:	Free Format Fixed
Dec. Places:	3

You can change the attributes of a variable at anytime except for the following circumstances:

- If a variable is currently being used in an analysis or in a formula definition you can not change its class or change its type to Category or String.

- If a column is being used in a compact variable you can not change any of its attributes except format and decimal places.

- If the source of the variable is analysis generated you cannot change the type or class.

Note the ⊠ symbol separating the attribute pane and the body of the dataset. The attribute pane functions as a split-pane window: pulling down the ⊞ control reveals the pane and closing it hides the pane. As a shortcut, double-click on the pane control to reveal the first five lines of the pane. When the attribute pane is open, the control appears as ⊠; when closed it appears as ⊞. If the attribute pane is closed, double-clicking on the pane control reveals the first five lines. If the attribute pane is open, double-clicking on the pane control closes it.

When you open the attribute pane, it pushes down the rows of the dataset so that row 1 always begins just below the bottom of the pane. You can scroll through the attribute pane and the body of the dataset independently. Open the attribute pane and drag the pane control below the first five lines of variable attributes to see summary statistics for each variable.

	City	State	Climate&Terrain	Housing	Health Care
Type:	String	String	Integer	Integer	Integer
Source:	User Entered	User Entered	User Entered	User Entered	User Entere
Class:	Informative	Nominal	Continuous	Continuous	Continuous
Format:	●	●	●	●	●
Dec. Places:	●	●	●	●	●
Mean:	●	●	662.000	10077.615	1029.115
Std. Deviation:	●	●	147.800	2720.186	992.920
Std. Error:	●	●	20.496	377.222	137.693
Variance:	●	●	21844.706	7399409.9...	985890.18
Coeff. of Variation:	●	●	.223	.270	.965
Minimum:	●	AZ	401	6440	210
Maximum:	●	WY	910	17158	5153
Range:	●	10.000	509.000	10718.000	4943.000
Count:	●	52	52	52	52
Missing Cells:	●	0	0	0	0
Sum:	●	●	34424.000	524036.000	53514.000
Sum of Squares:	●	●	23902768.000	56584031...	105352480
1	Phoenix	AZ	536	8921	
2	Tuscon	AZ	589	8548	
3	Salinas/Sea...	CA	843	13838	
4	Sacramento	CA	576	9855	
5	San Diego	CA	903	14465	
6	Oxnard/Ven...	CA	890	14000	
7	Stockton	CA	625	8474	
8	Fresno	CA	559	9291	

Western States Rated — Compact, Expand, Criteria: No Criteria — StatView 4.0

Attribute pane displaying all rows (fully open)

Data

Attribute pane control

For continuous variables, all the summary statistics are displayed: mean, minimum, maximum, standard deviation, standard error, variance, coefficient of variation, count, range, sum, sum of squares and number of missing cells. For nominal variables, only minimum, maximum, range, count and missing cells have information, the other cells contain missing values. No information is displayed for informative variables. When you open the attribute pane you always have complete and current summary information for your variables. You can copy the values in the attribute pane just as you can copy data in the dataset, and paste them into another application if needed.

When viewing summary statistics, double-click on the pane control to shrink the attribute pane so that only variable attribute information is displayed. Double-click again to close the attribute pane. Descriptive statistics are not calculated until you open the attribute pane. Therefore, if you plan to make several changes to your dataset, close the attribute pane to avoid the delay of frequent recalculation.

Variable names

You can edit variable names at any time. Names you give to dataset variables appear in the variable browser and as labels in results in the view. The default variable name is "Column *n*" where "*n*" is generally the number of columns in the dataset. Variable names must be unique, so if a new column is the fifth in the dataset, for example, yet there is already a "Column 5", the column will be named the next highest number that is a unique name. To edit a variable name, select the column by clicking in the box containing the name. Each variable name must be unique for that dataset.

With the column selected you can change its name by typing over it. To change a portion of the name, move the cursor over the variable name (the cursor changes to a text editing cursor), select the portion to edit and type in the new characters. If a variable name is selected, pressing Tab selects the next variable name.

Variable names cannot be longer than 80 characters and must be unique within the dataset. You cannot have a colon (:) in a variable name, and it is inadvisable to use quotation marks in variable names or begin a name with a digit if you plan to use the column in a formula.

Data type

Data type is set in the first row of the attribute pane. The data type identifies the nature of the data that will be entered into a column: real, integer, long integer, string, date/time, currency or category. When you set the data type of a variable, you will be able to enter only data of that type in the column.

You can change from any of these data types to any other at any time. For example, to change the data type of a variable from Real to Integer:

• Click on Real in the attribute pane. A pop-up menu of data types appears.

• Drag the cursor to Integer and release the mouse. The variable becomes an integer variable.

The input column has a default data type of Real. You can set the type to any of the following data types:

Data type	Description
Real	Numbers with fractional parts in the range from -1.1E4932 to 1.1E4932 with a smallest positive number of 1.9E-4951 and a largest negative number of -1.9E-4951. Set the number of decimal places in the Dec. Places pop-up menu.[*]
Integer	Whole numbers between 32,767 and -32,767.
Long Integer	Whole numbers between 2,147,483,647 and -2,147,483,647.
String	Alphanumeric data that documents the dataset (names, for example). Entries in string columns can be as long as 255 characters.
Date/time	Data that denotes points in time.
Currency	Data displayed in the format of any major currency. Set the number of decimal places in the Dec. Places pop-up menu.*
Category	Alphanumeric entries used to group data. When you assign a variable this data type, you must use an existing category or create a new category. The category's group labels are the only data that can be entered in the column. (See Categories later in this chapter for more details on creating a category.)

Data loss precautions

Caution is required when changing variable type if you have already entered data in the column. Some changes in data type cause data loss. For example, a change from Real to Integer truncates the real value to its integral part. Thus, when you change the Real number 1.456 to an integer, it becomes 1. If you choose Real again, the value 1 remains 1.000; the fractional portion is lost. If you change data type by mistake, immediately choose Undo from the Edit menu to avoid permanent data loss.

In general, you can lose data for one of four reasons during data type changes:

1. When the source data contains values that lie outside the bounds defined by the target data type, the out-of-bound source values are lost. Example: if you change a real number variable to an integer variable and the real number variable has values <-32767 or >32767, the out-of-bound values are lost and appear as missing value symbols (•).

2. When you convert source data containing a fractional portion to a numeric data type that does not contain fractions, the data is truncated or rounded up or down. Examples: 1.49 is truncated to 1, and 1.6 is rounded up to 2.

---

[*] The number of decimal places is for display purposes only; the full precision is used in all calculations and stored internally.

3. When you change a variable (other than Integer or String) to Category, a new category is created whose group labels are the unique values of the original data ordered by appearance in the dataset. Converting back to the original data type causes the values to appear as the ordinal values of the category. Example: A Real variable with the values 1, 3.45 and 6 becomes a Category with three levels: "Group for 1," "Group for 3.45," and "Group for 6." If the variable is changed back to Real, these values become 1, 2, 3.

When you change from an integer to a category, you are allowed to select a category or create a new category for the variable. Integer value 1 is converted to the first group label of the category, 2 to the second group label and so on. When you change from a string to a category, a new category is generated whose group labels are the unique levels of the string data. For example, a string variable with red, white and blue becomes a category variable with three group labels: red, white and blue.

4. When you change from String, the target data type must be able to recognize the string data or the string appears as a missing value. Example: the name Sims, H. is unrecognizable as a real number variable and the name is lost. It appears as a missing value symbol (•). The string data $1.23 is recognizable as currency (under a US operating system) and would be recognized as a currency data type.

Categories

Sometimes your data identifies a particular group rather than signifying a quantity. Data like this is a nominal variable. You can set any data type to nominal, but category data can be used *only* as a nominal variable. When you set a variable's type as category, you are prompted to provide information about the groups that make up the variable. For example, to enter the gender of patients in a study, you define a category in which Gender has exactly two group labels: Male and Female. The only data that can be entered into this column is Male and Female.

Using a category to enter your nominal data offers you specific advantages over other data types. The advantages are explained in the following section on Data class. See the sections on Nominal and continuous data class and Categories for more information.

Data source

Data source is specified in the second line of the attribute pane. The data source identifies the origin of data in the variable. It can be user-entered, created by a formula, or generated by an analysis.

Source	Description
User Entered	Data that you enter by hand; this is the default.

Dynamic Formula	Data created with the Formula, Recode, Series or Random Numbers commands. A dynamic formula variable changes whenever the variables or the formula used to define it change.
Static Formula	Data created by a formula and frozen. It does not change when you change the variables or formulas from which it was defined, although the formula definition remains. Changing a dynamic formula to a static formula stops recalculation of the formula, but you can change it back to dynamic formula at any time.
Analysis Generated	Data generated by an analysis: residuals, fitted and predicted values from a regression, factor scores from a factor analysis. Factor Analysis and Correlation/Covariance can create a new dataset containing a correlation matrix. See the appropriate analysis chapter for a discussion of analysis generated variables.

To change a variable's source from User Entered, for example, click on User Entered in the attribute pane. This pop-up menu appears:

Drag to either Dynamic Formula or Static Formula to change the source. You cannot change the source of a variable to Analysis Generated.

If a variable is created from a formula (dynamic or static), selecting the pop-up displays the formula dialog box that defines it. If a variable is created by an analysis, clicking on the pop-up and selecting Analysis Generated displays the analysis dialog box.

If the data source is not User Entered, you cannot edit the data. Also, changing from User Entered to either Dynamic or Static formula causes all entered data to be deleted and replaced by the data generated by the formula. Likewise, changing a formula from Dynamic or Static to User Entered retains all the data in the variable but causes all formula information to be lost.

Changing Analysis Generated variables to User Entered breaks the variable's link with the analysis that created it and allows you to save the variable with the dataset (this change is not permanent and can be undone). You can also change from Analysis Generated to Static or Dynamic Formula (again, with loss of linkage to the analysis).

Data class

Data class is specified in the third line of the attribute pane. You can assign variables a nominal, continuous or informative data class. An understanding of nominal and continuous variables is crucial and is discussed in an earlier section. When you first set the data type for a variable, the class for that variable defaults to continuous unless the variable is a category or a string type, in which case it defaults to nominal.

You can change data class for a variable at any time unless the variable is currently being used in an analysis or formula. Only data class choices compatible with the current data type selection can be made. Other choices are dimmed (inactive) in the Class pop-up menu.

Only variables with a numerical data type (integer, long integer, real, currency and date/time) can be continuous. Any type variable can be nominal or informative. Informative data cannot be used in an analysis or plot. As a result, the informative class should only be used for variables that are in a dataset strictly for informational purposes, such as patient names or identification numbers. Descriptive statistics are not calculated in the attribute pane for informative variables.

Changing data class from continuous to nominal is useful if you want the distinct values of the variable to identify groups rather than represent quantities in an analysis. To illustrate, three levels of a drug (10, 25 and 50 i.u.) can be seen as three drug administration groups (nominal variable), or as three values (continuous variables measured as 10, 25 and 50). Analyses uses the variable differently depending on whether its class is nominal or continuous. When you change a variable from continuous to nominal, the groups are sorted by magnitude (alphabetically for string columns).

Although you can use any data type as a nominal variable, category data offers some special advantages. If variables are always used to group data, choose Category. If you plan to use the variable as both nominal and continuous, choose a non-category type and change the data class. See the Categories section later in this chapter for more information.

The advantages of using a category variable for nominal data are:

- You can enter group labels using either the unique initial letter, the group label or the ordinal number of the label in the category definition.

- You ensure the accuracy of the group labels being entered, since only group labels defined by the category are accepted in the column.

- Categories use less memory to store information.

The advantages of using the Class control to specify nominal data are:

- You can use more than the 255 group labels allowed in a category.

- You can change data type back and forth between nominal and continuous.

Data format

Data format applies only to Real, Currency and Date/Time data and is specified in the fourth line of the attribute pane. The format you choose affects only the display of the data, not its contents. The format for Real data can be set to the following:

Format	Description
Free Format Fixed	Displays real numbers using the specified number of decimal places unless the column is not wide enough to display the entire number. If that occurs, the number is displayed in scientific notation.
Free Format	Chops off trailing zeroes to the right of the decimal point without regard to the number of decimal places specified.
Fixed Places	Displays the data using the number of decimal places specified. Data is not displayed in scientific notation.
Scientific	Displays data in scientific notation using the specified number of decimal places.
Engineering	Displays the numbers in scientific notation using exponents that are multiples of e3 and e-3.

Currency

Currency has its own choice of formats. If you choose the Currency data type, you may choose from among several major currency formats. Currency formats include those from the following countries:

Australia	Iceland
Belgium-Luxemburg	Italy
Denmark	The Netherlands
Finland	Norway
France	Portugal
French Canada	Spain
French Swiss	Sweden
Germany	Turkey
Greece	United Kingdom
Greek Swiss	United States

Date/Time

The Date/Time data type gives you options to display the time, day, date, month and year in a variety of combinations, formats and orders. The use of Date/Time variables in formulas is covered in the Managing Your Data chapter. If you use date/time data as a continuous variable, the date is translated as the number of seconds that have elapsed since January 1, 1904. (This is a standard originally established by Apple.)

Variable browser

Variables in the dataset are listed in the variable browser, a floating panel that appears in both the dataset and view. This section covers its use as a navigation aid in the dataset, where it enables you to:

Choose open datasets and open new datasets

Select variables

Create and expand compacted variables

You can show or hide the variable browser with the button in the upper right corner of the dataset and view, or with the Variables command in the Window menu. The button alternately shows and hides the variable browser, while the Variables command brings it to the front when it is hidden or obscured by another floating window. You can place the variable browser anywhere you like on-screen by clicking and dragging its title bar. You can resize it by clicking in the resize box and hide it by clicking in the close box in the upper left corner of the browser. The variable browser buttons change depending on whether you have a dataset or view frontmost. An example looks like:

Dataset   *View*

Variables are shown in the variable browser in a scrolling list. The symbols next to variable names indicate their data class. Continuous variables are shown with a ⓒ symbol to the right of their names. Nominal variables appear with a Ⓝ. Informational variables that cannot be used in an analysis are marked with a ◈ symbol. Compact variables are preceded by a triangle and followed by a ⓒ symbol. Click on the triangle to display the categories that identify the groups of the variable. These categories appear with a ⊞ symbol next to them. For example, a compact variable would appear as follows:

▷ Effectiveness   ☉

If you click on the triangle control, you display the nominal groups as well:

▽Effectiveness   ☉
        Time   ⊞

Select a variable using the variable browser by clicking on the variable name and clicking the Show button on the browser. This both selects the variable and scrolls the dataset so the variable is visible. To select several adjacent variables, click and drag the cursor over the desired variables. The dataset scrolls to the left-most selected variable when you click Show. To select discontiguous variables (variables that are not next to each other), hold down the Command key and click on the names. A shortcut: select dataset variables by double-clicking on their names in the variable browser.

You control the order in which the variables appear in the browser using the Order pop-up menu. The choices for order are:

Dataset order	The order in which the variables appear in the dataset's columns (left to right)
Alphabetical	Alphabetical order by variable name, with non-alphabetical names first
Variable type	Grouped in order by nominal, continuous, and compact
Usage	Ordered first by variable use in analyses and in alphabetical order within that classification. When a non-view window is the topmost window, the ordering is only alphabetical.

Two buttons at the top of the variable browser, Compact and Expand, enable you to create compact variables and expand variables that are compacted. They function exactly like the Compact and Expand buttons at the top of the dataset. See the Compact variables section later in this chapter for more information.

You can use the variables browser's Data pop-up menu to select among open datasets and to open new datasets. The name of the currently active dataset is shown. Click on the menu to choose another open dataset, and choose Other to get a file directory dialog box to locate and open a previously created dataset.

How to enter data

When you have set the attributes for a variable with the controls in the attribute pane, you are ready to enter the data for that variable in the dataset. Exercise 4 in the Quick

Start Tutorial chapter offers a thorough exercise in entering data. We recommend that you complete that exercise if you have not already done so and have questions.

• Move the cursor to the dimmed input cell and click to highlight it. The input row is the gray row that is always at the bottom of the dataset.

• Type a value.

When you enter a value into the input cell, a new input column appears to its right and a new input row appears at the bottom of the dataset. Your first variable is assigned the name "Column 1". (Remember that columns contain variables and rows hold cases.)

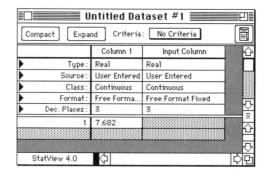

• Press Tab to highlight the input cell in the new input column.

• Set the desired variable attributes, type a value (into what is now Column 2), and press Tab.

A new input column appears on the right of the dataset. Continue setting attributes and entering values in input cells until you complete one row. To begin a new row:

• Select the first cell in the input row, or press Tab without entering a value in the input column of the previous row.

When you press Tab without entering a value in the input column, the cursor wraps back to the first column of the next row. You may begin entering values in the second row of your dataset as you did in the first. Now, though, you do not have to set attributes for each variable since they are already set.

By column

Entering data by column is much the same as entering it by row. After specifying the variable attributes and entering a value in the input cell for your first column, as described earlier, press Return.

Pressing Return rather than Tab selects the input row of the same column. Notice that a new input column still exists and a new input row now appears at the bottom of the dataset. You are working within the same column of the dataset in a new row.

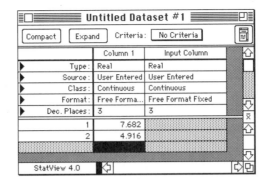

You may enter data for as many rows as needed until you are ready to begin a new column. To begin a new column, press Return without entering a value in the input cell. The cursor wraps to the first cell in the input column. You can now specify attributes for Column 2 and enter data as you did in the first column.

Missing values

A missing value, displayed by the "•" symbol, is entered by typing a period (.) or Option-8 (•) in a cell, unless the column has string as its data type. (String columns regard every character as data, so a missing value in a string column is simply an empty cell.) When you enter a value into an input row, missing values fill in the rest of the cells in the row. StatView lets you recode missing values to specified values by choosing Recode from the Manage menu (see Chapter 5, Managing Your Data).

Manipulating columns and rows

As described above, you create one column at a time by entering a value in the input column, pressing Tab and repeating the process. You create a new row by entering a value in the input row, pressing Return and repeating the process. Additional commands let you create several columns at one time as well as insert columns and rows into a dataset.

Add multiple columns

You can add several columns at once using the Add Multiple Columns command in the Manage menu. This is especially convenient for adding several variables with the same attributes. To add several columns:

• Choose Add Multiple Columns from the Manage menu.

• Enter the number of columns you want to create into the dialog box.

- Use the pop-up menus to set the attributes for these variables and click OK. For more details on variable attributes, see the Set variable attributes section earlier in this chapter.

The columns are appended to the right of existing columns. They are given default names of Column *n*, where *n* is usually the number of columns in the dataset. You can use the Undo command in the Edit menu to delete all the columns if you make an error. You must select Undo immediately after adding columns, before taking any other action.

Insert or remove columns

You can insert a column between two existing columns in the same dataset:

- Position the cursor between the variable names on the vertical line that separates the columns. The cursor changes to a cross with an arrow on its horizontal bar:

- Hold down the Command (⌘) key. The cursor changes to a thinner cross:

Ethnicity |↔|Test Type

- Click and a new column appears. Repeat to insert additional columns.

The newly inserted column has the same default variable attributes as the input column and is filled with missing values (•) until you enter data. You can remove a column at any time by selecting the column and choosing Delete from the Edit menu or by pressing Delete on your keyboard.

Insert row

You can insert rows in a dataset in a way similar to the method of inserting a column:

- Place the cursor over the horizontal line between two row numbers and hold down the Command (⌘) key.

- The cursor turns to a vertical version of the insert columns cursor: ↨

- Click once. The Insert Rows dialog box appears.

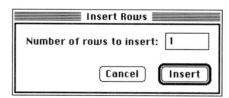

- Type the number of rows to add to the dataset and click Insert.

The rows are added to the dataset where you placed the cursor. Cells of the input rows contain missing values (•) until you enter data.

Resize column widths

To increase or decrease the size of columns:

- Position the cursor to the right of a variable name on the vertical line that separates columns. The cursor changes to a cross with arrows on its horizontal bar.

- Click on the line and drag it left to decrease the size of the column and right to increase it.

If a column is too narrow to display the data entered in its cells, pound signs (###) appear in place of numeric data. Ellipses (...) appear in place of alphabetic data (such as String data). The attribute names in the attribute pane are similarly abbreviated.

Cursor movement

The following tables indicate the keystrokes that control cursor movement within a dataset on normal and extended keyboards.

Normal keyboard

Keystroke	Cursor Direction
Tab	Right (with wrap-around)
Shift-Tab	Left (with wrap-around)
Return	Down, except in input row (with wrap-around)
Shift-Return	Up (with wrap-around)
Enter	Determined by Preferences command
Shift-Enter	Determined by Preferences command

The arrow keys move the cursor one cell. Holding down the Command key while pressing an arrow key scrolls the screen one page at a time without moving the cursor. Thus, Command-Down displays the next page of data, but does not move the cursor.

Extended keyboard

An extended keyboard with Page Up and Page Down keys enables you to page through the dataset without moving the selection from one cell to another.

Keystroke	Direction of Page Movement
Page Up	Up
Page Down	Down
Command-Page Up	Left
Command-Page Down	Right
Home	Upper left corner of dataset
End	Lower right corner of dataset
Command-Home	Upper right corner of dataset
Command-End	Lower left corner of dataset

Edit data

There is a dynamic link between datasets and views, so any changes made to your data are immediately reflected in any existing calculations in the view. You can edit individual values directly by clicking in the cell to be edited and typing in a new value. You can also use the standard Cut, Copy, Paste, Clear and Delete commands on selected cells in a dataset. If you need to see what you have selected, choose Show Selection from the Edit menu to scroll the dataset to the highlighted section. The cell in the upper left corner of the block is positioned in the upper left corner of the window. The following tables tell you how to select cells, rows and columns for editing.

Cells	How to select them
a single cell	Click in the cell.
adjacent cells	Click in one cell and drag vertically or horizontally to highlight all of them.
discontiguous cells	Select one cell. Hold down the Command key while selecting the other cells.
a small block of cells	Click in the corner cell and drag diagonally to highlight all of them.
a large block of cells	Select a cell in one corner of the block. Scroll to the location of the diagonally opposite corner of the block. Hold down the Shift key and click in that corner cell to highlight the entire block between the two corners.
discontiguous blocks of cells	Select one block as described in either method above. Hold down the Command key and drag to select another block.

Rows or columns	How to select them
all rows or all columns	Choose Select All Rows or Select All Columns from the Edit menu. These commands quickly select an entire dataset.

an entire row	Click once on a row number. Do not click twice on a row number, as this excludes the row from the analysis (and dims the row number). If you accidentally click twice on a row number, simply double-click to include it again.
an entire column	Click once on a variable name.
adjacent rows or columns	Click on a row number or variable name and drag the cursor over adjoining row numbers or variable names. This selects everything in between. To select a large block of data, select the first row or column, scroll to the row or column at the end of the group, hold down the Shift key and click. All rows or columns between the two selected rows or columns are selected.
discontiguous rows or columns	Click on the first row number or variable name, hold down the Command key and click on the other row number or variable names you want to select.
rows that meet a criteria	Hold down the Control key while selecting a user-defined criteria from the Criteria pop-up menu at the top of the dataset.

 There is a shortcut for deselecting any rows, cells or columns selected in the dataset. Click once in the empty rectangle above the row numbers and to the left of the first column heading. This removes any data selection.

Click here to
deselect all rows,
columns, and cells ————

	Teaching Effectiveness			
Compact	Expand	Criteria: No Criteria		
			Effectiveness	
	Teaching	0	1	2
1	Control	5.8	5.9	3.3
2	Control	5.7	5.0	4.5
3	Control	5.2	4.7	3.6
4	Control	5.6	5.2	5.4
5	Control	6.5	7.0	7.1
6	Control	2.7	2.3	3.8
7	Control	5.9	5.2	4.3
8	Control	4.0	4.2	4.0

StatView 4.0

Cut, clear and delete data

You can remove entire columns or rows using Edit menu commands or your keyboard.

Command	Action
Cut (Command-X)	Removes selected data to the Clipboard. If the data does not constitute an entire row or column, the row or column remains in the dataset. Cells where data has been cut contain missing value symbols. If an entire row or column is selected (including row number or variable name), Cut completely removes the row or column from the dataset. Rows below a cut row move up, and columns to the right of a cut column move left.

Clear (Command-B)	Removes selected data and replaces it with missing values. Data is permanently cleared unless you choose Undo (or Command- Z) immediately. Clear does not remove rows or columns.
Delete (Delete key)	Removes selected data and replaces it with missing values. If an entire row or column is selected, Delete removes them from the dataset. Deleted rows or columns are permanently removed unless you choose Undo immediately after deleting. With discontiguous rows or columns, the dataset shrinks by the number of deleted rows or columns.

Copy data

You can copy selected data to the Clipboard by choosing Copy from the Edit menu. You can paste data from the Clipboard back into a selected area of any active StatView dataset. When you cut or copy numeric data to the Clipboard, it is converted to text when you activate a desk accessory or switch to a different application using MultiFinder. (Other applications can only read data transferred as text.)

When data is converted from numeric to text format, only the number of decimal places currently displayed are saved. If you paste data outside of StatView, please display enough decimal places to meet your needs.

A yin-yang cursor appears while data is converted to text. You can cancel data-to-text conversion by pressing Command-Period while the cursor is displayed. By cancelling the conversion, the data is not available to the other application. When you return to StatView, the information is in the Clipboard (assuming you have not placed anything there from another application).

You can merge data from different datasets using the Copy and Paste commands. You must first create the number of empty rows and columns in one of the datasets. Then you can copy data from the other dataset and paste it into the empty cells. It is important to understand the constraints on pasting data which are described next.

Paste data

Pasting data into a dataset is much easier if you first familiarize yourself with the data you want to paste. The process is eased if you know the column by row size and the type of the data you plan to paste. There are three things to consider when pasting data from the Clipboard to a selected area of a dataset:

1. the size of the data relative to the size of the selected area

2. the type of data to be pasted and the data type in the selection area

3.   the location for the pasted data (such as the input row or the input column)

Size of the selected area

The selected area can have four basic sizes in relation to the data in the Clipboard:

- It can be the *exact* size of the data in the Clipboard. In this case, StatView pastes an exact copy of the data.

- It can be *smaller than the data* in the Clipboard. In this case, StatView pastes as much data as it can, starting in the upper left cell and leaving out the additional data.

For example, if the Clipboard contains an array of numbers 3 columns wide and 3 rows deep, and the selected area is only 2 by 2, only the first four data points of the source data is pasted (2 x 2). Paste does not shift cells to the right of the selected area further to the right, nor move the cells underneath the selected area down.

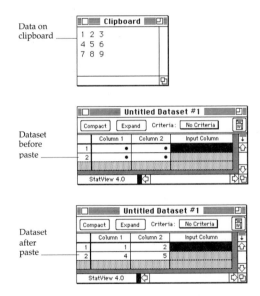

- It can be *larger* than the data in the Clipboard, and an exact multiple. In this case, StatView duplicates the data as many times as necessary to fill the selected area.

- It can be *larger* than the data in the Clipboard, but not an exact multiple. In this case, StatView copies the data only *once* and fills the remaining cells in the selected area with missing value symbols.

Data type to be pasted

When you paste data into a dataset, the pasted data is converted to the selected area's data type. (Recall that you can select data types in the attribute pane.) When you paste data of one type into a selected area of a different type, the conversion in data type can cause a loss of data. See the Data loss precautions section earlier in this chapter for help in avoiding data loss.

Location of pasted data

You can paste data into three areas of a dataset — the input row, the input column or the body of the dataset. When you paste data into the input row, the dataset grows to accommodate the new rows. However, if your source data has more columns than you have highlighted in the input row, the extra data is not pasted. To paste data into the input row of a dataset, highlight as many cells across the input row as your source data occupies and choose Paste from the Edit menu.

When you paste data into the input column, the dataset grows to accommodate the new column(s). The type of the new column(s) is determined by the same procedures used in importing data. To paste data into the input column of a dataset, highlight the entire column or as many cells as your source data occupies and choose Paste from the Edit menu. If you are pasting into a new dataset, simply highlight the input cell. The dataset adds the appropriate number of rows and columns to accommodate the data.

You can paste columns of data, rows of data or a block of data into existing dataset cells. In this case, data is only pasted into the highlighted area of the dataset. (See the earlier section, Size of the selected area.)

If you paste discontiguous data into a dataset, be sure to paste rows into rows, columns into columns and blocks into blocks with the same number of cells across and down. StatView joins discontiguous data in the Clipboard and cannot preserve the column/row structure of copied data unless it is pasted into areas the same shape as its origin. This capability is mainly useful for replacing rows or columns in one dataset with discontiguous rows or columns from another, or using discontiguous rows or columns from one dataset to form a new dataset. Pasting blocks of data into rows, columns or blocks of different shapes is not advisable.

Paste transposed data

Data in the Clipboard can be transposed while you paste. Use the Paste Transposed command to change entire rows into columns and entire columns into rows. For example, the following integers in a 3 x 3 section of a dataset:

1	2	3
4	5	6
7	8	9

transpose into:

1	4	7
2	5	8
3	6	9

To transpose data, choose Paste Transposed from the Edit menu. The block of cells in the target dataset should be as wide as the data to be transposed is deep. For example, if you have a 3 x 8 set of data to be transposed, you need a block of cells 8 x 3 for the transposed data. To transpose the following data:

1	2	3
4	5	6
7	8	9
10	11	12
13	14	15
16	17	18
19	20	21
22	23	24

you need to highlight the cells of the target dataset according to this 8 x 3 pattern:

1	4	7	10	13	16	19	22
2	5	8	11	14	17	20	23
3	6	9	12	15	18	21	24

If the target dataset does not have enough rows or columns to hold the new data, either create enough rows or columns to hold the data or highlight the correct number of cells in the input row or input column. If you paste into the input row or input column, the dataset automatically enlarges to hold the transposed data.

Categories

A category is a special, user-defined variable structure that is used only for nominal information. It allows you to create a set of specific group labels and give a name to this set. If you are familiar with the terms "factor" and "level," they often refer to the same concepts as category and group. You can associate one or more variables with a category to limit the variable's data points to one of the group labels of the category. A category variable can have up to 255 groups. For example, a category called Color has the group labels Red, Yellow and Green. Any variable associated with the Color category can contain only the values Red, Yellow and Green. Categories are used to:

- define the group labels that appear in a column whose type is category (see the Data type section earlier in this chapter)

- define the groups of a compact variable (see the sections on Dataset organization and Compact variables in this chapter for a discussion of compact variables)

- specify the groups when recoding a continuous variable to nominal groups (see Chapter 5 for more information on recoding).

You must use a category when you create a compact variable and when you recode data. It is optional when entering nominal information into a dataset, since you can change the class of any type of column to nominal. You may find, however, that using a category makes data entry easier and more accurate. Once you associate a variable with a category, the data you enter in the column must be one of the category's group labels. This prevents data entry mistakes. Using the Color example, you cannot enter "Redd," "Blue" or "4.3" in the column whose category is Color. You can enter the group labels of the category into a column by typing the first unique letter of a group or by typing a number corresponding to its order in the category. If you type 1, Red appears in the column, if you type G, Green appears in the column. Finally, you can associate a category with more than one column, eliminating the need to redefine a category for several columns or datasets.

Create a category

When a category is needed (for a category variable, compact variable, or when recoding continuous data to nominal groups) you see the following dialog box:

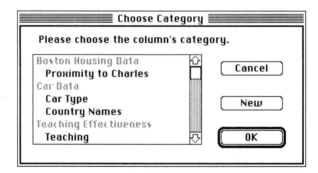

The scrolling list contains all available categories. These are categories used in the active dataset you are working on and all other open datasets. Categories are listed under their originating dataset. You can choose an existing category from this scrolling list or create a new category. To choose an already existing category, highlight it in the scrolling list and click OK.

In this exercise you will create a category and associate it with a variable in a new dataset.

- Open a new dataset by choosing New from the File menu. An empty dataset appears on the screen.

- Move the cursor over Real in the input column of the attribute pane. It turns to: ⊞.

- Click to open the pop-up menu for data type, and drag to select Category. The Choose Category dialog box appears.

If categories were listed in this dialog box now, you could choose one and apply it to the column. No categories are listed because you have not defined any for this dataset yet and no other datasets are open. After you complete this exercise, the category you define will appear in this dialog box and be available whenever the dataset is open.

- Click New to create a new category. The Edit Category dialog box appears:

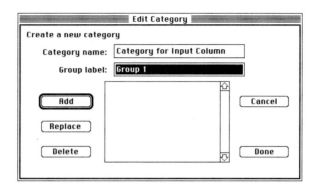

The Category name box is where you enter the name of the category, which can be as long as 255 characters. This name appears only in the list of categories shown in the previous dialog box, it does not show up in your dataset.

- Enter Animals in the Category name box and press Tab. The Group label box becomes highlighted. The labels you enter here represent the specific groups of the category. Group labels can be as long as 255 characters. They appear in the cells of your dataset (and as the sub-headings below the compact variable name when you use a category to define the groups of a compact variable).

- Enter Dogs in the Group label box and click Add or press Return. Dogs appears in the scrolling list.

- Repeat the same procedure using the names Cats and Mice. Remember to click Add after you type each group label in the text box. When you are through, the Edit Category dialog box looks like:

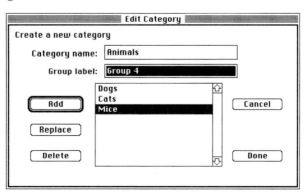

To replace or rename a label, highlight the group label in the scrolling list, type a new name into the Group label box and click Replace. To delete a group label, highlight the group label in the scrolling list and click Delete.

- Click Done to save the category with the active dataset. You have created a category called Animals consisting of three groups, Dogs, Cats and Mice.

- Place the cursor in the input cell of the dataset and type "d". The group label Dogs appears in the cell. Press Return. If you enter a letter that does not begin one of the group names, you get an alert box and nothing appears in the cell.

- Type "2" and press Return. The group label Cats appears in the second row of the input column.

- Choose Save from the File menu, assign a name to this dataset and click Save.

The category Animals will now appear in the Choose Category dialog box anytime this dataset is open and can be selected, even for use with another dataset.

To enter category data

You have two ways to enter data in a column with a category data type:

1. Type the first letter of a group label defined for that category. If the group label has a unique first letter, the entire group label is entered into the cell. If the first letter is not unique, type as many letters as you need to complete a unique group label.

2. Type the ordinal number assigned to the group label and the entire group label appears. Numbers are assigned to category group labels in the order the group labels were defined, beginning with 1.

For example, assume the group labels defined for a category are Low, Medium and High. To enter a category value:

- Type "L", and the category group label Low appears; type "M" and the group label Medium appears; type "H" and the group label High appears.

- Type "1" and the category group label Low appears; type "2" and the group label Medium appears; type "3" and the group label High appears.

Edit categories

You can edit categories using the Edit Categories command in the Manage menu. The following exercise demonstrates the editing functions: change a category name, replace a group label with a new label, add and delete group labels.

- Open the Tree Data in the Sample Data folder.

- Choose Edit Categories from the Manage menu. The Choose Category dialog box appears. The scrolling list displays the names of the categories in all open datasets.

- Select the category "root stock" from the scrolling list.

- Click Edit or press Return. The Edit Category dialog box appears. This dialog box is exactly like the dialog box used to create a new category.

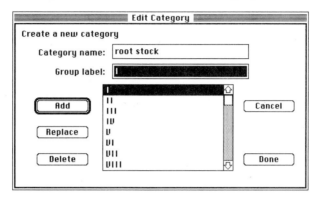

- Click in the Category name box and type "Variety" to rename the category.

- Highlight "IV" in the scrolling list to rename or replace it. The label IV appears in the Group label box.

- Type "Devon" and click Replace. The new group label replaces IV in the list.

- Type "Aston," a new group label, in the Group label box to add a new group to the category.

- Click Add or press Return. The new group label is added at the end of the list.

- Highlight "VII" in the scrolling list. The label appears in the Group label box.

- Click Delete. The group label is deleted from the list; "VII" is deleted from the category.

- You are finished with this exercise. Click Cancel and do not save any changes you have made to this dataset.

You should only delete group labels of categories that have been previously created but that have no data associated with them. If you delete a group label of a category that is in use in a dataset, the group does not disappear. Instead, it is *replaced* with the next group label and all groups adopt the label of the following group. The last group label is replaced by a generic "Group #." For example, a category called Color contains four group labels: Green, Blue, Red and Black. If all the group labels are used in a variable, and you delete the group label Red using the Edit Categories dialog box, every occurrence of Red is replaced with Black and every occurrence of Black is replaced with "Group 4."

Deleting unused categories

You may create a category and later delete the variable which used the category. Doing so do not cause the category to be deleted. It will continue to appear in the list of categories associated with the dataset unless you explicitly delete it. You must use the Edit Categories dialog box to delete these categories. You can delete only categories that are not used by any dataset. If you try to delete a category that is being used, an error message appears.

To delete an unused category:

- Open the dataset in which the category originated.

- Choose Edit Categories from the Manage menu. The Choose Category dialog box appears, displaying the names of the categories in any open dataset.

- Select the category you wish to delete and click Delete.

Compact variables

A compact variable is a data structure consisting of columns of continuous data identified by the groups of a category. Data you collect may contain information about the different classifications that group the observations. For instance data collected on the heights of opera singers might also include information on what part they sing: soprano, alto, tenor or baritone. A variable used to identify which group an observation belongs to is called a nominal variable, or grouping variable. Used by itself this nominal variable allows you to get a count of the number of observations that fall into the different groups. More often, this variable is used with other variables so you can compare values for the different groups.

In the opera singer example, you can use the nominal variable to see whether the singer's height depends on the part they sing. The method of entering singing part into a dataset has to allow an analysis to identify one part for each height value. There are two different ways to enter this data to convey the information to an analysis: nominal variables and compact variables. For more information on groups and nominal variables, see the Dataset organization section at the beginning of this chapter.

Scheme 1: Use a nominal variable to identify groups

In this layout, the heights of the opera singers appear in a single column. Another column contains the information about which group (singing part) is associated with each observation. The dataset has as many rows as there are singers, with each row representing a different singer. A dataset using a nominal variable looks like this:

```
┌─────────────────────────────────────────────┐
│ □ ═══════ Untitled Dataset #1 ═══════ ⊡▤    │
│ ┌─────────┐ ┌────────┐ Criteria: ┌──────────┐ ▤ │
│ │ Compact │ │ Expand │          │No Criteria│   │
│ └─────────┘ └────────┘          └──────────┘   │
│        │  Height  │   Part   │ Input Column │↕ │
│   1    │    62    │ Soprano  │              │⇧ │
│   2    │    62    │  Alto    │              │   │
│   3    │    64    │ Soprano  │              │   │
│   4    │    65    │  Alto    │              │   │
│   5    │    66    │ Soprano  │              │   │
│   6    │    66    │  Tenor   │              │   │
│   7    │    67    │  Alto    │              │   │
│   8    │    67    │  Alto    │              │   │
│   9    │    68    │  Alto    │              │   │
│  10    │    69    │  Tenor   │              │   │
│  11    │    70    │ Baritone │              │   │
│  12    │    71    │  Tenor   │              │   │
│  13    │    72    │ Baritone │              │   │
│  14    │    72    │  Tenor   │              │   │
│  15    │    76    │  Tenor   │              │⇩ │
│ ┌──────────────────────────────────────────┐  │
│ │ StatView 4.0   ◼ ◁ □               ▷◫   │
└─────────────────────────────────────────────┘
```

Scheme 2: Use a compact variable to identify groups

In this layout, there is a separate column of continuous data for each distinct group (singing part). The heights of the opera singers go into a particular column depending on which group they belong to. Rows of the dataset no longer represent different singers. A dataset with a compact variable looks like this:

```
┌──────────────────────────────────────────────────┐
│ □ ═════════ Untitled Dataset #1 ═════════ ⊡▤     │
│ ┌─────────┐ ┌────────┐ Criteria: ┌──────────┐  ▤  │
│ │ Compact │ │ Expand │          │No Criteria│     │
│ └─────────┘ └────────┘          └──────────┘     │
│       │          Height           │             │↕│
│       │Soprano│ Alto │ Tenor │Baritone│Input Column│⇧│
│   1   │  64   │  68  │  71   │  70   │            │ │
│   2   │  66   │  67  │  72   │  72   │            │ │
│   3   │  62   │  67  │  76   │   •   │            │ │
│   4   │   •   │  62  │  66   │   •   │            │ │
│   5   │   •   │  65  │  69   │   •   │            │⇩│
│ ┌────────────────────────────────────────────┐   │
│ │ StatView 4.0   ◼ ◁ □                 ▷◫   │
└──────────────────────────────────────────────────┘
```

In this dataset, Heights is a single compact variable. The four columns Soprano, Alto, Tenor and Baritone are directly analogous to the four group labels in the nominal variable, Parts, in the previous layout. Even though this compact variable consists of four individual columns, you can still select the entire variable by clicking on Heights, just as if you were selecting it in the normal layout.

As you can see, compact variables are drawn differently in a dataset than other variables. The top line shows the name of the compact variable — in this case the Heights of the singers. Below that are the individual columns which identify the different groups. The headings for the columns are the group labels which comprise the category associated with this compact variable.

Compact variables are not automatically created when you create a new column. To enter data using the first scheme above you simply create another column to contain the nominal information. To use a compact variable, you must tell the program that this collection of columns is related — has a particular structure — and identify the different groups labels and what they represent. The structure which identifies the groups of a compact variable is a category. If you have not read about categories yet, read the Categories section earlier in this chapter. The following discussion about creating compact variables assumes you have an understanding of categories.

Compact variables and the variable browser

Compact variables appear differently than other variables in the variable browser. The name of the compact variable appears as a single line in the browser, preceded by a triangle and followed by a ☺ symbol. Click on the triangle to the left of a compact variable in the variable browser to reveal the name of the category variable(s) which define the groups of the compact variable.

The variable browsers for the two previous datasets appear below:

Normal layout   *Compact variable*

In the first layout, both variables appear in the variable browser with nominal and continuous class indicators and there are separate lines for each variable. In the second layout, the name of the compact variable appears on a single line and indented directly below it appear the names of the category or categories that define the groups. As you can see, if the triangle next to the compact variable points down, the variable browser displays identical information. There will be as many lines in the variables browser for the compact variable (if the triangle is open) as there are for the same information using the standard layout.

You can select both the continuous and nominal portions of the compact variable in the browser by clicking on them. When you click on the continuous portion, Heights, in the variable browser it is exactly like selecting the Heights variable in a normal dataset layout. It will be used in any analysis, with the exception of Repeated Measures ANOVA, in the exact same manner as in the normal layout. (For more information on Repeated Measures ANOVA, see chapter 18.) You can select the nominal portion and assign it to an analysis if you need to identify the groups of the compact variable for an analysis or plot. For information on using compact variables in analyses, see the Data organization sections of Chapter 15, Unpaired Comparisons, and Chapter 18, Analysis of Variance (ANOVA).

Create a simple compact variable

A simple compact variable is one in which the compact variable contains just a single category to identify the nominal groups. The opera singer example above is a simple compact variable which uses a single category to identify the four singing parts. In this exercise you will create a compact variable that identifies two different groups in your data. This is useful when your dataset has values for each group in separate columns.

This dataset contains cholesterol measurements for male patients in the first column and those for females in the second column. To see if there is any difference between male and female cholesterol levels, you need to create a compact variable so the analysis will be able to identify and label the different groups. Creating a compact variable lets you keep the data in this layout and still perform analyses comparing groups. Analyses such as an unpaired t-test require a different data arrangement, which you can avoid by using a compact variable.

- Open the Simple Compact Dataset in the Sample Data folder. The dataset appears on the screen.

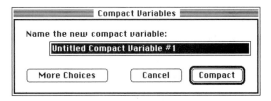

The two or more variables you select to compact do not need to be next to one another; however they all must be of the same type. To select the variables, click on the first variable name then drag to the last variable, or click on the first variable name and hold down the Shift key and click on the last variable. To select discontiguous variables, hold down the Command ( ) key while clicking.

- Select the Male and Female variables and click the Compact button at the top of the dataset or in the variable browser. The Compact Variables dialog box appears.

```
══════════════ Compact Variables ══════════════
Name the new compact variable:
┌────────────────────────────────────────────┐
│ Untitled Compact Variable #1                 │
└────────────────────────────────────────────┘

  [ More Choices ]        [ Cancel ]   [ Compact ]
```

- Type Cholesterol as the compact variable name and click Compact. The dataset looks like this:

The compact variable name, Cholesterol, appears as the top label in the dataset. It is the name you entered in the dialog box. The groups of the compact variable are labelled with the names of the individual variables you selected (Male and Female, in this case). The category which includes the group labels Male and Female appears in the variable browser as "Category for Cholesterol" (which may be truncated depending on the width of the variable browser).

The compact variable is displayed in its "closed" state on the left. On the right it is "open," displaying the group information with the default name of Groups for Cholesterol. You can now use this data in an analysis that compares groups by opening the compact variable, selecting both lines, and assigning it to the analysis.

When you create a compact variable, you automatically create a new category. Like all categories, this one remains associated with the dataset it was created for and can be referenced by any operation that uses categories. You can change the name of the category or of any groups choosing Edit Categories from the Manage menu as described in the earlier the section, Edit Categories.

Create a complex compact variable

A complex compact variable is one in which two different nominal variables define the structure of the compact variable. It is analogous to a dataset with two nominal variables and a single continuous variable. The intersection of the groups of the nominal variables defines a cell. In a compact variable there are as many columns as there are cells of the nominal variables. There are no analyses that *require* this variable structure, though you may find it useful if you prefer to enter your data with columns identifying different groups as opposed to using separate nominal grouping variables to identify groups. You can also create complex compact variables if your quantity of interest is arranged across several columns (e.g., the four columns young males, old males, young females, old females could be compacted by age and gender.)

Consider the opera singer data with one nominal variable dividing the data into singing parts (soprano, alto, tenor and baritone) and a second nominal variable dividing the data into left-handed and right-handed singers. A compact variable that captures all this information needs eight columns in the dataset to contain the continuous variable, height. Four parts x two hands = eight columns: left-handed sopranos, left-handed altos, left-handed tenors, left-handed baritones, right-handed sopranos, right-handed altos, right-handed tenors and right-handed baritones. In creating the compact variable you have to create two different categories — handedness and part — in order to identify all the groups.

- Open the Opera dataset in the Sample Data folder. The dataset appears on the screen.

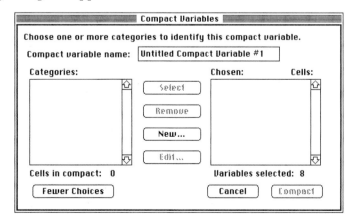

- Select all eight variables by clicking on LHS, holding down the shift key and clicking on RHB. The variables you compact do not need to be next to one another; however they all must be of the same type. To select discontiguous variables, hold down the Command key while clicking.

- Click the Compact button at the top of the dataset or on the variable browser. The Compact Variables dialog box appears.

- Since you are creating a complex compact variable, click More Choices. The following dialog box appears:

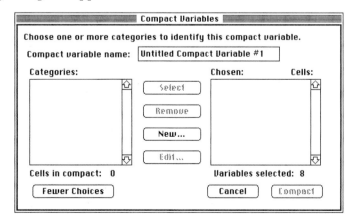

The scrolling list on the left contains the names of categories in all open datasets. The scrolling list on the right contains the categories that make up this compact variable (none, yet). Below this list is a piece of important information: the number of variables selected in the dataset. This number must equal the product of the number of groups in each chosen category before you can create the compact variable.

The number of groups in each category is listed to the right of the category name, in the cells column. Since you have eight columns selected in the dataset, representing two groups, you need two categories whose product equals eight. In this case, Handedness has two groups: left-handed and right-handed. Part has four groups: soprano, alto, tenor and baritone. The "Cells in Compact" for this compact variable will total eight: the product of the two levels of Handedness and four levels of Part (4 x 2 = 8).

The controls in the middle of the dialog box create categories and move them from one list to another as follows:

Control	Description
Select	Takes the selected category from the left-hand scrolling list and adds it to the scrolling list on the right.
Remove	Removes selected categories from the right-hand scrolling list.
New	Lets you create a new category which is added to both scrolling lists. You use this button to build a compact variable when the categories which describe the structure of the compact variable do not already exist (see the second example in the next section). For more details on creating categories, see the section, Categories, earlier in this chapter.
Command-New	Automatically creates a category using the names of the selected columns in the compact variable for group labels.
Edit	Allows you to edit selected categories from the right hand scrolling list. For more details on editing categories, see the section, Edit categories, earlier in this chapter.

If you select a category by mistake, click Remove to remove it from the definition of the compact variable. If you make a mistake in creating a category, use the Edit button to correct it.

- Type "Weight" in the Compacted variable name box at the top of the dialog box. This name later appears in the dataset as the name of the compact variable.

- Click New. The Edit Category dialog box appears.

- Type "Part" in the Category name box at the top and press Tab.

- Type "Soprano"in the Group label box and click Add. The name appears in the scrolling list below the text box.

- Type "Alto," "Tenor," and "Baritone," in that order, clicking Add after each until all the group labels of the first category are entered.

- Click Done when you are finished entering group labels.

The right-hand scrolling list in the Compact Variables dialog box contains the newly created category, "Part," and indicates it has four groups. The number of variables selected is eight, which is *greater* than the product of the number of cells defined by the "Part" category. Therefore, you need to define at least one more category. The number of additional categories you need to define at this point is dependent on the structure of your dataset.

- Click New again to create the second category. The Category dialog box appears.

- Type "Hand" in the Category name box at the top and press Tab.

- Type "Left"in the Group label box and click Add. The name appears in the scrolling list below the text box.

- Type "Right"in the Group label box, click Add and click Done.

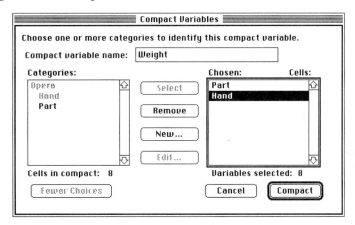

The right-hand scrolling list in the Compact Variables dialog box now contains two categories, Parts and Hands, with four and two groups, respectively. The product of their groups now equals the number of variables selected. Click Compact and the dataset appears.

| | Soprano | | Alto | | Tenor | | Baritone | |
	Left	Right	Left	Right	Left	Right	Left	Right
1	131	179	158	146	151	159	185	161
2	140	182	143	140	157	175	138	154
3	147	168	163	155	163	141	176	172
4	153	169	166	163	162	156	171	130
5	170	140	185	139	176	159	160	151
6	154	145	157	171	151	174	186	142
7	129	174	151	158	170	156	161	181
8	153	165	151	167	165	156	150	155
9	158	150	161	166	172	159	157	155
10	159	192	152	144	167	142	142	186

StatView 4.0

Expand a compact variable

You can remove the compact structure from a variable using the Expand button at the top of the dataset or in the variable browser. If you expand a compact variable by mistake, you can restore its compact structure using Undo in the Edit menu. To remove a compact variable:

- Select a compact variable by clicking on its name.

- Click Expand. The compact structure is removed from the variable and the original variable names reappear.

When you expand a complex compact variable that has more than one category defining it, the compact expands only one "level" when you click the Expand button. To expand the compact variable you created in the Opera dataset above, select it and click Expand. That leaves you with four simple complex variables (Soprano, Alto, Tenor and Baritone), each of which must be expanded individually.

Save datasets

You can save changes to any active dataset by choosing Save from the File menu. If you want to save the changed dataset under a different name and preserve the original dataset unchanged, choose Save As from the File menu. If the file is untitled when you choose Save, you get a directory dialog box to name it. The directory dialog box always appears when you choose Save As.

You can save your dataset in any of four formats using the pop-up menu in the directory dialog box. The normal format that StatView uses is StatView 4.x Data. You can also choose text file format (for transferring data to other applications), Old StatView Data (the format for saving StatView II, StatView SE+Graphics and StatView 512+ files) or SuperANOVA Data format.

StatView 4.x data

It is best to save files as StatView 4.x Data unless you plan to transfer data to another application. When you save as StatView 4.x Data, you retain all information about the dataset including formula definitions, criteria, the current selection, which rows are currently included, and so on.

Text

When you save data as text, only the actual data displayed is saved. For Real data, this means that only the decimal places currently displayed are saved. If you transfer data to another application, make sure to display enough decimal places to meet your needs before saving your data as a text file. Formula, Recode, Series and Criteria definitions are lost. When you select Text, this dialog box appears:

```
┌═══════════════ Export ═══════════════┐
│                                       │
│ Please specify how to save this text file. │
│ Separate items with:                  │
│ ◉ Tabs   ○ Commas  ○ Returns  ○ [    ]│
│                                       │
│ ☒ Save column names                   │
│ ☐ Enclose text items with quotes      │
│ ☐ Save Category columns as small integers │
│                                       │
│         [  Cancel  ]   (( Export ))   │
│                                       │
└═══════════════════════════════════════┘
```

Radio buttons at the top let you choose which character separates data points in the text file. Use the default of Tab, if possible. The other common options are commas or return characters. You can also enter another single character into the text box to the right of the buttons. The checkboxes let you save variable names with the dataset, enclose text in quotes and save category group labels as ordinal numbers. For more information on exporting data see the Importing and Exporting Data chapter.

If you are exchanging data with MacSpin from Abacus Concepts, you need to save and import data as delimited text. Do this using the Tab choice in the dialog box when saving as text or in the Import dialog box.

Old StatView data

Files saved as StatView 4.x Data cannot be read by StatView II, StatView SE+Graphics or StatView 512+. If you use any of these packages and would like to maintain file compatibility, save the files in Old StatView format. All numeric data will be saved, but you lose the following information:

> formula, recode, series and criteria definitions
>
> data class and data format attributes
>
> compact variable structures (these are saved in expanded format)

In addition, you will not be able to save Date/Time or Currency variables in a dataset unless you change the data type to something other than date/time or currency before saving.

SuperANOVA data

If you save a dataset in SuperANOVA format, nearly all information is kept intact except for the following:

Current selection of cells, rows or columns is lost.

The excluded rows distinctions are lost. All rows become included in the dataset.

Certain functions that appear in formulas in StatView are not available in SuperANOVA. (date/time functions, OneGroupChiSquare and ReturnChiSquare)

If your formulas contain functions that SuperANOVA does not recognize, SuperANOVA opens the Formula dialog box with the dataset and highlights the unknown function. You have two choices in this situation:

You can cancel the Formula dialog box. This retains the computed values in the formula column. If you save this dataset, you can read it back into StatView and all the formula information will be intact.

You can change the formula column from Dynamic Formula to User Entered. This removes the formula definition. If you read this dataset back into StatView 4.x after saving it in SuperANOVA, the formula definition is lost. If you do not save it in SuperANOVA first, it reverts to dynamic formula.

Close datasets

Close a dataset by clicking in the close box in the upper left corner of the dataset or choosing Close *name of dataset* from the File menu. You will be prompted to save any changes you have made since last saving the dataset.

If you attempt to close a dataset whose variables are used in an open view, you will be alerted to this fact. If you continue and close the dataset without closing the view first, all of the variables from the dataset will be removed from the view. We advise you to close views that use the variables of a dataset *before* closing the dataset. In addition, if you close an Untitled dataset (one not yet saved or a text file that has not been saved as a StatView document) and do not save it, StatView will not able to match the dataset with any view(s) that use the variables of that dataset.

If you close a dataset in StatView that was created by SuperANOVA, StatView 512+, StatView SE+Graphics or StatView II, you are asked whether you want to save changes. If you click OK, you get a directory dialog box. You have the option to rename the dataset or save the dataset under its original name. If you rename it, the original dataset will be preserved in Old StatView or SuperANOVA format. If you save it using the same name, you replace the old data format with StatView 4.X data format, in which case the dataset is no longer accessible to the other programs. Remember, that while StatView can read any dataset created by these programs, they cannot currently read a StatView dataset.

Open existing datasets

The Open dialog box has a pop-up menu that lets you specify which types of files are shown in the dialog box. The default choice is "All Available," meaning all types that StatView can open, including both datasets and views. You can use this pop-up menu to limit the choices to one of the following: All data (for all the types of data files that StatView can open) StatView 4.x data, SuperANOVA data, Old StatView data, Text and StatView 4.x View.

If you are opening a text file, you need to specify how to import the data. See the Importing and Exporting Data chapter for more information on importing text files.

Print a dataset

The dataset must be the front window when you want to print it. If the attribute pane is open, all attribute and summary statistics will print as well as the data. When you choose Print from the File menu, the entire dataset is printed. Row numbers and variable names always appear on printouts. You can also print a dataset (or a view) from the Finder by selecting the document's name or icon and choosing Print from the File menu.

Chapter

4

Importing and Exporting Data

StatView imports text files from other Macintosh applications such as Microsoft Excel or 4th Dimension, as well as from non-Macintosh applications such as dBase, Lotus 1-2-3 and SAS. StatView can access text files created by non-Macintosh applications by means of a terminal emulation program, a network, third party utilities such as DOS Mounter or Access PC, or Apple File Exchange for an MS-DOS disk.

 You do not need to set variable attributes in an empty dataset before importing your data. StatView automatically creates columns and sets attributes for your imported data by interpreting the data's structure from the format of the text file. If you need to combine several imported text files in one dataset, or add imported data to an existing dataset, you can do so by adding multiple columns or rows and using Copy and Paste.

Importing prerequisites

You need to save the data to be imported in a text file (ASCII format). Check the manual for your source application to see how to save a file in text format.

When importing a text file, StatView assumes that the data is organized in a row by column format, with each row (case) occupying a single line and each data point in a line separated by one or more separator characters such as a tab, comma or space. The default format expects data points separated by tabs with a carriage return at the end of each line. You can use double quotations (" ") to group complex data points.

StatView handles a wide range of separator characters. If the manual for your source application does not identify which ones are used, a text editor can display the symbols for them. If you do not have a text editor, a word processor is a suitable substitute if you choose the option to display all formatting symbols.

Import from Excel

This quick exercise shows how to save an Excel spreadsheet as a text file that StatView can import. If you have a file in another application, continue to the next section.

- First, make sure your Excel file has no formatting characters in it, such as percent signs %, slashes /, or other such characters (commas, decimal points and dollar signs $ are fine).

- In Excel with your worksheet open, choose Save As from the File menu.

- Click Options.

- Choose Text as the file format in the dialog box. Click OK.

- Type a name for the file.

- Click Save and quit from Excel.

Text file import

StatView imports text files from any Macintosh program or diskette containing Macintosh-formatted files. The following exercise uses a sample text file from the Sample Data folder.

- In StatView, choose Open from the File menu. This dialog box displays all the types of files StatView can open.

- Change the Show pop-up menu to Text, so only text files appear in the list.

- Select the Text File Example in the Sample Data folder (or use your own text file), and click Open. The Import dialog box appears.

```
╔══════════════ Import ══════════════╗
║ Please specify how this text file looks.        ║
║ Items may be separated with tabs and:           ║
║  □ spaces □ commas □ returns □ [      ]          ║
║  Number of variables:      [0   ]               ║
║  □ Convert small integers to Categories.        ║
║  □ Make variables with errors have type string  ║
║        ( Cancel )      (( Import ))             ║
╚═════════════════════════════════════╝
```

- The Text File Example from Word uses tabs as the separator character, as do text files from Excel, so leave the default settings and click Import.

StatView makes two passes through the data to place the data in the correct columns and assign the variables the correct data type (integer, real, currency, string, and so on). A dataset appears on the screen when the importing operation is complete.

Import dialog box options

The Import dialog box settings specify characteristics of the text file and how it is translated into a dataset. StatView recognizes tabs, spaces, commas, returns or any user-entered character as separator characters. Tabs are the default. If you used returns as separators, you need to enter the number of variables in the "Number of variables" text box.

The "Convert small integers to categories" option is useful if your source application uses integers rather than alphanumerics to code the levels of groups. For example, a text file variable of "1" and "2" representing Male and Female will be converted to a category with two groups: Group 1 and Group 2. Once the import is complete, you can edit the category and change Group 1 to Male and Group 2 to Female. Integer variables are converted to categories only if the integer variable contains less than 255 unique elements and the element with the lowest integer value is between 0 and 6.

The option to "Make variables with errors have type string" is helpful if your imported dataset appears with many missing values (•) that you think should not be there. Use this option if the number of importing errors StatView reports seems unusually high. This occurrence can indicate incompatible data in a variable, usually as a result of missing or incorrect separator characters. You can import the text file again with this option checked. Any variables with errors are imported as string variables so all data values are displayed. Now you are able to examine the variable, correct the errors and set it to the appropriate data type using the attribute pane. See the later section on Data type identification for more information on incompatible data types.

Variable name identification

The first line in your text file must meet both the following criteria in order to be recognized as variable names rather than as a row of data:

No purely numeric entries on the first line

All entries are unique within their respective columns

A purely numeric entry such as "1987" is not considered a variable name (even if it is enclosed in quotation marks), but a variable name can begin with a number, such as "2nd measurement." If the first line of data meets the first criteria, each entry is compared to all other entries in its column. If none of the first line entries are repeated within their columns, the first line appears as variable names in the dataset.

If any cell in the first line does not meet these criteria, all variables are given default names (Column 1, Column 2, etc.), and the first line of the text file is treated as data points. You can rename the variables by selecting them and typing the new name.

The data in the example below will import with default variables names, since the first entry in the middle column is also one of the groups in the category.

Type	Light	Score
A	None	43
B	Candle	49
B	None	38
A	Light	42
B	Candle	50

Data type identification

Each variable in the dataset is assigned a data type based on the number of data points of each type found in the text file's column. StatView assumes a variable consists wholly of the simplest data type, integer, until it reads a more complex data type. Each variable is considered separately, and each data point in the variable is counted as either integer, long integer, real, string, date/time or currency data. These counts are used to assign a type to the variable as follows:

- If either integers, long integers or reals have the highest count, the variable is assigned real if contains a single real value. If there are no real values, the variable is assigned long integer if there is a single long integer value. If there are no real or long integer values, the variable is assigned integer.

- If currency or date/time have the highest count, the corresponding type is assigned to the variable if more than 50% of the data points are currency or date/time. If they appear less than 50% of the time, the variable is assigned the type of the data value with the next highest count.

- If strings have the highest count, the variable is assigned string unless there are repeated values. If there are repeated values and less than 256 distinct strings appear in the variable, the variable is assigned category.

Most variables contain a single data type, so the assignment of type is straightforward. Sometimes, data entry errors or missing separator characters combine different types of data in the same variable. When a data point is incompatible with the data type assigned to the variable, it appears as a missing value (•). If you have a lot of missing values in a variable, use the last option in the Import dialog box, "Make variables with errors have type string." String variables can contain any data point, so you can examine the variable, determine what the problem is, fix it, and then change the type of the variable to the correct type.

The following exercise illustrates data type assignment and the effectiveness of the "Convert small integers to categories" choice in the Import dialog box.

- In a word processing application, open the Text File Example in the Sample Data folder. In Microsoft Word it appears like this:

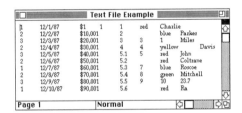

- In StatView, choose Open from the File menu, select the Text File Example from the Sample Data folder and click Open.

- In the Import dialog box, leave the default settings and click Import. The dataset appears on the screen.

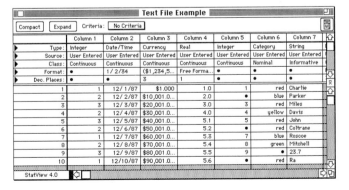

95

- Close this dataset without saving it, so you can import the text file again in the next exercise.

The following table illustrates the data type assigned to each variable and the reason for assigning this particular type.

Variable	Data type	Reason
1	Integer	All the values are integer.
2	Date/Time	All the values are date/time.
3	Currency	All the values are currency.
4	Real	Although nine out of ten values are integer, the variable contains a single real value.
5	Integer	All values are integer. The three missing values do not affect data type.
6	Category	Eight out of ten values are string but there are repeated strings (red and blue). The number 1 is interpreted as the first group label (red); 10 is converted to a missing value because there are only four groups.
7	String	Nine out of ten values are string and none are repeated. The number 23.7 is merely another string.

You can transfer more of the information from the text file to the dataset by using the "Convert small integers to categories" option in a second import.

- Choose Open from the File menu.

- Select Text File Example and click Open.

- In the Import dialog box, click the "Convert small integers to categories" checkbox and click Import The dataset appears again.

Column 1 and Column 5 are now category variables (column 1 contains Group 1, Group 2 and Group 3 rather than integers 1, 2 and 3). You can change the group labels for this category so they are more informative. See the Edit categories section in the Datasets chapter for details on editing category group labels.

Missing values

Two adjacent separator characters in a text file appear as a missing value in the dataset. For example, if you press these keys while creating a text file:

1 Tab 3 Tab 5 Tab 7 Tab Tab 11

The following data points would appear in the imported dataset:

$$1 \quad 3 \quad 5 \quad 7 \quad \bullet \quad 11$$

Most Macintosh spreadsheets and databases display missing fields (missing values) between two successive separator characters. There is one exception to this rule: Multiple *spaces* are not read as multiple missing values. They are compressed into a single space and read as a single separator. For example, if you enter the following values:

$$38 \quad \text{space} \quad 4 \quad \text{space} \quad 12 \quad \text{space} \quad \text{space} \quad \text{space} \quad 19$$

You might expect the three consecutive spaces to translate as two missing values in six variables:

$$38 \quad 4 \quad 12 \quad \bullet \quad \bullet \quad 19$$

Instead, the spaces are treated as one separator character, leaving four variables:

$$38 \quad 4 \quad 12 \quad 19$$

Export StatView data

Before exporting data to another application, consider how you want your data to appear in the destination file so you can make the appropriate choices in the export dialog box.

How to export

- With a StatView dataset open, choose Save As from the File menu. The directory dialog box appears.

- Use the Format pop-up menu to select Text.

- Type a name for the text file and click Save. The Export dialog box appears.

- Click the button denoting the separator character used in the receiving application. If that application lets you choose the separator character, select Tab.

- Click a checkbox to select one or more of the following options:

    save column names

    enclose text items with quotes

    save category columns as small integers (if the receiving application does not recognize alphanumeric data)

- Click Export. Refer to the receiving application's manual if you need help importing the text file.

Data exchange between Abacus Concepts products

Many StatView users also use StatView II, MacSpin or SuperANOVA. StatView reads files created by StatView II and SuperANOVA and can save files in those formats as well. You do not need to convert your datasets to text when moving between these packages. StatView cannot currently open or save files in the MacSpin file format, so you must transfer your datasets as text.

StatView automatically lists StatView II and SuperANOVA datasets in the directory dialog box. You open them directly from the File menu, with the Open command. You can list files of only a certain type in the directory dialog box. Select the desired file type from the pop-up menu to make it easier to locate a desired dataset.

To write a dataset that can be read by StatView II or SuperANOVA, select the desired file type from the pop-up menu in the directory dialog box.

Chapter

5

Managing Your Data

There are four commands in the Manage menu that manipulate your data. The Formula command creates new variables based on existing variables, the Recode command replaces missing values or changes continuous data to nominal data, and the Series and Random Numbers commands generate new variables based on a series or random distribution. All four command names are followed by ellipses (…) in the Manage menu, but appear in the manual text without ellipses.

Select the dataset

If you are working in a dataset when you choose Formula, Recode, Series or Random Numbers, the action you take applies to that dataset. If a view is the topmost window when you choose one of these commands, they apply to the open dataset (if there is only one open dataset). If several datasets are open, and a view is the topmost window, you choose the dataset from a dialog box that appears when you select one of these commands.

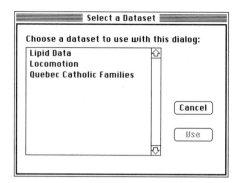

Preferences

You can set preferences for the size and font of the text in all of these dialog boxes (Formula, Series, Recode and Random Numbers) with the Preferences command in the Manage menu. The preferences apply to text derived from the dataset (variable names), function names and text that you enter in the dialog boxes, not the buttons and text of the dialog box itself. This is useful if you want to print the expressions from the dialog boxes in a font different than the default. To set the size and font of text:

• Choose Preferences from the Manage menu.

• From the scrolling list of preferences, choose Formula and click Modify. The Formula Preferences dialog box appears.

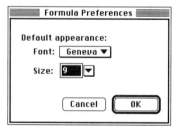

• Choose the preferred font and font size from the pop-up menus. You can type in a size different from the ones that appear on the size menu.

• Click OK. You return to the Choose Preferences dialog box.

• Click Done. The new preferences go into effect the next time you open a Formula, Recode, Random Numbers or Series dialog box.

Beware that enlarging the font size beyond 12 or 14 point may render the buttons in the keypad of the Formula dialog box illegible.

Formula

The Formula command in the Manage menu displays a dialog box containing a list of all the variables available for formula use, a list of all the functions and operators you can use, and a keypad. These are the building blocks of a formula variable. You can create a simple formula to sum two variables, or write a complex formula with many arguments.

There are over 100 functions to choose from, grouped by nine types: date/time, logical, mathematical, probabilities, random numbers, series, special purpose, statistical and trigonometric. You can find a complete list in Appendix B. In addition, the Hints window will display definition for each function as you select it in the list.

Formula variables you create are, by default, dynamically linked to the variables used to define them. For example, if you define a formula variable as "Age/10" and then change a value in the Age variable, the formula variable changes accordingly. You can turn this link on and off by changing the Source of the variable (in the attribute pane) from Dynamic Formula to Static Formula.

The Formula dialog box

When you choose Formula from the Manage menu, the Formula dialog box appears. The dialog box has five regions: the list of variable names, the list of functions, the Attributes button, the keypad and the formula definition.

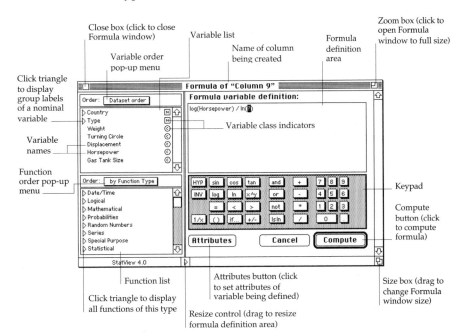

The parts of the formula appear in the definition area as you select them from the lists, type them, or use the keypad. Missing arguments are represented by questions marks. This dialog box behaves like a regular window: you can resize it, use Cut/Copy/Paste on the text, change character font, size and style, and move it behind or in front of other windows. When open, the Formula dialog box is listed in the Window menu where you can select it to bring to the front. You can double-click the top area beneath the title bar to bring the dataset it refers to frontmost.

The triangle at the bottom of the dialog box allows you to resize the function and variable name areas by clicking and dragging it from side to side. If you drag it all the way to the left, the variable and function areas disappear; you can still type in the definition area and use the keypad to create formulas.

You can print the formula definition by choosing Print from the File menu. The resulting document is titled the same as the Formula dialog box's title, and contains only the formula, not the rest of the dialog box. You can change the font and size of the text in this dialog box using the commands in the Text menu, or set the defaults using Preferences, described earlier in this chapter.

Click the Compute button to create the new variable defined by the formula. Click Cancel, Escape, or press Command-Period to cancel the creation of a new variable and close the dialog box. If you are editing an existing formula variable and cancel during the process, the original definition is restored. To access a variable's formula definition for editing, click Dynamic or Static formula in the dataset's attribute pane.

When you click the close box of the Formula dialog box, an alert message asks whether to save the formula. The buttons in the alert box correspond to the buttons in the Formula dialog box in their actions. Save is equivalent to Compute, Don't Save is equivalent to Cancel, and clicking Cancel in the alert box returns you to the Formula dialog box.

Variable list

The scrolling list in the upper left of the Formula dialog box shows the variables that you can use in a formula. You double-click on a variable name to add it to the formula definition where you placed the cursor in the definition. You can view the variable list in one of four orders by choosing from the Order pop-up menu above the list. Your choices are:

```
Dataset order
Alphabetical
by Class
by Usage
```

Each variable name has a class symbol beside it: either Ⓝ for nominal or Ⓒ for continuous. Click the triangle next to a nominal variable to display the variable's group labels in an indented list. The downward pointing triangle next to the nominal variable "Type" below indicates that the variable's groups are shown.

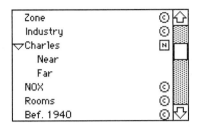

This mechanism provides an easy way to enter a group label from a nominal variable into a formula, which is particularly useful in formulas with if-then-else statements.

The variable list may not contain all the variables that appear in the dataset, and compact variables are listed differently from others. If your compact variable name is Weight and the individual column names (the groups of the category) are Before and After, the variable list in the Formula dialog box will show "Before Weight" and "After Weight." The following variables do not appear in the variable list:

- any variable whose class is informative
- the input column
- the variable whose formula is currently being edited
- any formula-based variables whose formula definition uses the variable currently being edited. For example, assume Kilograms is a formula-based variable whose definition is LBS /2.2, and LBS is the name of a variable in the dataset. If you change the class of LBS to Dynamic formula, Kilograms will not appear in the variable list in the LBS formula dialog box.

Keypad and function list

The keypad and the function list show all the operators and functions available for formulas. The keypad contains the most frequently used operators and functions, including the arithmetic operators +, -, *, and /, and the trigonometric functions sin, cos and tan. The function list contains over 100 other functions, all of which are listed in Appendix B and described in the Hints window.

All of the functions in the list are available when creating or editing a formula using the Formula dialog box. Some are also available in the Random Numbers and Series dialog boxes and when creating or editing a criteria. A complete definition for each function is available in the Hints window. To see a specific definition, select the function and display the Hints window. In the list, note that:

- All the non-hyperbolic trigonometric functions evaluate arguments or return results that are in radians (there are 2π radians in 360°).

- For the logical functions, the value False is represented by the zero (0) value. Any non-zero and non-missing value is equivalent to the value True.

- For the statistical functions, unless otherwise indicated, the first argument must be a variable name. The remaining arguments can be any value unless otherwise indicated. Many of these functions let you specify which rows of the dataset to use in the calculation: *AllRows* (the default), *OnlyIncludedRows*, or *OnlyExcludedRows*.

- The hyperbolic and arc trigonometry functions can be selected from the function keypad by first pressing the INV and HYP keys. For instance, to get the cosh function, press "HYP" then "cos". You can also use the INV key to generate ≤, ≥, and ≠.

The function list works like the variable names list. Enter an operator or function from the list into the formula definition by double-clicking on the function name. You can view functions alphabetically or grouped by function type by using the Order pop-up menu above the functions list. When viewing by function type, click the triangle next to each type to see all the functions of that particular type in an indented list.

Date/Time	Construct, return an integer for and calculate the difference between date/time values. See the section, Date/Time functions, in this chapter for information.
Logical	Make yes-no (true or false) decisions about data
Mathematical	Computational functions exclusive of trigonometric and statistical computations
Probabilities	Distribution functions and their inverses
Random Numbers	Generate random numbers
Series	Generate series
Special Purpose	An assortment of special functions
Statistical	Mathematical functions associated with statistical analyses
Trigonometric	Mathematical functions that relate to geometry

The keypad works just like a calculator keypad. Enter an operator or function into a formula definition by clicking on the appropriate button. The keypad functions listed in the following table can be modified by clicking on the Hyperbolic and/or Inverse keys before entering a function. These keys produce no output themselves, but remain selected until a function is entered after them. The HYP and INV keypad functions are for use only with keypad buttons. The following table lists the keypad symbols and the functions that appear in the definition area if you click them with no modifier, with the HYP modifier, with the INV modifier or with both modifiers. The • means that the modifier key has no effect for a symbol.

Keypad symbol	No modifier	With HYP modifier	With INV modifier	With both modifiers
sin	sin(?)	sinh(?)	arcsin(?)	arcsinh(?)
cos	cos(?)	cosh(?)	arccos(?)	arccosh(?)
tan	tan(?)	tanh(?)	arctan(?)	arctanh(?)
and	? AND ?	•	NOT(? AND ?)	•
+	? + ?	•	? + ?	•
log	log(?)	•	10 ^ ?	•
ln	ln(?)	•	e ^ ?	•
x^y	? ^ ?	•	? ^ (1/?)	•
or	? OR ?	•	NOT(? OR ?)	•
-	? - ?	•	? - ?	•
=	? = ?	•	? ≠ ?	•
<	? < ?	•	? ≥ ?	•
>	? > ?	•	? ≤ ?	•
not	NOT(?)	•	?	•
*	? * ?	•	•	•
1/x	1/?	•	?	•
()	(?)	•	•	•
if…	if?then?else?	•	•	•
+/-	- ?	•	+ ?	•
IsIn	? ElementOf ?	•	NOT(?ElementOf?)	•
/	? / ?	•	•	•

Keypad and function arguments

Most functions have "?" in their name, which represents an argument to a function. Arguments are the values that the operator or function uses to produce a new value. When you enter a function into a formula definition, you need to replace the "?" with the desired argument. This is also true for functions located in the keypad. For example, if you click the Log button, the function Log(?) appears in the formula definition area. Replace the "?" with the desired argument (usually a number or variable).

Many functions can take a varying number of arguments. Functions of this type contain ellipses (…) to indicate that they allow any number of arguments. The arguments to a function can be constants, variables or formulas themselves. For example, the function Sum(Weight, Ln(Age), 10) adds the values from the Weight variable, the natural log of the value from the Age variable and the number 10. Some functions contain default arguments which you can change, such as LinearSeries(1,1), which accepts two arguments. When you enter it into a formula it appears with a 1 for each of its arguments. You can change these default arguments to any values you want.

Attributes button

The variable created by the formula defaults to the name "Column *n*," containing real values with three digits following the decimal point. Click on the Attributes button to display the following dialog box which lets you change the default attributes (name, type, class, format, number of decimal places) of the computed variable.

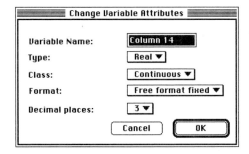

Enter the variable name into the text edit area. The Type, Class, Format and Dec. Places pop-up menus work exactly like the controls in the attribute pane. You can change the formula variable's attributes in this dialog box, or in the dataset's attribute pane later.

Formula definition

The formula definition area is a full text editing area. You can enter your formula here by a variety of methods: clicking on the keypad, double-clicking on variable and function name lists, typing, choosing Cut/Copy/Paste or any combination of these. When you click a button in the keypad or double-click either the variable or function name list, the selected operator is inserted into the formula definition.

When you insert a function name, the first available "?" in the name is automatically selected, indicating where the next argument will be inserted. If a variable name or a number is selected when you insert a function name, the selected item replaces the first "?" and the second "?" is highlighted. If you click an arithmetic operator on the keypad, a placeholder "?" is also inserted for the second argument. When you press Tab, you move to the next "?" or "…" in the function. Similarly, pressing Tab with the Command key down selects the previous "?" or "…".

Build a formula

The following are all valid formula expressions:

-3
1+2
1 + (2 - 10)
3 (4+6)
4^2
log(100)

The expression 3 (4+6) means "3 times the quantity 4 plus 6", or 30. The expression log(100) means "evaluate the base 10 log of the value 100" and it returns 2.00.

A formula can also include references to variables in the same dataset:

Age / 2
Log(Weight)

A formula of this type is evaluated on a row-by-row basis. For example, the expression "Age / 2" is first evaluated for row number 1 of the dataset, then row number 2, then 3 and so on. If the Age value in row number 1 is 10, the resulting formula for row number 1 is 5 (10 divided by 2).

Logical formulas can be created with the if-then-else function, such as:

if Age > 10
then 10
else Age

The result of this formula is "10" for each row of the Age variable with a value greater than 10. Otherwise the result is the existing value of the Age variable in that row.

Exercise

In this exercise you create a new formula variable which is the average of two variables: Triglycerides and Trig-3yrs.

- Open Lipid Data located in the Sample Data folder.

- Choose Formula from the Manage menu.

- Type Triglycerides in the formula definition area. As soon as you type "Trigl" the rest of the variable name is filled in. You type as few characters as are needed to distinguish a variable from all others.

- Click the ⊞ operator on the keypad. A highlighted placeholder is inserted for the second argument. The formula definition looks like this:

- Double-click Trig-3yrs in the variable list. The selected "?" is replaced and the variable name is automatically entered.

Variable names, dates, and nominal levels of a category appear in quotation marks if they are not purely alphabetic or contain spaces.

- Use the cursor to select the entire formula and click the ⬚ () operator on the keypad. The expression is enclosed in parenthesis:

$$\text{(Triglycerides + "Trig-3yrs")}$$

- Click following the closing parenthesis to deselect the expression.

- Click the ⬚ / operator and the constant ⬚ 2 on the keypad. A variable is now defined, with the formula (Triglycerides + "Trig-3yrs")/2.

- Click Compute. The new variable, the average of Triglycerides and Trig-3yrs, appears at the right of your dataset, to the left of the input column.

Shortcuts with formulas

As you saw in the preceding exercise, StatView automatically creates placeholders for arguments and anticipates the rest of a formula or function when you start typing. In a similar way, StatView anticipates arguments for the mathematical operators +, -, *, and /. For example, if you double-click on a variable and then click the + operator, the definition area highlights to indicate that it is ready to take the second argument:

In addition, if any part of a formula is already selected when you insert a function name, the selection is interpreted as the first argument of any function that can take arguments. For example, if you select Weight in the formula definition, and click the Sin button you see:

$$\text{sin(Weight)}$$

When you type variable names or functions in the formula definition, you have to type only the minimum number of characters to identify the word. For example, if you type the characters "w" and "e," and you have a variable named Weight, the remaining characters are automatically entered. However, if you have a variable named "Weight" and a variable named "Weight1," you have to type the whole word, since the letters "we" are not unique. When you begin to type the name of a function, the function is inserted, along with any arguments, and the first argument of the function is selected. If the formula is anticipated incorrectly, simply delete any incorrect characters.

Errors in formula

You get a warning after you click the Compute button if there is an error in the formula definition. The Hints window appears with information about your error and the problematic section of the formula is highlighted in the Formula dialog box. Most errors involve an invalid argument (i.e., a constant rather than a variable), the wrong number of arguments, or unknown variable names. Any formula with an error will not compute. If it is a new formula, missing values will remain in the column until the formula definition is corrected. If you edit the formula for an existing, valid formula variable and cause an error, the original definition remains. When you satisfy the requirements of the formula and click Compute, the formula calculates. Choose Hints from the Window menu for additional help while you are building your formula.

Dynamic vs static

The source of a variable is visible and can be changed in the attribute pane. When you define a formula, its source is *dynamic* by default, if you change data associated with the formula, the formula automatically recalculates. You can change this source to *static*, which keeps recalculation from recurring or *user-entered*, which deletes the formula information completely. You cannot edit the data in a dynamic or static formula variable. A formula variable behaves differently according to its source:

Source	Description
Dynamic formula	Changes every time the variables or formula used to define it change.
Static formula	Does not recalculate when you change the variables or formula used to define it. Changing a dynamic formula to a static formula controls the recalculation of the formula, with the option of changing the variable back to dynamic formula at any time. This is helpful if you plan to do a lot of editing in a dataset that contains formula variables.
User entered	Does not store formula information. Changing a variable from dynamic or static formula to user-entered loses all formula information and makes that variable editable again. Do this only if you do not plan to access the variable as a formula. For example, to change a variable from Inches to Centimeters, you can create a formula which converts inches to centimeters, change the new variable to user-entered and then delete the original variable.

If you delete a variable that is used in a formula, you are alerted to the fact that the variable is used in a formula definition. If you continue and delete the variable, the formula which references it will change to a static formula. This keeps the calculated values in the dataset. You can then change the column to user-entered or redefine the formula.

Logical functions

The logical functions available in StatView are listed in Appendix B and defined in the Hints window. When using two or more logical operators in a formula definition, always use a Boolean statement (AND, OR, XOR, IS) between them. For example, to determine whether a value in variable n falls between 0 and 10 you must enter: $(0 <$ variable n) AND (variable $n < 10$) rather than $(0 <$ Variable $n < 10$).

Also, if you are using a range (Value n:Value m) to determine if a value in a variable falls between the values n and m, you must use the ElementOf operator. The statement should be:

> If Weight ElementOf (150:160)   then ?   else ?

not

> If Weight = (150:160)   then ?   else ?

Missing values and functions

Boolean operators return a missing value whenever the truth or falseness cannot be determined in a completely consistent manner. Specifically, these functions treat missing values as follows:

NOT	Return missing if the argument is missing
OR	Return missing if both arguments are missing or if one argument is missing and the other false, but return true if one argument is missing and the other true
AND, XOR, <, >, ≤, ≥, =, ≠, ElementOf	Return missing if either argument is missing
if - then - else	Return missing if the first argument is missing

You can explicitly test for missing values with the IsMissing(?) function. This function returns true if the argument is a missing value, and false otherwise.

Date/Time functions

The date/time functions count time in seconds from 12:01 AM January 1, 1904 to 12:00 AM January 1, 2064. They cannot calculate a date or accept a date/time argument before or after these dates. These boundaries result from the inner workings of the Macintosh and the fact that date/time values are stored as long integers.

 Since time is measured in seconds, every date/time value you enter in a variable or formula is an exact second, whether you specify that second or not. If you enter the value "July 3, 1987", for example, StatView interprets that as exactly 12:00 AM on that date. If you specify only the month and year, "July, 1987," StatView interprets that as 12:00 AM of July 1, 1987. With only the year specified, StatView uses 12:00 AM January 1, 1987 for its calculations. It is important to be aware that an exact second is always used in calculations, and that if you do not include hours, minutes and seconds in an argument, calculations are based on the assumptions described here.

If you specify only a time (hour, minute, second) with no date information for an argument in a function that returns a date, StatView assumes the current day, month and year.

StatView provides you with ten date/time functions. When viewed by function type, they appear under the Date/Time list. There are three types of functions: selector functions, constructor functions and functions that calculate a difference. Selector functions extract fields from a date/time (e.g., the year). Constructor functions create a date/time from the fields (e.g., given a month, date, and year, they create the date/time month/date/year). There is only one function that calculates a difference (DateDifference), and its purpose is to compute the difference between two dates in specified units (e.g., the number of years between the two dates).

Selector functions simply return one part of a date/time value as an integer. Selector functions are:

> Month(?)
> Day(?)
> Year(?)
> Weekday(?)
> Hour(?)
> Minute(?)
> Second(?)

Selector functions take either a date/time constant or a date/time variable for an argument. When typing in a date/time constant for an argument, enclose the constant in quotation marks and separate the month, day and year with any combination of the following marks (with a U.S. system):

Slash /

Dash -

Period .

Space

Comma ,

If you are using StatView with an operating system from another country, you have a choice of date and time formats localized for that country. StatView automatically adopts foreign formatting conventions and allows you to enter date/time values in those formats. Your formatting choices in the attribute pane change also. For a complete list of countries, call Abacus Concepts technical support at (510) 540-1949 between 8:30 AM and 4:00 PM PST Monday through Friday.

The month in a date/time constant can be spelled or abbreviated or a numerical value; numbers can have one or two digits (i.e., 7 or 07); and the year can include or exclude the century. If the century is excluded, StatView assumes you mean the current century. In addition, if you leave the year off entirely, StatView assumes you mean the current year. All of the following are correct for a U.S. system:

"January-1-1987"	"Jan 1, 1987"
"1 1 1987"	"Jan 1"
"1/01/87"	"1/1"
"January/01"	"87 1 January"

In the last case above, "87 1 January," the year is the first value, the day the second and the month the last. You can use this order only if you spell out or abbreviate the month. The month cannot be a number in this date format (with a U.S. system).

If you wish to specify a time in addition to a date, type in the time before or after the date and separate it from the date with a space (not a character). Use the normal hour-minute-second format with colons as separators (with a U.S. system), and add "AM" or "PM" to indicate morning or afternoon. With AM/PM omitted, StatView assumes a 24-hour time cycle. You can also specify morning or afternoon by typing in time as a 24-hour value, i.e., "15:12:31" to mean 3:12:31 PM. These are both valid for the same date/time:

"5/21/89 4:28:15 PM"

"16:28:15 5/21/89"

When using a date/time function to construct a date, set the data type for the formula variable to date/time. You can do this with the Attributes button in the Formula dialog box or in the attribute pane after calculating the result. The functions that construct date/times are: Date(?,?,?) and Time(?,?,?).

StatView returns the date/time value specified, with midnight for the time of a date. The Date and Time constructor functions take integers for arguments. Date(?,?,?) requires the year, month and day, in that order. The month can be spelled or abbreviated or a numerical value; numbers can have one or two digits (i.e., 7 or 07); and the year can include or exclude the century. The second function, Time(?,?,?), requires the hour, minute and second, in that order. Enter a "+" or "-" operator and a constant after any argument to calculate a difference. You can add or subtract values for one or all of the arguments.

In general, when using a date/time constructor function, set the data type for the formula variable to Date/Time and choose a format appropriate for the result, i.e., that displays the result of the function in years, months, days and so forth. Click on the Attributes button in the Formula dialog box to set the data type and format for the formula variable, or change the data type and format in the attribute pane. (If you choose any data type other than Date/Time, StatView returns the number of seconds from midnight January 1, 1904 that the date/time result represents.)

The last date/time function returns a difference:

DateDifference(?,?,?)

This function calculates the difference between the first two arguments in the unit of time specified by the third argument. Enter date/time values in the first two arguments and a value in the third that specifies the unit of time. The units are:

1 = years
2 = months
3 = days
4 = weeks
5 = hours
6 = minutes
7 = seconds

Rules for entering date/time values for arguments in this function are the same as described earlier for date/time selector functions. The following example shows a valid DateDifference function:

DateDifference("7/21/89 11:02:51 PM", "9/13/86 15:02:32", 7)

This function tells StatView to return the difference in seconds between the first date/time constant and the second.

In general, when using the DateDifference function, be aware that this function can return fractional values. There is a fractional difference in years between two months of the same year, for example, or between different months of two years. If you set the data type to integer or long integer, StatView truncates a fractional value to its integral part, i.e., 12.5 becomes 12. (If you set the data type to Date/Time, StatView returns a date/time value corresponding to the number of seconds from midnight January 1, 1904 represented by the result.)

 Caution is required when calculating the difference between months. StatView measures a month as the number of seconds in a year divided by twelve (60 * 60 * 24 * 365.25/12). But months actually vary in length and cannot be exactly described this way. Thus, the differences between months appear as fractional values.

Random numbers

You can add variables to your dataset that contain random numbers generated from several commonly used distributions. These variables are static formula variables created with the Random Numbers command in the Manage menu. The Random Numbers dialog box looks like:

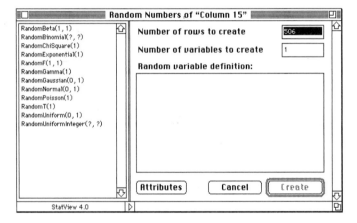

You can change the font and size of the text in this dialog box using the commands in the Text menu, or set the defaults using Preferences, described earlier in this chapter. There are four steps to follow in this dialog box:

1. Select a distribution
2. Replace the "?" or change the default values in parentheses
3. Type the number of rows and columns to create
4. Set the attributes that will apply to the new variable(s)

Distributions

You have a list of twelve distributions to choose from. If you need more information about each distribution, choose Hints from the Window menu. As you click on a distribution, the Hints window offers a brief description of the random numbers it generates. Double-click on a distribution to select it. It appears in the definition area to the right, where you can set the values in parentheses.

Some distributions have "?" in their name while others have default values. As with formulas, a "?" represents an argument which is to be replaced with a constant or formula. You can change the default values (0,1) in any of the definitions once you select one. The Hints window explains what each value or "?" represents.

Definition area

When you select a distribution by double-clicking on it, it appears in the definition area to the right. You can also type the distribution directly into the definition area, as it is a full text editing area. Additional information for the arguments of a distribution can be entered by clicking on the "?" or constant and typing a value or using Cut/Copy/Paste. To access the definition for a variable after it is created, click Static Formula in the attribute pane.

You can also use the Formula dialog box to generate random numbers, since its function list includes the Random Number functions as well. There is a complete list of StatView's functions and operators in Appendix B.

Number of rows and variables

You can create any number of rows and columns of random numbers in one operation. The number of rows created defaults to the number of rows currently in the dataset. You can specify any number of values to generate in the new variable. When you specify a number larger than the number of rows currently in the dataset, rows are added to the dataset and all other columns in those rows are filled with missing value symbols (•) unless they are formula variables and their definition specifies otherwise. The number of variables created initially defaults to one, but you can specify any number of variables you want to create.

Attributes button

The variable created by the random distribution defaults to the name "Column *n*," containing real values with three digits following the decimal point. Click on the Attributes button to display the following dialog box which lets you change the default attributes (name, type, class, format, number of decimal places) of the computed variable.

```
╔═══════════ Change Variable Attributes ═══════════╗
║                                                   ║
║   Variable Name:      [Column 15        ]         ║
║                                                   ║
║   Type:               [ Real ▼]                   ║
║                                                   ║
║   Class:              [ Continuous ▼]             ║
║                                                   ║
║   Format:             [ Free format fixed ▼]      ║
║                                                   ║
║   Decimal places:     [ 3 ▼]                      ║
║                                                   ║
║                     [ Cancel ]   [[  OK  ]]       ║
║                                                   ║
╚═══════════════════════════════════════════════════╝
```

Enter the variable name into the text edit area. The Type, Class, Format and Dec. Places pop-up menus work exactly like the controls in the attribute pane. You can change the random variable's attributes in this dialog box, or in the dataset's attribute pane later.

Variables created using the Random Numbers dialog box are created as static formulas. You can change their source to dynamic or user-entered, but cannot edit the data in a dynamic or static formula variable. A random number variable behaves differently according to its source:

> Static formula: This is the default. You cannot edit the variable.
>
> Dynamic formula: A dynamic formula variable changes every time the original variable used to define it changes or its formula definition changes.
>
> User-entered: Changing to user-entered loses all formula information. You can edit the variable.

Create the variable

Once you define the distribution and set the attributes and number of rows and variables to create, click Create to generate the new variable(s) and close the dialog box. Clicking Cancel cancels the whole process. The new variable of random numbers is appended to the right side of the dataset. You can move it anywhere else by inserting an empty column and using the Cut, Copy and Paste commands in the Edit menu to transfer the data. If there is an error in the definition of the distribution an alert appears in the Hints window when you click Create. For a discussion on errors see the earlier section, Errors in formula.

When you click the close box of the Random Numbers dialog box, an alert message asks whether to save the distribution. The buttons in the alert box correspond to the buttons in the Random Numbers dialog box in their actions. Save is equivalent to Create, Don't Save is equivalent to Cancel, and clicking Cancel in the alert box returns you to the Random Numbers dialog box.

Series

You can add new variables that contain numbers based on a series definition with the Series command in the Manage menu. These variables are static formula variables. The Series dialog box looks like:

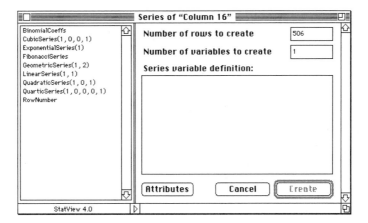

You can change the font and size of the text in this dialog box using the commands in the Text menu, or set the defaults using Preferences, described earlier in this chapter. There are four steps to follow in this dialog box:

1. Select a series
2. Replace the "?" or change the default values in parentheses
3. Type the number of rows and columns to create
4. Set the attributes that will apply to the new variable(s)

Series list

The list on the left contains eight series to choose from. If you need more information about each series, choose Hints from the Window menu. As you click on a series, the Hints window offers a brief description of the variable it generates. Double-click on a series to select it. It appears in the definition area to the right, where you can set the values in parentheses.

Some definitions have "?" in their name, while others have default values. As with formulas, a "?" represents an argument which must be replaced with a constant, formula or variable name. You can change the default values in a series when you select it. The Hints window explains what each value or "?" represents.

Definition area

When you select a series by double-clicking on it, it appears in the definition area to the right. You can also type the series name directly into the definition area, as it is a full text editing area. Additional information for the arguments of a series can be entered by clicking on the "?" or constant and typing a value or using Cut/Copy/Paste. To access the definition for a variable after it is created, click Static Formula in the attribute pane.

You can also use the Formula dialog box to generate series, since its function list includes the Series definitions.

Number of rows and variables

You can create any number of rows and variables of a series in one operation. The number of rows created defaults to the number of rows currently in the dataset. You can specify any number of values to generate in the new variable. When you specify a number larger than the number of rows currently in the dataset, rows are added to the dataset and all other variables in those rows are filled with missing value symbols (•). The number of variables created initially defaults to one, but you can specify any number of variables you want to create.

Attributes button

The variable created by a series defaults to the name "Column n," containing real values with three digits following the decimal point. Click on the Attributes button to display a dialog box which lets you change the default attributes (name, type, class, format, number of decimal places) of the computed variable.

Enter the variable name in the text edit area. The Type, Class, Format and Dec. Places pop-up menus work exactly like the controls in the attribute pane. You can change the random variable's attributes in this dialog box, or in the dataset's attribute pane later.

Variables created using the Series dialog box are created as static formulas. You can change their source to dynamic or user-entered, but cannot edit the data in a dynamic or static formula variable. A series variable behaves differently according to its source:

> Static formula: This is the default. You cannot edit the variable.
>
> Dynamic formula: A dynamic formula variable changes every time the original variable used to define it changes or its formula definition changes.
>
> User-entered: Changing to user-entered loses all formula information. You can edit the variable.

Create the variable

Once you define the series, click Create to generate the new variable(s) and close the dialog box. Clicking Cancel cancels the whole process. The new series variable is appended to the right side of the dataset. You can move it anywhere else by inserting an empty column and using the Cut, Copy and Paste commands in the Edit menu to transfer the data. If there is an error in the series definition of the series an alert appears in the Hints window when you click Create. For a discussion on errors see the earlier section, Errors in formula.

When you click the close box of the Series dialog box, an alert message asks whether to save the series definition. The buttons in the alert box correspond to the buttons in the Series dialog box in their actions. Save is equivalent to Create, Don't Save is equivalent to Cancel, and clicking Cancel in the alert box returns you to the Series dialog box.

Exercise

This exercise creates a new dataset with five variables, each containing one hundred observations.

- Choose New from the File menu. A new dataset appears.

- Choose Series from the Manage menu.

- Double-click on CubicSeries(1,0,0,1) in the series list. Leave the default settings intact.

- Type 100 as the number of rows to create and press Tab.

- Type 5 as the number of variables to create.

- Click the Attributes button.

- Type "Series 1" to name the first of the five variables.

- Click on the triangle next to Dec. Places, drag to 2 and click OK.

- Click Create. Five new variables are added to your dataset.

Recode data

You can recode data from an existing variable to a new variable. The original variable remains unchanged, and a new variable is added to the dataset. There are two types of recoding: you can change all missing values to a chosen value or assign values of a continuous variable to specified groups. When you select Recode from the Manage menu, the Recoding Data dialog box appears.

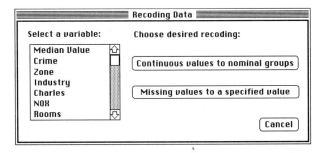

Select the original variable you want to recode from the list on the left. All variables in the dataset, except compacts variables and those whose class is informative, appear in the list. Click either button to choose the preferred recoding. (When you select a nominal variable, the "Continuous Values to Nominal Groups" button dims.) The recoding method you choose determines which dialog box appears for your recoding definition. Both dialog boxes behave as regular windows: you can resize them; use Cut/Copy/Paste on the text; change character font, size and style; and move them behind or in front of other windows. You can print the recode definitions by choosing Print from the File menu.

Missing values to a specified value

This choice lets you change the missing values in an existing variable to a value you specify. This value can be a constant or a function of the variable, such as the mean. The Recode Missing dialog box looks like:

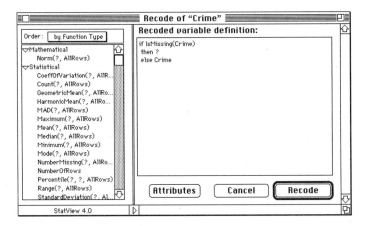

You can change the font and size of the text in this dialog box using the commands in the Text menu, or set the defaults using Preferences, described earlier in this chapter. You can resize the space allocated to the function list and definition area by dragging the triangle at the bottom of the dialog box. If you double-click on the triangle, the function list will toggle between being shown and hidden. When the list is hidden, the triangle is in the lower left and points downward.

Recode definition

The recoding dialog box appears with a formula already entered in the definition area. The formula displayed is:

> if IsMissing("Variable *n*")
>
> then ?
>
> else "Variable *n*"

where Variable *n* is the variable you selected from the previous dialog box. The "?" is a placeholder for the recode function (or constant) you plan to use. To access the Recode definition for a variable once it is created, click Dynamic Formula in the attribute pane.

You can accomplish the same recoding with the Formula command by entering the above if-then-else statement in the definition field of the Formula dialog box.

Recode function list

The list on the left contains different information depending on the class of the variable you are recoding. If your variable is nominal, it lists the levels of the nominal variable. If your variable is continuous, it displays the different types of functions you can apply to a variable when recoding missing values.

You can use the Order pop-up to list these functions by type or alphabetically. When they are listed by function type, click the triangle next to the type to display the list of functions. These functions all return some descriptor of the variable (such as mean, geometric mean, standard deviation). For a description of these functions, choose Hints from the Window menu.

Select the Recode function (or level name) by double-clicking on it. This automatically inserts the function at the correct place in the recode definition.

Attributes button

The variable created by recoding defaults to the name "Column *n*," with the same attributes as the original variable. Click on the Attributes button to display a dialog box which lets you change the default attributes (name, type, class, format, number of decimal places) of the computed variable.

Enter the variable name in the text edit area. The Type, Class, Format and Dec. Places pop-up menus work exactly like the controls in the attribute pane. You can change the random variable's attributes in this dialog box, or in the dataset's attribute pane later.

Variables created using the Recode dialog box are created as dynamic formulas. If you change data in the source variable, the recoded variable automatically recalculates. You can change the source of a recoded variable to static (in the dataset's attribute pane), which keeps it from recalculating, or to user-entered, which deletes the recoding information completely, but cannot edit the data in a dynamic or static formula variable. A recoded variable behaves differently according to its source:

> Dynamic formula: A dynamic recoded variable changes every time the original variable used to define it changes or the recode definition changes.

> Static formula: A static formula recoded variable is a frozen formula variable that does not change when you change the original variables used to define it. By changing a recoded variable from dynamic formula to static formula you prevent the recode from recalculating. You can change the variable back to dynamic formula at any time. This is helpful if you plan to do a lot of editing in a dataset containing recoded variables.

> User-entered: A user-entered variable does not store any recode information. Changing a variable from dynamic or static formula to user-entered retains all the numerical information but deletes all recoding information and makes that variable editable again. Do this if you plan to remove the original data from the dataset and only use the recoded data.

Create the recoded variable

Once you select a function or nominal group to replace the "?", click the Recode button to generate the recoded variable. The Recode dialog box remains open until you close it by clicking in its close box or by choosing Close from the File menu. The recoded variable is appended to the right side of the dataset. You can move it anywhere else by inserting an empty column and using the Cut, Copy and Paste commands in the Edit menu to transfer the data. Clicking Cancel, Escape, or pressing Command-Period cancels the new variable and closes the dialog box. If there is an error in the recode definition, an alert appears in the Hints window. For a discussion on errors see the earlier section, Errors in formula.

When you click the close box of the Recode dialog box, an alert message asks whether to save the recode definition. The buttons in the alert box correspond to the buttons in the Recode dialog box in their actions. Save is equivalent to Recode, Don't Save is equivalent to Cancel, and clicking Cancel in the alert box returns you to the Recode dialog box.

Continuous data to nominal groups

This recoding method derives a new nominal variable from continuous data. This is particularly useful when you have a range of numeric values that you want to reclassify in groups. For example, temperature measurements in degrees recode to hot, temperate or cold; response time measurements in seconds convert to slow, medium and fast. If your data is in date/time format you can recode dates from day/month/year to seasons.

When you click "Continuous values to nominal groups" in the Recode dialog box, you must specify a category to define the groups for the recode. The Category dialog box appears, and you can select an existing category or click New to create a new category with the appropriate group labels. For help with categories, see the Categories section in the Datasets chapter.

After you create or choose a category, the following Recode dialog box appears:

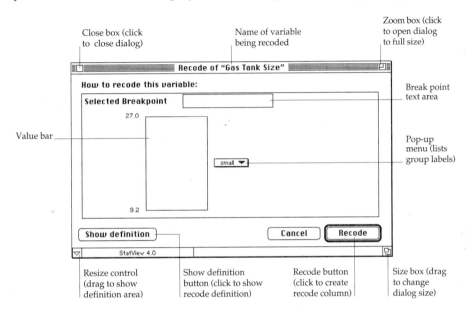

You can change the font and size of the text in this dialog box using the commands in the Text menu, or set the defaults using Preferences, described earlier in this chapter. Double-clicking on the triangle at the lower left of the dialog box splits the dialog box to display the recode definition. The triangle then becomes a split pane control. You can change the space allocated to the definition and the rest of the dialog box by dragging the triangle. Double-click on the triangle to hide the definition when it is showing.

Create the recode

The value bar represents the range of your data. Its top and bottom edges are labelled with the highest and lowest values in the variable you are recoding. You define the boundaries of your groups by setting breakpoints in this bar. You can set breakpoints by moving the mouse up and down in the bar, or by typing the desired breakpoint into the text box above the bar. Use the pop-up menus to the right of the bar to assign the appropriate category group to the range defined by the breakpoints.

To create breakpoints with the mouse:

- Move the cursor over the value bar. The cursor becomes a "+" and its location is displayed to the left of the value bar. As you move the cursor over the value bar its location is continuously updated.

- Click at the location of the desired breakpoint. A dotted line appears across the value bar to indicate the breakpoint. You can move a breakpoint to a new location by selecting and dragging.

To create breakpoints by typing:

- Type a value into the breakpoint text field.

- Press Return. A breakpoint is created at that location and appears in the value bar.

This dialog box is optimized for a category whose elements are ordered from lowest breakpoint value to highest value. If you construct your category in this way, simply type in your breakpoints from the lowest to the highest, pressing Return after each one.

Each breakpoint divides the data into an additional part. A recoding with one breakpoint divides your data into two groups, two breakpoints into three groups and so on. As you add a breakpoint, a new pop-up control appears, cycling through the groups of the category you selected for the data variable. To change the category group assigned to a range, click the pop-up menu control. Drag the mouse to the new group.

If a breakpoint is selected, its value is displayed in the breakpoint text area. Editing the text value will cause the breakpoint to change. To deselect a breakpoint, click in the dialog box outside the value bar.

Show expression

Clicking the Show definition button displays the formula corresponding to the recode you defined. This recode expression is what appears on paper if you choose Print from the File menu. You cannot change any values in here. If you wish to edit the recode formula, you can select the recode expression and use Copy and Paste to transfer it to a formula. (See the Formula definition section earlier in this chapter.)

Exercise

In this exercise, you create a variable that categorizes the risk of heart attack in patients as high, medium or low, depending on their measured HDL-Cholesterol values. The lower the HDL-cholesterol values the higher the risk of heart attack. Values below 35 denote high risk, between 35 and 60 denote medium risk and 60 and above denote low risk.

- Open Lipid Data in the Sample Data folder.

- Choose Recode from the Manage menu.

- Select the variable HDL and click "Continuous values to nominal groups."

- In the Category dialog box, click New and create a category called HDL risk with three group labels in the following order: High risk, Medium risk, Low risk. Click Done after you have created this category.

- In the Recode dialog box, type the number 35 and press Return.

- Type the number 60 and press Return. You have just recoded the HDL levels into the appropriate risk groups. The value bar indicates the breakpoints and the pop-up menus indicate the group associated with each range of values.

- Click the Show Definition button to see the corresponding formula:

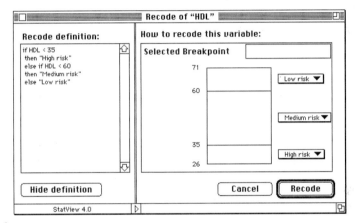

- Click Recode.

The recoded variable is appended to the right side of the dataset. It is currently a Dynamic Formula variable, which means that adding a value to the HDL variable automatically creates the corresponding group in the recoded variable.

6

Exploring Subsets of Your Data

There are several ways to divide your data into subsets for analysis. You can include or exclude any row from an analysis, apply a combination of criteria using logical operators, group criteria with parentheses and reorder data with ascending or descending multi-key sorts. The criteria you create are saved with the dataset and available for reuse through the Criteria pop-up menu at the top of the dataset.

Select the dataset

The Criteria and Sort dialog boxes described in this chapter all apply to the active dataset. If you are working in a dataset when you choose Create Criteria or Sort from the Manage menu, the action you take applies to that dataset. If a view is the topmost window when you choose one of these commands, they apply to the open dataset (if there is only one open dataset). If several datasets are open, and a view is the topmost window, you choose the dataset from a dialog box that appears when you select one of these commands. (If no datasets are open, the commands are dimmed in the Manage menu.)

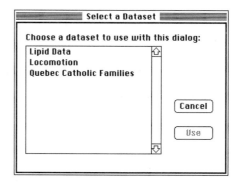

Choose the dataset you wish to use and click Use. The dialog box applies to that dataset. If you leave the Criteria or Sort dialog box open, any other Criteria and Sort dialog boxes you open apply to the same dataset.

Sort data

The Sort command in the Manage menu lets you sort the rows of your dataset in either ascending or descending order using one or more variables of the dataset as the Sort key. For example, when you sort the rows of Lipid Data in ascending order using Cholesterol as the sort key, the subject with the lowest cholesterol value appears in the top row and the one with the highest in the bottom row. When sorting, StatView sorts the entire dataset.

The Undo command in the Edit menu returns a dataset to pre-sort order *only* if you choose Undo immediately after the sort. Otherwise, once you sort your dataset you cannot return it to its original order unless you first take a simple precaution. Before you sort, create a new linear series variable using the Series command. Then you can always sort back to the dataset's original order using the series variable as the sort key. The Sort dialog box looks like:

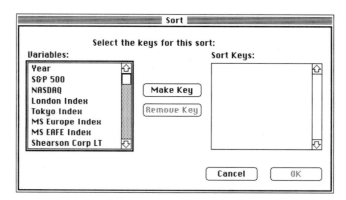

The list on the left contains the names of all the variables in your dataset. To choose the sort key variable, double-click on it or select it and click Make Key. (Typing its first few letters will select the variable.) The variable(s) you select appear in the Sort Keys list on the right. The rows in your dataset will be rearranged according to the order of data in these variables. An arrow precedes the name of each sort key. The arrow indicates whether to sort in ascending or descending order. An upward-pointing arrow indicates ascending order; a downward-pointing arrow indicates descending order. (In alphabetical sorts, A to Z is ascending order.) Click the arrow to toggle between the two.

To remove a variable from the list of sort keys, double-click on it or select it and click Remove Key. When a variable in either list is selected, the list appears with a highlighted line around it. After you have defined the sort, click OK to sort the dataset. You can abort the process mid-sort by typing Command-period.

Missing values are considered the largest values in a variable. Case and accent marks are ignored when sorting text. In string variables with mixed alphanumeric data, numbers are sorted as the smaller values. If you choose more than one sort key, the additional keys are applied only if two values are equal in the first sort.

Include and exclude rows

When you use a variable in an analysis, all the data in that variable is included in the analysis unless you exclude rows (cases). When a dataset is created, all rows are included. You can exclude one or many rows, creating a specific subset of your data for analysis.

You include and exclude rows using the Include Row and Exclude Row commands in the Manage menu. Select rows in your dataset to include or exclude by clicking on the row number (the numbers at the left side of your dataset). You can select any number of adjoining or discontiguous rows at one time. A shortcut to include or exclude all rows is the Select All Rows command in the Edit menu, followed by the Include or Exclude Row command.

You can tell whether a row is included or excluded by its row number. Included row numbers appear in regular, dark type. The row numbers of excluded rows are dimmed. These characteristics appear on a printout of your dataset as well as on the screen. Double-clicking on a row number toggles its state between included and excluded. Changing the state of any row does not affect any other row. The state of a row usually has no effect on the behavior of rows and variables in the dataset, only on its use or exclusion in an analysis. The exception occurs when a formula uses OnlyIncludedRows or OnlyExcludedRows as an argument.

Criteria

You can define criteria to exclude rows from an analysis based on characteristics of one or more variables. For example, you can exclude any patient whose weight is over 250 pounds or all customers who purchased a green car. The criteria you create and apply to your dataset can be as simple or complex as you like and can be saved to apply at any time in your analysis. All criteria are saved when you save a dataset. A list of all available criteria appears in the Criteria pop-up menu at the top of the dataset.

There are four ways to select and define a new criterion:

1. Choose New from the Criteria pop-up menu at the top of the dataset.

2. Use the Create Criteria command in the Manage menu.

3. Choose Edit/Apply Criteria from the Manage menu and double-click on New in the scrolling list in the resulting dialog box.

4. Choose Random from the Criteria pop-up menu at the top of the dataset.

When you do any of these, you get the Criteria dialog box The dialog box behaves like a window — you can resize it, use Cut, Copy and Paste in the text fields, change character font, size and style and move it behind or in front of other windows. When open, the Criteria dialog box is listed in the Window menu where you can select it to bring it to the front.

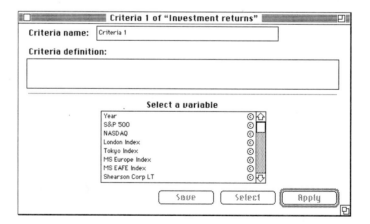

There are four steps to follow in this dialog box: name the criterion, select a variable, choose a comparison operator, and set a value or range of values. The name of the criterion defaults to "Criteria *n*". You can type any name you want to replace the default. This name appears in the Criteria pop-up menu at the top of the dataset.

Below the name rectangle is the definition area where you create and edit criteria. You can print a criterion definition by choosing Print from the File menu. A definition consists of three parts: a variable, a comparison operator and a value. You choose these three parts from the list below the definition, which shows a list of variables, a list of comparison operators, a list of the levels of a variable or a value bar, depending on which you need to choose. You can type in the definition area if you prefer to use the keyboard rather than the mouse.

StatView determines whether you need to see a list or the value bar by the position of the flashing cursor. When the dialog box opens and you have a blank definition area, a list of variables appears in the choices area. If the cursor is flashing after you select the variable, the choices area displays comparison operators. As you edit your criterion, the choices reflect your cursor location. Placing the cursor at the beginning of the criterion definition brings up the variables list again.

Select a variable

A criterion can use any variable in the dataset except the input variable and string variables whose class is informative. Double-click on a variable in the list to include it in the criterion definition. If you enter a variable name by typing, the name is filled in as soon as you have entered the first unique letters.

Choose a comparison operator

After you choose a variable, or if you place the cursor before an operator in an existing criterion, the list displays comparison operators:

Operator	Meaning
<	less than
=	equal to
>	greater than
ElementOf	is an element of
IS	equal to, or both are missing values
≠	not equal to (equivalent form is <>)
≤	less than or equal to (equivalent form is <= or =<)
≥	greater than or equal to (equivalent form is >= or =>)
ISNOT	not equal to, if neither value is missing, or one value missing and the other is not

All the comparison operators except ElementOf can be compared only to a single value. For example, the following are all single-value criteria:

height	>	72
eye color	=	blue

weight   ≤   152

Use ElementOf when you want the criterion to include a range or set of values. You may want to include all groups of a nominal variable except one in your analysis. In that case you use ElementOf and list all but one group in the criterion. Some examples:

Criterion Definition	Effect
weight ElementOf {[100:125]}	Include in the analysis any subject whose weight is greater than or equal to 100 and less than or equal to 125.
dosage ElementOf {(1:1.25], (2:2.25], (3:3.25]}	Include in the analysis any subject with a dosage level that falls in the following ranges: 1 <dosage ≤ 1.25 or 2 < dosage ≤ 2.25 or 3 < dosage ≤ 3.25.
eye color ElementOf {blue, green, brown}	Include in the analysis any subject with blue, green or brown eyes.

Any operation which produces a missing value results in the exclusion of the row. However, the operations IS and IS NOT let you compare values with missing values.

- IS is similar to the = operator, except that if both arguments are missing values, IS returns true rather than a missing value.

- IS NOT is like the ≠ operator, except that if both arguments are missing values, IS NOT returns false rather than a missing value. In addition, if one argument is not a missing value and the other is a missing value, IS NOT returns true rather than a missing value.

The following characters are used to define the values included in a set. These characters appear automatically as you use the value bar, or you can type them into the definition.

Operator	Meaning
{	Beginning of a set
}	End of a set
,	Separates the elements of a set
:	Separates the lower and upper values of the range
[	Include the lower value of the range
(	Exclude the lower value of the range
]	Include the upper value of the range
)	Exclude the upper value of the range

Set a value or range

The value you enter is determined by the comparison operator you use and the class of the variable (nominal or continuous). To aid in setting the values, the choices area displays information on the values you can set. If you choose a continuous variable, a value bar is displayed. If you choose a nominal variable, a scrolling list containing its levels is displayed.

Continuous variable

The value bar appears if the variable in your criterion is continuous. It is a linear representation of the bounds of the variable in the criterion. You use this bar to specify a single value and also to define the bounds of a range of values.

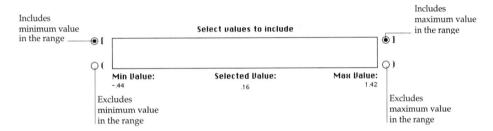

The lowest value in the variable is at the left, labelled Min Value. The highest value of the variable is at the right, labelled Max Value. As you move the cursor from side to side across the bar, the number below Selected Value reflects its position. The display format for these numbers mimics the variable's format.

When you define a range, use the bracket and parentheses at each end of the value bar to include or exclude the maximum and minimum values in the range. The brackets [ ] include values. The parentheses ( ) exclude values. For example, if a variable contains integers between 1 and 10, the range [4:6] contains the values 4, 5, 6, the range (4:6] contains the values 5 and 6 and (4:6) only contains the value 5. You can toggle between brackets and parentheses by clicking on an endpoint then clicking the bracket or parentheses button.

To specify a single value, move the cursor across the bar until the value you want appears under Selected Value, then click. To change the value, click on the vertical line in the bar and drag it to its new location. The Selected Value updates to correspond to the new location. When you use a comparison operator that takes a single value (=, ≠, IS or ISNOT) a single vertical line is drawn indicating the position of the value.

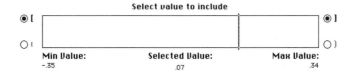

When you use an inequality operator that defines a range (<, >, ≤ or ≥), a left or right brace is drawn and the end of the value bar is fills with a gray pattern. The example below indicates that all values greater than or equal to a given value are included:

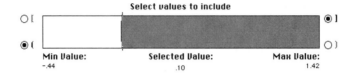

To specify a range of values, move the cursor across the bar until one end of the range appears as the selected value. Press the mouse, drag it to the other endpoint's value and then release it.

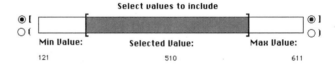

To move an existing range, click on it and drag the entire range across the bar. To change one of the endpoints of a range, click on it and drag the mouse to the new position. You can also change the range values by typing the ranges into the criterion definition.

Nominal variable

When the variable in your criterion is nominal, you see a list of its groups instead of the value bar. If the variable is a category variable, this will be a list of the group labels of the category.

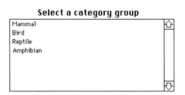

Double-click on the group label to select one or more groups. Use Command-Click to select more than one discontiguous group. If you need to define a criterion to include only rows with missing information for a certain variable, enter a missing value by pressing Option-8.

Combine criteria

A list of Boolean operators appears after you specify the value in a criterion. You can combine as many criteria as you like using AND, OR or XOR. To enter a Boolean operator, type the operator or double-click on it. You can also type & for AND and type | for OR. You can group expressions using parentheses.

Buttons: Apply, Save and Select

The buttons at the lower right corner of the Criteria dialog box give you three options when you are finished creating or editing criteria.

- apply the criterion to the dataset
- save the criterion and apply it later
- select the rows in the dataset which correspond to the criterion

All three buttons save the criterion with the dataset, add it to the Criteria pop-up menu, and bring the dataset to the front.

Button	Action
Save	The criterion is saved and included in the Criteria pop-up menu. The dataset comes to the front and the Criteria dialog box closes.
Apply	The criterion is evaluated and those rows which meet the criterion are included in the dataset. The criterion is saved and becomes the currently applied criterion, appearing selected in the Criteria pop-up menu. The dataset comes to the front, but the Criteria dialog box stays open behind it.
Select	The criterion is saved and appears in the Criteria pop-up menu, but is not applied. The rows in the dataset that meet the criterion become selected. The dataset comes to the front, but the Criteria dialog box stays open behind it.

If the criterion definition is incorrect, you cannot apply or save it. If that is the case, when you click Apply or Save an error message appears in the Hints window with information about how to correct the error.

When you click the close box of the Criteria dialog box, an alert message asks whether to save the criterion definition. The buttons in the alert box have the following actions: Save returns you to the dataset and saves the criterion definition. Don't Save returns you to the dataset without saving the criterion definition. Cancel returns you to the Criteria dialog box without affecting the criterion definition.

Criteria pop-up menu

The Criteria pop-up menu is at the top of the dataset. You can use it to apply pre-defined criteria, see which criteria are applied, define new criteria, remove criteria, or specify a random percentage of rows as a criterion. The Criteria pop-up menu lists all criteria defined for the dataset and highlights any that are applied. A criterion appears dimmed in the pop-up menu if it has not been saved or applied (because you are editing it) or if it is invalid (eg., you deleted a variable used in the criterion).

You can also use this pop-up menu to select the rows in a dataset that conform to a criterion. If you hold down the Control key while selecting a user-defined criterion from the pop-up menu, the rows that meet its requirements are selected in the dataset. This action does not apply the criterion, it merely selects the rows. If a different criterion is currently applied, there is no change in that criterion or in the inclusion of rows.

The Criteria pop-up menu contains three other choices above the dotted line: New, Random and No Criteria. No Criteria is the default, indicating that all dataset rows are included in any analysis. Choose New to see the Criteria dialog box and define a new criterion. Choose Random to include a specified percentage of the observations in a dataset. Choosing Random presents the following dialog box:

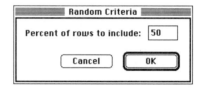

Enter the percent of data you want to randomly include in the dataset. The percent you specify is not applied exactly, i.e., if you specify 50% inclusion and you have 20 rows of data, on the average, ten rows will be included. Clicking OK creates a criterion entitled "x% Rows Included" and applies it to the dataset. Each time you apply a random criterion, a new random sample of the dataset is included.

When you close a dataset which contains a random criterion, the definition is saved with the dataset (the percent of rows), but the exact rows included by the criterion are not saved unless the random criterion is applied when you save. When you reopen the dataset and apply the random criterion, a new random sample of the dataset is included.

Edit, apply and delete criteria

There are two ways to apply an existing criterion. If a view is the active window, choose Edit/Apply Criteria in the Manage menu. In the dialog box, select the criterion and click the Apply button. If the dataset is the active window, choose the criterion from the list in the Criteria pop-up menu. If you want to apply a criterion, but have not yet defined it, choose New from the Criteria pop-up menu in the dataset. The creation of new criteria is covered at the beginning of this section.

To edit an existing criterion, choose Edit/Apply Criteria in the Manage menu. A dialog box appears, containing a list of all the criteria you have created.

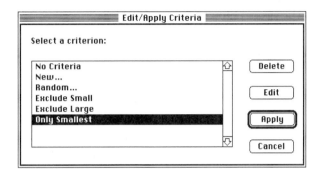

Select a criterion by clicking on it, and click the Edit button. If you are editing a criterion you defined, the Criteria dialog box appears, displaying the criterion definition. You can edit the definition by typing, or by selecting part of it and making another choice from the list or value bar. As you select part of the definition, the appropriate list or bar appears. You can double-click on any term in a list or click an drag a line in the value bar to change the definition. If you edit a criterion currently applied to the dataset, the dataset immediately reflects the change.

If you are editing a random criterion, the dialog box that appears looks very much like the Formula dialog box. It allows you to edit complex criteria. The definition of your random criterion appears in the definition area, and you can use the function list, variable list and keypad just as you do in the Formula dialog box, which is described in the preceding chapter.

To delete a criterion from the Criteria pop-up menu, so it is no longer saved with the dataset, choose Edit/Apply Criteria in the Manage menu. In the dialog box, select the criterion and click the Delete button. There are two ways to stop applying a criterion to a dataset. The first is to choose No Criteria from the Criteria pop-up menu in the dataset. The second is to choose Edit/Apply Criteria from the Manage menu, select No Criteria, and click the Apply button.

Exercise

In this exercise, you create two criteria, one to exclude all women from an analysis, a second to exclude all but men with a low lipid count from the analysis.

• Open Lipid Data located in the Sample Data folder.

• Choose Create Criteria from the Manage menu.

- Double-click on the following in succession:

  the variable Gender

  the = comparison operator

  the element Male

- Name the criterion Men and click Apply.

You have just created a criterion for the Male subjects in the experiment. Only that data for male subjects will be included in the analysis.

- Choose Create Criteria from the Manage menu again.

- Double-click on the following:

  the variable Gender

  the = comparison operator

  the element Male

  the Boolean operator AND

  the variable Cholesterol

  the comparison operator $\leq$

- Click in the value bar and move the control until the Selected Value is 200.

- Name this criterion Low Lipid Males and click Apply. The dataset comes to the front.

- Click in the Criteria pop-up and choose Men. Only those rows in the dataset with values for men are included, the rest have dimmed row numbers.

- Click in the Criteria pop-up and choose Low Lipid Males. Notice how the included rows change.

If you were using this dataset in some analyses, the tables and graphs in the view would change as you selected different criteria from the pop-up menu.

Chapter

7

Templates

There are two general techniques for generating analyses in StatView: specify all the details of the analyses yourself, or use a template containing pre-set specifications. A template is a blueprint of one or more statistical or graphical analyses, missing only the data. We recommend that you read this chapter, and learn to use the templates provided with StatView before you attempt to create your own (as described in Chapter 8). Since a template is an empty structure, like a macro or batch file, you need to specify the variables to be used in it. When you open a template, variable "slots" are shown in a dialog box along with a list of the variables in the dataset you are working with. To use a template, you open a template file, choose the dataset and slide the variables you wish to analyze into the slots.

Templates provided with StatView

StatView comes with a large selection of templates covering all the analyses in the analysis browser, and more. They offer you the ability to use StatView without the need to master the analysis and variable browsers. Much of what you want to accomplish with StatView can be done simply and quickly with templates. You can use templates individually or combine several templates in a single view.

Some templates consist of one analysis displayed as a single table or graph. At the other end of the spectrum are templates consisting of pages of analyses and results. Templates for each of StatView's statistical and graphical analyses are located in the StatView Templates folder. A representative sample of these templates is listed in the Analyze menu. You can customize this menu (see below) to include the analyses and graphs that you commonly use. All templates in the Templates folder can appear in the menu. Also, the Additional Templates folder offers examples of templates that combine frequently used analyses and enhance your presentations.

StatView Templates folder

StatView expects templates to be stored in a folder called StatView Templates that is in the same folder as StatView. You should place all templates you create in this folder. If you move the Templates folder to another directory and/or rename it, StatView will open a directory dialog box to locate it the next time you use a template. StatView then remembers the new location and the new name. If you change the name or location of the Templates folder, the only way to restore its default name and location is to throw away the StatView Library file. StatView will build a new Library containing the default folder name and location. Note that you lose all preferences you have set, as these are saved in the Library file.

The view

There are two window types in StatView: the dataset and the view. The view is where analyses are created and customized. All results appear in the view.

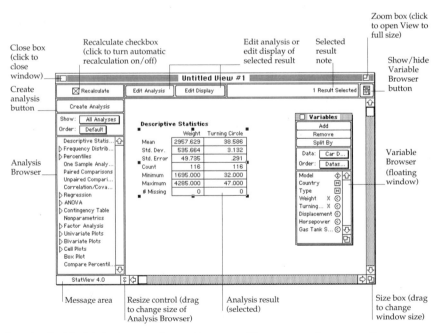

The view is divided into two main parts: a scrolling area where results appear and an analysis browser. You can resize the amount of area devoted to each. In addition, there are buttons that allow you to create analyses, edit analyses, and edit displays. There is also a checkbox to turn calculation on or off. The variable browser is a floating window that is used to assign and remove variables from an analysis. You can show and hide the variable browser using the control in the upper right hand corner of the view.

This chapter does not go into detail about the features of the view. Templates do all the work of creating analyses for you, so you do not need to know much about the workings of the view to use templates. In the next chapter, Building Analyses, you can learn about the analysis browser, variable browser and other features of the view.

When you select a template from the Analyze menu or from the Templates folder, the template's results appear in one of two places. If a view is not the topmost window, a new view automatically opens to contain the results. If a view is topmost, the results appear at the top of the view if it is blank, or below the last result if it already contains results.

Select a template

You may select a template directly from the Analyze menu, or from the Templates folder by using the Templates command in the Analyze menu. The two methods are interchangeable. Templates can easily be moved onto the Analyze menu as needed. It is easier to have frequently used templates listed in the Analyze menu, since it requires fewer steps to use them that way. In either case, once you choose a template, the Assign Variables dialog box appears, as described below.

From the Analyze menu

If the template you want to use is listed in the Analyze menu, select it. If a dataset is open, the Assign Variables dialog box appears. If no dataset is open, a directory dialog box appears. Locate and open the dataset containing the variables you want to use. When you have chosen the dataset, the Assign Variables dialog box appears (described below).

From the Templates folder

If the template you want to use is not listed in the Analyze menu, choose Templates from the Analyze menu. You see the Templates dialog box with a scrolling list of the templates in the Templates folder.

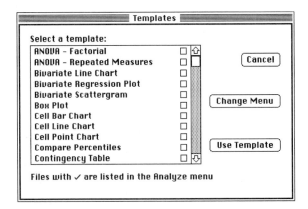

Choose the desired template from the scrolling list and click Use Template. Do not click the checkbox to the right of a template unless you wish to add it to the Analyze menu. These checkboxes indicate whether or not the template is listed in the Analyze menu. If you want to add a template to the Analyze menu, follow the instructions in the next section.

If a dataset is open, the Assign Variables dialog box appears. If no dataset is open, the directory dialog box appears. Locate and open the dataset containing the variables you want to use. When you have chosen the dataset, the Assign Variables dialog box appears (described below).

Add and remove templates in the Analyze menu

You can add templates to or remove templates from the Analyze menu at any time. Templates remain stored in the StatView Templates folder, but the Analyze menu offers a shortcut for their use. To add a template to the Analyze menu:

- Choose Templates from the Analyze menu. The Templates dialog box opens.

- Click the box to the right of a template name. A check mark appears in it.

- Click the Change Menu button to add the template to the Analyze menu. (Template names appear on the menu in alphabetical order.)

To remove a template from the Analyze menu:

- Choose Templates from the Analyze menu. The Templates dialog box opens.

- Click the box to the right of a template name to remove the check mark.

- Click the Change Menu button. The template is removed from the menu.

You can tailor the Analyze menu to include those templates you commonly use.

Assign variables

The Assign Variables dialog box is used to assign variables from one or more datasets to a template.

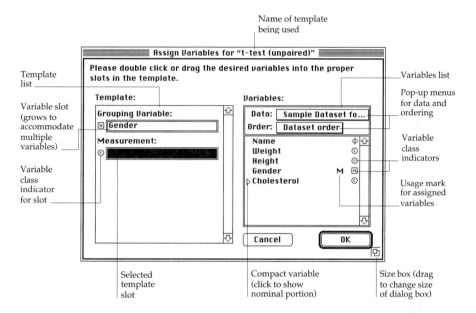

Name of template being used

Template list

Variable slot (grows to accommodate multiple variables)

Variable class indicator for slot

Variables list

Pop-up menus for data and ordering

Variable class indicators

Usage mark for assigned variables

Selected template slot

Compact variable (click to show nominal portion)

Size box (drag to change size of dialog box)

Variables list

The variables list on the right shows all the variables in any open dataset(s). You can switch between open datasets using the Data pop-up menu. To open a new dataset, select Other from the Data pop-up menu and use the directory dialog box to locate and open a dataset. You can order the variables in the list by dataset order, alphabetically or by variable class (continuous, nominal, informative) or usage using the Order pop-up menu. To the right of each variable in the list is a symbol indicating the data class of the variable. $\boxed{\text{M}}$ is for nominal, $\odot$ is for continuous, $\diamondsuit$ for informative. Compact variables have a $\triangleright$ to the left of their names. Clicking on this triangle displays a list of the nominal variables within the compact variable.

(There is a discussion of variable class and compact variables in the Datasets chapter.) An "M" usage mark appears next to any variable that has been assigned to a slot in the template.

Template list

The template list on the left displays slots for the variables used in the template. A slot can contain multiple variables and will grow as additional variables are assigned to it. To the left of each slot is a symbol indicating the data class of the variable that must be assigned to that slot to meet the variable requirements of the analysis. Match the class symbols of the variables with those of the variable slots. You cannot put a nominal variable in a continuous slot, or a continuous variable in a nominal slot. Informative variables cannot be placed in any slot. Only a compact variable can be placed in a compact variable slot, which is indicated by a ✳ symbol. You will only see a compact variable slot if your template includes a repeated measures ANOVA. In other analyses, the nominal and continuous portions of compact variables may be used in the same ways as other nominal and continuous variables.

There is a great deal of flexibility in the use of the template slots:

> You do not need to use every slot; some can remain empty.

> Each slot can hold more than one variable and grows to accommodate as many variables as you assign.

> You can assign the same variable to more than one slot.

Assign variables to a slot

There are several ways to assign variables from the variable list to slots in the template list:

- Drag a variable from the list into a slot.

- Double-click on a variable in the list to assign it to the highlighted slot. The slot immediately below then becomes highlighted. You can double-click on consecutive variables to assign them to consecutive slots.

  Holding down the Command key (⌘) and double-clicking assigns multiple variables to the currently highlighted slot.

- Drag a variable from one slot to another.

Press the Tab key to to move the selection from the currently highlighted slot to the one immediately below.

Assign multiple variables to a slot

You can assign multiple variables to a slot by dragging them into the slot or by holding down the Command key and double-clicking. The structure of the template does not lock you into a set number of variables. In a simple example, a template that generates descriptive statistics on one variable will yield a single table of results for three variables when you drag all three into the single slot.

Remove variables from a slot

If you mistakenly assign a variable to the wrong slot, just reverse the assigning process to remove it. You may explore different variable options for a slot and change your mind about which to include. You can remove a variable from a slot in two ways:

• Click on the variable in a slot and press the Delete key.

• Drag the variable from a slot back to the variable list.

Calculation and results

When you finish assigning variables and click OK, the template-generated results appear in a view. If the top window is a view, the results will appear in that view. If the top window is not a view, the results will be placed in a new, untitled view.

If a view has calculation disabled (the Recalculate box is not checked in the upper left corner of the view), graph and table placeholders appear rather than completed results. When you are ready to see your results, click the Recalculate box (an X in the box means calculation is enabled).

Modify template results

Once you have applied a template you can manipulate the results that appear in the view using the Analysis and Variable browsers, the Edit Display and Edit Analysis buttons, as well as the tools in the Draw menu.

The Building Analyses chapter and the chapters for each analysis discuss how the parameters of results can be controlled. Chapters 9 and 10 describe how the format of tables and graphs can be customized. See Chapter 8 for information on how to create and save custom templates tailored to your specifications.

Exercises

In this exercise, you apply one of StatView's templates to a sample dataset, Car Data, which is located in the Sample Data folder. You use a template to generate a basic set of descriptive statistics from this data, then continue by adding results from a regression template. To read about descriptive statistics and regression, see the Descriptive Statistics and Regression chapters later in the manual.

Descriptive statistics

You should have no datasets or views open before starting this exercise.

- Choose Descriptive Statistics from the Analyze menu.

- In the directory dialog box that appears, choose Car Data from the Sample Data folder and open it. The Assign Variables dialog box appears.

- Click on the continuous variable slot, labelled with the ☉ symbol, so you can assign continuous variables.

- Assign the four variables Weight, Turning Circle, Displacement and Horsepower from the variable list on the right to the template slot on the left by holding down the Command (⌘) key and double-clicking on each one in succession. They appear in the slot, which expands to accommodate all the variables.

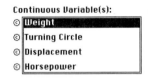

Both the slot and the variables in the list are marked with a ☉, signifying that the variables are continuous. Try double-clicking on a nominal variable in the list (marked by a 🅽) to assign it to the slot. An alert tells you that the class of the variable is incorrect for that particular slot.

- Click OK to create the results. A new view opens containing this table of basic descriptive statistics.

Descriptive Statistics

	Weight	Turning Circle	Displacement	Horsepower
Mean	2957.629	38.586	158.310	130.198
Std. Dev.	535.664	3.132	60.409	39.822
Std. Error	49.735	.291	5.609	3.697
Count	116	116	116	116
Minimum	1695.000	32.000	61.000	55.000
Maximum	4285.000	47.000	350.000	278.000
# Missing	0	0	0	0

Regression

Now you will see if there is a relationship between gas tank size and the weight of the car by performing a regression analysis. A Simple Regression analysis template is contained in the Analyze menu. Its results will be added to the view containing the descriptive statistics you just created, because that view is still active.

- Choose Regression—Simple from the Analyze menu. A dataset is open, so no directory dialog box appears. Instead, you see the Assign Variables dialog box with the first variable slot highlighted. The variables from the open dataset are listed on the right.

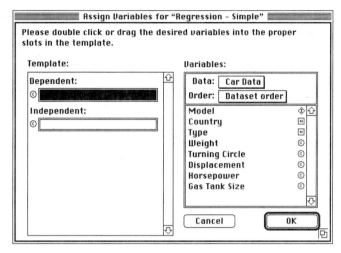

This template has two slots, both for continuous variables. Rather than double-click to assign variables, this time drag variables into their slots.

- Drag Gas Tank Size into the slot labeled Dependent. You want to see whether this variable changes in some predictable way in relation to the Independent variable, Weight.

- Drag Weight into the slot labeled Independent and click OK to create the results. The analysis calculates and results are added to the view below the descriptive statistics you earlier created.

Regression Summary
Gas Tank Size vs. Weight

Count	116
Num. Missing	0
R	.847
R Squared	.717
Adjusted R Squared	.715
RMS Residual	1.643

ANOVA Table
Gas Tank Size vs. Weight

	DF	Sum of Squares	Mean Square	F-Value	P-Value
Regression	1	780.014	780.014	288.914	<.0001
Residual	114	307.779	2.700		
Total	115	1087.793			

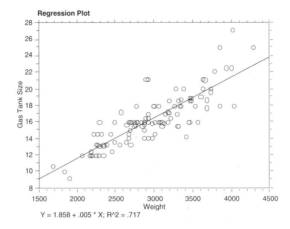

Regression Coefficients
Gas Tank Size vs. Weight

	Coefficient	Std. Error	Std. Coeff.	t-Value	P-Value
Intercept	1.858	.860	1.858	2.161	.0328
Weight	.005	2.860E-4	.847	16.997	<.0001

The results you see in the view are: Regression Summary, ANOVA Table, Regression Coefficients and Regression Plot. Scroll through the view to see all the results. Examine these results to interpret their significance about the relationship of the size of the gas tank to vehicle weight.

- Choose Save from the File menu and name this view "My Car Analysis" in the directory dialog box. Put the view in a folder of your choosing, and click Save.

- Close the view by clicking in the close box at the upper left.

- To re-examine the results, reopen the view with the Open command from the File menu. See the section, Use original variables, in the Building Analyses chapter for instructions on how to open a view with its original data.

Results can be saved as a regular StatView file, in text format, or as a PICT file for exporting. This is covered in greater detail in the next chapter, Building Analyses.

Your own templates

You are not limited to templates provided with StatView. You can also make custom templates of your own. The next chapter, Building Analyses, covers the tools you use to create your own analyses from scratch and how to save them for use as templates. Once you are adept at using the analysis and variable browsers and can negotiate the Edit Analysis and Edit Display dialog boxes, you are ready to design templates.

There are several situations in which it can be a great help to use your own templates:

- You can design a set of analyses and results tailored for your experiments and save it for regular reuse. Use these templates to avoid respecifying analysis parameters, graph and table formatting, etc. with each analysis.

- If you are not an expert on statistical analysis, you can take a problem to a statistician and have him or her set up a series of analyses in StatView as a template. In effect, that expert's statistical knowledge and expertise becomes available to you for use over and over again. All you have to do is provide the data.

- If you have statistical prowess that you would like to share with others, you can design a template that allows them to perform analyses in a mistake-proof manner. All they have to know is the simple procedure involved in opening a template and assigning variables.

- A template is a set of instructions that specifies everything about the results in a view. This means you can save any formatting and graph/table structure that you prefer for your analyses. In this way, if you want all your regression plots to appear in a particular size, or graph and table titles to be in a special font, or even have a certain title or logo appear at the top of every view, you can create all these features and save them in a template to apply over and over to your data.

  For example, if you need to generate a periodic report with data that changes each period (e.g., monthly figures), and your report format and structure is always the same, you can design a template with that format, complete with titles and pictures. Your reports will all be uniform, and generating them will take only the time needed to open a dataset and assign variables.

Chapter

8

Building Analyses

This chapter covers the use of the analysis browser and variable browser, tools you use to construct analyses without using a template. The chapter also explains how to use these tools to create your own templates containing the statistics and graphs you commonly work with as well as custom formatting. At the end of this chapter, you will be able to create your own templates and add them to the Analyze menu, customizing StatView to suit your needs.

All information in this chapter applies equally to results you create using the browsers and those generated with a template. Output generated using a template is identical to output you create "from scratch" using the analysis and variable browsers. You can mix both types of output in a view. If you prefer to use StatView without learning about the analysis and variable browsers, you can do so by using the templates provided in the StatView Templates folder. The preceding chapter covers the use of the templates that are shipped with the program.

The exercises in this chapter cover the following:

- Perform analyses either by assigning variables first, then creating the analysis; or by creating the analysis first and then assigning variables.

- Create additional output to better understand complex analyses.

- Expand existing analyses to analyze additional variables.

- Perform the same analyses on different sets of variables.

- Perform a sequence of analyses on one set of variables.
- Generate analysis results for subgroups of your data without changing the structure of your dataset.

Analysis building tools

The work of creating analyses and using templates is done in a window called a view, which is also where the results appear. A view looks like this:

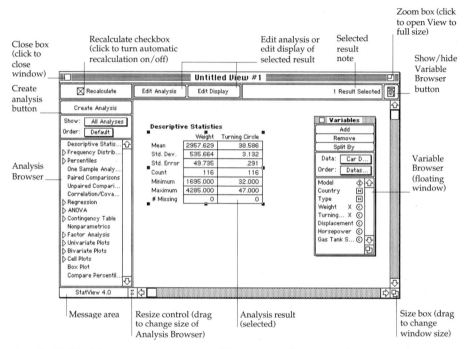

The view is divided into two parts: a scrolling area where results appear and an analysis browser. You can change the amount of area devoted to each function by dragging the Σ symbol at the bottom of the window. In addition, there are buttons to create analyses, edit analyses, and edit displays. There is also a checkbox which, when checked, tells the program to automatically recalculate after any change to an analysis or dataset. The variable browser is a floating window that is used to assign and remove variables from an analysis. You can show and hide the variable browser using the button in the upper right corner of the view. Each of these items is described in detail later in this chapter.

To open a new, empty view, choose "New View" from the Analyze menu. If you are working in a dataset, you may also double-click in the empty rectangle at the top left of the dataset (above the row numbers and attribute pane and to the left of the first variable name) to create a new view.

Overview of analysis process

There are several ways to use the analysis browser, variable browser and existing results to create new results in the view. All of them are covered in this chapter. The pathways for creating analyses are illustrated in the diagram below.

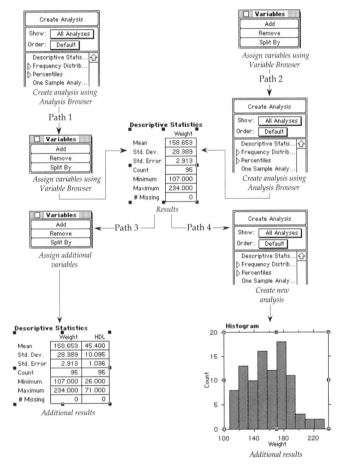

Paths of the analysis process

Paths 1 and 2 show the process of creating a new analysis. In Path 1 you create the analysis first using the analysis browser and then assign variables using the variable browser. In Path 2 you assign variables first, then create the analysis. There is no difference in the results generated by the two methods. Try both and use the one that feels more comfortable.

Paths 3 and 4 show the process of continuing an analysis by adding variables or creating additional results. In Path 3 you assign additional variables to an analysis via a selected result. In Path 4 you create a different analysis using variables from an existing result. Examples of all four paths are given later in this chapter.

Action objects

As the preceding diagram shows, the tables and graphs in the view play a central role in the process of generating analyses. All statistical output, whether tables or graphs, are "action objects." They retain the information used to create them: the variables you assigned and the analysis parameters you specified. When a result (action object) is selected, this underlying information is passed to your next action, reducing the number of steps that you would ordinarily repeat in order to create additional analyses. This feature is important to keep in mind as you read this chapter and use the program.

Analysis browser

The analysis browser is the directory you use to choose an analysis and select the particular tables or graphs you want as results. It lists every analysis you can perform. The analysis browser is at the left of the view, and its features are described below.

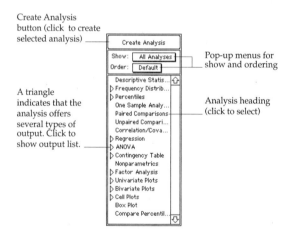

 You can make the analysis browser narrower or wider by dragging the Σ symbol at the bottom of the browser. Double-clicking on the Σ closes the browser completely, leaving a ⊞ symbol. Double-click on this symbol to reopen the browser. There is a setting in the Application Preferences dialog box to keep this browser closed until you want to open it. See the Overview and Requirements chapter for information about this preference.

Show and order pop-up menus

You can change what is listed in this browser with the Show pop-up menu. The All Analyses list is the default, showing all the analyses and graphs. The two subsets of that list are Basic Statistics and Graphs Only. Note that no analysis is offered in the Basic Statistics or Graphs Only list that is not available in the All Analyses list.

The Basic Statistics and Graphs Only lists are designed to simplify and speed the process of generating analyses. When you use these lists, you accept the default settings for the analysis, bypassing the dialog box in which you would otherwise set the parameters. The analysis chapters (11-22) explain the default settings. You can still change the analysis parameters by selecting the result and using the Edit Analysis button.

You can change the order of any of these lists from Default to Alphabetical using the Order pop-up menu. Default order groups the analyses before the graphs and orders them from simpler to more complex.

Create analysis button

To perform an analysis, you select it in the browser and click the Create Analysis button, or double-click on an analysis. Most selections are followed by a dialog box in which you set parameters for the analysis. The default results of the analysis appear in the view, to the right of the analysis browser. Results appear beneath the bottom result in the view. (The view automatically adds additional pages as they are needed.) You can assign variables before or after creating an analysis.

There are two ways you can bypass the analysis parameter dialog boxes and accept default parameters: you can press the Control key and click the Create Analysis button (or double-click on the analysis) or you can change the analysis browser Show pop-up menu to either Basic Statistics or Graphs Only and choose from these lists.

Analysis output

Analyses with triangles next to them offer several different types of output. Analyses without triangles generate a single summary table or graph. When you click on the triangle next to an analysis, it points down and the results appear listed beneath the analysis. Hold down the Command (⌘) key and click on any triangle to show or hide the lists of output for all analyses at once. For example, clicking on the triangle next to Regression displays the different tables and graphs that regression analysis can display.

▽Regression
    Regression Summary
    ANOVA Table
    Regression Coefficients
    Confidence Intervals
    Residual Statistics
    Regression Plot
    Residuals vs. Fitted
    Dependent vs. Fitted
    Residuals vs. Dependent

When the list is showing and you click *once* on the analysis heading, the tables and graphs that comprise the default output are selected. You create the default output if you select the heading and click the Create Analysis button. If you wish to create results other than the default, simply select them from the list. You can select more than one result by clicking on it and dragging the mouse. You can select discontiguous results by holding down the Command (⌘) key and clicking.

Variable browser

The variable browser is a floating window that lists the variables in open datasets, one dataset at a time. Use this browser to assign variables to and remove them from analyses. The variable browser looks like:

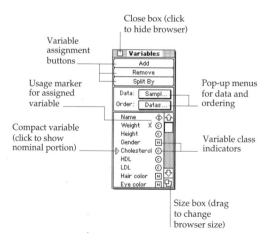

Since the variable browser is a floating window, you can move it around your screen, change its size, and show or hide it. The size of the browser is controlled through the resize box in the lower right corner of the browser. There are several methods you can use to show or hide the browser:

- Click the 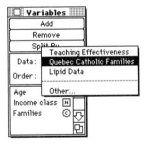 button at the top of the view to show the browser when it is hidden or hide it when it is visible.
- Choose Variables from the Window menu to show it when it is hidden.
- Click the close box to hide it when it is visible.

By default, the variable browser automatically shows itself the first time any dataset is open. However, there is a setting in the Application Preferences dialog box which keeps it from appearing until you tell it to show itself. See the Overview and Requirements chapter for information about this preference.

Data pop-up menu

With the Data pop-up menu, you control which dataset's variables are shown in the variable browser. You can use variables from different datasets in one view and toggle between variable lists without leaving the view. The Data pop-up menu lists all the open datasets, so you can select the dataset whose variables you want to see listed. You can open any other dataset by choosing Other from the list.

When you choose Other, a directory dialog opens so you can locate and open any dataset not currently open. The dataset will appear topmost on your screen so you can examine it before using any of the variables in your analysis.

Assign variables using buttons

The buttons at the top of the variable browser change depending on the analysis you choose. For most analyses, you use these three buttons:

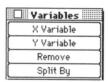

The Add button assigns the selected variable to the analysis and the Remove button removes it. The Split By button generates results for any group of a nominal variable or combination of groups for two or more nominal variables. You can split any analysis or graph. For example, if you have a variable that divides your dataset into male and female groups, by selecting this variable and clicking the Split By button you can get any analysis results broken down by gender. For more information on this command, see the Split-by section below.

The variable browser has two other states, one for regression and one for bivariate plots. The Independent, Dependent and Force buttons are used to assign variables for a regression. The X Variable and Y Variable buttons are used to assign variables for a bivariate plot. These buttons appear when you select a bivariate plot or regression in the analysis browser or select the output from these analyses in the view.

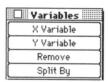

Bivariate plot buttons

Regression buttons

For more information about the analyses that use these buttons, see Chapter 17, Regression and Chapter 22, Plots. All variable browser buttons work the same way. You select a variable and click on the appropriate button to assign the variable to an analysis. An assigned variable gets a usage marker next to it to tell you what role it has in the analysis.

You can select more than one variable by clicking on it and dragging the mouse. You can select discontiguous variables by clicking on the first and then holding down the Command (⌘) key and clicking on another. You can also double-click on a variable to assign it. Double-clicking has the same effect as clicking the top button in the variable browser (either Add, Independent, or X Variable depending on the analysis).

There are several keyboard modifiers you can use in conjunction with double-clicking :

Keyboard action	Button it mimics
Double-click	Add, Independent or X Variable (top button of browser)
Option double-click	Split By

Control double-click	Dependent, Y Variable (or Add, if these buttons are not visible)
Option-Control double-click	Remove

Using Command-Shift to create a new analysis

Holding down the Command (⌘) and Shift keys when using the variable assignment buttons forces StatView to create a new analysis using the assigned variables, as opposed to assigning the variables to the existing analysis. This applies for all analyses which can take more than one variable of a particular usage. See the "Variable requirements" section of each analysis chapter for additional information about using these modifier keys.

Assigning variables from different datasets

You can assign variables from different datasets to the same analysis. If you do so, StatView applies the following rules while calculating the analysis:

- Variables with fewer values are padded with missing values at the end in order to give all variables the same number of observations.

- The excluded rows are the union of the excluded rows for the datasets which contain the variables. For example if variable A comes from dataset A with rows 3 and 4 excluded, and variable B comes from dataset B with rows 7 and 8 excluded, rows 3, 4, 7 and 8 will be excluded from each analysis that uses both variables.

Two analyses are the exception to these rules — descriptive statistics and one sample analyses (only if you do not have split-by variables assigned). For these two analyses, no missing values are padded and the exclusion applies to each variable individually. If you do have split-by variables assigned, they calculate the same as other analyses.

Variable class indicators

The symbol to the right of each variable in the browser identifies the variable's class. ⓒ denotes a continuous variable, Ⓝ denotes a nominal variable and ⬥ denotes an informative variable. Most analyses determine how to treat the data contained in a variable by the class of the variable—nominal or continuous (informative variables cannot be used in analyses). A variable's class is set in the dataset's attribute pane, usually when you create the dataset. The Datasets chapter explains variable class as it pertains to the data in a variable; variable class implications for analyses are discussed in the Understanding analyses section later in this chapter.

Compact variables

A compact variable can be thought of as the information in a continuous variable, arranged in groups by a nominal variable. Compact variables have at least two components in the variable browser: the compact variable (continuous), and at least one category that defines the groups (nominal). Compact variables appear with a triangle to the left of the variable name:

▷ Cholesterol ⓒ

Clicking on the triangle displays the categories that comprise the variable:

▽ Cholesterol ⓒ
Gender Ⓝ

Compact variables and their associated categories are just like other variables listed in the browser. You select and assign them to analyses using the assignment buttons. For more information, see Compact variables in the Datasets chapter.

Usage markers

A variable that is being used in an analysis has a usage marker to the right of it (to the left of the class indicator) in the browser.

Type   S Ⓝ
Weight   X ⓒ
Turning Circle Y ⓒ

Usage markers in the variable browser

Usage markers note the variable's use in the selected result(s). If you select a different result, the usage markers change to reflect the variable usages in that analysis. The table below describes the usage markers and their meaning.

Usage	Marker
A continuous variable in any analysis	X
An independent variable in a regression	
An X variable in a bivariate plot	
A nominal variable in a frequency distribution or descriptive statistics	
A dependent variable in a regression or ANOVA	Y
A Y variable in a bivariate plot	
A grouping variable	G
A split-by variable	S
A forced independent variable in a stepwise regression	F

| A variable with more than one usage. This will appear if you have multiple results selected that use the same variable in different usages. | ! |

Usage markers appear only when a view is the topmost window. If one or more results are selected in the view, the variable browser shows usages next to all variables used in selected results. If no results are selected, usage markers appear next to any variables that have been assigned and are awaiting the creation of the next analysis.

Order variables in the list

When you have many variables in your dataset, StatView offers different listing orders to help you easily locate the variables you want. The Order pop-up menu offers four choices for ordering the variable list:

1. Dataset order is the default. It lists the variables in the same order as variables appear in the dataset (left to right).

2. Alphabetical lists variables in alphabetical order. As long as you know the names of all your variables, this order can make them easiest to find.

3. By Variable Class lists continuous variables first, then nominal, and finally informative. This order can help you understand the components of your dataset.

4. By Variable Usage places variables that have usage markers at the top of the list in the following order X, F, Y, G, S, !. This order helps you quickly see what variables are used in the currently selected results.

Results browser

The results browser provides an index of all the tables and graphs in all open views. If a view contains a great deal of output or you are working with several views at once, it is easy to lose track of what you have done, what is currently selected and where particular results are located. Using this index, you can select a result from the scrolling list, click the Select button, and the view scrolls to and selects the result.

Bring the results browser to the front by choosing Results from the Window menu or by choosing Show Results Browser from the Layout menu. It looks like this:

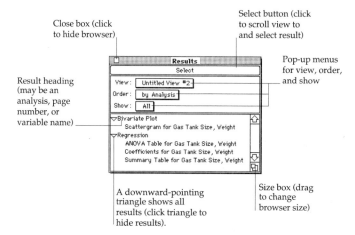

Close box (click to hide browser)

Select button (click to scroll view to and select result)

Pop-up menus for view, order, and show

Result heading (may be an analysis, page number, or variable name)

A downward-pointing triangle shows all results (click triangle to hide results).

Size box (drag to change browser size)

To hide the results browser, click the close box in the upper left corner. By default, the results browser remains hidden until you choose to show it. However, there is a setting in the Application Preferences dialog box which makes the browser automatically appear the first time you create a view. See the Overview and Requirements chapter for information about this preference.

The results are grouped under headings with triangles next to them. The heading is either an analysis, a page number or a variable name, depending on the order you select from the Order pop-up menu. Click on the triangle to hide or show the results listed under an individual heading. If you hold down the Command key and click on the triangle, all results lists are hidden or shown at once.

View pop-up menu

If you have several views open at once, you can see results from any of them listed in the results browser. The View pop-up menu lists all of the open views so you can select the view whose results you want to see listed. If you want to open a view not currently open, choose Other from the list and locate the view with the directory dialog box.

Scroll to and select results

With a lot of tables and graphs in a view, it may not be easy to find the one you want. Since selecting a result is one way of choosing variables or an analysis, you need to be able to navigate to the result you want quickly. The results browser is a good tool for that, useful for scrolling to and selecting results in a view. To select a result, double-click on it or choose it from the scrolling list and click the Select button. When results are selected in the browser they are selected in the view and they may be deleted or used as action objects (see the later section on action objects).

To choose several adjacent results in the browser, drag the cursor. To select results that are not listed next to each other under one heading, or are listed under different headings, hold down the Command (⌘) key while clicking on them. Choosing a heading and clicking the Select button selects all the results under that heading. You can select all the results containing a certain variable, all the results from a single analysis, or all the results appearing on a particular page by choosing the heading(s) they are listed under and clicking the Select button.

Order pop-up menu

Using the Order pop-up menu in the results browser, you can list results by Analysis, Location or Variable. Changing the order of results in this browser has no effect on their position in the view. The different orderings are:

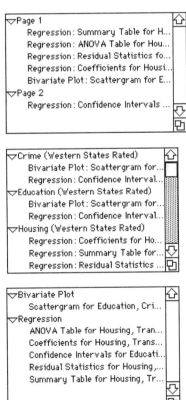

Location

Results are grouped by page, in order of their appearance in the view. The location of a result's title determines what page it is on; a result that lies across a page break is listed under the page the title is on.

Variable

The variable name and dataset are listed in the headings. Any results which use these variables are listed below. This is the only ordering in which results can appear more than once.

Analysis

Each table and graph is listed under the particular analysis which created it.

Show pop-up menu

Since selection plays such an important role in the analysis process, knowing what is currently selected helps you understand what will happen when you create a new analysis or assign or remove variables. Using the Show pop-up menu, you can list in the results browser all the results that appear in a view or just results that are selected. By showing selected results in the results browser, you can easily see which variables are used in the selected output. To choose between all results and selected results, choose All or Selected from the Show pop-up menu.

Additional features

Results Selected note

All results (tables and graphs) generated by the program are action objects. When a result is selected, information from the selected result is passed to your next action. For this reason it is useful to be able to tell at a glance whether any results are selected. The selection note in the upper right corner of the view gives you instant feedback about the number of results currently selected. If no results are selected, this area is blank.

You can use the results browser (listed by selected results) to see which particular tables and graphs are selected. The results browser is discussed in the preceding pages. The variables in the variable browser can also be ordered by "usage" to show which variables are in use.

Application progress message

While StatView performs an operation, the message area in the lower left corner of the view keeps you informed of its progress. It displays "StatView 4.0" when the program is awaiting your next action.

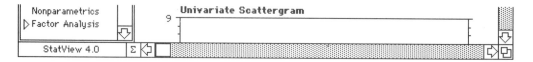

A variety of messages appear during calculation, to mark the program's progress. Here is a sampling: Change Variables, Update Displays, Create New Analysis, Build SSCP Matrix, Edit Parameters, Request Displays, Change Graph.

Recalculate checkbox

You can control calculation of results in the view with the Recalculate checkbox in the upper left corner of the view. There is a dynamic link between a view and the datasets it uses, so any changes made to the data cause immediately recalculation. New views have recalculate turned on. Click the checkbox to disable calculation (the X disappears). When recalculate is on (checked), all tables and graphs are recalculated following any of these actions:

- any action that changes a value of a variable used in an analysis
- deleting a variable from the dataset that is used in an analysis
- adding, deleting or clearing rows in a dataset
- applying a criteria to the dataset
- assigning variables to or removing them from an analysis

 If you plan to make several changes to an analysis, table, graph or to variables in the dataset, it is a good idea to turn off recalculation. This way, you can make your changes without waiting for recalculation after every single change. In particular, univariate or bivariate plots which display a great number of observations have to replot every point with each change you make.

Cancelling calculation

 Anytime the cursor appears as the rotating yin-yang symbol ☯ you can cancel the operation you are performing by pressing the Command-Period keys. If a view is topmost, pressing Command-Period will also turn recalculation off.

Recalculate in the background

 You can use other applications on your Macintosh while your analysis calculates if you use MultiFinder or System 7. StatView can perform calculation in the background, so you can switch to another application (by clicking the icon in the upper right of your Macintosh screen). When the calculation is finished you are notified by a flashing Σ near the Apple menu.

Updating and placeholders

StatView ensures that all results appearing on the screen are consistent with the current analyses, variables and state of the dataset. If recalculate is on and the analysis or data is changed, all tables and graphs are updated. However, if recalculate is not on and the analysis or data changes, tables and graphs are replaced with placeholders until you turn recalculate on. A placeholder is an empty graph or a box with an X in it.

Edit Analysis

When you click the Edit Analysis button, you get a dialog box that lets you modify the analysis parameters for each table and graph selected in the view. Holding down the

Option key and double-clicking on a result has the same effect. If you prefer to access this dialog box by simply double-clicking, you can set this as a view preference. Each analysis has different parameters, so the dialog boxes are different. Each analysis chapter contains a full explanation of the pertinent analysis dialog box.

If you change the parameters of an analysis, all results associated with that analysis change as well. For example, if you generate a frequency distribution analysis and display both a table and a histogram, changing the number of intervals of the frequency distribution causes both the summary table and histogram to update.

Edit Display

When you click the Edit Display button, you get a dialog box that lets you modify the selected table or graph. Double-clicking on a result has the same effect. If you prefer to see the analysis parameter dialog box rather than the display dialog box when you double-click, you can set this as a view preference. In that case, the display dialog boxes will be accessible by holding down the Option key and double-clicking. A discussion of editing tables and graphs appears in the next chapter.

Window menu

The Window menu helps you keep track of all the windows you have open, and makes it easy to switch between them. You can bring any window to the front by choosing it from the Window menu. It lists:

- All open datasets and views in front to back order
- The Clipboard (whether open or not)
- Any open Formula, Series, Random, Recode or Create Criteria dialog boxes
- The variable browser and results browser
- The Hints window

The active window has a check mark next to it.

Above the list of windows is the Zoom Up/Down command. This command is the equivalent of clicking in the zoom box in the upper right corner of a window. It toggles the active window from its original size to the full size of the screen and back.

The three commands at the bottom of the menu (Variables, Hints, Results) show the three StatView floating windows: the variable browser, hints window and results browser. The order of these three in the Window menu changes to reflect the order in which they are open on your screen; the topmost window is first on the list. See the Troubleshooting chapter for a discussion of Hints. The variable and results browsers are discussed earlier in this chapter.

Understanding analyses

Performing an analysis in StatView is a two-step process: you create an analysis and assign variables to it. You can do these things in either order. It is important to understand the different parameters and variable requirements of each analysis before analyzing your data.

Analysis parameters

Each analysis presents its own dialog box in which you set the analysis parameters. In the descriptive statistics dialog box, for example, you choose which descriptive statistics to calculate, while the regression dialog box offers a choice between types of regression models. The analyses, their parameters, variable requirements and dialog boxes are described in Chapters 11 through 22. When you have a question about an analysis dialog box, take advantage of the explanations in the Hints window. See the Troubleshooting chapter for information about Hints.

Variable requirements

Each analysis requires certain variables before it can calculate. Two factors determine whether the variable requirements for an analysis have been met: variable usage and the number of variables assigned. The discussion below provides an overview of these two factors.

For a detailed explanation of the variable requirements for each analysis see the appropriate analysis chapter later in this manual. In addition, when you create an analysis, a message below each table or graph placeholder tells you what variables are required for that analysis.

Usage

Variable usage is the way an analysis treats the data contained in a variable. Most analyses determine usage by the class of the variable—nominal or continuous. (You set the class of a variable in the dataset's attribute pane.) For some analyses, however, class alone does not provide enough information to tell the analysis how to use the variable. When you create one of these analyses, special usage buttons replace the Add button in the variable browser (see the section on the variable browser above.) The concept of variable usage is illustrated in the following examples and in the exercises later in the chapter.

An example of variable usage based on class occurs in ANOVA. To generate an ANOVA, you use the Add button to assign one continuous and one or more nominal variables. StatView automatically treats the continuous variable as the dependent variable.

Since nominal variable(s) make sense only as grouping variables in ANOVA, this usage is given to any nominal variable you assign. Once a variable has been assigned to an analysis, its usage is indicated by a marker in the variable browser. In the above example, the continuous variable would have a Y next to its name signifying dependent; any nominal variable would have a G next to it showing that it is a grouping variable or factor.

The analyses which cannot assign roles to variables based on class alone are regression and bivariate plots. Consider an example in which you want to quantify the relationship between Displacement and Horsepower, two continuous variables, in a car dataset. You hypothesize that horsepower is linearly dependent on engine displacement. You can test this hypothesis using a simple regression. The regression analysis needs to identify which variable is dependent and which is independent in the hypothesis. Both variables have the same class (continuous) so class alone cannot be used to specify usage. Therefore, the Add button in the variable browser is replaced by two buttons: Dependent and Independent.

Number of variables

Some analyses can handle any number of variables in one result. Some accept only a specific number. Still others can handle multiple variables with one usage, but only a single variable of another usage. The number of variables an analysis requires is the determining factor in what happens when new variables are assigned to an existing analysis.

For example, an unpaired t-test requires a single continuous and a single nominal grouping variable. What happens if you assign another continuous variable to the analysis? A new, separate analysis is generated that performs a t-test on the new continuous variable using the groups identified by the original nominal variable. The result appears as an additional table in the view.

On the other hand, a descriptive statistics table and a correlation matrix analyze multiple variables. As you assign new variables, the tables expand to include the new variables; a separate table is not created. In order to understand what will happen when you assign new variables to an analysis, you need to know the number and class of variables it requires.

Summary table

The following table indicates the variable requirements (class and number), variable browser buttons and usage markers for each analysis. No analysis calculates until its variable requirements are met. Analyses that can be assigned one or more variables analyze additional variables in the same table or graph. Those that accept only a set number of variables create a new result for each new variable assigned. The analysis chapters, 11 through 22, discuss the variable requirements for each analysis in more detail.

Analysis	Variable class	Number of variables	Browser button	Usage marker[*]
Descriptive Statistics	continuous or nominal	one or more	Add	X X
Frequency Distribution (histogram, pie chart)	continuous or nominal	one	Add	X X
Percentiles	continuous	one or more	Add	X
One Sample Analysis	continuous	one or more	Add	X
Paired Comparisons	continuous	two or more	Add	X
Unpaired Comparisons	nominal continuous	one one	Add Add	G X
Correlation/Covariance	continuous	two or more	Add	X
Regression—Simple/Polynomial	continuous continuous	one one	Independent Dependent	X Y
Regression—Multiple/Stepwise	continuous continuous continuous	one or more one (optional)	Independent Dependent (Force)	X Y (F)
ANOVA (factorial design)	nominal continuous	one or more one	Add Add	G X
ANOVA (repeated measures)	nominal compact	optional one	Add Add	G X
Contingency Table (coded raw data)	nominal	two	Add	G
Contingency Table (coded summary data)	nominal continuous	two one	Add Add	G X
Contingency Table (two way table)	continuous	two or more	Add	X

[*]Analyses that compare different groups—unpaired comparisons, ANOVA, contingency table, two group unpaired nonparametric tests, cell plots, box plots and percentile comparisons—treat nominal variables as grouping variables ("G "). Analyses that describe information—descriptive statistics, frequency distribution, univariate and bivariate plots—treat nominal and continuous variables the same ("X ").

Nonparametric—one sample	continuous	one	Add	X
Nonparametric—two group paired	continuous	two	Add	X
Nonparametric—two group unpaired	nominal	one	Add	G
	continuous	one	Add	X
Nonparametric—Freidman	continuous	three or more	Add	X
Nonparametric—Kruskall Wallis	nominal	one	Add	G
	continuous	one		X
Factor Analysis	continuous	two or more	Add	X
Univariate Plots	continuous or nominal	one or more	Add	X
				X
Bivariate Plots	continuous or nominal	one or more	X Variable	X
	continuous or nominal	one or more	Y Variable	Y
Cell Plots	continuous	one or more	Add	X
	nominal	optional	Add	G
Box Plot	continuous	one or more	Add	X
	nominal	optional	Add	G
Compare Percentiles Plot	continuous	one or more	Add	X
	nominal	one	Add	G

You can force creation of a new analysis when you assign variables, if the analysis can take more than a single variable. To do so, hold down the the Command (⌘) and Shift keys before clicking a variable browser button. For example, with a bivariate plot selected, Command-Shift and click the X Variable button to create a new bivariate plot using the newly assigned X variable and the previously assigned Y variable. (Otherwise, the new X variable is added to the existing plot.) See the Variables section of each analysis chapter (Chapters 11-22) for additional information about using these special modifier keys.

Split by

The Split By button in the variable browser is a tool for splitting your analysis to examine subgroups of your data. When you assign a nominal variable as a split-by variable, the analysis is performed for each group of the nominal variable. You can split analyses or graphs by assigning multiple nominal variables to see information on each cell defined by the combination of the groups of the nominal variables. For information on how each analysis uses split-by variables see the variable requirements section of the appropriate analysis chapter.

Splitting analyses

For some analyses, all information on each group and for the total is shown in a single table. These analyses are descriptive statistics, frequency distribution (summary table only), percentiles (summary table only), one sample analyses, paired comparisons and unpaired comparisons. The other analyses show information for each group in separate tables.

Some analyses — frequency distribution, regression, ANOVA, and factor analysis — include plots as optional output. These analyses create a separate plot for each cell in any split-by variable(s) assigned.

Splitting plots

Some plots are offered in the analysis browser as distinct analyses: univariate and bivariate plots, cell plots, box plot, and compare percentiles. For these analyses, information for the different groups appear in a single plot, with groups identified with dissimilar points or fill patterns.

Action objects

Results are central to the analysis process in StatView because all statistical output generated by the program, tables and graphs, are "action objects." They retain information about the variables and analysis parameters that were specified when they were created. This information can then be used to quickly generate subsequent analyses. When you click the Create Analysis button or assign a variable with the variable browser, StatView uses information contained in the action object to determine what to do next:

- If no results are selected, a new analysis is created.
- If a result is selected and you create a different analysis, StatView assigns the variables used in the selected result to the new analysis. You do not have to repeat the step of assigning the variable(s).
- If a result is selected and you assign new variables, StatView either expands the analysis or creates a new one depending on that analysis' variable requirements. You do not have to repeat the step(s) of specifying the analysis parameters.
- Note that newly created results are selected when added to the view.

An awareness of which results are selected in the view is therefore crucial for a smooth work flow. The picture below illustrates how a selected result appears in the view. The eight black squares are selection handles.

Regression Summary
Gas Tank Size vs. Weight

Count	116
Num. Missing	0
R	.847
R Squared	.717
Adjusted R Squared	.715
RMS Residual	1.643

There are several ways to get feedback on which results are currently selected. When a result is selected in the view, a note appears in the upper right corner of the view. If no note appears, no results are selected. You can also use the results browser for information about selected results.

The results browser is an index of all results in a particular view. It can list all the results that appear in the view or only currently selected results. You can see which analyses are selected and what variables are assigned to them. The results browser is discussed in detail earlier in this chapter.

You also need to know which variables are used in selected results. You can find this information in the variable browser as well as the results browser. The usage markers to the right of variables in the variable browser change to reflect usage in the currently selected result. You can list variables by usage, making it easier to see which are used. This reorders the variable names, placing those with a usage marker at the top of the browser. The variable browser and reordering variable names are explained in greater detail earlier in this chapter.

Exercise

The exercise below is divided into seven parts, each dependent on the preceding one. They walk you through the analysis process, demonstrating the interaction of the analysis and variable browsers and action objects. In order to get the greatest benefit from the exercise and gain a thorough understanding of these important concepts, it is best to complete the entire exercise.

Create an analysis

Creating an analysis from scratch is a simple, two-step process involving the variable and analysis browsers. To create any analysis, you must select an analysis from the analysis browser and assign variables to it from the variable browser. You can use the browsers in either order. Try both and use whichever feels more comfortable.

Create an analysis, then assign variables ...

In this exercise, you select an analysis with the analysis browser then use the variable browser to assign variables.

- Open Car Data in the Sample Data folder. The dataset appears on the screen.

- Choose New View from the Analyze menu, or double-click in the empty rectangle above the row numbers in the dataset. A blank view appears on the screen.

If you are interested in the degree of correlation among several continuous variables in this dataset, a good place to begin your analysis is with a correlation matrix.

- In the analysis browser, select Correlation/Covariance and click the Create Analysis button. The Correlation/Covariance dialog box appears, so you can set parameters for the analysis.

- You want to generate a correlation matrix, so leave the default settings and click OK. A table placeholder appears in the view, with the message that you still need to specify variables.

- In the variable browser, select the variables Turning Circle, Displacement, Horsepower and Gas Tank Size by clicking on the first variable and dragging the mouse down the variable list.

- Click the Add button to assign the selected variables to the analysis. The analysis calculates and the table updates in the view.

Correlation Matrix

	Turning Circle	Displacement	Horsepower	Gas Tank Size
Turning Circle	1.000	.747	.482	.618
Displacement	.747	1.000	.764	.719
Horsepower	.482	.764	1.000	.666
Gas Tank Size	.618	.719	.666	1.000

116 observations were used in this computation.

… Or assign variables, then create an analysis

In the previous exercise, you created the analysis first then assigned the variables. You could just as well have assigned the variables first, then created the analysis. The order in which you perform the two steps does not matter.

The next exercise is a continuation of the preceding one. You assign variables to an analysis that requires you to specify variable usage, a simple regression between two variables in the Car Data. You begin by assigning variables, then create the analysis. The results will appear in the same view as the correlation matrix created in the previous example.

- Make sure that no results are selected in the view by clicking in blank space. Also, make sure the dataset used in the previous example is still open. (Check the Window menu to see if the dataset is listed.)

- In the analysis browser, select Regression. Notice that the variable browser automatically replaces the Add button with Independent and Dependent buttons. You use these buttons to assign variables and specify variable usage simultaneously.

- In the variable browser, select Displacement and click the Independent button, then select Horsepower and click the Dependent button. The usages of Displacement and Horsepower are indicated in the variable browser by an X and Y, respectively.

- Since Regression is already selected in the analysis browser, click the Create Analysis button. The Regression dialog box appears so you can set parameters for the analysis.

- You want to generate a simple regression, so leave the default settings and click OK. The default output for a simple regression of Horsepower vs. Displacement appears in the view.

Regression Summary
Horsepower vs. Displacement

Count	116
Num. Missing	0
R	.764
R Squared	.584
Adjusted R Squared	.580
RMS Residual	25.796

ANOVA Table
Horsepower vs. Displacement

	DF	Sum of Squares	Mean Square	F-Value	P-Value
Regression	1	106510.675	106510.675	160.061	<.0001
Residual	114	75859.765	665.437		
Total	115	182370.440			

Regression Coefficients
Horsepower vs. Displacement

	Coefficient	Std. Error	Std. Coeff.	t-Value	P-Value
Intercept	50.444	6.744	50.444	7.480	<.0001
Displacement	.504	.040	.764	12.652	<.0001

More information from the same analysis

When you select a result, you are, in effect, selecting its analysis parameters and its variable assignments (see the earlier section on Action Objects). If you then create another analysis with the analysis browser, StatView uses the variables from the selected result and combines them with the new analysis.

If, on the other hand, you select a result and then assign variables from the variable browser, StatView takes the analysis parameters from the selected result and combines them with the newly assigned variables to generate a new result.

Add additional output

This exercise is a continuation of the preceding exercises. In the previous exercise, you generated only the default results for a simple regression. Regression has a triangle next to it in the analysis browser, indicating that several tables and graphs are available as output. In this exercise, you add additional output from the regression analysis to the default results.

- Click on the triangle next to Regression to see all the output available for a regression analysis. There are nine results in the indented list.

- The results from the previous example should still be selected, since all new output remains selected until you deselect it. The selection note in the upper right corner will say "3 Results Selected" if this is the case. If not, select all three of them while holding down the Shift key.

- Double-click on Regression Plot in the analysis browser. A scattergram of the two variables with the calculated regression line is added to the view.

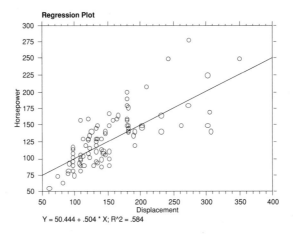

Regression Plot

Y = 50.444 + .504 * X; R^2 = .584

In this way you can generate additional output for most analyses. You can choose those results that interest you most rather than having all the results associated with an analysis appear in the view at once.

Expand an existing analysis by assigning a variable

This exercise is a continuation of the preceding exercises. There are many analyses that can incorporate multiple variables in a single analysis (see the summary table earlier in the chapter). When any of these analyses are selected in the view, they expand to incorporate the new variables assigned to them.

For example, if you select the correlation analysis created in the example above, you can assign more variables to the matrix by selecting the new variables in the variable browser and clicking on the Add button.

- Select the correlation matrix by clicking on it.

- Highlight the variable Weight in the variable browser, then click Add (or just double-click on Weight). The correlation matrix immediately recalculates:

Correlation Matrix

	Turning Circle	Displacement	Horsepower	Gas Tank Size	Weight
Turning Circle	1.000	.747	.482	.618	.752
Displacement	.747	1.000	.764	.719	.830
Horsepower	.482	.764	1.000	.666	.707
Gas Tank Size	.618	.719	.666	1.000	.847
Weight	.752	.830	.707	.847	1.000

116 observations were used in this computation.

Create a new analysis by assigning a variable

Some analyses require only a specific number of variables. When you select a result from one of these analyses and assign a new variable from the variable browser, you get a separate result. This result has the same characteristics of the original analysis, but has the new variable substituted in an appropriate usage. The simple regression analysis created earlier is such an analysis.

Select any one of the three tables created from the previous regression analysis example. The next variable you assign will use these same analysis parameters.

- In the variable browser, assign Weight to the analysis by selecting it and clicking the Independent button. A completely new regression analysis uses Horsepower as the dependent variable and Weight as the new independent variable. The four regression outputs are created (Regression Summary, ANOVA Table, Regression Coefficients and Regression Plot). The Regression Summary table is shown below.

Regression Summary
Horsepower vs. Weight

Count	116
Num. Missing	0
R	.707
R Squared	.499
Adjusted R Squared	.495
RMS Residual	28.299

As you see, this process saved you from having to reassign Horsepower as the dependent variable, and let you bypass the Regression dialog box. The process is efficient because the analysis you select forwards information for use in the analyses that follow it.

Use previously assigned variables in new analyses

This exercise is a continuation of the preceding exercises. The variables in a selected result can be used in a completely different analysis, just as they can be used to create additional output for the same analysis.

- Select the correlation matrix previously created.

- In the analysis browser, double-click on Frequency Distribution. Accept the default dialog box settings by clicking OK. The default output for frequency distribution is added to the view. (Your results will appear in a single verticle column in the view. We arranged them side by side here to conserve space.)

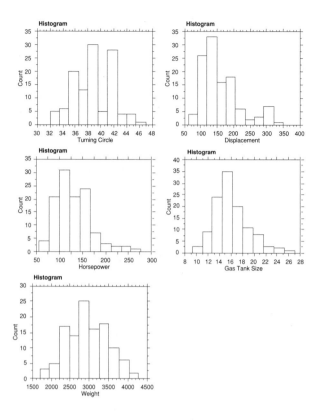

You can see that when results are selected in the view and you choose a new analysis, the variables used in the selected results are assigned to the newly created analysis.

Analyses of data subgroups: split by

You can see the results of any analysis broken down by groups of a nominal variable in a way that is completely interactive and does not require reorganizing your dataset. (Note that StatView allows you set criteria which restrict the analysis to a subset of your dataset. For more information on criteria, see Chapter 6, Exploring Subsets of Your Data.) To illustrate this capability, you can generate a separate correlation matrix for each of the countries in the Car Data.

• Select the correlation matrix you generated in the earlier exercise.

• In the variable browser, assign the nominal variable Country to the analysis by selecting it and clicking the Split By button. A separate correlation matrix appears for each country represented in the dataset:

Correlation Matrix
Split By: Country
Cell: Japan

	Turning Circle	Displacement	Horsepower	Gas Tank Size	Weight
Turning Circle	1.000	.760	.649	.752	.738
Displacement	.760	1.000	.944	.932	.920
Horsepower	.649	.944	1.000	.864	.822
Gas Tank Size	.752	.932	.864	1.000	.908
Weight	.738	.920	.822	.908	1.000

30 observations were used in this computation.

Correlation Matrix
Split By: Country
Cell: Other

	Turning Circle	Displacement	Horsepower	Gas Tank Size	Weight
Turning Circle	1.000	.448	.313	.564	.603
Displacement	.448	1.000	.845	.791	.859
Horsepower	.313	.845	1.000	.768	.748
Gas Tank Size	.564	.791	.768	1.000	.786
Weight	.603	.859	.748	.786	1.000

37 observations were used in this computation.

Correlation Matrix
Split By: Country
Cell: USA

	Turning Circle	Displacement	Horsepower	Gas Tank Size	Weight
Turning Circle	1.000	.679	.450	.581	.765
Displacement	.679	1.000	.801	.658	.793
Horsepower	.450	.801	1.000	.432	.545
Gas Tank Size	.581	.658	.432	1.000	.845
Weight	.765	.793	.545	.845	1.000

49 observations were used in this computation.

This is how easy it is to calculate statistics for different subgroups of your data. It is a flexible and interactive process, and it follows the way you think. Best of all, you do not need to touch the dataset to do it.

View preferences

There are many aspects of the program that you can customize to your liking with the Preferences command in the Manage menu. View preferences are discussed here, Preferences for the formatting of tables and graphs are discussed in detail in the next chapter. Preferences that determine whether the analysis, variable and results browsers appear automatically are covered in Chapter 1, Overview and Requirements.

You can set preferences in the view that govern text, the size of lines when printed, the size of the document (for exporting to MacDraw II), whether results are saved with a view, and what happens when you double-click on results. These choices apply to both tables and graphs.

To get to the View Preferences dialog box, choose Preferences from the Manage menu, select View in the Choose Preferences dialog box and click Modify. After you make your selections in the dialog box, click OK, and then click Done in the Choose Preferences dialog box. The new settings do not affect currently open views.

```
┌══════════════ View Preferences ══════════════┐
│ ┌─Default text──────────┐                      │
│ │                        │   Sample            │
│ │  Font:  Geneva ▼      │                      │
│ │                        │                      │
│ │  Size:  9      ▼       │                      │
│ └───────────────────────┘                      │
│                                                 │
│  ☐ Print and copy lines at 1/4 width           │
│  ☐ Limit document size to MacDraw II           │
│  ☒ Save analysis results with view             │
│  ☐ Templates appear using view text defaults   │
│  Double-click on table/graph same as           │
│      ⦿Edit Display   ○ Edit Analysis           │
│                     ┌────────┐  ┌──────────┐   │
│                     │ Cancel │  │   OK     │   │
│                     └────────┘  └──────────┘   │
└═════════════════════════════════════════════════┘
```

Text

In the box labelled Default Text, you can specify the default font and size for all analysis output by choosing from the appropriate pop-up menus. The word "Sample" to the right of the box changes to reflect the choices you make. These settings affect all the text in tables and graphs generated using the analysis browser: headings, numbers, axis labels, and legends. You can override these settings for an element of any table or graph using the Text menu. These settings also determine the defaults for text added with the text tool in the Draw menu.

Print and copy at 1/4 width

This option affects only printed results; there is no discernible difference on the screen. Clicking "Print and copy lines at 1/4 width" reduces all single line widths by approximately 1/4 when they are printed out on a printer that can print hairlines. Otherwise the lines are single-pixel lines. The hairline widths carry over when tables, graphs or drawn objects are copied to another application and printed from there as well as when you print from StatView. Once you set this 1/4 width preference, it applies to all documents you copy or print, regardless of whether you created them before or after you set the preference.

Limit document size

If you save your views as PICT files and read them into MacDraw II, you need to constrain the document size so it does not exceed the capabilities of MacDraw II. Clicking "Limit document size to MacDraw II" limits the total number of pages in a view to the number of pages that MacDraw II can contain. (MacDraw drawing size is 9 pages high by 17 across on a LaserWriter, a bit less than 100 square inches. StatView's document size is roughly 227 square inches, or about 23 pages high by 30 pages across.)

Save analysis results with view

By default, calculations are saved when you save a view so the results do not need to be recalculated when the file is reopened with its original dataset. You can turn this option off in order to lessen the size on disk of saved view files. If you create a view to use as a template, it makes more sense *not* to save the results with the view so the template file is smaller.

Template text

By default, when you use a template, the font and size of all output text is the font and size that you used to create the template. This is what you would expect a template to do. You may, however, wish to override these settings and use the default text as set in the view preferences. This is useful if you are using the analysis templates provided with StatView (which were created using Geneva 9 point font) and you wish the output to appear in another font or size.

Saving a view

You can save an active view at any time by choosing Save or Save As from the File menu. In the directory dialog box, name the file, select the appropriate format and save it in the desired folder. When you save a view as the default format (StatView 4.x View), you save all aspects of your work — the analyses, variables used, anything you have drawn, etc. When you reopen the view you can resume your work at the point you left it. Since all characteristics are retained with a saved file in view format, you can use any view as a template.

 If you save a view whose associated dataset is Untitled (it has not been saved or is a text file that has not been saved as a StatView document), StatView cannot match the dataset with the view when the view is reopened. When you try to save the view, you get an alert so you can save the dataset first. If you close a dataset whose variables are used in open views, those variables will be removed from the results. You get a warning when this is about to occur and can cancel and not close the dataset.

As a template

You can use any view you save as a template. A list of situations in which templates are helpful is given at the end of the preceding chapter. There are several points to take into consideration if you plan to use a view as a template. Consider the advice given in the Templates section later in this chapter before you design a template for repeated use.

If you plan to use the view as a template, save it in the StatView Templates folder. You can then add it to the Analyze menu for easier access. You do not need to save calculated results with a view if it is to be used as a template. In the View Preferences dialog box, leave "Save analysis results with view" unchecked– that saves disk space.

As a text file

Text files contain all the text and data from tables but no representation of graphs nor any of the text in graphs. Text files can be read by word processors and any programs that can read text.

As a PICT file

PICT files contain a PICT representation of all of the information in the view (tables, graphs, all text and drawn objects). These PICT files can be read by any program that can read PICT information, such as drawing programs and some painting and word processing programs.

Reopen your work

Any view you create can be saved and reopened. You can use the original dataset or choose a different dataset (and assign new variables) when you reopen it. Whether you use the original dataset or a different one, you have the option to assign different variables than were used originally. You can also combine variables from several datasets, including the original one. When you reopen a view you may continue to work in the original view or add its contents to an open view (if it is the topmost view.)

The Open command in the File menu displays a directory dialog box to locate and open a view. Choose "StatView 4.x View" in the pop-up menu if you want to see only view files listed. When you open a view, you get the Opening a View dialog box:

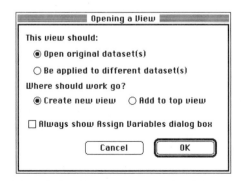

The most common use of this dialog box is to leave the default settings and click OK.

The setting "Open original dataset" selects the dataset(s) whose variables were saved with the view. The original dataset must have the same name and be exactly where it was the last time you saved the view for StatView to find it easily.[*] For this reason, if you need to rename a dataset, it is advisable to rename a *copy* of it, and keep one under the original name. If you move the view and dataset to another disk, keep the dataset in the same location relative to the view. If StatView cannot locate the dataset, it opens a directory dialog box for you to locate it.

The Opening a View dialog box offers the choice whether to display the results in a new view by themselves, or add them to the topmost open view. The setting "Create new view" displays the results in a new view. If you add them to the top view, they appear at the end, following all existing tables and graphs. Creating a new view is the default setting, and reopens your work by itself, as you left it. If no views are open, the "Add to top view" choice is dimmed.

You need to show the Assign Variables dialog box only when you want to assign variables other than those originally used in your view (see below).

Use original variables

To open your work exactly as you left it, using the same variables, leave the default settings: Open original dataset and Create new view, and click OK. If you check "Always show Assign Variables dialog box," the original variables are assigned to their respective slots when that dialog box appears.

Assign different variables

...from the original dataset

If you want to use the original dataset, but assign variables other than those used in the original view, check the box at the bottom to show the Assign Variables dialog box, and click OK. When the dialog box appears, the original variables are assigned to their respective slots. Drag them back to the variables list and replace them with the variables you want to use.

...from different datasets

There are two ways to use variables from datasets other than the original one when you reopen a view. The first option is to select "Be applied to different dataset" and click

---

[*] This doesn't apply to System 7.0 users. StatView can locate a dataset moved to another location with System 7's file ID.

OK. This brings up a directory dialog box so you can choose the dataset. Once you choose a dataset, the Assign Variables dialog box appears.

The second method is easier if you want to use variables from several datasets including the original one. Leave "Open original dataset" selected, check "Always show Assign Variables dialog box" and click OK. You can then use the Data pop-up menu in the Assign Variables dialog box to select different datasets.

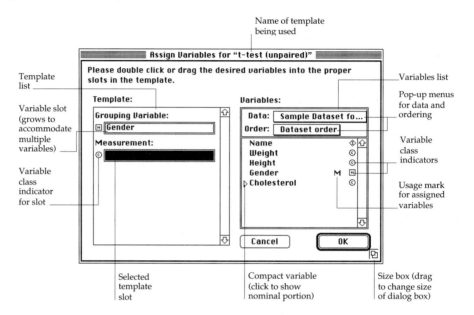

The Assign Variables dialog box lists all the variables in the dataset, and all the variable slots that need to be filled for this view. You assign variables from the variables list into slots by dragging or double-clicking. This process is covered in the preceding chapter, Templates.

Print a view

There are several things to consider before you print. The two most important are the page settings and the position of tables and graphs relative to page breaks.

The page settings control the printing of each page in the document. Changes you make affect only the active view, since page setup information is stored with the file when you save it. To perform page setup, choose Page Setup from the File menu. The type of dialog box displayed depends on the type of printer currently selected in the Chooser.

Before you print, scroll through the view to see if tables, graphs or text are cut by a page break (the horizontal hashed lines in the view). You can avoid printing the top of a result on one page and the bottom on another by using the Clean Up Items command in the Layout menu. The checkbox labelled "Ignore page breaks" should not be checked.

A third thing to check is the number and configuration of pages specified for your document. Use the Drawing Size command in the Layout menu to set the size and shape of the overall document. This determines how many pages will be printed. If a table extends horizontally onto an adjacent page not included in the Drawing Size dialog box, the overhanging part will not print.

To print the information in a view, choose Print from the File menu. The standard Print dialog box appears for the printer type currently selected in the Chooser. In the appropriate text boxes, enter the number of copies and number of pages to print and click OK, or press Return to start printing. You can also print a view (or a dataset) from the Finder, without having the document open, by selecting the file and choosing Print from the File menu. While printing, StatView displays a dialog box that allows you to cancel printing or suspend printing on non-LaserWriter printers. For further details on printing, refer to your Macintosh Reference Guide.

StatView offers the option of printing lines in tables and graphs as hairlines on printers. This option affects only printed results; there is no discernible difference on the screen. Clicking "Print and copy lines at 1/4 width" in the View Preferences dialog box reduces all single line widths by approximately 1/4 when they are printed on a printer that can print hairlines. Otherwise the lines print as single-pixel lines.

Templates

There are many advantages in using templates. Think of templates as the way to use this program to create macros. You can set up custom formatting for graphs and tables, set preferences for analysis parameters, perform analyses in batch mode, apply complex analyses repeatedly, and duplicate the structure of reports even though you have different data. This section provides tips to consider when making a template, followed by two examples of different templates you might create.

StatView ships with many templates installed and listed in the Analyze menu. You can remove templates you do not use often from this menu, and add others. You are not limited to using the templates provided with the program. You can, and should, create templates of your own that help you keep from repeating steps you always perform in an analysis. The Additional Templates folder provides examples of useful applications of templates, such as combining frequently used analyses and enhancing your presentations.

The preceding chapter, Templates, provides all the details about using templates. We recommend that you read that chapter before continuing with this discussion. The preceding sections of this chapter describe how to use the analysis browser and variable browser to create analyses and assign variables. Those skills are all you need, since the process of creating a template is the same process used to create results and save a view.

There is no magic involved in creating a template; you follow the same steps you use to create an analysis. You create the structure that you wish to use as a template in the same manner as you create all analyses and graphs. You customize the output, add drawings to the view, and save the view in the StatView Templates folder to make accessing this information easier.

StatView templates folder

The StatView Templates folder is a special folder. Any views that appear in this folder can be added to the Analyze menu and accessed through the Templates command in the Analyze menu. When you use a template, either by choosing from the menu or from the Templates dialog box, you bypass the automatic use of the original dataset; instead, you are automatically asked to locate the dataset to use with the template and then shown the Assign Variables dialog box. See Chapter 7 more more information about the StatView Templates folder.

File menu vs. templates folder

Saved views may be accessed in two ways. If you place a saved view in the StatView Templates folder, it is accessed through the Analyze menu. Views that are saved to a location other than the StatView templates folder can be opened using the Open command from the File menu in the same way as any other Macintosh file. Views saved in these two ways have different properties.

Templates and saved views are used for different purposes. Templates are meant to be reused with different variables and datasets than those used to create it. Saved views simply save your work in progress to be reopened and continued at a later time.

When you open a template, you are presented with the Assign Variables dialog box in which you select the dataset and variables to assign to the template. Template output automatically goes to a view if it is topmost, or into a newly created view.

When you open a saved view from the File menu, on the other hand, you are presented with the Opening a View dialog box which offers the option of using the original dataset and variables and allows you to choose where output is to be placed.

Template tips

When you create a view to reuse as a template, there are several things to take into consideration. Some characteristics that are helpful in working views get in the way when you use them as templates, and vice versa.

Variable slot names

You use the Assign Variables dialog box to assign variables from any dataset to the slots in the template. The templates list contains separate slots for each variable that was used in the view which was saved to make the template. Therefore, when you create your template, consider giving your variables generic names that you can apply to any dataset rather than names that have a meaning for one specific dataset. The picture below shows both of these situations:

X Variable:	Weight:
⊙ [ ]	⊙ [ ]
Y Variable:	Cholesterol:
⊙ [ ]	⊙ [ ]
Generic variable names	*Specific variable names*

Since the slots take their names from the dataset used when the template was created, if you plan to use generic names, you may need to change the names of the variables in the dataset used when creating the template, or create a dummy dataset with generic names.

It is important to note that when the Assign Variables dialog box first appears, it will pre-assign variables to slots if the names match. So if you are repeating an analysis on datasets with the same variable names, it is worthwhile to use specific variable names. This will save you the trouble of having to drag the variables into the correct slot. The ordering of slots in the dialog box corresponds with the creation order of the variables in the dataset which was used to create the template.

Do not save results

You can minimize disk storage space for your templates by not saving the results with the view. In the View Preferences dialog box, do not check "Save analysis results with view" as one of the options. This will make the file smaller and you need only the structure to use it as a template, not the results. You should remember to turn this option on again so that your regular views will be saved with their results.

Turn Recalculate off

You may want to disable calculation when adding results from several templates to one view so you do not have to wait for each set of results to calculate before adding results from another template. If you add template-generated results to a view with Recalculate off (see the section, Recalculate checkbox, earlier in this chapter), graph and table placeholders appear in the window rather than completed results. When you are ready to calculate the results, click the Recalculate checkbox in the upper left corner of the view. The analyses then calculate and the results appear.

Formatting and templates

There are a few cases in which the formatting information saved with a template will not apply to all output. These situations are as follows:

- For analyses that generate new tables or graphs for additional variables (as opposed to those that incorporate additional variables in the same table or graph), formatting information applies only to the number of tables or graphs present when the template was created.

  If you create a template for an unpaired t-test that analyzes a single continuous variable and a single nominal variable, then assign two continuous variables to the template, only the analysis using the first continuous variable will be formatted as in the template. The analysis using the second variable will generate a new table using the default table formatting. If you would like the formatting information to be retained, create the template using the maximum number of variables you plan to assign. For the example above, if you created the template using two continuous variables, the customizations would apply to both variables. Remember, that you do not need to fill all the slots in order to use a template.

- Analyses that show information for each split-by group in separate tables or plots (as opposed to the same table or graph) will not use any formatting information saved with template if the template uses a split-by variable.

 For information on how an analysis handles additional variables and split-by variables see the Variable Requirements section in each analysis chapter. Also, note that many default formatting instructions can be globally set using View, Table and Graph preferences.

Example templates

There are many different ways to use templates to help your work. Below are two different examples of how you might use templates, with exercises to create them.

Customize the format of a graph

A template lets you name and save all the features of a particular graph. If you are writing an article for publication, you may want all the scattergrams in it to have exactly the same format. You can customize a single scattergram, save the view to the StatView Templates folder, and use it to create all the scattergrams. There is no need to repeat all the formatting for each new scattergram.

When you use a scattergram template, the Assign Variables dialog box contains a single slot for the variable assigned to each axis. The labels for these slots are the names of the variables used to create the initial scattergram. If you want these names to be generic, change the names of the variables to X variable and Y variable. If you want them to be specific to a certain project, use specific variable names. The template below uses generic variable names.

- Open Tree Data in the Sample Data folder. The dataset appears on the screen.

- Select the variable name "Trunk Girth" and type "X Variable." Rename the Weight variable as "Y Variable" in the same manner.

- Choose New View from the Analyze menu. A blank view appears on the screen.

- In the analysis browser, select the Show pop-up and change it to Graphs Only.

- In the analysis browser, click on the triangle next to Bivariate Plots. The results appear indented beneath it.

- Select Scattergram and click the Create Analysis button. By choosing Bivariate Plots from the Graphs Only list rather than the All Analyses list you bypass the Bivariate Plot dialog box. A graph placeholder appears in the view until you assign variables.

- In the variable browser, select X Variable from the list and click the X Variable button. Select Y Variable from the list and click the Y Variable button. The scattergram appears in the view.

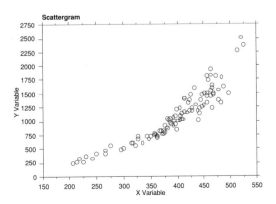

189

Chapter 8: Building Analyses

In the following steps, you will customize X and Y axis lengths, change the font and size of the axis values and labels, and change the position of major and minor tick marks.

To set the axes to a specific length:

- Make sure the graph is selected and click the Edit Display button.

- Type "3" in the Vertical text box and "5" in the Horizontal text box. Click OK.

To change the font and size of the axis values, labels and graph title:

- Make sure the graph is still selected.

- In the Text menu, change the Font to Helvetica (or some other font if you do not have Helvetica installed in your System) and change the size to 12.

- Click in blank space in the view to remove the current selection. Select both axis labels again by holding the Shift key while you click on them. Change their style to bold, using the Text menu again.

To change the tick mark styles:

- Select the Y axis and click the Edit Display button. In the first Numeric Axis dialog box, click the More Choices button. In the second dialog box, use the pop-up menus to change the major and minor tick marks to the last choice and click OK.

- Repeat this process for the horizontal axis (X axis).

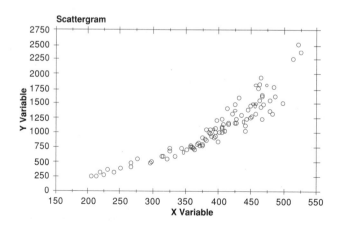

- Click once in blank space in the view to deselect the axis. Otherwise it would be selected when you reopened this template.

You have finished customizing the graph and are now ready to save this view as a template. First, change one of the preference settings so the template will use less hard disk space.

- Choose Preferences from the Manage menu.

- In the Choose Preferences dialog box, select View and click Modify.

- Make sure the box labelled "Save analysis results with view" is not checked, and click OK. This ensures that only the structure of the view is saved, not the results as well. (Remember to change this back after you have saved the template so that your future results will be saved with the view.)

- Click Done in the Choose Preferences dialog box.

- Choose Save from the File menu. In the directory dialog box, change the name of the view to My Scattergram and save it in the StatView Templates folder.

- Close both the view and the dataset. Do not save the changes to the dataset.

You are now ready to use this template to format a new scattergram. You can use this template with any dataset.

- Open Car Data in the Sample Data folder. The dataset appears on the screen.

- From the Analyze menu, choose Templates. In the dialog box, select My Scattergram and click the "Use Template" button.

- In the Assign Variables dialog box, double-click on Turning Circle to assign it to the X Variable slot. Assign Displacement to the Y Variable slot in a similar manner. Click OK.

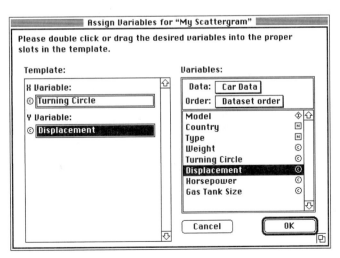

A new view is created. The scattergram plotting Turning Circle vs. Displacement appears in the view with the same format you specified earlier.

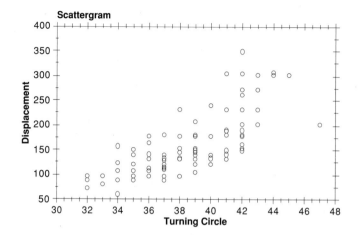

- Close this view and Car Data. You do not need to save changes to either.

The scattergram template can be modified at any time, if you need additional or different formatting.

Customize the parameters and output of an analysis

A template lets you name and save all the parameters and output of a particular analysis. You can modify parameters for any of the templates that ship with StatView, as well as add additional output. You can also start from scratch and build your own analysis template with the parameters and results you desire.

The exercise below shows you how to construct a Simple Regression template of your own that differs from the one supplied with StatView. The template you will create includes the intercept in the analysis and displays the Summary Table, Coefficients, Regression Plot and Plot of Residuals vs. Fitted Values.

When you use this template, the Assign Variables dialog box will contain one slot for the Independent variable and one for the Dependent variable. The labels for these slots are the same as the ones for Simple Regression. If you want these names to be generic, you can create a dataset with two columns named Dependent and Independent. If you want them to be specific to a project you are working on, use specific variable names. The template below uses generic variable names.

- Choose New from the File menu to create a new dataset.

- Select the heading of the input column. Type Dependent to create the first column. Press Tab and Type Independent to create the second column. Press Return so the variable browser updates with the new variable name.

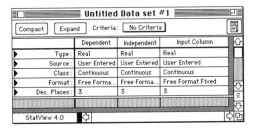

- Choose New View from the Analyze menu. A blank view appears on the screen.

- In the analysis browser, click on the triangle next to Regression. The results appear indented beneath it.

- Select Regression Summary table, hold down the Command key and select Regression Coefficients, Regression Plot and Residuals vs. Fitted.

- Click the Create Analysis button. The Regression dialog box appears.

- Because you are performing a simple regression, leave the default setting "Simple." Click the "No intercept in model" checkbox and click OK to specify that the regression line will pass through the origin.

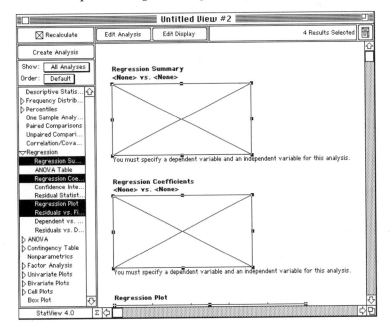

- In the variable browser, select Dependent from the list and click the Dependent button. Assign Independent to the analysis by selecting it and clicking the Independent button.

The dataset contains no data, so no calculations occur even though the Recalculate box is checked. This is acceptable because you have specified all you need to create this template. You are now ready to save this view as a template.

- Choose Save from the File menu. In the directory dialog box, change the name of the view to Simple Regression—No Intercept and save it in the StatView Templates folder. When you click Save, this alert appears:

> ⚠ You have not yet saved a dataset which depends on this file. If you decide to proceed, StatView 4.0 will have difficulty locating the dataset when the file is reopened. You may avoid this by first saving the dataset.
>
> Cancel   Continue

- You do not need to save the changes to the dataset because it was only created to make the two variable names. Click Continue.

- Close both the view and the dataset.

You are now ready to use this template with any dataset to format a simple regression.

- From the Analyze menu, choose Templates. Select Simple Regression—No Intercept and click the "Use Template" button.

- In the directory dialog box, double-click on Car Data in the Sample Data folder.

- In the Assign Variables dialog box, assign Gas Tank Size to the Dependent slot by double-clicking on it or dragging it into the slot. Assign Weight to the Independent slot in the same manner.

- Click OK. A new view is created and the output of the template is placed in the view. The simple regression that is calculated contains no intercept and the output you have chosen appears in the view.

Chapter

9

Customizing Graphs and Tables

StatView includes all the features of a graphing program, allowing you to enhance the appearance of graphs and tables for clarity and visual impact. You can format each table and graph individually or set global preferences that govern every graph and table you create. You format using individual dialog boxes, tools in the Draw menu or commands from the Text menu.

Formatting options for graphs include changing: axis bounds, tick marks, interval widths, labels and symbols, grid lines, fills, colors, patterns, line widths and text formats. You can also flip the horizontal and vertical axes.

Formatting options for tables include changing table style and text formats, controlling line widths, color and pen patterns, and transposing rows and columns.

Use of dialog boxes

Many of the formatting changes you make to tables and graphs are controlled through a dialog box that appears after you click the Edit Display button. There are two important features to know about using these dialog boxes.

Shortcut to Edit Display

You normally invoke formatting dialog boxes by selecting a table or graph component and clicking the Edit Display button. You can bypass the button with the following shortcut: hold down the Option key and double click on the graph/table component.

Show button

Formatting dialog boxes have a "Show" button which lets you preview formatting changes as you make them.

After making changes in a dialog box, click "Show" to see the effects on the selected graph. The dialog box does not close or move, but the table or graph updates to reflect the settings in the dialog box. If you do not like the changes you have made, you can change them while the dialog box is still open. Click OK to implement the changes you have made and close the dialog box; click Cancel to exit the dialog box and leave the table or graph in its original format.

Draw menu

The Draw menu contains a tool palette for drawing shapes in the view, and pop-up menus that lets you customize tables and graphs. The pop-up menus for fill, pen, line point, size and color as well as the text tool are discussed in this chapter as they pertain to tables and graphs; the drawing tools are all explained in the next chapter.

The Draw menu is a tear-off menu. You can place it anywhere on the screen so it does not obscure your work. Hold down the mouse to display the Draw menu, move the cursor down into the body of the menu, and move the mouse to drag it to the desired position. As you position the menu, an outline indicates where the menu will appear when you release the mouse.

When you attempt to tear off the menu, a pop-up menu may unexpectedly appear (such as color or line choices). Release the mouse and try again. This time, drag the cursor across the menu more rapidly or tear the menu off to the left.

If the menu ever hides your results, move it elsewhere in the view by clicking on the top bar of the menu and dragging it. Close it by clicking the close box in the upper left hand corner. The menu automatically closes when you do not have a view frontmost.

You can use the Draw menu just like a standard pull-down menu if you do not want it as an added window on your screen. You can select any of the drawing tools by clicking on Draw, dragging to highlight the desired drawing feature and releasing the mouse.

Undo of format changes

It is important to remember that any formatting that you perform, whether through a dialog box, draw menu, mouse movement or menu command, can be undone if you choose Undo from the Edit menu before you perform another action. If you make a mistake, choose Undo immediately to return your graph to its previous state.

Graphs

Graphs have many aspects you can format. You can set global preferences to govern the appearance of all your graphs, or change the format of an individual graph. Some components of a graph are customized in dialog boxes that appear when you select them and click the Edit Display button. Other components are customized by selecting them and using options from the Draw and Text menus. Some formatting changes apply to the entire graph, others to particular components of the graph.

A graph is composed of many different components. Understanding what these components are and how they fit together helps make it easy to achieve a desired formatting result. A graph is pictured below with each of its components labeled. The following table describes these components.

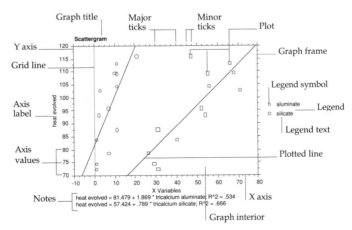

Component	Definition
Title	The text at the upper left of a graph, which identifies the analysis and variables involved

Frame	The border around a graph, a closed rectangle or an L-shape
Interior	The area inside a graph but outside the plot
X axis	The horizontal axis or abscissa
Y axis	The vertical axis or ordinate
Axis values	The numbers or words along an axis that label points on the axis
Tick marks (major, minor)	Marks on an axis which indicate intervals on the axis scale
Axis labels	The labels below the X axis and to the left of the Y axis that indicate what variable or quantity is plotted on that axis
Plot	The points, bars, lines, or boxes in a graph
Grid lines	The vertical and horizontal dotted reference lines that can be added to a graph
Plotted lines (straight or curved)	The plotted line and confidence bands in regression plots or scattergrams and the normal distribution curve in a histogram
Legend	An object outside a graph, containing legend symbols and text identifying the symbols corresponding to the variables or groups in the graph
Notes	Text below the X axis label that gives information about a graph, such as a regression equation or variable requirements
Reference Lines	Lines indicating mean and standard deviation, etc., on a univariate plot, percentiles on a percentile plot, or equal X and Y on a compare percentiles plot

Selecting parts of a graph

Graphs and their component parts can be moved, resized and customized. Any time you want to change something, it must be selected first. There are two types of selection: selecting the graph as whole or selecting a component of the graph. With the whole graph selected you can:

Change all the line widths, colors and the font, size and style of all text

Fill the interior of the graph to give the graph a different background

Change the structure of the graph (click the Edit Display button to get a graph dialog box)

To select the graph as a whole:

- Click on the selection tool of the Draw menu if it is not already selected.

- Click directly on the frame of the graph or click in the interior of a graph but not on a bar, point, line, etc. Eight selection handles (small squares) appear on the border to show that the whole graph is selected.

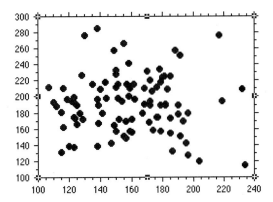

Graph with eight selection handles on frame

There are many components of a graph, and it is important to click in the right place to select the component you want to modify. You can select more than one component by holding down the command key and clicking on additional components. Selection for some components is indicated by a light gray border which appears around it.

Selection for other components is indicated by square black handles around the object. We call these selection handles.

Weight

Make sure the cursor is shaped like an arrow when you are trying to select something. If you have been using the Draw menu, click on the selection tool (arrow) if it is not already selected.

Component	How to select it	What you can format	Tool to use
Title	Click on the text	font, size, style of text color	Text menu Draw menu
Frame	Click on the frame	L-shape or rectangle line width, pen, color	Edit display Draw menu
Interior	Click in blank space in the graph interior	color and fill	Draw menu

X or Y axis	Click on the axis numbers	font, size, style of text	Text menu
		line width, pen, color	Draw menu
Axis values	Click on the axis numbers	bounds, intervals, scale, format, decimal places	Edit Display
		font, size, style of text, color	Text menu
Tick marks	Click on the axis numbers	length, width, position	Edit Display
Axis labels	Click on the label	font, size, style of text	Text menu
		color	Draw menu
Plot	Click on any object in the interior of the graph	line width, pen, fill, point type, point size, color	Draw menu
Grid Lines	Click on the axis numbers	position, presence	Edit Display
Plotted lines	Click on the line	line width,pen and color	Draw menu
Legend	Click anywhere in the legend	layout, frame, add shadow box, corner type	Edit Display
Legend symbols	Click on the symbol	point type, point size, color	Draw menu
Legend text	Click on the text	font, size, style of text	Text menu
		color	Draw menu
Notes	Click on the text	font, size, style of text	Text menu
		color	Draw menu

Moving a graph or a graph component

You can move an entire graph or any component of a graph. To move the entire graph, click anywhere in the interior of the graph or on the graph frame and drag your mouse to a new location. The entire graph and all its components are relocated. Do not drag any of the selection handles (small black squares), as this will resize the graph rather than moving it.

You can move most components of a graph: the title, legend, axis, axis labels, notes. If you move the axis, it is constrained to the respective horizontal or vertical direction. To move any component of a graph, select the component and drag it to a new location.

Moving a component does not move the entire graph. However, if you move the graph as a whole, all components move and stay in the same position relative to each other.

Keyboard shortcuts

You can use the arrow keys to move any selected component or the graph as a whole. Each keystroke moves the component or graph one unit in the direction of the arrow. If the grid is turned on, the unit of movement equals the distance between tick marks on the view's ruler. If the grid is off, the unit of movement is one screen pixel.

Overlay graphs

You can merge the plots from separate graphs, to create a double layer graph. Select only the plot of one graph and drag it into position in the other graph's frame. If one obscures the other, make sure the plot you drag has the fill "None." (Check the fill in the Draw menu.)

Resizing a graph

To resize any graph, select the whole graph, click on any of the eight selection handles and drag the mouse to the new location. The graph resizes differently depending on which handle you drag. If you drag any of the four corner handles, you can resize the graph horizontally and vertically at the same time. If you drag the handle in the middle of either of the sides, the graph will resize horizontally. If you drag the handle in the middle of the top or bottom of the frame, the graph resizes vertically.

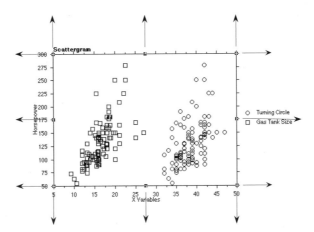

Arrows indicate which way graph enlarges

All components of the graph move to stay in the same relative location to the graph.

Formatting and editing graph text

You can change the font, size, style and color of graph titles, notes, axis labels, axis values and legend text. You can also change the orientation of all text except in legends. You can apply these changes to an individual component or for all the text of the graph.

If you want to format all the text in a graph at once, select the entire graph. If you want to edit only a single component, select only that component. The text editing commands and pop-up menus are in the Text menu. The color choices are in the Draw menu.

You can edit all text in a graph except axis values, using the text tool in the Draw menu.

- Click on the text tool (the letter A) in the Draw menu.

- Place the cursor over the text you want to change, and click. The text is enclosed by a box.

- The entire title, label or word is now editable. You can delete words or letters and type anywhere in the box.

- When you finish, select the arrow cursor in the Draw menu. The box around the text disappears, leaving the text you added.

 If you use the text tool to edit any text, the text in that object will no longer automatically update if you alter the analysis. The exception to this occurs if a change to the analysis is so great that it forces the graph to completely reformat. If you clear or cut the title or legend, you can bring it back using the "Show title" or "Show legend" checkboxes in the dialog box accessible through the Edit Display button.

Setting graph preferences

You can set general preferences that control the default appearance of all graphs. When you change these preferences, existing graphs do not change to conform to the new settings. All changes to the preferences apply to the next graph you create. The Graph preferences dialog box controls the size, frame, point size, order of plotting symbols, fills, and colors. You can also control whether to use different symbols and fills or colors to distinguish variables.

Using the Graph Preferences dialog box

To set graph preferences, choose Preferences from the Manage menu. From the scrolling list of preferences in the dialog box, choose Graph and click Modify. The Graph Preferences dialog box appears:

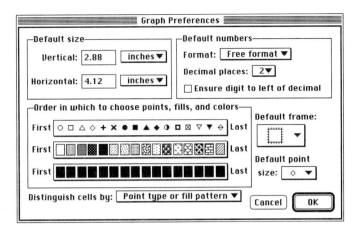

When you finish making your choices (described in the following table), click OK. You return to the Preferences dialog box. Click Done to execute the new settings. They go into effect for the next new graph.

Preference	How to set it
Graph size	Specify length of the vertical (Y) and horizontal (X) axes by entering values in the text boxes and choosing scale units (inches, centimeters, picas or points) from the pop-up menus.
Axis numbers format and decimal places	Select a format and number of decimal places from the pop-up menus. If you always need to display a digit to the left of the decimal point (0.25 vs. .25), click the checkbox below the decimal places pop-up menu.
Frame style	Select a graph frame from the Default Frame pop-up menu.
Point size	Choose a size from the points in the Default Point Size pop-up menu.
Order of point types used in line charts and scattergrams Order of fills used in bars, pies, box plots, etc. Order of colors used for points and fills	The point, fill and color bars work the same. Click on the position (between first and last) you want to modify, and edit it by dragging to the desired option in the pop-up menu. Do not drag across the bar itself. As you change the position of one color, point, or fill in the order, the others adjust. For example, if you want to use black for your first variable, click on the first color in line and drag to the black square on the pop-up menu.
How to distinguish between multiple variables in a graph	Choose "Point type or fill pattern" to distinguish variables by point type in a scattergram or line chart, and by fill pattern in all other graphs.

Choose "Color" to distinguish each variable with different colors. The first point type or fill pattern will be used for all variables

Choose "Point/Fill and Color" to distinguish variables by both point type and color in a scattergram or line chart, and by fill pattern and color in all other graphs.

Controlling font and line preferences

There are two preferences governing graphs that are set in the View preferences, rather than in the Graph preferences. One controls the size and font of the text in graphs, the other determines whether the lines in graphs are printed and copied as thin lines rather than the width that appears on the screen.

To set these preferences, choose Preferences from the Manage menu. From the scrolling list of preferences in the dialog box, choose View and click Modify. The View Preferences dialog box appears:

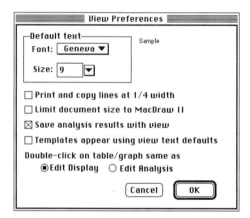

This dialog box controls preferences for tables as well as graphs. Specify the default font and size for text by choosing from the appropriate pop-up menus. The word "Sample" in the upper right reflects the text settings you choose.

Clicking "Print and copy lines at 1/4 width" makes all single line widths appear as thin lines when they are printed on a printer that can print hairlines. This will happen if you copy a graph to another application and print from there as well as when views are printed from StatView. All line widths (tables and graphs) will be reduced by approximately 1/4 from what you see on the screen. Hairlines have a more professional look on a printed page, particularly when the graph is accompanied by text.

Changing graph structure

While StatView displays many different graphs, each one has an overall structure that you control through the Graph dialog box. You can alter the frame style, transpose the two axes, hide or show the title and legend, and set the graph dimensions. To change any of these characteristics, select the graph as a whole and click the Edit Display button. The Graph dialog box appears:

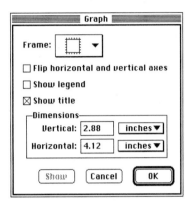

The changes you make in this dialog box apply only to the graph you selected. If you want to make changes to several graphs, you can select them all (hold down the Shift key while selecting them). You will get a series of Graph dialog boxes, one for each graph, in the order in which you selected the graphs.

Command	Formatting Action
Frame	Choose from three different styles in the pop-up menu.
Flip horizontal and vertical axes	Check this box to exchange the horizontal and vertical axes, changing the orientation of the graph. For example, cell bar charts change in orientation and become column charts, as shown here.
Show legend	Check the box to display legends for graphs with more than one variable. Hide the legend by leaving this checkbox blank.
Show title	Graphs are automatically given titles reflecting the analysis and variables. The checkbox in the Graphs dialog box governs whether a title is displayed or hidden.

| Dimensions | You can specify the horizontal and vertical dimensions in inches, centimeters, picas or points. |

Formatting certain plots

There are formatting changes you can make for three types of plots: box plots, univariate line charts and cell line charts. To change the formatting, you click on the plot (the box or the line within the graph) and click the Edit Display button. The plots and their dialog boxes are discussed below.

Box plot

You can choose between four different styles of box plots by clicking on the appropriate icon. The Show button applies your selection to the box plot selected in the view, but without closing the dialog box so you can change your mind.

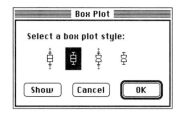

The first choice shows the default style. The second choice excludes outliers from being plotted. The third choice allows you to display notches that represent a 95% confidence interval on the medians. The fourth choice allows you to display notches but exclude outliers.

Univariate and cell line chart

You can control how points are connected for both univariate line charts and cell line charts.

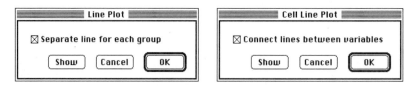

If the univariate plot displays information on several groups, you can control whether or not the lines between each group are connected. Examples of both are shown below; the default shows separate line segments for each group.

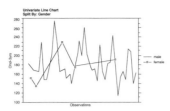

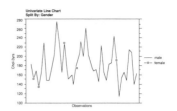

Separate line for each group   *One line for all groups*

If the cell plot displays information on several variables, you can control whether or not lines connect the variables. Examples of both are shown below; the default is to connect the variables.

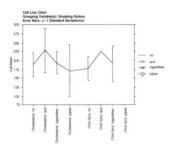

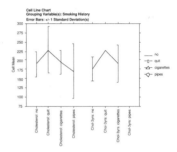

Connect lines between variables   *Do not connect lines*

Axes

StatView displays three different types of axes: a numeric axis for displaying continuous measurements, a cell axis for displaying information on groups or combinations of groups, and an ordinal axis for displaying the order of a point in a dataset. Each type of axis has a different dialog box to control its format, and different options you can change. You can tell whether an axis is numeric or cell by its values. Numeric axes are numbered; cell axes show intervals as words (group labels).

Bivariate plots can have either numeric or cell axes; univariate plots can have those and ordinal axes as well. Frequency distributions, percentile plots, and comparison percentiles always have two numeric axes. Cell plots and box plots have a numeric and a cell axis. Pie charts do not have axes.

Cell axis

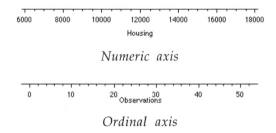

Numeric axis

Ordinal axis

The axis values appear at major intervals along both vertical and horizontal axes. The formatting choices for tick marks, interval width, and axis values are discussed separately for each type of axis. All formatting for axes is controlled through the Edit Display button, when an axis is selected. The only exception is the orientation of axis values. This text can be rotated using the commands Rotate Right and Rotate Left in the Text menu. When you have long axis values, they are legible only when rotated to be perpendicular to the axis.

Numeric axes

You can control almost all of the formatting of a numeric axis. To make any change, select the axis and click the Edit Display button. StatView offers two dialog boxes: a smaller one with fewer choices and a larger dialog box with more choices.

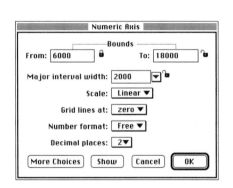

Small dialog box with fewer choices

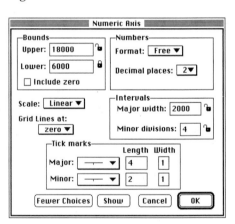

Large dialog box with more choices

The small dialog box includes basic formatting options. The large dialog box contains all the options of the fewer choices dialog box, plus some additional ones. Whichever dialog box you last used to format a numeric axis is the one you get by default the next time you format one. You can switch between the two dialog boxes using the Fewer Choices/More Choices buttons.

Bounds

You can change the upper and lower bounds of an axis by entering new values in the text boxes. When you create a graph, the bounds are such that the entire range of points appears. You can changes these bounds by entering values into the text boxes. In the small dialog box the boxes are labelled "From" and "To." In the large dialog box they are labelled "Upper" and "Lower".

When you enter a value into the text box, the lock changes from 🔓 to 🔒 signifying that the axis is locked to this value and will not change. If a bound is locked and you later add values to the dataset which are outside the bounds, they will not appear on the graph. To unlock a bound, click on the lock and StatView will once again automatically set the bound value.

In the large dialog box, you can click the Include Zero checkbox so zero will appear in the axis. This option does not lock either bound. StatView still determines the upper and lower bounds automatically; however, if zero does not fall between these bounds, the upper or lower bound will be adjusted to include zero.

Major and minor intervals

Numeric axes have major and minor intervals. Values appear at major intervals, while minor intervals are indicated by tick marks between the major interval values. You can specify the width of the major interval and the number of minor intervals between each major unit. For instance, the following illustration shows a numeric axis with major intervals of twenty and four minor intervals between each major interval.

You can determine the width between major intervals, which defines where numbers are displayed on the axis. You can also control the number of minor divisions that appear between the major intervals. Major intervals can be changed in either dialog box; minor intervals only in the large dialog box.

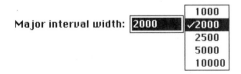   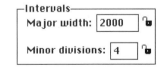

In the small dialog box   *In the large dialog box*

When you create a graph, the major intervals default to a width that is appropriate for the axis bounds and the minor intervals are based on the major intervals. If the axis bounds change, the major interval width automatically updates and so will the number of minor divisions. You change the intervals by typing in the text boxes. The smaller dialog box has a pop-up menu of suggestions for alternate "good" major interval widths.

When you enter a value into the text box, the lock changes from to signifying that the interval width is locked to this value and will not change. If the interval width is locked it will not update if you change the axis bounds. To unlock the interval width, click on the lock and StatView will once again automatically set the width.

Tick marks

You can specify the placement, length and width of tick marks. Tick mark formatting choices appear only in the large dialog box (More Choices). The placement options are the same for both major and minor tick marks. They can lie across the axis, extend in from the axis, extend out from the axis or not appear at all. Select from the choices in the pop-up menu, shown at right.

The length you enter in the text box determines how far major and minor tick marks extend from the axis in points. It is common to make major tick marks longer than minor tick marks. The default is four points for major tick marks and two points for minor ones.

You can specify the width of major and minor tick mark lines in pixels by entering the appropriate value in the text box. The line tool in the Draw menu also controls line width and can be used on tick marks. See the next chapter for more details.

Scale

The axis scale is linear by default, but you can change to any of three log-based scales. For a logarithmic scale, choose "Log base 10", "Log base e" or "Log base 2" from the pop-up menu of either dialog box.

Grid lines

Graphs can have horizontal grid lines to help you see where the plotted information falls. The default setting shows a grid line at zero. You can choose from the pop-up menu to display grid lines at major or minor ticks, at zero, or not show any grid lines. The histogram below has lines at major ticks.

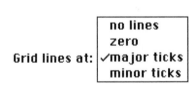

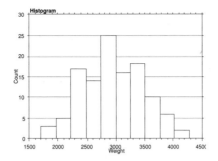

Number format and decimal places

The default number format and decimal places for the axis are set in the View preferences dialog box (see the earlier section, Preferences, for more information). You can control both of these using the pop-up menus in either the large or small dialog box, though you may not set number formatting if the axis contains integers. Your number format options are:

Free format	no trailing zeroes regardless of the number of decimal places specified.
Free format fixed	with the number of decimal places specified unless too many, then the number is displayed in scientific notation.
Fixed places	with the number of decimal places specified.
Scientific	scientific notation with the specified number of decimal places.
Engineering	scientific notation using powers of 10 that are multiples of 3.

Cell axes

Your formatting choices for cell axes are not as extensive as for numeric axes. You can change the style of tick marks, the position of axis values, how many of them are shown, and determine whether or not to show grid lines. There is only one dialog box for cell axes. To make any of these changes, select the axis by clicking on its values and click the Edit Display button. The following dialog box appears:

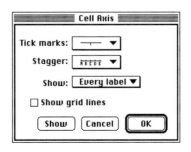

Axes for nominal variables are inherently different from numeric axes since a cell axis does not define a range of values but instead lists the labels of groups or the names of variables. Cell axes use tick marks to identify different groups. The tick marks for a cell axis are equally spaced and have no relation to a numeric width. The distance between the tick marks is controlled by the number of groups displayed in the graph.

Pop-up menus in the dialog box offer the formatting choices. There are six options for displaying tick marks. By default they extend outside the graph, but you can make them extend into the graph, or cross the axis.

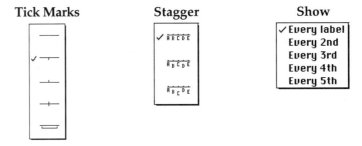

You can choose from three patterns for staggering axis values to make them more legible. The Show pop-up menu lets you choose which values to show along the axis. The checkbox labelled "Show grid lines" lets you place grid lines at each tick mark on the graph.

Ordinal axes

Ordinal axes are used only by univariate plots, which are discussed in Chapter 22, Plots. An ordinal axis in its default appearance has no tick marks or values. An ordinal axis displaying values assigns a number to each observation, marking the order in which it appears in the dataset. To toggle between these two display options, select the axis and click the Edit Display button. The Ordinal Axis dialog box appears:

If you choose to add values, they will range from 0 to the count of values for the variable.

Legends

When a graph contains more than one variable or shows more than one group, a legend is needed to identify the variables or groups. The legend serves as a key to the graph and also to control the formatting of the lines, points, bars, etc., that are drawn in the interior of a graph.

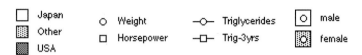

Examples of different legends

The legend is composed of both text and graphic objects or symbols. The text identifies the variables and groups in a graph. The symbols are identifiers and controls, and are displayed differently depending on what is plotted in the graph: filled rectangles for bar charts and pie charts, points for scattergrams, points with lines for line charts, and rectangles with points in them for grouped box plots.

Change symbols and text in legends

There are two ways to select the plotting symbols of a graph for modification. You can select the interior of the graph, or select symbols in the legend. The legend acts as a control area used to select the points, fills, patterns, colors and pen of a graph. More information on changing these attributes is offered in later sections, Point size and style and Change lines and fills in graphs.

When you select a symbol in the legend, it appears with a gray border around it.

Turning Circle

If the graph is a scattergram, you can change point size, type or color. If the graph is a bar chart, pie chart or box plot, you can change the fills, colors, line widths or pen patterns. If the graph is a line chart you can modify the lines and the points. Any formatting changes you make apply to the plotting area of the graph identified by the legend symbol.

You can change all the symbols or all the legend text by selecting the entire legend. Click in the interior so the legend appears with a gray border around it.

With the entire legend selected you could change every single point to a particular size or color, for example. You can also change the format of the legend text using the Text menu. The text can be selected individually if you want to modify only one item in the legend. You can type a new label in a legend using the text tool. (This new label may revert back to one automatically assigned when you change the analysis.) If you cut or clear the legend, you can bring it back using the Edit Display button.

Legend format

There are three different legend layouts to choose from, and two frame options as well. To change the layout or frame, select the entire legend by clicking anywhere in it, and click the Edit Display button. The Legend dialog box appears:

The layout pop-up menu determines whether the legend text and symbols are stacked vertically or horizontally. You have three choices:

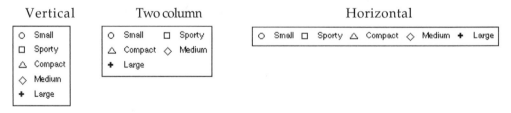

You can also draw a frame around the legend and control whether the frame has rounded corners or is shadowed. The different possibilities are:

Once you change the layout and frame style of the legend, you may want to move it below or above the graph (particularly with horizontal legends). You can move it anywhere in the view by selecting the legend and dragging it to a new location.

You can change the fill and color of the legend using the Draw menu. The legend text can be modified just as any other text in the view. Select the text by clicking on it, and then change the text, font, style or color. The legend symbols change only when you make changes within the graph, as described in the preceding section.

Point size and style

Points are used as plotting symbols in scattergrams, line charts, percentile plots, compare percentile plots and in box plots. When you create a graph, point styles are used according to the settings in the Graph Preferences dialog box. If you are using a template, the point styles and sizes are in the order saved with the template.

You can change the style and size of selected points using the Draw menu. (Changing color is discussed later). The lower portion of the menu contains the point and size modification pop-up menus:

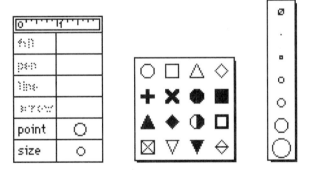

The Draw menu and the point and size pop-up menus

The point pop-up menu contains sixteen choices of point types that you can use. The size pop-up menu contains the seven choices for point size. Choosing ⊘ at the top means no point. Choosing ⊘ is useful when you have a line plot and do not wish to see the points. To change a point, select it and choose the the preference type or size form the pop-up menus. You can select the point you want to change two ways:

- If the graph has a legend, select the corresponding point in the legend.
- Select the point by clicking in the interior of the graph over a point. A dotted gray line appears around the entire plot.

215

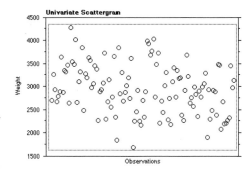

If the graph has a legend you can still click in the interior of the graph over any point to select that point. However, if the graph contains a split-by variable, you can only change the point and size of all points at once.

Change lines and fills in graphs

Three pop-up menus found in the Draw menu (fill, pen, and line) are handy tools for highlighting aspects of your data for publication, or emphasizing the implications of your results. You can widen lines and fill them with patterns, or add patterns to the plotted shapes within a graph. You can also add a fill to the interior of a graph, making the plot itself stand out more. The Draw menu shows the fill, pen and line currently used in the graph you select. When you make a selection from the pop-up menus, this section of the Draw menu updates.

Make sure you select the appropriate graph component before you try modifications. You may want to refer to the earlier section on selecting parts of a graph.

Fill

You can add a pattern to the interior of an entire graph, or to any of the following plotting shapes: the bars in a bar chart and histogram, the slices of a pie chart, and the box of a box plot. The 39 fill patterns are shown at the right, in the pop-up palette from the Draw menu. When you create a graph, the order in which fills are used in a graph is determined by the settings in the Graph Preferences dialog box. If you are using a template, the fill patterns are saved with the template.

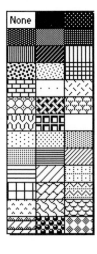

To add a background fill to a graph, select the entire graph by clicking on the frame or in blank space in the graph interior. In the fill pop-up menu of the Draw menu, drag to the square containing the desired fill. The fill you choose will occupy the blank interior of the graph:

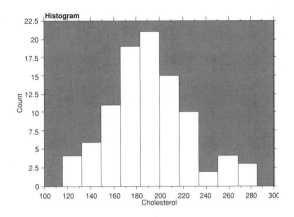

A graph with its interior filled

Line width

The line pop-up menu offers five widths to choose from, the dotted line at the top being a representation of an invisible line. You can change the width of the following lines: a graph frame, tick marks, boxes in a plot, pie chart divisions, bars in a chart, the simple and polynomial regression lines and the normal curve of a histogram. All line widths default to a single point line. (If you want all lines to print as hairlines, check the appropriate box in the View Preferences dialog box.)

Pen pattern

All the lines in a graph whose width you can change can also be filled with any of the sixteen choices in the pen pop-up menu. All lines default to a solid black pattern. Changing the pen pattern of a line has a greater visual impact with wider lines. The pattern is only as wide as the line, so you see virtually no effect with a single point line. (PostScript printers interpret some patterns as halftones, so a single pixel screen line may print as a gray line with some patterns.)

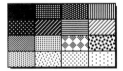

Changing lines

To change the line width, pen pattern, or both for the entire frame of a graph, click on the frame to select it. The width and pattern you choose change all four sides of the graph and all the tick marks. You can make the same changes for reference lines: the simple and polynomial regression lines in bivariate plots or regression plots, and the normal curve that is added to a histogram. To change the outline of a plot (box, bar, or pie), select the plot. Click on any part of the box, bar or pie so a gray line surrounds the plot in the graph interior, or click on the legend if there is one. Any line changes you make will change the outline of the plotted shape.

Changing plots

The plot is the shape inside the graph: the bars of a bar chart, the boxes of a box plot, the wedges of a pie chart. You can change the width and pattern of their outlines, as described above. You can also fill them with a pattern.

There are two ways to select a plot for adding fill: click on it in the graph, or select it using the legend symbol. If a particular legend symbol is selected, the fill applies to only the corresponding part of the plot. If the entire legend is selected or the entire plot is selected, the fill applies to the entire plot.

For example, suppose you would like to use color, as opposed to fill, to distinguish the bars of a bar chart. You could change the fills of all the bars to black by clicking in the interior of the graph. You could then change the color of individual bars using the legend. For more information on using the legend to control format changes, see the section, Legends, earlier in the chapter.

Color in graphs

The pop-up menus that control color are at the bottom of the Draw menu. You can change the color of any graph component using these menus. The program defaults to black and white, black for the pen and fill colors and white for the color of the view. For each component you select, the pen and fill color menus change different aspects of the graph.

The table below describes the components that can be selected and what each pop-up menu controls.

Component	How to select	Pen color	Fill color
Frame	Click on the frame	All lines connected to the frame including axis tic marks	The interior of the graph
Axis	Click on an axis value	Axis values, axis line, tick marks, grid lines	n/a

Plot	Click on the plot	Points or lines in the plot	The fill of bars, boxes or pies
Regression line or normal curve	Click on the line	The line	n/a
Legend symbol	Click on the symbol	Points or lines in the plot	The fill of bars, boxes or pies
Legend as a whole	Click in the interior of the legend	Points or lines in the plot, legend text	The fill of bars, boxes or pies
Any text	Click on the text	The text	n/a

To change the color of both aspects at once, hold down the Command (⌘) key while selecting either color rectangle in the Draw menu. That selects both, and your color choice will apply to both pen and fill of the selected graph component.

Tables

Tables have many aspects you can format. You can set global preferences to govern the appearance of all your tables, or change the format of an individual table. Before manipulating a table it is important to understand that it is composed of many different components. A table is pictured below with each of its components labeled.

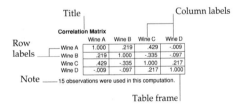

Selecting parts of a table

Tables and their components can be moved, resized and customized. Before you can move, resize or change a particular component of a table, you must select it. You need to know where to click to select the right component, so your modifications have the effect you want. First, make sure the cursor is shaped like an arrow when you are trying to select something. If you have been using the Draw menu, click on the selection tool (arrow) if it is not already selected.

The components of a table that you can select are:

Component	How to select it	What you can edit	Tools to use
Entire table	Click anywhere inside the table or on the row and column labels	table format, row height, row and column orientation	Edit Display
		line width, pen pattern, color of lines and text	Draw menu
		font, size and style of text inside the table	Text menu
Title	Click on the title	font, size and style of text	Text menu
		color of text, wording	Draw menu
Notes	Click on the note	font, size and style of text	Text menu
		color of text, wording	Draw menu

You can select more than one component by holding down the command key while clicking on additional components. Selection for all components is indicated by square black handles surrounding them.

Table with all components surrounded by black selection handles

Moving a table or a table component

You can move the entire table, its title or the note below it. To move the entire table, click anywhere in the interior of the table or on a row or column header and drag your mouse to the new location. When you do this, the entire table, its title and notes are moved, but stay in the same orientation relative to each other.

If you want to move only the title or the note, select whichever one you want to move and drag it to a new location. Moving a title or note has no effect on the body of the table.

Keyboard shortcuts

You can use the arrow keys to move any selected component or the table as a whole, once it is selected. Each click of an arrow key moves the component or table one unit in the direction of the arrow. If the grid is turned on, the unit of movement equals the distance between tick marks on the view's ruler. If the grid is off, the unit of movement is one screen pixel.

Resizing a table

There are three ways to resize a table. You can change individual column widths, change all the row heights at once, and stretch or shrink an entire table. Row height is one of the parameters you can set in the Table Preferences dialog box, so it will be standard for all tables you create. When you want to override that preference, you can change all the row heights in the Table dialog box that appears when you click the Edit Display button. The other two types of resizing are done directly in the view.

To change the width of a column in a table, first select the table. Move the cursor until it lies on the vertical line between two columns. When the cursor changes to ✛, click and drag to adjust the column width.

To stretch or shrink a table, first select the table. Then grab any of the handles and move the mouse. A dotted line appears as you drag, showing the size the table will be when you release the mouse.

Descriptive Statistics

	Weight	Turning Circle
Mean	2957.629	38.586
Std. Dev.	535.664	3.132
Variance	286935.418	9.81
Count	116	116
Minimum	1695	32
Maximum	4285	47

Dotted line while dragging

Descriptive Statistics

	Weight	Turning Circle
Mean	2957.629	38.586
Std. Dev.	535.664	3.132
Std. Error	49.735	.291
Count	116	116
Minimum	1695.000	32.000
Maximum	4285.000	47.000
# Missing	0	0

Stretched table

Formatting and editing text of tables

You can change the attributes of the text inside the table, as well as the text of the title and notes. The column and row headers are considered part of the body of the table, so their text changes along with the numbers inside the table. The font, size, and style pop-up menus in the Text menu apply to all text, as does the color pop-up palette in the Draw menu.

To format a title or note, select just that text, then use the appropriate menu choices. To format the text of row and column headers and the numbers inside the table, select the entire table.

Table titles and notes appear by default, though you can use the text tool in the Draw menu to edit them. To change the content of either of them, click on the text tool in the Draw menu, select the text you wish to change, and type the new text. You cannot edit row or column headers or values in tables.

If you use the text tool to edit any text, the text in that object will no longer update if the analysis changes. If you cut or clear the title, you can bring it back using the Edit Display button.

Table preferences

You can set general preferences that control the default appearance of tables. All changes to these preferences apply to the next table you create. The two preferences dialog boxes that affect the appearance of tables are Table Preferences and View Preferences. The View Preferences dialog box sets the defaults for the font and size of text in the view, and whether lines are reduced to a quarter of their width when printed or copied to another application. View preferences are discussed earlier, in the section, Controlling font and line preferences, since some of these settings pertain to graphs as well.

You get to the Table Preferences dialog box by choosing Preferences from the Manage menu. From the scrolling list of preferences in the dialog box, choose Table and click Modify. The Table Preferences dialog box appears:

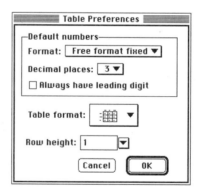

The Table preferences govern several structural characteristics of tables as well as the formatting of numbers within the table. The structural characteristics are: the format of the table's grid, the height of the rows, and whether rows and columns are transposed from their default orientation. These are all discussed in the next section.

The number formatting choices govern the format of numbers, the number of decimal places to display, and whether fractional numbers are always preceded by a zero to the left of the decimal point. Use the pop-up menus to set the decimal places and default format choices for numbers as follows:

Free format	no trailing zeroes regardless of the number of decimal places specified.
Free format fixed	with the number of decimal places specified unless too many, then the number is displayed in scientific notation.
Fixed places	with the number of decimal places specified.
Scientific	scientific notation with the specified number of decimal places.
Engineering	scientific notation using exponents that are multiples of e3 and e-3.

Clicking "Always have leading digit" adds a leading zero to numbers whose non-fractional part is zero. For example, this option will change the number .05 to 0.05.

Table format

The Table format pop-up menu choices appear in two places, the Table dialog box you get when you click the Edit Display button, and the Table Preferences dialog box accessed through the Preferences command in the Manage menu. The pop-up menu works the same in both places. It shows you ten different formats using graphic representations of the tables:

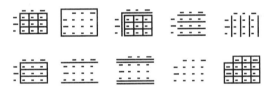

If none of these formats suit you, choose "Other" at the bottom of the list. This will bring up the Borders dialog box so you can design your own format.

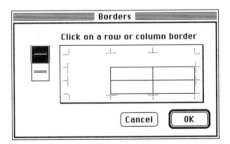

Use this dialog box to determine where borders occur in the table and whether they appear as single or double lines. Click on the single or double line icon to choose a line style, and click between cells to toggle borders on and off.

Two additional structural characteristics of tables are found in the Table dialog box you see when you select a table and click the Edit Display button:

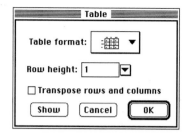

You can set row height so each row in the table is a multiple of the height of a single row as determined by the point size of the text in the table. Select a number from the pop-up menu or enter a number into the text field.

The checkbox "Transpose rows and columns" flips the orientation of the table so the columns become rows and rows become columns.

Descriptive Statistics

	Mean	Std. Dev.	Variance	Count	Minimum	Maximum
Weight	2957.629	535.664	286935.418	116	1695	4285
Turning Circle	38.586	3.132	9.81	116	32	47

Original table

Descriptive Statistics

	Weight	Turning Circle
Mean	2957.629	38.586
Std. Dev.	535.664	3.132
Variance	286935.418	9.81
Count	116	116
Minimum	1695	32
Maximum	4285	47

Transposed table

Line widths and pen patterns of tables

You may want to emphasize or de-emphasize the grid of a table by changing the width of the lines and filling them with any of sixteen pen patterns. When you create a table, the default line width is the narrowest option and the pen pattern is solid black. If you are using a template, the line widths and pen patterns are saved with the template. To change the line width and pen pattern of a table, select the entire table. Choose the new line width or pattern from the pop-up menus in the Draw menu.

Line width

The line pop-up menu offers five widths to choose from, the dotted line at the top being a representation of an invisible line. You cannot change selective lines, but must change the width of all lines in a table at once. All line widths default to a single point line. If you want all lines to print or copy at a quarter of the width you see on the screen, check the appropriate box in the View Preferences dialog box.

Pen pattern

You cannot change selective lines, but must change the pen pattern for all lines in a table at once. All lines default to solid black. Changing the pen pattern of a line has a greater visual impact with wider lines. The pattern is only as wide as the line, so you see virtually no effect with a single point line. (PostScript printers interpret some patterns as halftones, so a single pixel screen line may print as a gray line with some patterns.)

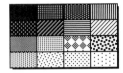

Color of tables

The pop-up menus that control color are at the bottom of the Draw menu. You can change the color of a table, its title or notes. The program defaults to black and white, black for the pen and fill colors and white for the color of the view. For each component you select, the pen and fill color menus change different aspects of the table.

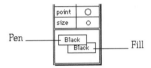

The table below lists the components of a table and what each pop-up menu controls.

Component	How to select	Pen color	Fill color
Table	Click in the interior of the table, on a number or the grid	Row, column headers and numeric text	All grid lines
Title	Click on the title	Color of text	n/a
Notes	Click on the note	Color of text	n/a

To change the color of both aspects at once, hold down the Command (⌘) key while selecting either color rectangle in the Draw menu. That selects both, and your color choice will apply to both pen and fill of the selected table component.

Cut, clear, copy, paste and duplicate commands

You can use the standard Macintosh Cut, Copy, Paste and Clear commands with tables and graphs. It is very important to note that any StatView table or graph that is copied into the clipboard becomes a static picture when it is pasted back into a view. This picture is not a dynamic object. It will not change if the variables, analysis or dataset are changed. You should not use these commands to move objects around. They should be used only to produce a picture of a result for comparative purposes.

Cut and copy

These commands apply to the component that is selected. Cut removes the component, table or graph from the view and places a copy into the clipboard. Copy places a copy of the component, table or graph into the clipboard, leaving the original in the view. (If you cut the title or legend you can bring them back using the Edit Display button while the entire graph or table is selected.)

Duplicate

Duplicate places a copy of the table or graph into the view. This command applies to the component that is selected. When a component, table or graph is first duplicated, the duplicate appears below and to the right of the original by one grid unit (whether gridding is turned on or not).

Clear

The Clear command (or the delete key on the keyboard) removes the table, graph or selected component from the view and places a copy into the clipboard. The Clear command applies to the individual component and does not always apply to the graph or table as a whole.

The individual components of a table or graph that you can clear by selecting them are: the title, legend (as a whole), axis label, and any notes. If the plot, axis, whole graph, or whole table are selected, the entire table or graph gets cleared. If you delete any text associated with a graph, the default text will reappear if the analysis is updated. If you clear the title or legend you can bring them back using the Edit Display button while the entire graph or table is selected.

Paste

Paste places the contents of the clipboard into the view, depending on the last mouse click. If the position of the last mouse click is within the visible portion of the view, the pasted object will be centered on that position. If it is not visible, the pasted object will be centered in the view. Remember, when you paste a table or a graph you get only a picture of the table or graph, not a dynamic object.

10

Drawing and Graphics

StatView includes all the features of a drawing program to help you manage the output of your analysis. These drawing features are so complete that you do not need another program to customize your output. The advantage of staying with StatView as your drawing program is twofold. You can change the analysis, have your results update and not have to redo the formatting of graphs and tables. You can save your formatting and drawing in template format and reapply it to different data. This chapter discusses how to use the Draw menu to add shapes and text to a view and use other commands to arrange shapes and results within a view.

Draw menu

The Draw menu contains a tool palette for drawing shapes in the view, and pop-up menus for customizing tables, graphs and shapes. The drawing tools are discussed in this chapter; the pop-up menus are explained in the preceding chapter as they pertain to tables and graphs, and in this chapter as they pertain to shapes. Keep in mind that you can undo and redo your most recent action using the Undo command in the Edit menu.

The Draw menu is a tear-off menu. You can place it anywhere on the screen so it does not obscure your work. Hold down the mouse to display the Draw menu, move the cursor down into the body of the menu, and move the mouse to drag it to the desired position. As you position the menu, an outline indicates where the menu will appear when you release the mouse.

When you try to tear off the menu, a pop-up menu may unexpectedly appear. Release the mouse and try again. This time, drag the cursor across the menu more rapidly or tear the menu off to the left.

If the menu ever hides your results, move it elsewhere in the view by clicking on the top bar of the menu and dragging it. Close it by clicking the close box in the upper left hand corner. The menu automatically closes when you activate a dataset.

You can use the Draw menu just like a standard pull-down menu if you do not want it open on your screen. Select a drawing tool by clicking on Draw, dragging to highlight the desired drawing feature and releasing the mouse.

Selection tool

The selection tool ![arrow] activates the arrow cursor that you see on your screen most of the time. When you use the Draw menu, be sure to re-select this tool to select objects you want to modify or change. Clicking on the selection tool changes the cursor to an arrow so you can select tables, graphs and text or geometric figures you have added.

Selecting tables and graphs and their components is discussed in detail in Chapter 9, Customizing Graphs and Tables. To select a shape, click on the outline of the shape. A shape or text that is selected appears with a set of handles surrounding it. To select a second object, hold down the Shift key while clicking on the shape.

As you click in the blank space of a view, the cursor changes to a finger: ☞ Select multiple objects by dragging a selection rectangle around them with this finger cursor. A dotted outline, which represents the selection rectangle, grows as you drag the pointing finger. When you release the mouse, the objects inside the rectangle are selected.

ANOVA Table for Turning Circle					
	DF	Sum of Squares	Mean Square	F-Value	P-Value
Type	4	531.778	132.945	24.745	<.0001
Residual	111	596.359	5.373		

Model II estimate of between component variance: 5.546

Move selected objects by clicking inside the frame with the selection tool and dragging them to a new location. To select all objects in the view, choose Select All from the Edit menu. This command selects everything in the view: objects you have drawn as well as tables and graphs generated by the program.

Shapes and lines

You can draw the following shapes using the associated drawing tools:

Tool	Shape	Shortcut
⟋	line	Hold down the Shift key while drawing to constrain to a straight line at a 45 or 90 degree angle.
⟍	arc	Hold down Shift key while drawing to constrain to fit within a square.
☐	rectangle	Hold down the Shift key while drawing to constrain to a square.
◻	rounded rectangle	Hold down the Shift key while drawing to constrain to a square with round corners.
◯	ellipse	Hold down the Shift key while drawing to constrain to a circle.
⊿	polygon	Hold down the Option key to close the polygon.
♡	free-form curve	Hold down the Option key to close the spline.

To draw a shape (other than a polygon or a free-form curve):

• Select the tool for that shape.

• Position the cursor where you want the shape to start.

• Hold down the mouse and drag until the shape is the desired size.

The cursor changes back to the selection tool as soon as you release the mouse. To draw more than one shape of the same type or add text to more than one location, hold down the Command key and the cursor reverts to the last tool used.

The corner/center control lets you draw some shapes beginning either in the shape's center or at its corner. To choose the starting point of a rectangle, rounded rectangle, ellipse, arc or line, click on the control in the Draw menu to toggle it between the two different states: ⊡ indicates you are drawing from the center; ◰ indicates you are starting from the corner.

You resize or reshape most shapes by clicking on the shape's outline to select it and dragging one of its handles. You can change the shape into its constrained shape by selecting the shape and holding down the Shift key as you drag. Shapes are resized according to the state of the corner/center control in the Draw menu. As you drag the cursor to resize a shape, a dotted outline appears, indicating the size and placement you will see when you release the mouse.

Rounded rectangle

Once you have drawn a rounded rectangle, you can control the amount of rounding at its ends. Double-click on the rounded rectangle or select it and click the Edit Display button to see this dialog box:

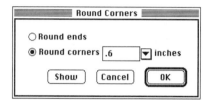

You can round the ends of the rectangle or just round the corners. If you click the button for round corners, you can specify the radius of the corner arcs in the pop-up menu. The pop-up menu provides commonly used radii, or you can type your own. The units of measure and the radius suggestions in the pop-up menu are in centimeters or inches, depending on your custom ruler settings. (See the later section on rulers.) Below are example of both types of rounded rectangles.

Rounded ends   *Rounded corners*

Arcs

There are two ways to change the shape of an arc: using the Reshape command in the Edit menu or dragging the arc's selection handles. Reshape mode applies to polygons and splines also, and is covered following the discussion of those two shapes. When you select an arc (without using the Reshape command), it is surrounded by eight selection handles rather than just one at each end. Dragging any of these selection handles changes the configuration of the arc. This is easier to understand by doing rather than reading about it. The shape of the arc is defined by the rectangle of selection handles around it. As you change the shape of the rectangle by dragging a selection handle, the arc adapts itself to the new shape.

Polygons

Polygons are drawn and reshaped differently than other shapes. To draw a polygon:

- Select the polygon tool ![polygon tool icon].

- Click and release the mouse where you want the first line to begin.

- Move the cursor to where you want the first vertex and click the mouse. Make a polygon with as many vertices as you want by clicking wherever you want a vertex.

- Double-click on the last point to end an open polygon or click on the starting point to make a closed polygon.

Open polygon   *Closed polygon*

Holding down the Option key while drawing a polygon will display a closed polygon. To open a closed polygon, hold down the Command (⬛) and Option keys and click on the segment you want to open. Similarly, to close an open polygon, click on one of the two free end vertices while holding down the Command and Option keys.

Reshape a polygon

Choosing the Reshape command in the Edit menu changes the cursor to the reshaping cursor ✛ . (Press the Control key while double-clicking on the polygon as a shortcut to display this cursor. The reshape cursor disappears when you release the Control key.) Reshape mode applies to arcs and splines too, and is covered following the section on splines. Once in Reshaping mode, to delete a vertex, click on a vertex while holding down the Option key. To add a vertex between two vertices, hold down the Option key and click on the desired section of the polygon. The new vertex becomes the selected vertex.

Free-form curves

The spline tool lets you draw free-form curves based on cubic splines, similar to Bezier curves. Once you have drawn a spline curve, it acts like any other shape. You can select it by clicking on the line and you can drag the selection handles to resize the entire spline. You can also reshape the curve by moving individual vertices and by adjusting the amount of curve between vertices.

- Select the spline tool ![spline tool icon] in the third row of tools in the Draw menu. The cursor becomes a crosshair.

- Click where you want the first vertex. Move the tool along the path that you want the curve, clicking at each change in direction to add a new vertex. You can add as many vertices as you want and move them later to adjust the curve.

- Double-click where you want the last point, if you want an open curve. If you want a closed curve, click once on the first point in the curve. To finish drawing a closed curve without having to click again on the first point, hold down the Option key and double-click.

Reshape a spline curve

You can resize splines directly by dragging on any of the eight selection handles. You reshape them using the Reshape command in the Edit menu. Reshape mode also applies to arcs and polygons and is covered in the next section.

There are two actions that change the shape of a curve: moving a vertex and moving a velocity handle. A vertex is a point connecting two arcs of the curve. Velocity handles determine the angle of the arcs between vertices. Moving a vertex changes its distance from adjoining vertices, so can alter the overall shape of the figure. Moving a velocity handle leaves the vertex in place and changes the angle of the arcs that connect it to adjoining vertices. As you drag a vertex or velocity handle to a new location, the curve continuously updates.

- Click on the line of a spline to select it.

- Choose Reshape from the Edit menu. The cursor changes to the reshaping cursor and the selected spline displays all of its vertices as square handles.

- Click on a vertex with the reshape cursor. Its velocity handles appear. The velocity handles are the two lines emanating from the vertex:

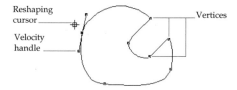

Each vertex has two velocity handles. Initially these handles emerge from the vertex in opposite directions and have equal length. As you drag the end of a velocity handle, you alter both the angle of the tangent line to the curve at the vertex and the velocity of the curve at that point. Normally, the opposite velocity handle will remain aligned to the one you are dragging, but by holding down the Option key, you can drag one velocity handle without changing the direction of the other, thus creating a corner.

To delete a vertex with the reshaping cursor, click on a vertex while holding down the Option key. To add a vertex between two vertices, hold down the Option key and click on the desired section of the curve. The shape of the curve should not change appreciably and the new vertex becomes the selected vertex, with velocity handles displayed.

To open a closed curve with the reshaping cursor, click on any segment with both the Command and Option keys held down. If the curve was previously closed, it will now be open. (Nothing happens if the curve was already open.) To close an open curve, click on one of the endpoints of the curve with both the Command and Option keys held down.

Reshape mode

The Reshape command in the Edit menu is used to change the shape of arcs, polygons and splines. When you select this command, the cursor changes to the reshaping cursor

⊹ . (Holding down the Control key is a quick way to get into Reshape mode when you only need to use it for a short while. The reshape cursor disappears when you release the Control key.) The Reshape command remains checked in the Edit menu until you select it again. Double-click on the Arrow tool in the Draw menu as a shortcut to display the reshaping cursor. Double-click again to return to the arrow cursor.

The reshaping cursor lets you alter the shape of an arc, polygon or spline by moving their vertices. The specifics of each shape are discussed in the preceding sections.

Color for shapes

You can control the color of two areas of a shape, the line around the shape and the fill. You can also change the background color of the view as a whole. Add or change the color of a shape using the color menus at the bottom of the Draw menu:

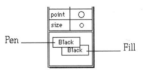

The top rectangle in the color palette controls the pen color, the second rectangle controls the fill color. Color for tables and graphs is discussed in the previous chapter.

The pen color of a shape is the color of the border that surrounds the shape (the line that surrounds an ellipse or a rectangle).

The fill of a shape is defined as the interior of the shape (the color of whatever fill you choose for a shape). A white fill or a fill of "None" will not show color.

To change the color of both the pen and fill of a shape at the same time, hold down the Command (⌘) key while selecting the color. To change the color of a shape:

• Select the shape.

- Change the fill (in the Draw menu) to solid (black), so your color choices will be visible.

- Select the pen or fill portion of the color menu. A pop-up color menu appears.

- Drag to a color and release the mouse. The pen or fill changes to the selected color.

When nothing is selected in the view, a background color is labelled in the Draw menu, representing the view background color. To change the color of the view background:

- Make sure there is nothing selected in the view.

- Select the background portion of the color menu.

- Drag to a color and release the mouse.

Cut, copy, paste, duplicate and clear shapes

StatView provides the standard Macintosh Cut, Copy, Paste and Clear commands to use with shapes. For information on using these commands with tables and graphs, see Chapter 9, Customizing Graphs and Tables.

To edit a shape, select it and choose the appropriate command from the Edit menu.

- Cut removes the shape from the document and places a copy into the clipboard.

- Clear (or delete from the keyboard) removes the shape from the document.

- Copy copies the shape to the clipboard.

- The Duplicate command makes a copy of the shape. The first time the duplicate command is used, the duplicate appears below and to the right of the original by one grid unit (whether gridding is turned on or not). If you move the duplicate shape (with the mouse, arrow keys on the keyboard, or both) to some new position and duplicate it, this second duplicate will be offset from the first duplicate by the same amount that the first duplicate is offset from the original. This makes producing such things as the arrows shown below very easy.

The pasted location of a shape depends on the last mouse click. If the position of the last mouse click is within the visible portion of the view, the pasted shape will be centered on that position. If it is not visible, the pasted shape will be centered in the section of the view that is visible.

Text

You can add text anywhere in the view, to label or comment on a result.

- Select the text tool **A** from the Draw menu. The cursor changes to an I-beam.

- Click where you want to enter text. You see a text box with an insertion point:

- Type your text in the box. As you type, the box expands to the right.

- To return the insertion point to the beginning of the next line, press Return. (If you press Enter instead, you exit text mode and return to the arrow cursor.)

The border of the text box extends downward when text reaches the bottom of the box. It expands both horizontally and vertically until you specifically resize it, at which time its size becomes static. When text in a static text box reaches the right border, the cursor moves to the beginning of the next line. When it reaches the bottom of the box, the box enlarges downward.

You can set the size of the text in advance of typing if you prefer, by resizing the empty box. Click in the lower right corner and drag to resize.

To define the size of the text box:

- Choose the selection tool and click inside the text box. The border changes to a set of handles (the small squares around the box).

- Drag one of these handles to resize the border of the text. When you have finished adding text, click anywhere outside the box. To add more text, click on the text tool, then click where you want to add more text and begin typing.

Change text attributes

To change the look of the text, use the pop-up menus for font, size, and style from the Text menu. You can change text as a whole or select only part of the text before you change the attributes. Just select the characters to modify and then choose commands in the Text and Edit menus.

At the bottom of the Size pop-up menu (in the Text menu) is a choice called Other. If you choose this you see the following dialog box and can enter any text size.

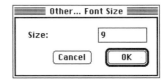

You can change the alignment of letters within a text box using the Left Justify, Center Justify and Right Justify commands from the Text menu. The Rotate Left and Rotate Right commands in the Edit menu let you display rotated text. You can edit rotated text just as you do normal text. While you are editing rotated text, StatView displays the text in normal position. When you are finished editing, the text again appears rotated.

You can change the color of all text within a text box by selecting the text box, selecting foreground color from the draw menu and dragging to the desired color in the pop-up menu. To change the color of a single character or group of characters, select them and follow the same procedure.

Fills, lines, and arrows

The Draw menu has pop-up menus you use to change the fill, pen pattern, line width, and arrows of your drawings. The current attributes for a selected shape are displayed in the pop-up menu next to the attribute name. If nothing is selected, the default drawing attributes are displayed. You can change the defaults by clicking on the background of the view and changing the attributes. These attributes will be in effect for the next shape you draw.

Fill

Fill refers to the pattern inside a shape. Choosing None makes the shape transparent, which is the default for all shapes. For a solid fill color, choose black. You have 39 fill patterns to choose from. You can add a fill pattern to the interior of shapes that remain unenclosed (such as arcs, polygons and free-hand shapes).

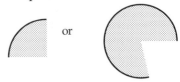

Using fills with tables and graphs is covered in the preceding chapter.

Pen		The pen is the pattern on the border of a shape. Changing the pen pattern of a line has a greater visual impact with wider lines. The pattern is only as wide as the line, so you see virtually no effect with a single point line. You can fill any line with one of 16 choices in the pen pop-up menu. All lines default to a solid black pattern.
Line		Line refers to the thickness of the lines used in the shape. You have five choices of lines. The dashed line at the top (- - - -) makes a line invisible. You can later select the invisible line and change its attributes. All lines default to a single point width, the second choice from the top in the pop-up menu.
Arrow		Arrow refers to the four choices of arrow heads you can add to lines and arcs. You can specify that a line or arc has no arrows, an arrow at the beginning, at the end or at both ends.

There is an option in the View Preferences dialog box that changes the way lines appear when printed or copied (see the section, Setting graph preferences, in the preceding chapter). If you select this option, all lines in the view, including those of shapes, print at one quarter the width you see on the screen. This obviously affects the visual impact of line widths and pen patterns you choose. No difference appears on the screen, you only see it when the shape is printed or copied to another application.

Imported objects

You can paste objects from other applications into the view from the Clipboard. Objects copied from other applications and pasted into StatView behave differently depending on their composition. Text can be manipulated like any text created by StatView. Non-text objects are pasted into StatView as pictures whose elements, if any, cannot be manipulated. You cannot change the attributes of any picture except to resize it. Double-clicking on a pasted picture that has been altered in size returns it to the original size.

Move and align objects

Cursor placement is important when you are moving shapes. Once you select an object by clicking on its outline, handles appear around the shape. If you click on one of these handles, you resize or reshape the shape as you drag the cursor. To simply move the shape, click on the outline between the handles.

Lock and unlock

You can lock an object to prevent it from being accidentally moved or edited. A locked object cannot be moved, edited or changed in shape or size, but can still be selected and copied. To lock an object, select it and choose Lock from the Layout menu. To unlock objects so you can move or edit them, select the objects and choose Unlock from the Layout menu.

Overlap and overlay objects

All objects in the view are layered in front of or behind other objects. The first object drawn or created by StatView is behind everything else. Each successive object you draw or create is placed in front of all previous objects. When objects do not overlap, their order makes no difference. However, if objects overlap, the objects in front obscure objects behind. You can change the order of objects using the commands in the Layout menu, or with the controls in the Draw menu.

To move an object, select it and choose the appropriate command from the Layout or Draw menu. If you select several objects, they move as a group.

Tool	Command	Action
	Move to back	Moves the selected object behind all other objects in the view.
	Move to front	Moves the selected object in front of all other objects in the view.
	Move Backward	Sends the object one layer back in the stack.
	Move to Back	Sends the object to the bottom of the stack. It appears behind all objects in the view.
	Move Forward	Moves the object one layer up in the stack.
	Move to Front	Moves the object to the top of the stack. It appears in front of all objects in the view.

Tables and graphs are considered objects as well. The following exercise demonstrates the technique of highlighting a table by layering it above a drawn, filled object to create a frame.

- Create any table in the view. (We use an ANOVA table in the pictures that illustrate this exercise.)

- In the Draw menu, click on the rectangle tool.

- Place the cursor above and to the left of the table, click and drag diagonally down and to the right to surround the table with a rectangle.

	DF	Sum of Squares	Mean Square	F-Value	P-Value
Subject	27	181.976	6.740		
Time	2	18.926	9.463	7.093	.0018
Time * Subject	54	72.040	1.334		

- With the rectangle still selected, in the Draw menu click on the word "None" next to fill, and drag to select the middle fill in the second row. When you release the mouse, the rectangle is filled, obscuring the table.

- With the rectangle still selected, in the Draw menu click on the middle tool in the bottom row 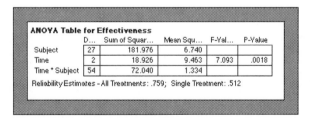 to move the rectangle behind the table. The table is now barely visible.

- Use the rectangle tool in the Draw menu again to draw a second, smaller rectangle within the first one.

- With this second rectangle selected, change its fill to plain white using the fill palette in the Draw menu as before. Now you see a white rectangle within a darker one and the table is once again obscured.

- In the Layout menu, choose Move Backward, to move the white rectangle behind the table.

ANOVA Table for Effectiveness

	D...	Sum of Squar...	Mean Squ...	F-Val...	P-Value
Subject	27	181.976	6.740		
Time	2	18.926	9.463	7.093	.0018
Time * Subject	54	72.040	1.334		

Reliability Estimates – All Treatments: .759; Single Treatment: .512

What you see here is a layering of three objects: the dark rectangle at the back, the white rectangle in the middle, and the table in front.

Rulers and grid lines

The ruler and grid commands in the Draw menu let you line up text and shapes you add as well as tables, graphs, and text generated automatically. These commands are in a pop-up menu that appears when you click on the ruler in the middle of the Draw menu.

		Show Rulers
fill	None	Turn Grid Off ⌘Y
pen	■	Show Grid Lines
line	—	Hide Page Breaks
arrow	—	Custom Rulers...
point		Align to Grid
size		Align Objects...

The first four choices are toggles. Their names change depending on the state of the view. For example, if rulers are showing, the top choice appears as Hide Rulers. If rulers are not displayed, the top choice appears as Show Rulers. The two menu states of these commands are: Show Rulers/Hide Rulers, Turn Grid On/Turn Grid Off, Show Grid Lines/Hide Grid Lines, Show Page Breaks/Hide Page Breaks.

You can align objects by moving them freehand to line up with measurements on the ruler, or turn the grid on so objects snap into alignment according to a grid based on the units of your ruler. You can change the units of the ruler, and elect to see the grid when it is on, or have it invisible.

When rulers are present, as you move the pointer around in the window, its position is indicated on the rulers by dotted lines. Since you can tell where the cursor is, it is easier to align objects. To align the tops of two objects using rulers:

- Click on the ruler icon in the Draw menu and drag to the Show Rulers command.

- Select the first object by clicking on its outline.

- Move the pointer to the top of the first object.

- Click between the handles and drag the object to the desired location.

- Select the second object.

- Move the cursor to the line at the top of the object and drag it until the indicator line for the second object is at the same place on the ruler as the first object.

When the grid is on, you must draw or move objects at intervals of your ruler gradation. Grid lines appear as dotted lines that are drawn every inch, if your ruler displays inches, or every centimeter if your ruler displays centimeters. If you positioned an item with the grid turned off you can later align the item to the grid by selecting the object(s) to align, turning the grid on and choosing the Align To Grid command.

The Turn Grid On/Off command is in the ruler pop-up menu of the Draw menu. (Command-Y is the keyboard shortcut for turning the grid on and off.) When the grid is on, you can choose to have the grid lines visible or invisible using the Show/Hide Grid Lines command in the same menu. Grid lines are never printed.

You can move the zero point of a ruler by clicking on the thick black line at zero and dragging the mouse to the desired location. To reset the zero point back to the beginning of the ruler, click in the box at the intersection of the two rulers. To change the units of measure on the ruler, select the Custom Ruler command from the ruler pop-up menu in the Draw menu. You will see this dialog box:

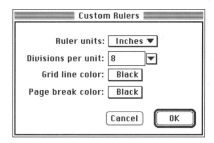

You can display rulers in inches or centimeters, with any number of divisions per unit. Set the color for page breaks and grid lines, which affects only what you see on the screen since neither of them are printed.

Align objects to one another

The Align Objects command in the ruler pop-up menu of the Draw menu will vertically align tops, centers or bottoms and horizontally align left sides, centers or right sides of shapes and tables and graphs.

To align objects to one another:

• Select the objects you want to align.

• Click on the ruler in the Draw menu and drag to the Align Objects command. You see this dialog box:

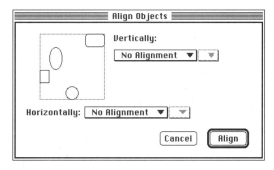

- Choose Align from either the Vertically or Horizontally pop-up menu. The pop-up menu to its right becomes active so you can choose the alignment. As you choose, the sample objects in the dialog box move to reflect the alignment that will appear in your view.

- Click Align to align the objects.

Group objects

You can select two or more objects and join them together so they act as one object. Grouped objects can be a combination of results, drawn shapes, and text. You may want to group graphs with arrows or illustrations to keep them intact while you move or reorganize your results. The applies specifically to the Clean Up Items command in the Layout menu. Unless shapes are grouped with the tables, graph or text they refer to, they will not be moved with those objects when the window is cleaned up. Grouped objects are moved, selected, resized, cut, copied, cleared and pasted as single objects.

You can group one or more grouped objects. When ungrouped, the subgroups remain intact; they do not become individual objects again until individually ungrouped. To group objects, select them and choose Group from the Layout menu. To ungroup objects, select a group and choose Ungroup from the Layout menu.

Grouped objects are not only linked graphically but also analytically. Selecting any object in the group applies any subsequent command to all objects in the group. When you change variables, analysis parameters, display characteristics, etc., it affects all the results.

Color preferences

StatView takes advantage of the color capabilities of your system and will display any of the sixteen million colors in each palette slot. If you have a non-color monitor, you can still print in color on a color printer. On a color system, you can edit the color palette as follows:

- Choose Preferences from the Manage menu.

- In the Choose Preferences dialog box, select Color Palette from the scrolling list and click Modify. The Color Palette dialog box appears (in color, of course):

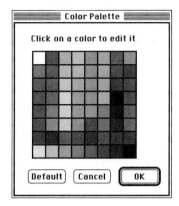

- Click on the color you want to modify. The standard color wheel dialog box appears. (It is described in your Macintosh reference manual.) At the upper left of this dialog box, a colored rectangle shows the color you selected.

- To select a new color, click on a color in the color wheel. The rectangle at the upper left changes. Its bottom half shows the color you started with; its top part shows the new color you chose from the color wheel.

- To increase or decrease the brightness of the new color, drag the scroll bar at the right of the color wheel. Moving it up makes the colors brighter; moving it down darkens them. You can also modify the new color by clicking on the up/down arrows next to hue, saturation and brightness, as well as red, green and blue. This changes the numerical values associated with the colors.

- When you are done selecting and modifying the new color, click OK in the color wheel dialog box. You return to the Color Palette dialog box.

- Click OK if you are done, or repeat the steps above to change another color.

- When you are finished choosing new colors for your palette, click OK to save the new colors. (The Default button returns the color palette to StatView 's default palette.)

- Click Done in the Choose Preferences dialog box to execute your new preferences.

The colors you choose are saved in the StatView Library file. You get these colors each time you start StatView. New color preferences take effect immediately.

Clean up the view

The Clean Up Items command in the Layout menu lets you rearrange the graphs, tables, shapes and text in the view. You can avoid page breaks so your results are not split between pages when you print. You can arrange results by their location, group them by analysis, or according to several other guidelines. The Clean Up dialog box looks like:

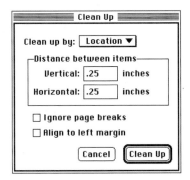

This dialog box keeps results from overlapping and ensures that results do not fall over page breaks when you are copying or printing. When you clean up, results are arranged from the top left corner down the length of the page. Drawn shapes and added text are not moved unless you have grouped them with a table or graph. You have four options for choosing how to clean up the items:

Clean up by location	Keeps results in the same relative order.
Clean up by analysis	Groups results by analysis in the order analyses occur in the view, beginning at the location of the first result.
Distance between items	Specify the gap between items by entering values in inches in the Vertical and Horizontal text boxes. The default is .25 inches.
Ignore page breaks	Allows items to cross page breaks. This is not advisable when you print, but it saves space in the view while you examine your results on the screen. Page breaks look like this on the screen: ╲╲╲╲╲╲╲╲╲╲╲
Align to left margin	Places the first result in the upper left corner of the first page and lines all results against the left margin as specified in the Distance Between Items box. The default starts page cleanup at the current location of the first result.

Page and document settings

As you produce results in the view, new pages are automatically added to the bottom of the view. If you want to enlarge items horizontally beyond one page, you must create the additional pages using the Drawing Size dialog box. This gives you added flexibility for creating very large presentations. You can also use the Drawing Size command to remove extra blank pages in a view after deleting results.

A view document can be a single page or as large as 49 x 49, which is about 2009 pages of 8.5" x 11" paper. If you change page size in the Page Setup dialog box, the maximum number of pages changes. You cannot set the drawing size less than the number of pages that your results require. One page is the default. Change the size of your document by choosing Drawing Size from the Layout menu. The Drawing Size dialog box appears:

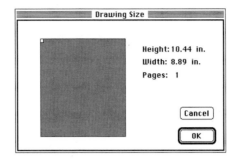

Each small white square represents one page in your document. Click on squares to include or exclude them from the document, or drag to increase or decrease document size. Click OK to execute a new drawing size. The pages are added to or removed from the active view.

You can select any square and StatView automatically selects the squares between the upper-left corner and the one you select. In the Drawing Size dialog box below, a page area totaling 323 pages has been selected with a height of 177.48 inches and a width of 168.91 inches.

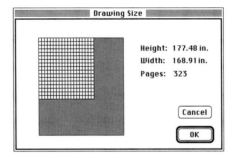

If you export your results to MacDraw II, it is advisable to check the setting "Limit window size to MacDraw II." This checkbox in the View Preferences dialog box constrains the size of your StatView document to the requirements of a MacDraw II document, which differ depending on the page size.

11

Descriptive Statistics

Descriptive statistics compute numbers that summarize data rather than making comparisons between the data or its sources. Descriptive statistics fall into three categories:

- measures of central tendency, which give an idea of the average value of a number or other quantity (where average can take on a variety of meanings)

- measures of variability, which convey whether most measurements are clustered within a narrow range of values or spread over a large range

- measures of an overall distribution property indicated by a single number

You can use descriptive statistics on measurements representing a sample of some underlying population, anecdotal evidence, available data, or the entire population. This population may be real (people who live in a particular city) or theoretical (all the plants of a particular type). The size of a population or the destructive nature of the measurement method usually makes it undesirable to undertake measuring the entire population. Descriptive statistics can be merely descriptive, but are more often estimates of usually unmeasurable quantities known as population statistics. Since descriptive statistics are calculated from a sample of the population, they are often called sample statistics. Later references are to sample statistics unless otherwise stated. Sample statistics characterize the population on which they are based.

Discussion

Measures of central tendency

A descriptive statistic summarizes data with a single number. One approach uses the mean, or arithmetic average, to summarize the central tendency of a set of numbers.

Mean

The mean is the sum of the observations divided by the number of observations. The sum of the differences between each observation and the mean is zero. Each observation plays a part in the calculation of the mean, so difficulties can arise if your data contains outliers, observations that are distant from the bulk of your data. Outliers can be discarded or corrected *if* they arise from an obvious error in data collection; but often they are important to the data and should not be ignored. A simple example concerns the salaries of employees of a small company. There are five employees: two clerks each making $12,000 per year; two sales reps making $15,000 and $18,000; and the owner of the company, whose salary is $100,000. (In practice, measurements based on a sample of only five observations should be regarded with caution.) The mean of the salaries is $31,400. This is not an accurate reflection of the "average" employee salary of the company. The owner's salary distorts the value of the mean since it is so much larger than the other salaries, yet all are given equal weight. The same problem occurs with the "average" price of homes in a neighborhood; several expensive homes may inflate the mean price of homes, giving the consumer a distorted image of the cost of neighborhood housing.

Median

An alternative measure of central tendency that can solve this problem is the median. The median is the middle value in a set of observations that is ordered from lowest to highest value. When there is an even number of observations, the median is the average of the two numbers on either side of the middle. By definition, half of the observations are less than or equal to the median, while the other half is greater than the median. For the salary example given above, the median salary is $15,000, a much better estimate of an "average" employee salary. The effect of outliers is eliminated because the order of the observations, rather than their values, determines the median. The importance of most other observations is eliminated along with the outliers since only the order of the observations is ever used in calculating the median.

Trimmed mean

A measure of central tendency that provides an alternative to discarding all the observations except the central one or two is the trimmed mean. This statistic is a compromise between the mean, which uses all the data, and the median, which focuses on only one or two central values. The observations that are most distant from the center of the data are eliminated (trimmed) before the mean is calculated. You decide the amount of data to be trimmed before the remaining observations are averaged. The amount of data that is ignored at both extremes of the dataset is expressed as a percentage. In an example of 100 observations, 10% of which are trimmed, the 10 largest and the 10 smallest (20 observations in all) are eliminated from consideration, and the mean is calculated from the remaining 80 observations. By default, the percentage of data trimmed in StatView is 10%; other values can be specified.

Mode

Another measure of central tendency is the mode, the value that occurs most often in a dataset. Your chances of guessing the value of an observation correctly are best if you choose the mode. The mode has a number of shortcomings when used as a measure of central tendency. Data collected using a continuous measurement scale (such as height or weight) may not contain observations with the same value. In such a case, the data has to be grouped before a meaningful value of the mode is determined. Alternatively, a dataset can have several modes, making it difficult to decide the appropriate value to use. Nevertheless, the mode may be a useful measure of central tendency for a variable that takes on a limited number of values, or where the values are mostly in one clump. Any variable containing negative values will return missing values for the mode.

Geometric and harmonic mean

Two less common measures of central tendency are the geometric mean and harmonic mean. These measure the central tendency of a mathematical transformation of the original observations. The transformed data may have more desirable statistical properties than the raw data. With variables like economic indices and bacterial counts, for example, which exhibit more variability as their values increase, the logarithm of the data often behaves better than the untransformed data. The geometric mean is calculated from the logarithm of the variables and re-transformed to the original scale of measurement. The harmonic mean is calculated similarly, but uses a reciprocal transformation (transforms a value by dividing one by that value). The harmonic mean is sometimes used to report the central tendency of rates or ratios.

If a variable contains a zero neither the harmonic or geometric mean can be computed. Also, any variable containing a negative number will return missing values for both these measures.

Measures of variability

A measure of central tendency alone generally does not provide enough information to summarize a set of numbers. For example, if every value in one dataset has the same value, but the values in a second dataset are spread over a wide range, the mean, median or trimmed mean for the two datasets can still be the same. The mean of the dataset containing identical values is more representative of the sample's central tendency than the mean of the more diverse sample. One effective way to display the spread or variability of a set of numbers is a histogram (a bar chart representing a frequency distribution). There are also several descriptive statistics that summarize variability. See Chapter 12, Frequency Distribution, for more information about histograms.

Minimum, maximum and range

A simple expression of the variability of a set of numbers is a report of the minimum (the smallest value in the set of numbers), the maximum (the largest value) and the range (the difference between the minimum and maximum). These values may not be representative of the rest of the dataset, so providing only the minimum, maximum and range can be misleading, but their easy interpretation might make it useful to report them in addition to other measures of variability.

Variance

It is usually better to report some average measure of the difference between each value in a variable and the mean. You cannot calculate a simple average because, by the definition of the mean, the average difference between each observation in a dataset and the mean must be zero. One of the most common measures which gets around this problem is the variance.

The variance does this by squaring the differences between the observations and the mean before averaging. The sample variance, which is the type of variance most commonly used, is usually calculated by dividing these squared differences by one less than the number of observations. The population variance is calculated by dividing the squared differences by the number of observations. StatView defaults to calculating the sample variance. If the data you are analyzing is an entire population as opposed to a sample of a population, you can choose to divide by the number of observations by choosing "n" as opposed to "n-1" as the denominator for the variance in the Descriptive Statistics dialog box. Use of the square of the differences increases the influence of observations far from the mean in calculating the variance. This may or may not be desirable, depending on the nature of your dataset. For example, if your data contains many outliers, the variance might be considerably larger than if you did not have outliers. The variance is often used as a measure of variability when the mean is used as a measure of central tendency because the sum of squares of differences from a set of data and any single value is minimized when that value is the sample mean.

Standard deviation

A consequence of using the square of the differences is that the variance is reported in the square of the original unit of measurement and can be difficult to interpret. For example, if the height of a group of plants is measured in centimeters, the variance is expressed as square centimeters. To overcome this problem, variability is usually reported as the standard deviation (the square root of the variance). This represents an "average" deviation from the mean in the same unit of measurement as the original observations. Data from a normal (Gaussian or bell-shaped) distribution follows the empirical rule of statistics: 68% of the data is contained in the range of the mean plus or minus the standard deviation; 95% in the range of the mean plus or minus twice the standard deviation; 99.7% in the range of the mean plus or minus three times the standard deviation. Thus, a quick rule of thumb for normally distributed data is: the vast majority of observations (95%) fall within two standard deviations of the mean.

Coefficient of variation

The coefficient of variation is a unitless expression of variability calculated by dividing the sample standard deviation by the sample mean. It is especially useful when comparing the variability of several measurements, or when measurements are in different units. When the mean is numerically small (near zero), the coefficient of variation may be very large, even though the variation in the data is not excessive.

Standard error of the mean

The standard deviation of a set of observations estimates the variability of the underlying population. For example, the empirical rule described above relates to the proportion of individual values that will fall within a particular range. However, it is often more meaningful to consider the variability of the sample mean, since it is the statistic that is actually used to gain insight into the central tendency of the data. The standard error of the mean is a statistic that estimates the variability you expect if you take repeated samples of the same size from the population. It is calculated by dividing the standard deviation of the observations by the square root of the number of observations. Since it is unlikely that a sample of observations would all be unusually high or low, we would expect the variability of the mean to be less than that of an individual value.

For example, a dataset contains the weights of 100 ten year old boys. You could calculate the standard deviation of the data to get an idea of the variation in weights for these individual boys. But if you repeatedly sample 100 boys from a theoretical population of ten year olds, it is unlikely that you would ever get a sample where most or all of the boys are unusually light or heavy; thus the variability of the mean will be less than the variabilities of the individual values.

To apply the empirical rule to the mean of a group of measurements, use the standard error of the mean instead of the standard deviation. In such a case, you estimate the standard deviation of a hypothetical population of means, and interpret the standard error of the mean relative to the mean just as you would the standard deviation relative to the observations.

Interquartile range

In the presence of outliers, the median or trimmed mean provides a measure of central tendency. Similarly, a variety of measures of variability are appropriate when outliers are present. One measure closely related to the median is the interquartile range, labelled in the Descriptive Statistics table as "IQR." Recall that the median is the value greater than or equal to one half of the data and less than the other half. The median is an example of a group of measures called percentiles. The nth percentile is the value such that n% of the data is equal to or less than the percentile. Thus, the median is the 50th percentile, and 90% of all values are found at or below the 90th percentile. The interquartile range is calculated by subtracting the 25th percentile from the 75th. Thus, it is the spread of values containing the central 50% of the data and, like the median, ignores the outermost points in a dataset.

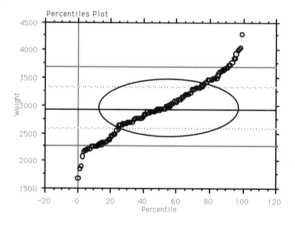

interquartile range circled

Median absolute deviation (MAD)

The median absolute deviation (MAD) is a measure of variability that incorporates all the data, but does not give as much influence to outliers as the standard deviation. The MAD is the median of the set of differences between each data point and the median of the data. The MAD is often a useful measure of variability when the median is used to describe the central tendency of the data.

Measures describing overall characteristics of a distribution

While measures of central tendency and variability are useful for succinctly describing the characteristics of data, sometimes more information is needed. It may be of interest to know if the outlying values are mostly very large or very small, or if most of the values are close to the central values. Two useful statistics that describe these properties of a set of data are skewness and kurtosis.

Skewness

Skewness is a reflection of the symmetry of the distribution, that is, the parts of the distribution above and below the mean. For a symmetric distribution of values, the mean and the median coincide. A histogram of the data will show one side of the data as a mirror image of the other side, with the value of the mean as the "mirror." A symmetric distribution has a skewness value of zero. Deviations from symmetry are reflected in changes in the skewness value.

When the number of extreme values larger than the mean is less than the number of extreme values smaller than the mean, the distribution is skewed to the left, or negatively skewed. In this case the tails will "stretch out" more on the left (lower) side of the distribution. The skewness value is less than zero and the mean is less than the median. In the opposite case, when the number of smaller values is less, the distribution is skewed to the right, or positively skewed. The skewness value is greater than zero and the mean is greater than the median. For negative skewness values, the left tail spreads out further than the right; for positive values the reverse is true. When skewness equals zero, the tails of the distribution look the same.

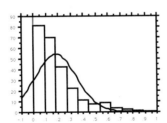 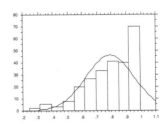

Positively and negatively skewed distributions

Kurtosis

Kurtosis is a measure of the amount of data in the tails (as opposed to the central part of the distribution). Kurtosis is scaled such that normally distributed data has a kurtosis value of zero. Positive kurtosis values indicate that the data is squeezed into the middle of the distribution (the tails of the distribution are slim and there are few extreme values). Negative values indicate the data has many extreme values spread out over a wide range (the tails are fat). There are terms to describe these three situations: mesokurtic, for kurtosis values near zero; platykurtic, for negative kurtosis values; and leptokurtic, for positive kurtosis values.

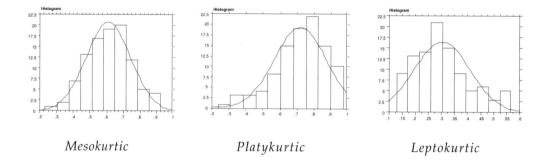

Mesokurtic   *Platykurtic*   *Leptokurtic*

Dialog box settings

When you create or edit descriptive statistics, you set the analysis parameters in two dialog boxes, a small one with few choices and an expanded one with many choices. In the first of the two, you can select either a subset of the descriptive statistics (Basic) or all the descriptive statistics (Complete) and click OK.

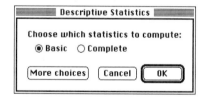

If you click the More choices button, you see an expanded dialog box listing all the descriptive statistics.

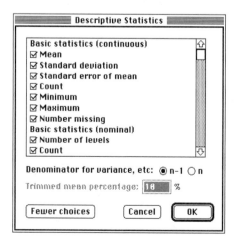

Using this dialog box, you can pick and choose from all the available descriptive statistics by clicking in the checkbox. The statistics are displayed in three separate groups: Basic statistics (continuous), Basic statistics (nominal) and Additional statistics. If Basic is selected in the fewer choices dialog box, than only the basic statistics are checked in the expanded dialog box. If Complete is selected, then all statistics will be checked in the expanded dialog box. Those statistics with a check mark next to them are included in the summary table. Using the expanded dialog box, you can customize which statistics to display by clicking to remove the checkmark.

Additional dialog box setting

The first choice at the bottom governs which value to use in calculating the variance. The default calculates a sample variance. See the previous discussion on the variance for more information. The second choice sets the percent of observations to exclude at the high and low ends of of the distribution when calculating the trimmed mean. The default is 10%, which trims the highest and lowest 10% of the observations before calculating the mean.

Variables

Requirements

Descriptive statistics can be generated for one or more nominal or continuous variables.

Variable browser buttons

Add — To generate descriptive statistics, select the variable(s) that you wish to analyze and click Add.

Split By — When you assign one or more split-by variable to a descriptive statistics table, results for each cell in the split-by variable(s) as well as totals for all groups are displayed in a single summary table.

Additional variables

Add — When you select a descriptive statistics table and assign additional variables, they are added to the summary table which expands to include the new variables.

By holding down the Command (⌘) and Shift keys simultaneously and then clicking Add, you create a new summary table for additional variables rather than expanding the selected table. Any split-by variables will automatically be assigned to the new table. By holding down the Command and Shift keys and then clicking Split By, you create a new summary table containing the original variables split by the new variable.

Results

For explanation of the results, please see the preceding discussion.

Basic continuous	Table containing the mean, standard deviation, standard error of the mean, count, minimum, maximum, and the number missing for continuous variables.
Basic nominal	Table containing the number of levels, count, number missing and mode for nominal variables.
Additional statistics available	Table containing the variance, coefficient of variation, range, sum, sum of squares, geometric mean, harmonic mean, skewness, kurtosis, median, interquartile range, model, trimmed mean, and median absolute deviation for continuous variables.

Templates

StatView offers many options for customizing all aspects of your statistical output, including which statistics are used and the appearance and location of tables and graphs. These customizations can be saved as templates and re-used.

A sample template for descriptive statistics is included in the StatView Templates folder. You may wish to use this template as is or create your own descriptive statistics templates which contain the statistics you commonly use. For more information on templates, see Chapter 7, Templates and Chapter 8, Building Analyses.

Exercise

In this exercise you create a set of descriptive statistics using the sample Car Data. It contains information about weight, gas tank size, turning circle, horsepower and engine displacement for 116 cars from different countries. You will generate descriptive statistics that will allow you to make comparisons between the cars of different countries.

- Open the Car Data in the Sample Data folder. The dataset appears on the screen.

- Select New View from the Analyze menu. A blank view appears on the screen.

- In the analysis browser, double-click on Descriptive Statistics. The Descriptive Statistics dialog box appears for you to set analysis parameters.

- For this example, you will create a basic set of descriptive statistics for several variables in your dataset. Basic statistics are selected by default in the Descriptive Statistics dialog box. Click OK to create the analysis. A table placeholder appears in the view until you add variables.

- In the variable browser, click on Country and drag down to Gas Tank Size, selecting all the variables in between.

- Click the Add button. X usage markers appear next to the variables in the browser. The results are calculated and these tables appear in the view.

Descriptive Statistics

	Mean	Std. Dev.	Std. Error	Count	Minimum	Maximum	# Missing
Weight	2957.629	535.664	49.735	116	1695.000	4285.000	0
Turning Circle	38.586	3.132	.291	116	32.000	47.000	0
Displacement	158.310	60.409	5.609	116	61.000	350.000	0
Horsepower	130.198	39.822	3.697	116	55.000	278.000	0
Gas Tank Size	16.238	3.076	.286	116	9.200	27.000	0

Nominal Descriptive Statistics

	# Levels	Count	# Missing	Mode
Country	3	116	0	3
Type	5	116	0	4

StatView calculates two tables, one for the continuous variables and one for nominal. For a discussion of nominal and continuous data class, see Chapter 3, Datasets. Spend whatever time you wish examining these results. When you are through, go on to the next part of this exercise.

It is useful to compare the subgroups of one variable that are defined by the levels of another variable. For example, comparing Turning Circle for cars from various countries will show which country makes the largest cars. To do this, you must first deselect the tables you just created. This avoids using the variables from existing tables in the new analysis. (New analyses are always created using the variables in any selected results.)

- Click in a blank space in the view. The tables are deselected. When deselected, the black handles around the tables disappear and the variables in the variable browser lose their usage markers.

- With Descriptive Statistics selected in the analysis browser, click the Create Analysis button. The Descriptive Statistics dialog box appears.

- Click the More choices button to customize the choice of statistics. An expanded Descriptive Statistics dialog box appears.

This Descriptive Statistics dialog box contains a scrolling list of statistics under three headings: Basic statistics (continuous), Basic statistics (nominal) and Additional statistics. Since Basic was selected in the first dialog box, all the basic statistics are selected in the expanded box. You will remove check marks from the statistics you do not wish to calculate. For this analysis, you will use only four descriptive statistics: mean, standard deviation, maximum and minimum.

- Uncheck the following in the continuous list: Standard error of mean, Count, and Number missing by clicking their checkboxes.

- Click OK to create the analysis. A table placeholder appears in the view until you assign variables.

- In the variable browser, select Turning Circle and click the Add button. It appears highlighted with an X usage marker next to it. The analysis calculates with this variable.

- In the variable browser, select Country and click the Split By button. It appears highlighted with an S usage marker next to it indicating you have assigned a split-by variable. The existing table updates showing the statistics broken down by the groups of the nominal variable.

Descriptive Statistics
Split By: Country

	Mean	Std. Dev.	Minimum	Maximum
Turning Circle, Total	38.586	3.132	32.000	47.000
Turning Circle, Japan	37.233	2.956	32.000	42.000
Turning Circle, Other	36.676	2.199	33.000	42.000
Turning Circle, USA	40.857	2.318	36.000	47.000

These results indicate that cars from the USA have the largest turning circle, and cars from Japan and other European countries have turning circles smaller than average. You are now finished with this exercise. You may save the view to any folder and open it with the same dataset to perform any further analyses you wish.

Chapter

12

Frequency Distribution

A frequency distribution graph (pie chart or histogram) can be a useful visual tool in getting a sense of the distribution of your data. These graphs divide your data into a number of ranges and display a bar or pie slice for each range. The height of each bar or size of pie slice is proportional to the fraction of your data which falls in that range. A frequency distribution can help you identify some characteristics of your data which may influence the choice of the descriptive statistics and other analyses you will use.

Discussion

Histograms and pie charts

The graph of a frequency distribution is one of the quickest and easiest ways to get a picture of your data and perform a visual test for normality. A histogram divides your data into bars whose height is proportionate to the amount of data which falls in the range of the bar. A pie chart accomplishes the same thing with pie wedges. The advantage of a histogram is that the X axis has meaning, so you have two visual cues rather than one.

A pie chart is better suited for showing large differences. A pie chart gives an excellent gross overview but will not illustrate fine differences. It is easier to compare bar heights than to compare pie wedges, particularly when the differences between bars or wedges is small. When one range dominates your data, as in the percentage of the U.S.

budget spent on defense, a pie chart offers a much more dramatic demonstration. When there are small differences between ranges, a histogram allows you to rank the ranges with greater ease.

Z-score histograms

A z-score histogram converts the values so the mean is zero and the standard deviation is one. The scale is the same for all z-score histograms, regardless of the original units of measurement. This graph is particularly useful when you compare two measurements which were made on different scales. If the data are normally distributed, fewer than 1 out of 100 points will be higher than 3 or lower than -3, and only 5% of the points will be larger than 2 or smaller than -2.

Dialog box settings

When you create or edit frequency distribution results, you see the Frequency Distribution dialog box, in which you set or change the analysis parameters.

```
╔═══════════════ Frequency Distribution ═══════════════╗
║                                                       ║
║  Number of intervals:  [10]      ☐ Show normal comparison ║
║                                                       ║
║  Do you wish to enter your own interval information?  ║
║  ◉ no  ○ yes   width: [      ]    initial value: [      ] ║
║                                                       ║
║  Intervals indicate: [ Count ▼ ]    include: [ Lowest value ▼ ] ║
║  ...................................................  ║
║  Tables show:  ⊠ Counts  ☐ Percents  ☐ Relative frequencies ║
║  Histograms show: [ Counts ▼ ]                        ║
║                              [ Cancel ]   [[ OK ]]    ║
╚═══════════════════════════════════════════════════════╝
```

Intervals

The top half of the dialog box controls the intervals in the analysis. The number of intervals is equal to the number of bars or pie slices in the resulting graph. The number of intervals defaults to 10 for continuous variables; you can enter a different number. The number of intervals for nominal variables is determined by the number of unique values of the variable. For continuous variables you can also set the interval width and the starting point. The width defaults to the range of the data divided by the number of intervals, and the initial value defaults to the lowest value in the variable, so the entire range is displayed. When you set a different width and initial value, the graph might not display the full range of the data. If this is the case, a note appears under the graph.

Changing interval width and initial value is useful when you want to examine one part of the distribution of your data more closely. The histogram on the left below was created using the defaults. The one on the right gives a closer look at the lower end of the distribution, since the interval width is set at 10 and the initial value at 250.

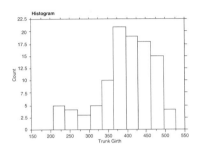

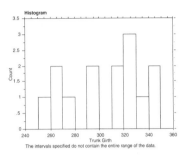

When values in your data fall on an interval boundary, you can set the intervals to include the lowest value (which is the default) or the highest value. Suppose two adjacent intervals extend from 10 to 20 and 20 to 30 respectively. If one of your data values is 20, you need to know which interval to include it in. If intervals include their lowest value, 20 will go in the second interval; otherwise it will go in the first. Intervals can also be cumulative, rather than count, which is the default. Cumulative intervals are inclusive of the totals of previous intervals, shown below.

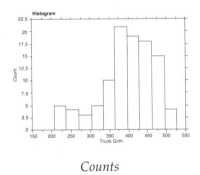

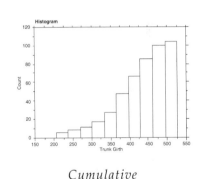

Counts   *Cumulative*

Normal comparisons

The checkbox for showing normal comparisons applies only to continuous variables. If you check this option StatView draws in the histogram the expected frequency curve for a normal distribution with the same mean and standard deviation as the variable. Normal counts, percents and relative frequencies will also appear in the summary table.

Counts, percents and relative frequencies

You can display interval values as counts, percents or relative frequencies, in both the table and the histogram. The histogram can show only one scale; tables can include all three. Counts is the frequency for each interval; percents is the percentage of total values comprised by the interval; relative frequencies is the relative frequency for each interval.

Variables

Requirements

Frequency distributions can be generated for nominal or continuous variables.

Variable browser buttons

Add
To generate frequency distributions, select one or more nominal or continuous variables and click the Add button.

Split By
When you assign one or more split-by variables to a frequency distribution table, results for each cell in the split-by variable(s) as well as totals for all groups are displayed in a single summary table. When you assign split-by variable(s) to a histogram or pie chart, a separate graph is generated for each cell.

Additional variables

Add
Each additional variable assigned creates a new table or histogram.

Results

For explanation of the results, please see the preceding discussion. The histogram is the default result for a frequency distribution.

Summary Table
Table containing the upper and lower values and the count, relative frequency or percentage of total observations for each interval. A comparison to a normal distribution may also be displayed using the dialog box.

Histogram
Graph showing the percent, relative frequency, or number of observations in each interval as a bar chart. Comparison to a normal distribution may also be displayed using the dialog box.

| Z Score Histogram | Graph showing the frequency distribution normalized so that the mean is zero and the standard deviation is one. |
| Pie Chart | Graph showing the number of observations in each interval as slices in a pie. |

Templates

StatView offers many options for customizing all aspects of your statistical output, including which statistics are used and the appearance and location of tables and graphs. These customizations can be saved as templates and re-used.

A sample template for frequency distribution is included in the StatView Templates folder. You may wish to use this template as is or create your own frequency distribution templates with the parameters and output you most commonly use. For more information on templates, see Chapter 7, Templates and Chapter 8, Building Analyses.

Exercise

In this exercise you will create a frequency distribution using the sample Car Data. It has information on weight, gas tank size, turning circle, horsepower and engine displacement for 116 cars from different countries. You will generate a frequency distribution of horsepower to determine whether horsepower follows a normal distribution.

- Open Car Data in the Sample Data folder. The dataset appears on the screen.

- Select New View from the Analyze menu. A blank view appears on the screen.

- In the analysis browser, click on the triangle next to the Frequency Distribution heading. The results appear in an indented listed beneath it.

- Select Histogram and Summary Table and click the Create Analysis button. The Frequency Distribution dialog box appears.

- Click in the checkbox next to "Show normal comparison." This setting overlays a normal distribution curve (sometimes called a bell-shaped curve) in the histogram and adds normal counts to the summary table. Click OK to create the analysis. Placeholders appear in the view until you assign a variable.

- In the variable browser, select Horsepower and click the Add button. The variable appears highlighted with an X usage marker next to it. The analysis calculates and the results appear in the view.

Frequency Distribution for Horsepower

From (≥)	To (<)	Count	Normal Count
55.000	77.300	4	7.255
77.300	99.600	21	14.976
99.600	121.900	31	22.774
121.900	144.200	21	25.516
144.200	166.500	24	21.063
166.500	188.800	7	12.809
188.800	211.100	3	5.738
211.100	233.400	2	1.893
233.400	255.700	2	.460
255.700	278.000	1	.082
	Total	116	112.567

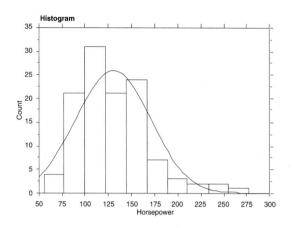

These results, particularly the histogram, show that the data is positively skewed, relative to a normal distribution. In other words, there are more cars with high horsepower than with low horsepower. The histogram tells us there are no cars with horsepower in the lowest 10% or so of the hypothetical normal distribution curve.

You are now finished with this exercise. You may save the view to any folder and open it with the same dataset to perform any further analyses you wish.

13

One Sample Analysis

StatView offers two one sample hypothesis tests: the t-test and the chi-square test. The t-test can be used to test the hypothesis that the mean of a normally distributed variable is equal to a value which you specify. The chi-square test can be used to test the hypothesis that the variance of a normally distributed variable is equal to a value which you specify. In each case, you can set a significance level and choose between one-tailed and two-tailed tests, as explained below.

Discussion

One sample t-test

The one sample t-test compares a sample mean to a hypothesized mean and determines the likelihood that the observed difference between the sample and hypothesized mean occurred by chance. The chance is reported as the p-value. A p-value close to 1 means it is very likely that the hypothesized and sample means are the same, since it is very likely that such a result would happen by chance if the null hypothesis of no difference is true. A small p-value (for example, 0.01) means it is unlikely (only a one in 100 chance) that such a difference would occur by chance if the two means were the same. In such a case we would say that the sample mean is statistically different from the hypothesized value. The t-value reported in the table expresses the difference between the mean and the hypothesized value in terms of the standard error.

Confidence interval

An alternative is to form a confidence interval around the mean of the sample. A confidence interval reports a range of values within which a particular parameter would likely occur if samples were taken repeatedly from the same distribution. If the sample mean is not statistically different from the hypothesized value, the hypothesized value is likely to be included in the confidence interval. Alternatively, when the hypothesized value is not contained in the confidence interval, the sample mean is probably not equal to that value, and the two means can be declared statistically different. Thus, the t-test and the confidence interval procedures provide similar information in different ways. Confidence intervals can be created using the One Sample Analysis dialog box.

Chi-square test

The chi-square test tests the hypothesis that the variance of a sample from a normal distribution is equal to some hypothesized value. The test compares the sample variance with the hypothesized variance and determines the likelihood that the observed difference between the two occurred by chance. This likelihood is reported as the p-value. A p-value close to 1 means it is very likely that the hypothesized and sample variances are the same, since it is probable that such a result would happen by chance if the null hypothesis of no difference is true. A small p-value (for example, 0.01) means it is unlikely (only a one in 100 chance) that the observed difference would occur by chance if the two variances were the same. In such a case we would say that the sample variance is statistically different from the hypothesized variance.

Confidence interval

An alternative is to form a confidence interval around the variance of the sample. A confidence interval reports a range of values within which a particular parameter would most likely occur if samples were taken from the same distribution over and over again. If the sample variance is not statistically different from the hypothesized value, the hypothesized value is likely to be included in the confidence interval. Alternatively, when the hypothesized variance is not contained in the confidence interval, the sample variance is probably not equal to that value, and the two can be declared statistically different. Thus, the chi-square test and the confidence interval procedures provide similar information in different ways. Confidence intervals can be created using the One Sample Analysis dialog box.

Tail

You can perform the t-test or chi-square test as a one-tailed or two-tailed test. The One Sample Analysis dialog box offers the choice of upper, lower or both tails. By default, the tests consider both possibilities: that the sample's mean/variance is larger than the hypothesized mean/variance, and that the hypothesized mean/variance will be larger than the sample's. Such a test is called a two-sided or two-tailed test. A one-tailed test considers a difference in only one direction; that the difference is either greater than (upper), or less than (lower) the hypothesized mean or hypothesized variance.

There are rare instances in which only one direction of difference is possible. In such cases, a one-sided test is more sensitive to differences than a two-sided test since it considers differences in only one direction. A great deal of knowledge about the nature of the problem at hand is necessary for the one-sided test to be valid. It is essential to be sure that a difference in the other direction is physically impossible.

Dialog box settings

When you create or edit one sample analysis results, you set the analysis parameters in this dialog box:

```
╔═══════ One Sample Analysis ═══════╗
║  ┌─Mean──────────────────────────┐ ║
║  │ ⊠ t-test                      │ ║
║  │   Hypothesized mean: [0     ] │ ║
║  │   □ [95  ] % confidence interval│ ║
║  │   Tail: [ Both ▼ ]            │ ║
║  └───────────────────────────────┘ ║
║  ┌─Variance──────────────────────┐ ║
║  │ □ chi square test             │ ║
║  │   Hypothesized variance: [1  ] │ ║
║  │   □ [95  ] % confidence interval│ ║
║  │   Tail: [ Both ▼ ]            │ ║
║  └───────────────────────────────┘ ║
║              [ Cancel ]  [[ OK ]]  ║
╚════════════════════════════════════╝
```

You can elect to perform an analysis of means (t-test) or variances (chi-square test) and set confidence intervals for both. If you choose a t-test, you compare the sample mean to a hypothesized mean, which you enter yourself in the text box. If you choose a chi-square test, you compare the sample variance to a hypothesized population variance, which you enter yourself in the text box. The hypothesized mean or variance embodies the question that you want the analysis to answer; you have reason to suspect that the mean or variance has a certain value.

For both tests, you can specify whether the test/confidence interval is two-tailed or one-tailed, and if two-tailed, which tail is to be used in the analysis. If you intend to use a one-tailed test, please read the caution in the earlier section on tails.

Variables

Requirements

A one sample analysis (t-test or chi-square) requires one or more continuous variables.

Variable browser buttons

Add
: To generate a one sample analysis, select one or more continuous variables and click the Add button.

Split By
: When you assign one or more split-by variable to an one sample analysis table, results for each cell in the split-by variable(s) as well as totals for all groups are displayed in a single summary table

Additional variables

Add
: Each addition continuous variable assigned is added to the existing table.

Results

For explanation of the results, please see the preceding discussion. The hypothesis being tested is shown in the title of the table.

Mean

One Sample t-test
: Table generated if only t-test is selected. This table shows the sample mean, the degrees of freedom, and the t-value and the p-value for the difference between the actual and hypothesized value.

Confidence Interval
: Table generated if only confidence interval is selected. This table shows the sample mean and the upper and lower confidence intervals as set in the dialog box.

One Sample Analysis
: Table generated if both t-test and confidence interval are selected. This table combines the above tables.

Variance

Chi-square test	Table generated if only chi-square test is selected. This table shows the sample variance, the degrees of freedom, and the chi-square and the p-value for the test.
Confidence Interval	Table generated if only confidence interval is selected. This table shows the variance, and the upper and lower confidence intervals as set in the dialog box.
One Sample Analysis	Table generated if both chi-square test and confidence interval are selected. This table combines the above tables.

Templates

StatView offers many options for customizing all aspects of your statistical output, including which statistics are used and the appearance and location of tables and graphs. These customizations can be saved as templates and re-used.

A sample template for one sample t-test is included in the StatView Templates folder. You may wish to use this template as is or create your own templates which contain the one sample analyses you commonly use. For more information on templates, see Chapter 7, Templates and Chapter 8, Building Analyses.

Exercise

In this exercise you perform a one sample t-test. The data used in this exercise comes from blood lipid screenings of medical students. You are concerned with one variable: Cholesterol. You want to find out if the mean cholesterol level of the students is significantly greater than 190, a point above which cholesterol levels may be unhealthy. You will test the null hypothesis that the mean value for cholesterol is less than 190. If you reject the null hypothesis, you can conclude that the mean is significantly greater than 190.

- Open Lipid Data in the Sample Data folder. The dataset appears on the screen. Scroll through the dataset to examine its contents.

- Select New View from the Analyze menu. A blank view appears on the screen.

- Select One Sample Analysis in the analysis browser and click the Create Analysis button. The One Sample Analysis dialog box appears.

- The test you want to perform, a t-test for means, is the default. Enter "190" in the hypothesized mean text box, as this is the value to which you compare the mean of the sample group.

- You want to see if the mean is greater than 190, but a one-tailed test is inappropriate since you cannot assert that it is impossible for student cholesterol values to be less than 190. Leave the Tail pop-up menu setting at Both and click OK to create the analysis. A table placeholder appears in the view until you assign the variable.

- In the variable browser, select Cholesterol and click the Add button. The variable name appears highlighted with an X usage marker next to it, indicating you have assigned a continuous variable to the analysis. A table appears in the view.

One Sample t-test
Hypothesized Mean = 190

	Mean	DF	t-Value	P-Value
Cholesterol	191.232	94	.336	.7373

From this result you can see that the mean is slightly higher than the hypothesized value of 190. However, although the mean is in fact higher, you cannot reject the null hypothesis that the mean is 190 or less because 191.232 is well within the range of sampling variance. The p-value indicates you would see a difference of this magnitude by chance more than 73% of the time.

You are now finished with this example. You may save the view to any folder and open it with the same dataset to perform any further analyses you wish.

Chapter

14

Paired Comparisons

There are several ways you can compare two samples of experimental units. One approach compares the means of the two samples by performing a t-test. If the samples are naturally paired in some way, a paired t-test is appropriate. The most common case is a comparison of two measurements taken from the same experimental unit at different times or under different conditions.

 If instead you want to compare average measurements for the two groups, rather than paired variables, an unpaired t-test is appropriate. Unpaired comparisons are described in the next chapter. Note that the paired t-test is the equivalent of a repeated measures ANOVA (Chapter 18) for two repeated measurements.

Another approach examines the relationship or closeness of association between properties of paired experimental units. For example, a researcher may question how closely a bird's body length follows its wing span. This can be done using a correlation analysis. The paired t-test and correlation analysis are described below. These tests assume that both samples are normally distributed and have the same variance. Extensions of these techniques for dealing with more than two groups or data that is not normally distributed are discussed in the ANOVA and Nonparametrics chapters.

Discussion

Paired t-test

The most common use of a paired t-test is the comparison of two measurements from the same individual or experimental unit. The two measurements can be made at different times or under different conditions. The paired t-test tests the hypothesis that the mean of the differences between pairs of experimental units is equal to some hypothesized value, usually set at zero. An hypothesized value of zero is equivalent to the hypothesis that there is no difference between the two samples. The paired t-test compares the two samples and determines the likelihood of the observed difference occurring by chance. The chance is reported as the p-value. A small p-value (for example, 0.01) means it is unlikely (only a one in 100 chance) that such a mean difference would occur by chance under the assumption that the mean difference were zero. In such a case we would say that there is a statistically significant difference between the two groups. The t-value reported in the table expresses the difference between the mean difference and the hypothesized value in terms of the standard error.

A paired t-test is more powerful than the unpaired t-test because it takes into account the fact that measurements from the same unit tend to be more similar than measurements from different units. For example, in a test administered before and after a training program, the usual (unpaired) t-test may not detect consistent but small increases in each individual's scores. The paired t-test is more sensitive to the fact that one measurement of each pair essentially serves as a control for the other.

The paired t-test is also appropriate when some other natural pairing exists. For example, a survey of husbands and wives is designed to test for differences of opinion on particular issues. Each couple's responses are viewed as a pair and tested for differences with a paired t-test. In some designed experiments, subjects are selected for similarities of age, race or sex. A paired t-test is appropriate to use on such measurements. The critical issue is whether a pair's responses are more likely to be similar than responses from random experimental units. When the pair's responses are likely to be consistently more similar, a paired t-test is more powerful than an unpaired t-test.

You may also may wish to examine your data graphically using a cell plot. See Chapter 22 for a discussion of cell plots.

Mean difference confidence interval

An alternative is to form a confidence interval for the mean of the difference between the two measurements for each experimental unit. When the two measures are not statistically different, the value of zero is likely to be included in the confidence interval. Alternatively, when zero is not contained in the confidence interval, the difference is probably not zero, and the measures can be declared statistically different.

Tail

You can perform the paired t-test as a one-tailed or two-tailed test. The Paired Comparisons dialog box offers the choice of upper, lower or both tails. By default, the tests consider both possibilities: that the first group's mean is larger than the second group's mean, and that the second group's mean will be larger than the first's. Such a test is called a two-sided or two-tailed test.

There are rare instances in which only one direction of difference is possible. In such cases, a one-sided test is more sensitive to differences than a two-sided test since it considers differences in only one direction. A great deal of knowledge about the nature of the problem at hand is necessary for the one-sided test to be valid. It is essential to be sure that a difference in the other direction is physically impossible.

A one-tailed test considers a difference in means in only one direction; that the difference is either greater than (upper tail), or less than (lower tail) the hypothesized difference or hypothesized correlation.

Z-test for correlation coefficients

The paired t-test is used to compare the means of measurements of the same variable taken at different times. Comparison of two variables which measure different things requires a different approach. The z-test tests the hypothesis that the correlation coefficient is equal to an hypothesized value, usually set at zero. An hypothesized correlation coefficient of zero is equivalent to the hypothesis that there is no correlation between variables. The z-test compares the two groups and determines the likelihood of the observed correlation occurring by chance. The chance is reported as the p-value. A small p-value (for example, 0.01) means it is unlikely (only a one in 100 chance) that such a correlation would occur by chance. In such a case we would say that there is a statistically significant difference between the two groups.

The most powerful tool for examining relationships of this sort is the bivariate scattergram (see bivariate plots in Chapter 22). A bivariate scattergram plots the values of one variable on the X axis and the values of the other on the Y axis. It is easy to see whether a relationship exists. For example, this scattergram shows a near linear relationship between two variables:

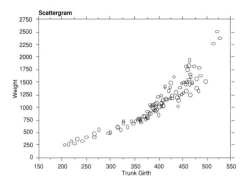

Correlation coefficient

The correlation coefficient is a more quantitative measure of the relationship between two variables than the bivariate scattergram. A correlation coefficient of -1 indicates that large values of one variable are exactly associated with small values of the other variable. A correlation coefficient of +1 indicates large values of one variable are exactly associated with large values of the other variable. The scattergram above has a correlation coefficient of .916.

The distinction between statistical significance and practical significance is important when using the correlation coefficient. The level of correlation that is practically significant varies from situation to situation. Generally, unless the absolute value of the correlation is greater than 0.5, the relationship between variables is not important. However, a correlation of 0.1 may be statistically significant with a large enough sample. This seems contradictory, but it means that a large enough sample size lends significance to a weak correlation. The statistical significance indicates that the value of the correlation coefficient is not zero; the decision remains whether the correlation is large enough to be important.

Correlation is useful for testing the relationship between more than two variables. The correlation of many variables can be displayed as a correlation matrix (table). The Correlation/Covariance analysis, discussed in Chapter 16, produces such a table. A correlation coefficient for all pairs of variables appears in the cell at the intersection of the variables' respective row and column. A partial correlation matrix removes the linear effect of one or more variables before examining the relationships of the other variables. For more information about correlation, see chapters 16 (Correlation and Covariance) and 20 (Nonparametrics).

The correlation coefficient measures only the *linear* relationship between variables. It cannot reveal anything about non-linear relationships and can be misleading if used with them. Polynomial relationships can be examined using polynomial regression (see Chapter 17). In some cases, you may be able to transform the data (using the formula capability) so that the relationship becomes linear. If it is possible to divide the independent variable into groups, you can test for the presence of a more general relationship than simply linear between these groups and a dependent variable, by using ANOVA (see Chapter 18).

Tail

You can also perform a z-test as a one- or two-tailed test. The Paired Comparisons dialog box offers the choice of upper, lower or both tails. By default the test considers both possibilities: that the correlation coefficient is either smaller or larger than an hypothesized value. A great deal of knowledge about the nature of the problem at hand is necessary for the one-sided test to be valid. You must be certain before you start the experiment that a difference in only one direction is possible.

Data organization

The data for each sample of the paired comparison must be located in a single continuous variable (column). Each row entry for the two columns being analyzed must be a measure for the same subject or for observations that are naturally paired.

For an introduction to dataset organization, see Chapter 3, Datasets. In addition, the exercise at the end of this chapter will help you see how to organize your data for this analysis.

Dialog box settings

When you create or edit paired comparison results, you set the analysis parameters in this dialog box:

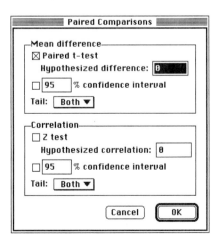

You can choose to analyze the mean difference, correlation, or both, by clicking in the appropriate checkboxes. The paired t-test computes a paired t-value between two variables when the row entry for each variable is a measure on the same subject. The z-test uses Fisher's R to Z transformation to test the hypothesis that the correlation between two variables is equal to the specified value. You can set confidence intervals for both tests, and designate either as two-tailed or one-tailed (upper or lower). Please read the caution in the discussion section if you are using a one-tailed test.

Variables

Requirements

Paired comparisons require two or more continuous variables. If more than two continuous variables are assigned, paired comparisons are calculated for all possible variable pairs.

Variable browser buttons

Add	To generate paired comparisons, select a two or more continuous variables and click the Add button.
Split By	When you assign one or more split-by variable to a paired comparisons table, results for each cell in the split-by variable(s) as well as totals for all groups are displayed in a single summary table.

Additional variables

Add	Each additional variables is added to the summary table which expands to include the new variable(s).

Results

For explanation of the results, please see the preceding discussion. The hypothesis being tested is shown in the title of the table.

Mean difference

Paired t-test	Generated if only paired t-test is selected. This table shows the mean of the differences between pairs, the degrees of freedom, and the t-value and the p-value for the mean difference.
Confidence Interval	Generated if only confidence interval is selected. This table shows the difference between the group means and the upper and lower confidence intervals for that difference as set in dialog box.

| Paired Means Comparison | Generated if both paired t-test and confidence intervals are selected. This table combines the above tables. |

Correlation

| Fisher's R to Z | Generated if only z-test is selected. This table shows the correlation between variables, the number of paired observations, and the z-value and the p-value for the correlation. |

| Confidence Interval | Generated if only confidence interval is selected. This table shows the correlation coefficient, and the upper and lower confidence intervals as set in the dialog box. |

| Correlation Coefficient | Generated if both z-test and confidence intervals are selected. This table combines the above tables. |

Templates

StatView offers many options for customizing all aspects of your statistical output, including which statistics are used and the appearance and location of tables and graphs. These customizations can be saved as templates and re-used.

A sample template for paired comparisons is included in the StatView Templates folder. You may wish to use this template as is or create your own templates which contain the paired comparison analyses you commonly use. For example you may wish to combine a z-test with a bivariate plot in a template. For more information on templates, see Chapter 7, Templates and Chapter 8, Building Analyses.

Exercises

Paired t-test

In this exercise you will perform a paired t-test. The data used in this exercise comes from blood lipid screenings of medical students. You will determine whether initial triglyceride levels are different from those measured in the same subjects after three years.

- Open Lipid Data in the Sample Data folder. The dataset appears on the screen.

- Choose New View from the Analyze menu. A blank view appears on the screen.

- In the analysis browser, select Paired Comparisons and click the Create Analysis button. The Paired Comparisons dialog box appears for you to set the parameters.

- The test you want to perform, a t-test for means, is the default. Leave the hypothesized difference as 0, as you are testing the hypothesis of no difference between the means. Click OK to create the analysis. A table placeholder appears in the view until you assign variables.

- In the variable browser, assign Triglycerides and Trig-3 yrs to the analysis by selecting them and clicking the Add button. The variables appear highlighted with X usage markers next to them indicating they have been assigned to the analysis. The analysis calculates and a table appears in the view.

Paired t-test
Hypothesized Difference = 0

	Mean Diff.	DF	t-Value	P-Value
Triglycerides, Trig-3yrs	3.419	42	.386	.7015

From this paired t-test, you can accept the hypothesis of no difference between means of the two groups. The mean difference is so small the p-value indicates you are likely to see a difference of this magnitude by chance 70% of the time. You are now finished with this example. You may save the view to any folder and open it with the same dataset to perform any further analyses you wish.

Z-test

The previous exercise compares the means of groups with the same variable: triglyceride levels. Comparison of two variables which measure different things on the same or paired experimental units requires a different approach.

In this exercise you create a scattergram and calculate a correlation coefficient to determine the degree of linear relationship between two variables. The data you use rates a number of different western cities by nine criteria. You will discover whether better climate is accompanied by an increase in housing costs.

- Open the Western States Rated dataset in the Sample Data folder. It appears on the screen. Scroll through the dataset to examine its contents. (For Climate & Terrain, a higher score is better; for Housing, the lower the score the better.

Your first step is to create a bivariate plot to see how linear the relationship is between the two variables in question.

- Select New View from the Analyze menu. A blank view appears on the screen.

- In the analysis browser, click on the triangle next to Bivariate Plots. The output appears in an indented list beneath the heading.

- Select Scattergram and click the Create Analysis button. The Bivariate Plot dialog box appears for you to set parameters.

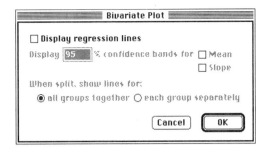

- The default parameters are appropriate, so click OK. A graph placeholder appears in the view until you assign variables.

- In the variable browser, select Climate&Terrain and click the X Variable button. The variable appears highlighted with an X usage marker next to it indicating you have assigned a variable to the X axis.

- In the variable browser, select Housing and click the Y Variable button. The variable appears highlighted with a Y usage marker next to it indicating you have assigned a variable to the Y axis. The graph appears in the view.

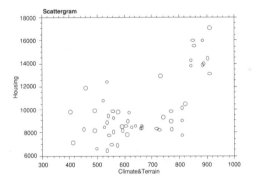

From this scattergram you can see that there is some degree of linear relationship between higher housing costs and more desirable climate (as defined by the criteria of the study). To confirm this judgement, examine the correlation coefficient for these two variables by performing a paired comparisons test.

You can avoid the step of assigning the Climate&Terrain and Housing variables again. by keeping the scattergram selected and then requesting Paired Comparisons. The next analysis you choose uses the variables in the selected result.

- With the scattergram still selected in the view, double-click on Paired Comparisons in the analysis browser. The Paired Comparisons dialog box appears for you to set parameters.

- Deselect Paired t-test, the default, and select Z test under Correlation. Leave the hypothesized correlation "0", as you are testing the hypothesis of no relationship between the variables. This test will produce a correlation coefficient and a p-value indicating the likelihood of this correlation occurring by chance.

- Click OK. The table appears in the view.

Fisher's R to Z
Hypothesized Correlation = 0

	Correlation	Count	Z-Value	P-Value
Climate&Terrain, Housing	.659	52	5.533	<.0001

From this test, you can conclude that a positive correlation exists between Climate&Terrain and Housing because of a significant correlation coefficient and a p-value that indicates a very low likelihood that this degree of correlation could occur by chance. You are now finished with this example. You may save the view to any folder and open it with the same dataset to perform any further analyses you wish.

Chapter

15

Unpaired Comparisons

Unpaired comparisons are comparisons made between the average measurements of two groups rather than between paired variables within those groups. StatView performs an unpaired t-test for comparing two means and an unpaired F-test for comparing two variances, both under the assumption that your data is normally distributed. If you want to compare paired measurements of the variables rather than averages for the two groups, read about paired comparisons in the preceding chapter.

Discussion

A measurement taken from two different groups raises the question: on the average, are the measurements for one group different from the measurements for the other group? This can be answered by performing an unpaired t-test on the measurements.

Unpaired t-test

The unpaired t-test compares the means of two groups and determines the likelihood of the observed difference occurring by chance. The chance is reported as the p-value. A p-value close to 1 means it is very likely that the two groups have the same mean, since it is very likely that such a result would happen by chance if the null hypothesis of no difference between groups is true. A small p-value (for example, 0.01) means it is unlikely (only a one in 100 chance) that such a difference would occur by chance if the two groups had the same mean. In such a case we would say that there is a statistically significant difference between the two means. The t-value expresses the difference between the mean difference and the hypothesized value in terms of the standard error.

You may also wish to examine your data graphically using a cell plot. See Chapter 22 for a discussion of cell plots.

Confidence interval

An alternative is to form a confidence interval for the difference between the means of the two groups. When the two means are not statistically different, the value of zero is likely to be included in the confidence interval. Alternatively, when zero is not contained in the confidence interval, the difference is probably not zero, and the measures can be declared statistically different. Confidence intervals can be created using the dialog box.

Tail

The unpaired t-test assumes that two groups are normally distributed and have the same variance. It is usually difficult to predict the direction in which the differences will lie. By default, the t-test considers both possibilities: that the first group's mean will be larger than the second group's mean, and that the second group's mean will be larger than the first's. Such a test is called a two-sided or two-tailed test.

A one-sided test is more sensitive to differences than a two-sided test since it considers differences in only one direction. A great deal of knowledge about the nature of the problem at hand is necessary for the one-sided test to be valid. You must be certain before you start the experiment that a difference in only one direction is possible.

F-test

A comparison of the variance of groups of measurements can be useful to validate the assumptions of the t-test, and for other purposes. For example, a mechanical part is manufactured by two different methods. You want to know if the size of the part differs between the two methods, and also whether one method or the other produces more consistent results. The F-test for variances shows whether the variance of one group is smaller, larger or equal to the variance of the other group.

The F-test depends on two parameters: the degrees of freedom for each of the two groups. This will be equal to the number of observations in the group minus one. Since the F-test is formed as a ratio of the two variances, the parameters are referred to as numerator degrees of freedom and denominator degrees of freedom.

Confidence interval

An alternative is to form a confidence interval for the ratio of the variances of the two groups. When the two variances are not statistically different, the value of 1 is likely to be included in the confidence interval. Alternatively, when 1 is not contained in the confidence interval, the variances are probably not equal and can be declared statistically different. Confidence intervals can be created in the dialog box.

Tail

It is usually difficult to predict the direction in which the variance differences will lie. By default, the F-test considers both possibilities: that the first group's variance will be larger than the second group's, and that the second group's variance will be larger than the first's. Such a test is called a two-sided or two-tailed test.

A one-sided test is more sensitive to differences than a two-sided test since it considers differences in only one direction. A great deal of knowledge about the nature of the problem at hand is necessary for the one-sided test to be valid. You must be certain before you start the experiment that a difference in only one direction is possible.

Data organization

To compare groups, your data must be organized in a way that allows the unpaired comparison analysis to identify which group an observation belongs to. This can be done using a column containing a separate nominal grouping variable or by using a compact variable. For an introduction to dataset organization, see Chapter 3, Datasets. In addition, the exercise at the end of this chapter will help you see how to organize your data for this particular analysis.

Standard layout

The dataset below shows one way to organize your data if you wished to perform an analysis comparing cholesterol levels for males and females.

	Name	Gender	Weight	Cholesterol
1	J. Suds	Male	145	168
2	H. Fitz	Female	123	167
3	R. Blunt	Male	245	265
4	T. Stout	Male	223	187
5	S. Small	Female	142	202

The cholesterol values for *both* males and females appear in a single column. The variable Gender is a separate nominal column and acts as a grouping variable that identifies the group (Male or Female) for each Cholesterol measurement. There will be one row in the dataset for each subject in the analysis.

Compact variable

If you are more comfortable placing different groups in separate columns, StatView offers an alternative to the data organization shown above. In this dataset organization, the observations for each group appear in a single column. Your dataset will contain as many columns as there are groups being compared. If you enter your data this way, you must create a simple compact variable in order for the analysis to know which group each observation belongs to. The cholesterol measurements for male and female from the above dataset look like this in a compact variable format:

	Cholesterol	
	Male	Female
1	168	167
2	265	202
3	187	•

The male cholesterol measurements are all placed in one column and the female cholesterol measurements in another. The column identifies the group, not the row. If there are unequal numbers of observations in the two groups, missing values (•) are automatically inserted in the column with fewer observations. These missing values are ignored in the analysis.

If you plan to use a compact variable, please read the discussion on compact variables in Chapter 3, Datasets, and Chapter 8, Building Analyses.

Dialog box settings

When you create or edit unpaired comparisons results, you set the analysis parameters in this dialog box:

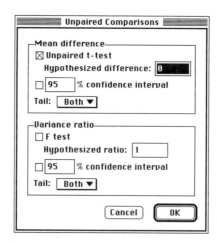

You can choose to analyze the mean difference, variance ratio, or both by clicking in the appropriate checkboxes. The unpaired t-test defaults to a hypothesized value of zero. The F-test tests the hypothesis that the ratio of the two variances is equal to the hypothesized ratio, which defaults to one. You can set confidence intervals for both tests, and designate either as two-tailed or one-tailed (upper or lower). Please read the caution in the discussion section if you are using a one tailed test.

Variables

Requirements

Unpaired comparisons require a single nominal grouping variable with two or more groups and one continuous variable. If the nominal variable contains more than two groups, unpaired comparisons will be calculated for all possible pairs of groups.

Variable browser buttons

Add
: To generate unpaired comparisons, select a single nominal grouping variable and a single continuous variable and click the Add button.

Split By
: When you assign one or more split-by variable to an unpaired comparisons table, results for each cell in the split-by variable(s) as well as totals for all groups are displayed in a single summary table.

Additional variables

Add
: Each additional nominal variable assigned creates a new analysis using the new nominal variable and the old continuous variable. Each additional continuous variable assigned creates a new analysis using the new continuous variable and the old nominal variable.

Results

For explanation of the results, please see the preceding discussion. The hypothesis being tested is shown in the title of the table.

Mean difference

Unpaired t-test
: Generated if only unpaired t-test is selected. This table shows the difference between the group means, the degrees of freedom, and the t-Value and the P-Value for the mean difference.

Confidence Interval	Generated if only confidence interval is selected. This table shows the difference between the group means and the upper and lower confidence intervals as set in dialog box.
Unpaired Means Comparison	Generated if both unpaired t-test and confidence intervals are selected. This table combines the above tables.
Group Info	Always generated and shows the count, mean, variance, standard deviation, and standard error for each group.

Variance ratio

F-test	Generated if only F-test is selected. This table shows the ratio of the group variances, the degrees of freedom in the numerator and denominator, and the F-value and p-value for the variance ratio.
Confidence Interval	Generated if only confidence interval is selected. This table shows the ratio of the group variances, and the upper and lower confidence intervals as set in the dialog box.
Variance Comparison	Generated if both F-test and confidence intervals are selected. This table combines the above tables.
Group Info	Always generated and shows the count, mean, variance, standard deviation, and standard error for each group.

Templates

StatView offers many options for customizing all aspects of your statistical output, including which statistics are used and the appearance and location of tables and graphs. These customizations can be saved as templates and re-used.

A sample template for unpaired comparisons is included in the StatView Templates folder. You may wish to use this template as is or create your own templates which contain the unpaired comparison analyses you commonly use. For example, you may wish to combine a cell plot with an unpaired t-test in a template. For more information on templates, see Chapter 7, Templates and Chapter 8, Building Analyses.

Exercise

In this exercise you perform an unpaired t-test on census information for 506 housing tracts in the Boston area. You will examine two groups of housing tracts, those near the Charles River and those farther away from it. You will find out whether the median value of owner-occupied homes varies depending on how far houses are located from the river. To do this, you will test the null hypothesis that no difference in median housing prices exists.

- Open Boston Housing Data in the Sample Data folder. The dataset appears on the screen. Scroll through the dataset to examine its contents.

- Choose New View from the Analyze menu. A blank view appears on the screen.

- In the analysis browser, select Unpaired Comparisons and click the Create Analysis button. The Unpaired Comparisons dialog box appears for you to set parameters.

- The test you want to perform, an unpaired t-test for means, is the default. Leave the hypothesized difference 0, as you are testing the hypothesis of no difference between means of the two groups. Click OK to create the analysis. Table placeholders appear in the view until you assign variables.

- In the variable browser, select Median Value and click the Add button. An X usage marker appears next to it, indicating a continuous variable has been assigned to the analysis.

- In the variable browser, select Charles and click the Add button. It appears highlighted and a G usage marker appears next to it indicating you have assigned it as a grouping variable to the analysis. These tables appear in the view.

Unpaired t-test for Median Value
Grouping Variable: Charles
Hypothesized Difference = 0

	Mean Diff.	DF	t-Value	P-Value
Near, Far	6.346	504	3.996	<.0001

Group Info for Median Value
Grouping Variable: Charles

	Count	Mean	Variance	Std. Dev.	Std. Err
Near	35	28.440	139.633	11.817	1.997
Far	471	22.094	77.993	8.831	.407

From these results, you can reject the null hypothesis of no difference between the price of houses near to and far from the Charles River. The mean value is significantly higher for housing near the river than for housing far from it. The low p-value indicates a probability of only one in 10,000 that such a difference would occur by chance.

16

Correlation and Covariance

Correlation and covariance values indicate the degree of linear relationship between two variables. Computing these values generally requires a single sample with two sets of observed values on each subject or sampling unit. Correlation and covariance measure only the linear relationship between two variables. If the relationship is other than linear, these coefficients can be very misleading. Before relying on the correlation or covariance of two variables as a measure of their association, you should examine a scattergram of the two variables. In this way you can make sure there is not some nonlinear relationship which the correlation or covariance would not detect.

Discussion

Correlation coefficient

The correlation coefficient has an absolute value between 0 and 1, with 1 indicating a perfect linear relationship and 0 meaning no linear relationship exists. When two variables increase or decrease proportionately (as one variable increases, the other variable increases; when one decreases, so does the other), a positive correlation between them exists. When one variable increases when the other decreases proportionately, there is a negative correlation (inverse relationship). A correlation of exactly 0 almost never occurs in practice. If an exact linear relationship exists among some of the variables, the matrix is said to be singular. A singular matrix is not invertible, so it is not possible to compute partial correlations or Bartlett's test of sphericity. If this occurs, an error message tells you the correlation matrix is singular.

Correlation matrix

When many variables are measured, it is useful to display the correlation coefficients in a correlation matrix, a table in which each row or column represents a different variable in the dataset. The cell at the intersection of a row and column contains the correlation coefficient for the two variables the row and column represent. In an exercise later, you will create and interpret a correlation matrix. Other values, such as the probability that a particular correlation is different from 0, may also be displayed in similar tables.

1.000	•	•	•	•	•	•	•
.846	1.000	•	•	•	•	•	•
.805	.881	1.000	•	•	•	•	•
.859	.826	.801	1.000	•	•	•	•
.473	.376	.380	.436	1.000	•	•	•
.398	.326	.319	.329	.762	1.000	•	•
.301	.277	.237	.327	.730	.583	1.000	•
.382	.415	.345	.365	.629	.577	.539	1.000

Correlation matrix

When you perform a correlation analysis, you have the option of saving the correlation matrix as a new dataset.

Fisher's r to z

To determine if a correlation coefficient is statistically different from zero, a Fisher's r to z transformation is carried out on the correlation. This transforms the correlation coefficient to a variable with a standard normal distribution, allowing a probability level (p-value) to be calculated for the null hypothesis that the correlation is equal to zero. One caution about judging correlation coefficients based on their significance levels: for a large enough sample, any correlation coefficient that is not exactly equal to zero will have a significant probability level.

The distinction between statistical significance and practical significance is important when using the correlation coefficient. The level of correlation that has practical significance will vary from situation to situation. Generally, unless the absolute value of the correlation is greater than 0.5, the relationship between two variables is probably not of much importance. On the other hand, with a large enough sample, a correlation of 0.1 may be statistically significant. This may seem contradictory. It simply means that when the sample size is large enough, even a weak correlation can safely be considered different from no correlation at all. The statistical significance simply indicates that the value of the correlation coefficient is not 0; it is up to you whether the magnitude of the correlation is large enough to be of importance.

Bartlett's test of sphericity

One special correlation pattern which may exist among a set of variables is sphericity. It means that all the variables in question are uncorrelated with each other, resulting in a correlation matrix with zeroes everywhere except the diagonal. You can test to see if a correlation matrix conforms to this pattern by requesting Bartlett's test of sphericity. A high chi-square and associated low p-value imply that the null hypothesis of no correlation between variables can be rejected. If the matrix is singular (an exact linear relationship exists among some of the variables) it is not possible to compute Bartlett's test and you see an error message noting that the matrix is singular.

Confidence intervals

You may also form a confidence interval for the correlation between pairs of samples of experimental units. When two variables are not correlated, the value of zero is likely to be included in the confidence interval. Alternatively, when zero is not contained in the confidence interval, the correlation is probably not zero, and the measures may be declared statistically correlated. You create confidence intervals using the dialog box.

Listwise/pairwise deletion

Sometimes a correlation coefficient in a correlation matrix may not agree with a value reported as a single correlation when the correlation coefficient is calculated for just two of the variables included in the matrix. This discrepancy may arise because StatView, by default, eliminates all rows that have a missing value for any of the variables for which correlations are calculated. This procedure is called listwise deletion. Such a correlation matrix has certain desirable statistical properties when used in further calculations, even though the deleting of cases may obscure some relationships in the data. You can override this by choosing the pairwise deletion option in the Correlation/Covariance dialog box.

Covariance

When several variables are studied simultaneously, it is often of interest to determine if any or all of the variables are related to each other. One way of doing this is to calculate a measure of how much changes in one variable affect the values of the other variables. When we consider changes in the linear sense, the measure is known as covariance. By a linear sense, we mean that a straight line on a graph would be a good representation of the relationship between the two variables. As one variable increases, the other consistently either increases or decreases. The covariance between two variables is measured on a scale which is heavily influenced by the magnitudes of the variables involved, and may be hard to interpret if the variables being studied are measured on vastly differing scales. For this reason, the correlation coefficient is usually preferred as a measure of linear relationships, because it is standardized to be in the range of -1 to 1, and is not affected by the scale of measurement.

Partial correlation

A correlation matrix may involve many variables. Since the entries in the matrix only address the relation between two variables at a time, there are many situations where the correlation coefficient may not accurately measure the strength of the relationship of interest. For example, suppose we have a dataset consisting of age, weight and a score on a fitness test.

The correlation between weight and the fitness score may mislead us into believing that there is a strong relationship between these two variables, when in fact it may be just the effect of age, since that is related to both weight and fitness score. What we would like is a measure of correlation between weight and fitness score with the effects of age removed. This is the basic idea behind partial correlation. The partial correlation of two variables with respect to a third is the correlation of the two variables after the linear effect of the third variable has been removed. Notice that, like the regular correlation coefficient, if non-linear relationships exist, the partial correlation coefficient may not be valid. Nevertheless, the partial correlation coefficient can be a useful tool when you are studying a set of closely related variables.

If the correlation matrix is singular (an exact linear relationship exists among some of the variables) it is not possible to compute partial correlations and you will see an error message noting that the matrix is singular.

Dialog box settings

When you create or edit a correlation or covariance analysis, you set the analysis parameters in this dialog box:

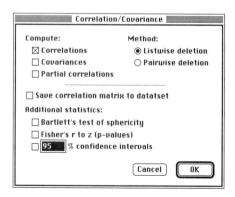

Select from correlation, covariance and partial correlation by clicking in the checkboxes at the top. Rows are eliminated from the analysis if they contain a missing value (listwise deletion) unless you select pairwise deletion instead. (A matrix formed with the pairwise method should not be used as input for a factor analysis.) For a further discussion of listwise and pairwise deletion, see the preceding section, Listwise deletion.

At the bottom of the dialog box you can choose to generate the following additional statistics: Bartlett's test of sphericity, Fisher's r to z (p-values), and a user specified confidence interval around the correlation coefficient.

Saving a correlation matrix

If you check save correlation matrix, the computed correlation matrix is saved to a new dataset titled Correlation Matrix. The dataset will have as many columns and rows as variables assigned to the correlation. The names of each column are Cor "Variable name" where "Variable name" is the name of one of the assigned variables for the correlation.

Note that the correlation matrix dataset is a very special dataset with many features. The dataset is linked to the correlation analysis. If you change the parameters of the analysis or any of the input data, the dataset will *automatically* update to reflect the new correlation matrix. If you close the view that contains the correlation analysis, this correlation dataset will close as well. When the view is reopened, the correlation matrix dataset is automatically recreated. Please note that because this dataset is linked to your analysis, it is a "read only" dataset; you can not change any value in the dataset (except the formatting) until you break the link between the dataset and the analysis. If you plan to use this correlation matrix as an input to another analysis, such as factor analysis, the analysis must appear in the same view as the correlation analysis that dataset is associated with.

You cannot close the matrix dataset, but can hide it by clicking the close box. It is merely hidden and is accessible through the Window menu. To sever the link between the dataset and the correlation analysis, you need to choose Save As from the File menu and save the dataset under a different name. This will save on the disk a copy of the correlation matrix as a dataset. You can then open this dataset as you would any other dataset. When you save a copy of the correlation matrix dataset to your disk, StatView automatically appends the letters "UE" to the beginning of the column names to indicate that these columns are now user entered.

Variables

Requirements

Correlation and covariance require two or more continuous variables.

Variable browser buttons

Add
To generate a correlation, select the continuous variable(s) that you wish to analyze and click the Add button.

Split By
When you assign one or more split-by variable to a correlation or covariance analysis, results for each cell in the split-by variable(s) as well as totals for all groups are displayed in a separate tables.

Additional variables

Add
When you select a correlation or covariance result and assign additional variables, they are added to the summary table which expands to include the new variables.

Results

For explanation of the results, please see the preceding discussion.

Correlation Matrix
Matrix of correlation coefficients for all pairs of variables in the analysis.

Covariance Matrix
Matrix of covariances for all pairs of variables in the analysis.

Partial Correlation
Matrix of partial correlation coefficients for all pairs of variables in the analysis.

Correlation Analysis
Generated if confidence interval and/or Fisher's r to z is selected in the dialog box. This table shows the correlation coefficients and the associated confidence intervals and/or p-values for all pairs of variables.

Bartlett's Test of Sphericity
Table containing the degrees of freedom, determinant of the correlation matrix, the chi square statistic, and p-value.

Templates

StatView offers many options for customizing all aspects of your statistical output, including which statistics are used and the appearance and location of tables and graphs. These customizations can be saved as templates and re-used.

A sample template for correlation and covariance is included in the StatView Templates folder. You may wish to use this template as is or create your own templates which contain the correlation and covariance analyses and plots you commonly use. For more information on templates, see Chapter 7, Templates and Chapter 8, Building Analyses.

Exercise

In this exercise you perform a correlation analysis on data in which different western cities are rated by nine criteria. You will discover whether there is a linear correlation between any two of the criteria by creating a correlation matrix. Then you will graph correlated and uncorrelated variables in order to see a graphic representation of a high and low correlation.

- Open the Western States Rated dataset in the Sample Data folder. The dataset appears on the screen. Scroll through the dataset to examine its contents. For all but two of the variables, the higher the score, the better. For Housing and Crime, the lower the score the better. The origin of the data and the components of each variable are described in Appendix C.

- Choose New View from the Analyze menu. A blank view appears on the screen.

- In the analysis browser, select Correlation/Covariance and click the Create Analysis button. The Correlation/Covariance dialog box appears for you to set parameters.

- For this analysis, use the default parameters. Correlations is the default, with the matrix calculated using each complete case (row) in the dataset. All rows in this dataset are complete. Click OK to create the analysis. A placeholder for the result appears in the view because you have not yet added variables.

- In the variable browser, select all the continuous variables (those with a ⊙ next to them) and assign them to the analysis by clicking the Add button. (Only continuous variables can be used in a correlation analysis.) The selected variables appear highlighted with X usage markers next to them. The analysis calculates and a correlation matrix appears in the view.

Correlation Matrix

	Climate&Terrain	Housing	Health Care & Environment	Crime	Transportation	Education	The Arts	Recreation	Economics
Climate&Terrain	1.000	.659	.445	.042	.086	.151	.442	.260	-.122
Housing	.659	1.000	.575	.147	.313	.177	.533	.397	.366
Health Care & Environment	.445	.575	1.000	.520	.399	.477	.949	.470	.262
Crime	.042	.147	.520	1.000	.289	.233	.553	.303	.239
Transportation	.086	.313	.399	.289	1.000	.302	.398	.454	.161
Education	.151	.177	.477	.233	.302	1.000	.455	.169	-.069
The Arts	.442	.533	.949	.553	.398	.455	1.000	.525	.189
Recreation	.260	.397	.470	.303	.454	.169	.525	1.000	.222
Economics	-.122	.366	.262	.239	.161	-.069	.189	.222	1.000

52 observations were used in this computation.

Scroll the window from side to side to see the complete matrix. The broken vertical line through the right side of the matrix indicates the right margin of the first page. Each cell at the intersection of a row and column contains a correlation coefficient for the two variables represented by the row and column. Scan the matrix to see where a correlation coefficient may be high enough to indicate a linear relationship between variables. Remember, 0 means no correlation and 1 means a perfect one to one relationship. A negative value means an inverse relationship.

Health Care & Environment and The Arts have a correlation of .949, a very high score. Most other correlations are fairly low, between .3 and .5. Climate&Terrain and Crime have a very low correlation, .042. To get a better idea of what these correlations mean, look at scattergrams of the variables with high and low correlations.

- Deselect the correlation matrix by clicking in blank space in the view. Otherwise all the variables in the correlation matrix will be used in the next analysis you create. The square black handles around the table disappear when the matrix is deselected, and the variables in the variable browser lose their usage markers.

- In the analysis browser, click on the triangle next to Bivariate Plots. The output appears in an indented list beneath the heading.

- Select Scattergram and click the Create Analysis button. The Bivariate Plot dialog box appears for you to set parameters for the graph.

- You are using the default parameters for this graph, so click OK to produce the scattergram. A graph placeholder appears in the view until you add variables.

Notice that the buttons in the variables browser have changed. The Remove and Split By buttons are the same, but the Add button has become two buttons: X Variable and Y Variable. This has happened because bivariate plots require you to assign variables to different axes. You must assign at least one X and one Y variable to complete the analysis.

As mentioned, Health Care & Environment and The Arts are the two variables with the highest correlation coefficient in the matrix. Begin by creating a scattergram with these two variables.

- In the variable browser, select Health Care & Environment and click the X Variable button. It appears highlighted with an X usage marker next to it indicating you have assigned it to the X axis.

- In the variable browser, select The Arts and click the Y Variable button. It appears highlighted with a Y usage marker next to it indicating you have assigned it to the Y axis. The analysis calculates and the bivariate scattergram appears in the view.

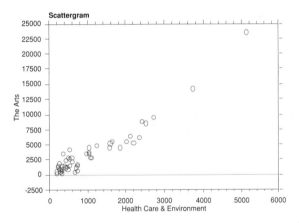

The plotted values of these variables occur along a fairly straight line, indicating that a high correlation exists between them. If there were a perfect linear relationship between Health Care & Environment and The Arts, a coefficient of one, the values would form a perfectly straight line.

If you look at a scattergram of two variables with a very low correlation, such as Climate&Terrain and Crime, you will notice that this scattergram differs from the preceding one showing a high correlation. In this one, points are scattered all over the graph rather than clustered along a fairly straight line. This graph provides visual evidence of a very low correlation between Climate&Terrain and Crime as determined in the correlation matrix. The correlation coefficient for these two is only .042.

You are finished with the examples for this chapter. You may now save the view to any folder and open it with the same dataset to perform any further analyses you wish.

17

Regression

Regression analysis explains or predicts the value of a dependent variable from one or more independent variables. All variables must be continuous. In regression modeling, the predictors are independent variables; they predict the dependent variable. StatView can perform these regressions:

> Simple
> Polynomial
> Multiple
> Stepwise (forward and backward)

Regression modeling is useful when all of the following conditions apply:

1. There is a linear relationship between the variable of interest (the dependent variable) and the variables used as predictors (the independent variables). As the value of any independent variable increases, the value of the dependent variable must increase or decrease consistently.

2. All observations (values for the dependent and independent variables) are independent of each other. If this is not the case (observations measured on the same object over time, for example), regression analysis can be used to examine relationships within your data, but the probability values for hypothesis tests will not be valid.

3. The portion of the dependent variable not explained by the independent variables is due to random error that follows a normal distribution with a constant variance. There

are diagnostics to help identify cases that do not follow this distribution and transformations that can help correct the problem. These are discussed in the later section, Criteria for model quality.

Discussion

Regression analysis is a tool for discerning relationships between variables. Given one or more variables, regression can predict a related value and illuminate the nature of the relationship between variables. You can predict a stock index based on unemployment rates or other economic indicators. You can estimate the yield of a chemical reaction using temperature, pressure and quantities of input materials.

Simple and multiple regression

Simple regression is appropriate when you wish to model your dependent variable with exactly one independent variable. One of the appealing features of simple regression is that you can verify the linearity of the relationship between the variables by looking at a scattergram of the two variables. With more than one independent variable, the appropriate technique to use is multiple regression. This takes into account the linear effect of several independent variables in predicting the dependent variable. As the name implies, this case is more complex than simple regression, since relationships among the independent variables may make it difficult to interpret the results (see the section on collinearity below). If you have many independent variables, you may want to consider a model selection procedure (described later under stepwise regression).

Polynomial regression

When the relationship between your dependent variable and your independent variable is not linear, polynomial regression may be a useful tool. As stated earlier, a linear relation implies that the dependent variable's values must consistently increase or decrease as the value of the independent variable increases. By including independent variables in which represent the square, cube, fourth power, etc. of the original variables, this strict linear relation is no longer required. For example, if you include the square of a variable as an independent variable, then the dependent variable may rise and fall (or fall and rise) once as the original variable's value increases. Similarly, the cube of a variable will allow for two changes in direction of the dependent variable as the independent variable increases. In addition, a polynomial regression can be useful when the relationship between a dependent variable and an independent variable follows a curve, for example if the dependent variable's rate of increase is less as the value of the independent variable increases.

Remember, however, that polynomial regression is just a mathematical tool for fitting a curve, and while it may be very useful for prediction, care should be taken before assuming that the underlying relationship between the two variables being studied is actually a polynomial.

Model selection: stepwise regression

In regression analysis, a model selection procedure helps choose the independent variables that are most useful in explaining or predicting your dependent variable. StatView offers two model selection procedures: forward stepwise and backward stepwise selection.

Forward selection starts with an empty model and adds independent variables in order of their ability to predict the dependent variable. Backward selection starts with all the independent variables in the model and at each stage removes the one that is least useful in predicting the dependent variable. The criteria for adding and deleting variables is the partial F-ratio. It is the square of the value obtained from a t-test for the hypothesis that the coefficient of the variable in question is equal to zero.

The forward procedure starts with no variables in the model (except the intercept, if present). The backwards procedure starts with all the variables in the model (step 0). Both procedures use the same algorithm to assign and remove variables. First, the partial F-ratio for each variable in the model is examined. If the minimum of these values is less than the F-to-remove you specify, the corresponding variable is removed, completing the current step. Otherwise, the partial F-ratio for each variable not in the model is examined. If the maximum of these values is greater than the F-to-enter you specify, the corresponding variable is entered. If no variable is either removed or entered, the stepwise procedure stops.

Force

Variables can be forced into the model using the Force button on the variable browser. In the forward procedure, all forced variables are entered at step 0; in the backward procedure, *all* variables are entered at step 0. In either procedure, forced variables are never removed from the model regardless of the value of their partial F-ratio.

Stepwise regression summary

At each stage of the model selection procedure, StatView displays a regression summary table to help you assess the quality of the regression model up to that stage. This table is reported for all regression models, but if the model is a stepwise model, it is available at each step. A different table, the stepwise regression summary table, is displayed only for stepwise models. It reports the number of steps, the number of variables entered, the F to enter and the F to remove.

The default criteria are appropriate for most models, but you can adjust them to suit your needs. For example, if you wish to build a model containing only variables that seem very useful for prediction (i.e., a model containing a very small number of variables), then raise the criteria for entering variables by increasing the value of the F-to-enter and F-to-remove.

Collinearity

Forward and backward stepwise selection techniques do not always choose the same model due to the close relationship between independent variables in regression studies. When a variable is considered for addition or deletion, its importance may be highly influenced by the presence of other variables in the model. You can identify sets of related variables by using both forward and backward selection and comparing the chosen models. If variables appear in one model but not the other, they may be too closely related to provide useful information; one of them should be removed. This phenomenon is known as collinearity.

When you perform a regression with many variables, some of the independent variables are inevitably related. If the relationships are not too strong (if the maximum correlations between any two independent variables are less than 0.8), this is not likely to cause problems. However, if there are strong relationships between some of the independent variables, your results can be difficult to interpret or even useless. In a stepwise regression, one indication of collinearity is the sign of the estimated coefficient for a particular variable changing depending on which other independent variables are included in the model.

Model coefficients and intercept

An intercept corrects for differences in units of measurement between the dependent and independent variables. It is the expected value of the dependent variable if all the independent variables had values of zero.

StatView automatically includes an intercept as part of a regression model unless you specify otherwise. The Regression dialog box contains a checkbox labelled "No intercept in model" which removes the intercept, forcing the model through the origin. It may be appropriate to remove the intercept from the model, but do so with caution. Sometimes there is a physical reason to remove the intercept: it is known ahead of time that if the independent variable(s) are 0, the dependent variable must be 0 (the weight of a tree must be 0 if its height is 0). Some of the statistics produced by StatView have a different interpretation when the intercept is removed from the model. You can test for significance of the intercept; the coefficients table provides a p-value for the intercept along with the coefficients for the variable(s). The error of the intercept is also provided in the coefficients table.

A regression model is an equation y = b0 + b1 * x1 + b2 * x2 + b3 * x3 + ... + error, where y is the dependent variable, x1, x2, ... are the independent variables, and b0 is the intercept. The model intercept and coefficients (b1, b2...) for each variable are listed with their standard errors in the model coefficient table. Note that in a simple regression, the intercept and coefficient of the independent variable in the model coefficient table are the intercept and slope of the regression line.

Standardized regression coefficients

Since the magnitudes of independent variables may vary widely, it is difficult to compare the relative importance of a regression coefficient for one variable with that of another variable. For this reason, standardized regression coefficients are often useful in determining which independent variables in a regression are most important in helping to predict the dependent variable. Standardized coefficients are calculated as if all of the independent variables had means of zero and variance of 1; thus two standardized coefficients can be directly compared, regardless of differences in the scale of the variables involved.

Criteria for model quality

R squared

The simplest statistic used to assess the quality of a regression model is the R^2 value, also called the coefficient of determination. It is the proportion of the dependent variable's variability that is explained by the independent variables (with a maximum value of 1). Thus, an R^2 of .80 means that 80% of the dependent variable's variation is explained by the independent variable(s). An R^2 close to one can be achieved by including many independent variables in the model. If the number of independent variables in a model is close to the number of observations, interpret the R^2 with extreme caution.

One problem with the use of R^2 is that the number of variables is not explicitly included in the formula used to calculate R^2. Thus, when you assign an additional independent variable to an existing regression, the value of R^2 is guaranteed to increase. A modification of R^2, known as the adjusted R^2, attempts to remedy this situation by applying a "penalty" to the R^2 value based on the number of variables assigned. The adjusted R^2 is especially useful for comparing a variety of models with different numbers of independent variables.

t-test

You can assess the adequacy of each independent variable in the model with a t-test. This tests the hypothesis that there is no linear relation between the dependent variable and the independent variable. This differs from the hypothesis of no correlation between the two variables (read about z-tests in Chapter 14, Paired Comparisons). The t-value displayed through the regression takes into account the other variables in the regression model, whereas correlation is performed for only two variables at a time. t-values and associated p-values for the intercept and each model coefficient can be found in the model coefficients table.

ANOVA statistics

Another measure of model quality is the regression ANOVA table. This table uses the sum of squares and mean squares to calculate an F statistic, as a standard ANOVA (Chapter 18) does. The probability of the F-statistic for a regression is a guide to how important the independent variable(s) are in explaining the behavior of the dependent variable; a low p-value associated with an F-statistic means it is unlikely that an F-statistic as large as the one calculated would have happened by chance. Thus we assume that the variable(s) in question are important in helping to explain variation in the dependent variable.

Residuals

Because a regression model rarely estimates the value of the dependent variable exactly, there is a difference between the predicted or fitted value of the dependent variable and its actual value. This difference is known as the residual.

Residual plots

Residuals are useful in helping you identify outliers, observations that behave very differently than the bulk of the observations. The residuals from a regression represent the part of the data that is not explained by the model. In the residual plots described below, any point that is distant from most of the points on the plot is considered an outlier and its origin investigated. If it is clear that the observation is an error (for example a mistake in data transcription or entry), then you correct it or delete it from the analysis. The fact that an observation does not fit in with the other observations in the analysis does not justify its removal. Before removing outliers, always investigate the source of the outlier to provide justification based on the context of the data collection process. If an unusual residual is the only reason for deleting an observation, it is best to leave it in the model and continue to investigate the cause of the unusual residual. Sometimes these observations contain important information about your data.

One useful residual plot is the plot of residuals versus fitted values. The following are some different shapes for this plot.

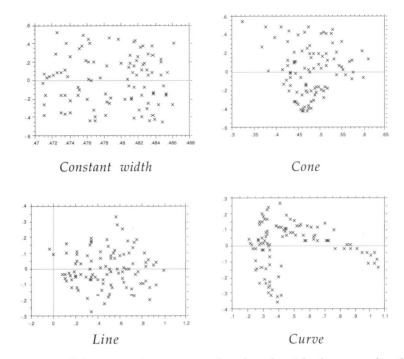

Constant width

Cone

Line

Curve

If the assumptions of the regression are met, the plot of residuals versus fitted values will show a band of constant width independent of the fitted value. The cone shape is a common deviation from this pattern, as in the upper right plot where the spread of residuals is wider for larger fitted values. This tells you that the variance of the observations increases as the mean increases. That generally indicates a need to transform the dependent variable by a logarithmic or square root transformation before regression is carried out. If the data are counts, for example, a square root transformation is often helpful.

Another useful residual plot uses the residuals plotted against each of the independent variables in the model. Once again, the expected pattern, if the assumptions are met, is a band of residuals of constant width throughout the range of the regressor. If the assumption of a purely linear relationship between the dependent and independent variable is not appropriate, the residual plots will display a systematic deviation from the constant width pattern. For example, if the residuals tend to lie in a band that curves either upward or downward, as in the lower right plot, the addition of a new term representing the square of the regressor may improve the fit. Similarly, the cone shape pattern described previously suggests that a transformation of the regressor in question may be in order. The plot of residuals versus independent variables may be useful when collinearity is suspected among the independent variables.

The assumption of independence of observations may be violated when observations are measured across time. As with the other violations of assumptions, a residual plot can help make this clear, though the observed pattern of the residuals may be more subtle.

A plot of residuals versus a variable representing time should, as always, show no discernible pattern. Any regularity, such as noticeable cyclical patterns, indicates that a more complex analysis is necessary to accommodate the time series nature of the data.

Residual statistics

Along with residual plots, StatView produces statistics which help summarize the behavior of the residuals. These include the number of residuals greater than zero and less than zero. Since the mean value of the residuals is guaranteed to equal zero, these two numbers can give you a feel for the symmetry of the residuals. If they are symmetric, the two numbers should be approximately equal. If not, the residuals may be skewed, and a transformation or a different model may be appropriate.

The remaining residual statistics help assess the level of first degree autocorrelation within the residuals, i.e., the level of correlation between each residual and the residual immediately before it in the dataset. Thus, they are only of value if the observations in your data are ordered in a meaningful way. These statistics are labelled SS[e(i) - e(i-1)], Durbin-Watson, and Serial Autocorrelation. An autocorrelation close to -1 or 1 implies a high degree of correlation between the residuals.

Dialog box settings

When you create or edit a regression analysis, you set the analysis parameters in two dialog boxes, a small one with few choices and an expanded one with many choices. In the first of the two, you can select simple, polynomial, multiple or stepwise regression and click OK to accept the default parameters.

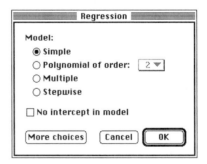

If you choose polynomial, you must specify an order or degree of the polynomial between 2 and 9. If you choose stepwise, your model will be created using the default stepwise parameters (forward stepwise with an F-to-Enter of 4.000 and an F-to-Remove of 3.996). You can change these parameters in the expanded dialog box by clicking More Choices. The checkbox at the bottom lets you remove the intercept from the model. Please read the cautions earlier in this chapter before doing so.

If you edit a multiple or stepwise regression analysis by selecting a result and clicking Edit Analysis, you will not be able to change the model to simple or polynomial regression. Those choices will be disabled in the dialog box.

To see the expanded dialog box which offers additional choices for regression analysis, click the More choices button. The expanded dialog box with many choices also contains all the choices present in the smaller dialog box. You can return to the smaller dialog box by clicking the Fewer choices button.

```
┌─────────────────────────────────────────────────┐
│ ▤▤▤▤▤▤▤▤▤▤▤▤ Regression ▤▤▤▤▤▤▤▤▤▤▤▤            │
│                                                   │
│  Model:  [ Simple ▼ ]   Order:  [ 2 ▼ ]          │
│  ☐ No intercept in model                          │
│  ................................................ │
│  Stepwise parameters:  ◉ Forward  ○ Backward      │
│  F-to-enter: [4    ]    F-to-remove: [3.996  ]    │
│  ................................................ │
│  Save to dataset: ☐ Residuals ☐ Fitted ☐ Predicted│
│  Compute values for:  ◉ included rows  ○ all rows │
│  ................................................ │
│  Confidence level: [95   ] %                      │
│  Plot confidence bands for:  ☐ Mean  ☐ Slope      │
│                                                   │
│  [ Fewer choices ]        [ Cancel ]  [[  OK  ]]  │
└─────────────────────────────────────────────────┘
```

The top section of this dialog box contains the information from the smaller dialog box. The other sections are described below.

Stepwise parameters

The section below that is available only if you choose stepwise regression. You can specify forward or backward, and set the partial F-ratio criteria for entering and removing variables. The F-to-remove defaults to 3.996, and must be lower than the F-to-enter, which defaults to 4.

Residual, fitted, and predicted values

There are checkboxes allowing you to generate and save residual, fitted and predicted values. These values are saved to the dataset containing the dependent variable and are dynamically linked to the analysis. They are assigned the name Fitted "Dependent", Residual "Dependent", or Predicted "Dependent", where "Dependent" is the name of the dependent variable for the regression. StatView identifies the source of these columns that are generated as part of an analysis as Analysis Generated variables (additional information on analysis generated variables is provided below).

StatView distinguishes fitted and predicted values as follows:

- Fitted values are values of the dependent variable predicted by the analysis using the data with which the regression model was fit.

- Predicted values are values of the dependent variable predicted by the regression model using new data. You enter this data into the columns which contain the independent variable(s), leaving missing values in the dependent column. These values can be entered into any row in the independent variable(s). The predicted values will appear in the same row in the Predicted "Dependent" column. Note that predicted values will also be generated for any row that contains a missing value for the dependent variable if predicted values is checked in the dialog box. However, predicted and fitted values as well as residuals will have a missing value if any row is missing a value for the independent variable.

Features of analysis generated variables

An analysis generated variable is dynamically tied to the regression analysis that created it. If you change the parameters of the model or any of the data in the independent or dependent variables, the analysis generated variable in the dataset will automatically update. In addition, the variable is associated with the view that contains the analysis, not the dataset in which they appear. This means that it will automatically be added to the dataset which contains the dependent variable when the view which contains the regression is reopened and the regression analysis recalculated. If you close the view, the variable will be removed from the dataset. Note that one consequence of this is that if you plan to use an analysis generated variable in a formula you need to open the view which contains the regression analysis in order for the formula to compute.

Because these variables are dynamic, you can generate a graph or statistic using the residual, fitted, or predicted values, that will also automatically update when the model or underlying data changes. You can create a histogram or box plot showing the distribution of your residuals and the plot will stay current with any changes you make to your model. Note that any result created using analysis generated variables must be located in the same view as the regression analysis.

To break the link between an analysis generated variable and the analysis, change its source to User Entered. This causes all ties to the analysis to be broken and the letters "UE" appended to the front of the variable name to indicate that it is now user entered. Any change to the regression that created it will have no effect on the variable, and they act just as any user-entered variable would. If you delete any of these analysis generated columns it is equivalent to un-requesting it from the dialog box.

Using included rows or all rows

You can choose whether to compute residual, fitted and predicted values using all the rows in the dataset, or for only the included rows. If you select Included rows, the values are calculated for just the included rows of the dataset; excluded rows contain missing values. If you select all rows, the values are calculated for all rows in the dataset regardless of their included or excluded state.

Confidence bands and intervals

The bottom choices in the dialog box allow you to plot confidence bands for the mean, slope or both in the simple regression plot. The confidence level text box specifies the level for the mean and slope for the regression plot and is also used with the confidence interval table.

Variables

Requirements

Simple and polynomial regression require one continuous independent and one continuous dependent variable. Multiple and stepwise regression require one or more continuous independent variables and one continuous dependent variable.

Variable browser buttons

Simple and polynomial regression

Independent	Select the continuous variable which is the independent variable for the model and click the Independent button. Simple and polynomial regression require a single independent variable in each analysis.
Dependent	Select the continuous variable which is the dependent variable for the model and click the Dependent button. Simple and polynomial regression require a single dependent variable in each analysis.
Force	The Force button is the same as the Independent button for all regression analyses except Stepwise regression (see below).
Split By	When you assign one or more split-by variables to any regression results, results for each cell in the split-by variable(s) are displayed in separate tables and plots.

Multiple and stepwise regression

Independent   Select the continuous variables which are the independent variables
                for the model and click the Independent button. Multiple and
                stepwise regression analyze one or more independent variables.

Dependent   Select the continuous variable which is the dependent variable for
                the model and click the Dependent button. Multiple and stepwise
                regression analyze a single dependent variable.

Force   The Force button allows you to force continuous variables into a
                stepwise regression. Each forced variable will automatically be an
                independent variable of the model even if these variables do not
                meet the model criteria. For a multiple regression, the Force button is
                the same as the Independent button.

Split By   When you assign one or more split-by variables to any regression
                results, results for each cell in the split-by variable(s) are displayed
                in separate tables and plots.

Additional variables

Independent   For simple and polynomial regression, each additional independent
                variable assigned creates a new analysis with the new independent
                and the previous dependent variable. For stepwise and multiple
                regression, additional independent variables are added to the
                model.

Dependent   For all regression models, each additional dependent variable
                assigned creates a new analysis using the new dependent variable
                and the old independent variable(s).

Results

For explanation of the results, please see the preceding discussion. The Regression
Summary, ANOVA table, and Regression Coefficients table are the default output for
this analysis.

Regression   Table containing count, number missing, correlation coefficient (R),
Summary R^2, adjusted R^2, and RMS residual.

ANOVA   Table containing the degrees of freedom, sum of squares, mean
Table   squares, F-value, and p-value for the regression ANOVA.

Regression   Table containing the coefficients of the regression equation.
Coefficients   Standardized coefficients, standard error, t-value and p-value are
                also displayed.

Confidence Intervals	Table containing both regular regression coefficients and their upper and lower confidence intervals as set in the dialog box. This table is not available for stepwise regression.
Residual Statistics	Table containing the number of residuals ≥ 0, < 0, and auto correlation statistics.
Regression Plot	Graph available only for simple and polynomial regression. It plots a scattergram of the dependent vs. the independent variable and includes the regression line and equation. Confidence intervals can be added for the mean and slope using the dialog box.
Residual Plots	Graphs of residuals vs. fitted dependent and dependent and of dependent vs. fitted dependent are available. For a stepwise regression, these plots will include information for the last step.

For further options on plotting scattergrams with fitted simple regression lines see the section on bivariate plots in Chapter 22.

Additional stepwise regression results

The following tables appear only if stepwise regression is selected. The Stepwise summary always appears. The Variables in Model and Variables Not in Model tables appear if regression coefficients are requested.

Stepwise Regression Summary	Table containing F-to-enter, F-to-remove, number of steps, variables entered, variables forced and the stepwise procedure used.
Variables in Model	Table containing the names and coefficients of the variables entered into the model at each step. Standardized coefficients, standard error, and the F-to-Remove are also displayed.
Variables Not in Model	Table containing the Partial correlation and the F-to-Enter of the variables not entered into the model at each step.

Templates

StatView offers many options for customizing all aspects of your statistical output, including which statistics are used and the appearance and location of tables and graphs. These customizations can be saved as templates and re-used.

A sample template for each regression model is included in the StatView Templates folder. You may wish to use these as is or create your own templates which contain the regression models with the parameters, tables and plots that you commonly use. For example, you may wish to combine a bivariate plot with a regression template. For more information on templates, see Chapter 7, Templates and Chapter 8, Building Analyses.

Exercises

The data you use in the first part of this exercise is Tree Data from the 1930s. The weight and trunk girth was measured for eight specimens from each of thirteen root-stocks for a total of 104 tree specimens.

Simple and polynomial regression

You will perform a simple and polynomial regression to predict the weight of trees from their girth. This makes it possible to get accurate estimates of weight without having to cut trees down and weigh them, a destructive and difficult process. Your first step is to perform a simple regression to see whether there is a linear relationship between weight and girth. A high R squared (R^2) would indicate a strong linear relationship.

- Open Tree Data, in the Sample Data folder. The dataset appears on the screen.

- Choose New View from the Analyze menu. A blank view appears on the screen.

- In the analysis browser, click on the triangle next to Regression. Scroll the analysis browser to reveal all the regression output listed beneath the heading.

- Select Regression Summary, hold down the Command (⌘) key and select Regression Coefficients, then click the Create Analysis button. The Regression dialog box appears for you to set parameters for the analysis.

- Since you are performing a simple regression analysis, leave the default setting Simple and click OK. A table placeholder appears until you assign variables.

- In the variable browser, select Trunk Girth and click the Independent button. This is the variable being used to estimate Weight. It appears highlighted with an X usage marker next to it.

- In the variable browser, select Weight and click the Dependent button. This is the variable being estimated. It appears highlighted with a Y usage marker next to it. The analysis calculates and these tables appear in the view.

Regression Summary
Weight vs. Trunk Girth

Count	104
Num. Missing	0
R	.916
R Squared	.840
Adjusted R Squared	.838
RMS Residual	183.606

Regression Coefficients
Weight vs. Trunk Girth

	Coefficient	Std. Error	Std. Coeff.	t-Value	P-Value
Intercept	-1225.413	102.361	-1225.413	-11.971	<.0001
Trunk Girth	5.874	.254	.916	23.101	<.0001

You can see from the high R^2 value in this summary table that there seems to be a clear linear relation between Weight and Trunk Girth. Now, to examine the relationship and to confirm the notion that it is linear, create a regression plot. This is a bivariate scattergram of Weight vs. Trunk Girth with a regression line added.

- With both tables still selected, select Regression Plot in the analysis browser and click the Create Analysis button. The plot appears in the view.

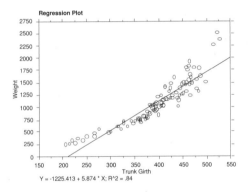

Regression Plot

$Y = -1225.413 + 5.874 * X; R^2 = .84$

Notice that you did not need to assign variables to this plot. The preceding table was selected when you created this plot, so StatView treats the plot as additional output from the existing regression analysis, rather than a newly requested analysis you are creating from scratch.

The regression plot shows that the weight of trees increases faster than it would if there were a strictly linear relationship with trunk girth. The spread of points is curved with values at the ends being above the regression line and those in the middle being below it. The relationship between Weight and Trunk Girth may be better explained by adding a quadratic term in Trunk Girth. You can test this hypothesis by changing the current analysis to a polynomial regression.

- With one of the results selected, click the Edit Analysis button at the top of the view. The Regression dialog box reappears. Changing the settings here will turn your current results into results for a polynomial rather than simple regression.

- Select "Polynomial of order" and leave the order set to 2 in the pop-up menu. Click OK. The analysis recalculates and new results appear in the view.

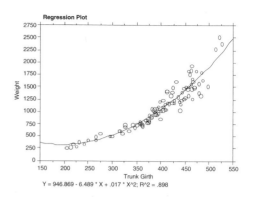

Regression Summary	
Weight vs. Trunk Girth	
Count	104
Num. Missing	0
R	.948
R Squared	.898
Adjusted R Squared	.896
RMS Residual	147.192

Regression Coefficients
Weight vs. Trunk Girth

	Coefficient	Std. Error	Std. Coeff.	t-Value	P-Value
Intercept	946.869	297.493	946.869	3.183	.0019
Trunk Girth	-6.489	1.640	-1.012	-3.956	.0001
Trunk Girth^2	.017	.002	1.944	7.597	<.0001

$Y = 946.869 - 6.489 * X + .017 * X^2; R^2 = .898$

In these results, the p-value of <.0001 for the squared term shows that the quadratic term is useful for explaining the relationship between the two variables. The graph clearly shows how accurately the second order polynomial regression fits the data.

Predicted values

Now you can use this model to predict a tree's weight based on its trunk girth. StatView will predict a value for any row in the dataset that has a value for the independent variable and a missing value for the dependent variable.

- Click the Recalculate checkbox to disable calculation. This prevents calculation of predicted values one at a time as you add each independent value to the dataset. Enable calculation after adding all the new independent values to the dataset.

- To create a column for predicted values make sure that one of the regression results is selected. Click the Edit Analysis button and in the Regression dialog box click the More choices button.

- In the larger dialog box, select Predicted (following "Save to dataset") and click OK.

- Bring the dataset to the front by choosing Tree Data from the Window menu. A new column titled "Predicted Weight" has been added to the end of the dataset containing missing values ("•").Your predicted values will appear in this column.

- Add four new rows to the dataset by entering the following values at the bottom of the Trunk Girth column (after row 104): 500, 600, 700, 800. Use the Return key to move down the column after entering each number.

- Bring the view to the front by selecting it from the Window menu. Click the Recalculate checkbox to calculate predicted values.

- Return to the dataset to see the predicted values by choosing Tree Data from the Window menu.

In the Predicted Weight column of the dataset, the following values appear:

500	◆	1909.081
600	◆	3111.125
700	◆	4649.705
800	◆	6524.818

The second order polynomial regression model predicts these values for weight based on the trunk girth values you entered. You are now finished with this example. You may save the view to any folder and open it with the same dataset to perform any further analyses you wish. Close the dataset without saving changes.

Multiple regression

In this exercise you will perform a multiple regression. The dataset you will use is Car Data. It has information on 116 cars compiled by *Consumer Reports*. This information includes data about weight, gas tank size, turning circle, horsepower and engine displacement for cars from different countries. You will find out if there is a relationship between gas tank size and other variables.

- Open Car Data in the Sample Data folder. The dataset appears on the screen. Scroll through and examine its contents.

- Choose New View from the Analyze menu. A blank view appears on the screen.

- In the analysis browser, click on the triangle next to Regression. The output appears in an indented list beneath the heading.

- Select Regression Summary and hold down the Command (⌘) key to select Regression Coefficients. Click the Create Analysis button. The Regression dialog box appears for you to set parameters.

- To specify a multiple regression, select Multiple and click OK. Two table placeholders appear in the view until you assign variables.

- In the variable browser, select the variable you are predicting, Gas Tank Size, and click the Dependent button. It is highlighted with a Y usage marker next to it.

- Select the four variables you are using to predict the value of Gas Tank Size and click the Independent button. They are: Weight, Turning Circle, Displacement and Horsepower. They appear highlighted with X usage markers next to them. These tables appear in the view.

Regression Summary
Gas Tank Size vs. 4 Independents

Count	116
Num. Missing	0
R	.852
R Squared	.727
Adjusted R Squared	.717
RMS Residual	1.637

Regression Coefficients
Gas Tank Size vs. 4 Independents

	Coefficient	Std. Error	Std. Coeff.	t-Value	P-Value
Intercept	2.551	2.553	2.551	.999	.3200
Weight	.004	.001	.781	7.820	<.0001
Turning Circle	-.021	.082	-.021	-.256	.7985
Displacement	-.001	.006	-.019	-.176	.8610
Horsepower	.011	.006	.139	1.689	.0940

The p-values in the Regression Coefficients table tell you that Weight is the only variable useful in predicting gas tank size. In addition, an adjusted R^2 value of .717 indicates a fairly strong overall relationship. To confirm the relationship between Gas Tank Size and Weight graphically, you might like to plot these two variables using a bivariate plot. You are now finished with this example. You may save the view to any folder and open it with the same dataset to perform any further analyses you wish.

Stepwise regression

In this exercise you perform a stepwise regression using census data for 506 housing tracts in the Boston area. You will determine what factors are most useful in predicting the median value of homes. The data's origin and variables are described in Appendix C.

- Open Boston Housing Data in the Sample Data folder. The dataset appears on the screen. Scroll through the dataset to examine its contents.

- Choose New View from the Analyze menu. A blank view appears on the screen.

- In the analysis browser, click on the triangle next to Regression. The output appears in an indented list beneath the heading.

- Select Regression Coefficients and click the Create Analysis button. The Regression dialog box appears for you to set parameters.

- Select Stepwise. (This setting produces a forward stepwise regression with an F-to-Enter of 4.000 and an F-to-Remove of 3.996. If you would like to change these parameters, do so by clicking the More Choices button to see a dialog box that allows you enter different values.) Click OK to create the analysis. Two table placeholders appear in the view until you assign variables.

- In the variable browser, use the Command (⌘) key to select all continuous variables (marked with a ⊙) except for Median Value and click the Independent button. The variables appear highlighted with X usage markers next to them.

- In the variable browser, select Median Value and click the Dependent button. It appears highlighted with a Y usage marker next to it. The analysis calculates and results appear in the view. Because there are many cases and variables, this may take some time.

- The Stepwise Regression Summary table indicates that nine variables were entered into the model in nine steps.

Stepwise Regression Summary
Median Value vs. 11 Independents

F-to-Enter	4.000
F-to-Remove	3.996
Number of Steps	9
Variables Entered	9
Variables Forced	0
Stepwise Procedure	Forward

- To see which variables were entered and which were not, scroll to the bottom of the view and examine the information for step 9. All variables were entered in the model except Industry and Before 1940.

Variables In Model
Median Value vs. 11 Independents
Step: 9

	Coefficient	Std. Error	Std. Coeff.	F-to-Remove
Intercept	42.003	4.950	42.003	72.002
Crime	-.128	.033	-.120	14.943
Zone	.046	.014	.117	11.142
NOX	-.173	.036	-.219	23.339
Rooms	3.712	.413	.284	80.751
Dist. Empl.	-1.552	.189	-.355	67.295
Highways	.300	.064	.284	21.698
Tax Rate	-.013	.003	-.243	14.975
Pupil/Teacher	-.964	.131	-.227	53.854
Low status	-.554	.048	-.430	133.711

Variables Not In Model
Median Value vs. 11 Independents
Step: 9

	Partial Cor.	F-to-Enter
Industry	.025	.300
Bef. 1940	.020	.200

This result guarantees that all nine variables entered in the model are somehow significant in explaining the dependent variable, Median Value. It does not provide you with any details about the individual variables themselves. You can examine this data further with the Dependent vs. Fitted plot.

- With at least one result selected, select Dependent vs. Fitted in the analysis browser and click the Create Analysis button. The performs a residual analysis and produces the following graph:

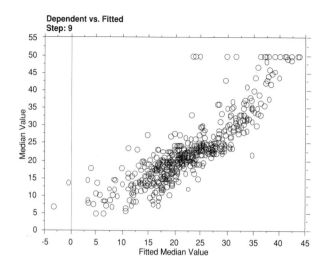

The houses with the highest median values cluster at the top of the graph in a straight line of points suggesting that their predicted values have no relation to the actual values. This suggests that we should reanalyze the data using two separate models: one for high value houses and one for all other values. Using the Recode command, you can create a nominal variable from Median Value that divides the dataset into two such groups. You can then assign this variable as a split-by variable to perform such an analysis.

You are now finished with this example. You may save the view to any folder and open it with the same dataset to perform any further analyses you wish.

Chapter

18

Analysis of Variance (ANOVA)

An analysis of variance (ANOVA) studies the effect of independent variables on a continuous dependent variable when the independent variables are nominal rather than continuous. A nominal variable can take on only a limited number of values, whereas a continuous variable can take on any value over a wide range. (In regression analysis, the independent and dependent variables are continuous, and contingency table analysis has only nominal variables.)

These restrictions hold for ANOVA in StatView: You can solve only full interaction models. A full interaction model contains each factor as a main effect and every possible combination of the factors as interaction effects. Repeated measure experiments can have no more than one within factor and those with two or more grouping factors must be balanced. A balanced model has equal numbers of cases in each combination of factors. In other words, a model whose two factors are group (I and II) and treatment (A and B) must have equal numbers of subjects in all four categories: group I receiving treatment A, group I receiving treatment B, group II receiving treatment A and group II receiving treatment B.[*]

---

[*] For those who routinely use more complex models, Abacus Concepts offers an application titled SuperANOVA that will solve any general linear model. Contact Abacus Concepts for information.

Discussion

ANOVA statistics

Analysis of variance determines the significance of the effects in a model by calculating how much of the variability in the dependent variable can be explained by the effect in question. It does this by calculating a quantity called the mean square, which is mathematically similar to the variance. This quantity is calculated by dividing the sum of squares of deviations from the means by the degrees of freedom for the effect (the number of parameters that the model is estimating to test for the significance of the effect). For main effects, the number of degrees of freedom is one less than the number of discrete values for the factor in question. The degrees of freedom for an interaction is the product of the degrees of freedom of each of the factors contained in the interaction. Finally, this mean square is divided by an estimate of variance known as the residual mean square. This ratio (mean square of the effect divided by residual mean square) results in an F-statistic that can be used to test the importance of the effect in question.

The probability (p-value) of the F-statistic for an effect is a guide to how important that effect is in explaining the behavior of the dependent variable; a low probability value associated with an F-statistic for an effect means it is unlikely that an F-statistic as large as the one calculated would have happened by chance. Thus we assume that the effect in question is important in helping to explain the dependent variable.

ANOVA models may be useful with a continuous independent variable if it is known or assumed that the relationship between the independent variable and the dependent variable will not easily be explained by a polynomial, linear or other easily linearized relationship. For example, increasing the concentration of a fertilizer increases yield of a plant up to a certain point, but the yield remains constant after that point. Such a relationship, called a plateau, is not linear. In cases like this, you can create a new nominal variable from the original independent variable by dividing the original independent variable's values into a few non-overlapping categories and using this new variable as one of the factors in your ANOVA model. For information on how to do this, read about recoding in Chapter 5, Managing Your Data.

Compared to regression

One advantage of ANOVA models is that they can detect more complex relationships between the independent and dependent variables than the simple linear relationships of regression models. ANOVA is always used when an independent variable is nominal such as hair color (black, brown, blonde, red) or the state in which subjects live (California, New York, Texas, Ohio). In such cases it is impossible to calculate a linear relationship (upon which regression analysis is based) between the value of the independent variable, such as black, brown or blonde, and the dependent variable, which must always have a continuous (numerical) value.

It might seem possible to use hair color as a regressor (an independent variable in a regression) if you recode hair color values so black becomes 1, brown 2 and so forth. In fact, you should not recode a discrete value to use in a linear model as a regressor. When you add an independent variable to a linear model as a regressor, you assume that an increase in the independent variable will cause a proportionate increase or decrease in the dependent variable (see Chapter 17, Regression). By arbitrarily recoding a discrete variable to a continuous variable, this will not typically be the case.

Interactions

One benefit of using ANOVA models is that they can detect interactions among the factors in your model. An interaction between two or more factors means that the effect of one of the factors differs depending on the level(s) of the other factor(s) involved in the interaction. You can graph interaction effects in a line chart or bar chart to see if this is the case. The first exercise, later in the chapter, illustrates the use of interaction plots.

You can create interaction plots for bars, lines and point separate from an ANOVA analysis using cell plots as described in Chapter 22, Plots.

For example, in a study on the effect of different types of fertilizer on the yield of different varieties of corn, some types of fertilizer might be more effective on some varieties of corn than on others. The interaction test of variety by fertilizer, indicated in the ANOVA table as variety*fertilizer, tests the null hypothesis that the effect of fertilizer is the same regardless of the variety of corn considered. This is exactly equivalent to testing the hypothesis that the effect of variety of corn is the same regardless of the fertilizer considered. A main effect test of type of fertilizer would average out the effects of variety and not address the question of what effect each fertilizer has on each type of corn. The main effect test for variety would similarly average out the effects of fertilizer, testing the null hypothesis that the means for the different varieties are the same.

Post hoc testing

When your ANOVA determines that some of the effects in your model are significant, it is usually of interest to examine the mean values of the dependent variable for each level of the factor(s) in question to determine why there was a significant difference (which means are different from each other). Referring back to the corn variety/fertilizer example, it would be helpful to examine the mean value of yield for each level of variety and fertilizer, and each of their combinations, in order to determine which types of fertilizer and/or corn variety result in the highest yield. When you are testing effects that contain a single factor, known as main effects, there are several tests available to help you find out where the differences in the dependent variable's values are coming from. These tests, known as post-hoc tests, or multiple comparisons, are specifically designed to make many comparisons among a group of means and still present results that are accurate at the significance levels that they report. StatView offers the following multiple comparison tests for main effects[*] : Fisher's PLSD, Scheffé's F and Bonferroni/Dunn. The post-hoc table gives you the following information:

Fisher's PLSD for Displacement
Effect: Country
Significance Level: 5 %

	Mean Diff.	Crit. Diff	P-Value	
Japan, Other	14.430	20.578	.1673	
Japan, USA	-54.953	19.417	<.0001	S
Other, USA	-69.383	18.242	<.0001	S

The title indicates the test name, the effect, and the significance level. The first column contains the mean difference between the groups. The second column reports the mean difference that would be required for it to be significant at the level you set in the dialog box. The third column reports the probability that the difference between the groups is significant. The "S" to the right of a row appears only when the difference is significant at the level you chose.

If you determine that an interaction among some of the factors in your model is significant, you would still examine the means of the dependent variable for each combination of the factors in question to get more insight into what the interaction means. But there are no statistical tests like the multiple comparisons tests for main effects described here. If you need a statistical test in this situation, you can split your data by one of the factors and perform a multiple comparisons test on the other factor to help determine where the significant interaction is arising from, but keep in mind that such a test does not use all of your data, so it may not be powerful enough to establish where the differences lie. In many cases, more insight can be gained by examining the means graphically, with an interaction plot, or through a table of means.

Fisher's Protected Least Significant Difference

Assuming that a significant F-ratio has been defined[**] , this procedure evaluates all possible pairwise comparisons with a multiple t-statistic. This multiple t-test assumes that the means have been ordered from smallest to largest. It determines the critical value to be exceeded, for any pair of comparisons, on the basis of the maximum number

---

[*] If your experiment is a repeated measures ANOVA, post hoc tests are available only for the between factors.

[**] An F-ratio is significant if the reported p-value is less than a pre-specified significance level.

of steps between the smallest and largest mean. This procedure has been implemented in a general way for use with unequal as well as equal sample ns. The original PLSD assumes equal sample size.

The PLSD is the most liberal post-hoc procedure of the three available in StatView. By insisting that the associated main effect be significant, $p < \alpha$, Fisher argued that the associated probability of a type I error across all pairwise comparisons would be approximately α.

It is possible for an effect to have a significant F-ratio associated with it but not have any significant pairwise comparisons. This occurs when the contrasts of some linear combinations of the means, not necessarily pairwise, are significantly different. The probability of a type I error will also be inflated when the sample sizes are unequal.

Scheffé's F

Scheffé's F (1953) procedure for post-hoc comparisons is very robust to violations of the assumptions typically associated with multiple comparison procedures. It may be used when you have unequal cell ns as well as when you have heterogeneous variances, that is, in the case where the variances of the cells are not equal. (In the case of heterogeneous variances, the basic assumptions of the analysis of variance are violated, and the significance levels associated with all the hypothesis tests must be interpreted with caution). This procedure was developed with the assumption that all possible comparisons would be made; in StatView, the procedure has only been implemented to make pairwise comparisons of means.

The Scheffé is the most conservative of these three paired comparison procedures. However, because it was the first paired comparison procedure with demonstrated robustness to assumption violations, it has enjoyed long term popularity and is still used by many researchers.

Bonferroni/Dunn

The Bonferroni/Dunn procedure is a multiple comparison procedure for making all possible pairwise contrasts amongst a collection of means. There are $(p(p-1)/2)$ comparisons when you implement the Dunn as a procedure for comparing all pairwise differences for p means. It has no limit on the number of comparison means that may be contrasted. This procedure tends to be less conservative than Scheffé's F; it is more likely to determine that differences are significant.

Repeated measures ANOVA

Like regression, the usual analysis of variance assumes that each observation in the analysis is independent of each other observation. In many cases, however, observations are not independent because they represent measurements taken on the same object or individual over a period of time . To correctly analyze experiments like these, the calculations for the analysis of variance must take into account the fact that variability among observations taken from the same experimental unit (like a person or a plant) is smaller than the variability measured between different experimental units. Such an analysis is known as a repeated measures analysis of variance. To analyze a repeated measures model in StatView, each of the repeated measurements for a given subject must be part of the same observation (row) in your data set, along with any grouping variables that are used in the analysis. StatView will calculate hypothesis tests for the repeated measure main effect, the interaction between the repeated measure and the grouping factors, along with the full factorial analysis for the grouping factors.

A term labelled "Subject(Group)" is automatically added to your ANOVA table. It is a within subjects error term, which you may see referred to as "within subjects error" or "error(a)" in other sources. StatView must calculate more than one estimate of variability to accurately assess the importance of the different effects in a repeated measures design, since the variability of measurements taken on the same individual is generally smaller than that of measurements taken on different individuals, For those effects which compare differences among the grouping variables (sometimes called between subjects tests), the usual estimate of residual error will be appropriate. But for tests involving the repeated measure itself (sometimes called within subject tests), a separate estimate of error must be calculated.

Within and between factors

There are two types of variables, or factors, in a repeated measures design: within factors and between factors. A between factor distinguishes the characteristics of the subjects in the experiment. A within factor represents the different conditions under which each subject is measured. StatView handles repeated measures designs with one within factor and up to thirteen between factors.

A within factor requires several columns, one for each of its levels. Every subject has a measurement in each level of the within factor, i.e., one in each column. All the columns of the within factor are formed into a compact variable, so they act as one factor in the analysis (see chapter 3, Datasets, for a discussion of compact variables and "Data organization" below). For example, temperature can be a within factor. The number of levels is equal to the number of different temperatures at which measurements are taken. If your dependent variable is measured at $50°$, $60°$, $70°$, $80°$ and $90°$, you have five columns (one for each temperature) representing the five levels of the factor temperature.

Data organization

In order to perform an ANOVA, your data must be organized in a way that allows StatView to identify which group(s) the observations belong to. For a repeated measures design, you must create a simple compact variable to identify the groups of the within factor. For an introduction to dataset organization including compact variables, see Chapter 3, Datasets. In addition, the exercises at the end of this chapter will help you see how to organize your data for both factorial and repeated measures experiments.

Factorial

In a factorial experiment, you assign one or more nominal variables and a single continuous variable (the dependent variable) to the ANOVA analysis. The nominal variables are the independent variables for the analysis. Your dataset needs to be organized so that all the values of the dependent variable appear in a single column. Each nominal variable will appear in a separate column. The nominal variables divide your dependent data into groups. There will be one row in the dataset for each subject or other experimental unit in the analysis.

	Height	Gender	Weight
1	Tall	Male	145
2	Tall	Female	123
3	Short	Male	245
4	Tall	Male	223
5	Short	Female	142

The dataset above shows the organization for a factorial ANOVA. All observations for the dependent variable, Weight, are in a single column. The grouping variable Height is a separate nominal column identifying the group (tall or short) for each Weight measurement.The variable Gender is another separate nominal column that identifies the group (male or female) for each Weight measurement. Each row in the dataset represents a separate, unique, subject in the experiment.

Some users may wish to use compact variables to identify the groups of the between factors for their factorial ANOVA. In a compact variable, the values of the columns (variables) in the usual dataset organization become the rows in the dataset with the compact variable. If you plan to use a compact variable, please read the discussion on compact variables in Chapter 3, Datasets, and in Chapter 8, Building Analyses.

Repeated measures

In a repeated measures experiment, you have a single within factor as well as one or more between factors. The within factor must be set up as a *compact variable*. To enter the within factor, you need to create a column for each group of the within factor. Any between factors are entered as separate nominal columns.

Consider an experiment testing the mobility of six athletes, male and female, at four temperatures (60, 70, 80 and 90 degrees). The dataset for this experiment would have six rows, one for each subject in the experiment, and five columns. One column would indicate the gender of the subject. This nominal column would be a between factor in the repeated measures experiment. The other four columns would record the mobility measurements taken at the four different temperatures. There would be a separate column for each separate temperature. These four columns are the within factor.

In order for StatView to understand that these four columns are related and represent a different group (or level) of the within factor, they need to be made into a compact variable before analyzing the repeated measures experiment. To create a compact variable, you select the columns that represent the groups of the within factor and click the Compact button at the top of the dataset. You then need to enter a name for the variable. A dataset containing this information might appear as follows:

	Column 1	60	70	80	90
1	male	2.40	3.60	4.80	5.00
2	male	4.30	4.50	5.00	4.25
3	female	5.30	6.00	2.60	5.10
4	female	4.50	2.70	6.00	4.00
5	male	4.70	1.50	4.70	3.65
6	female	2.30	4.00	2.15	4.00

If your experiment had additional between factors, there would be an additional nominal column for each factor up to 13 factors. The compact variable would remain unchanged. For more information on compact variables, see Chapter 3, Datasets.

Dialog box settings

When you create or edit the results of an ANOVA, you set the analysis parameters in this dialog box:

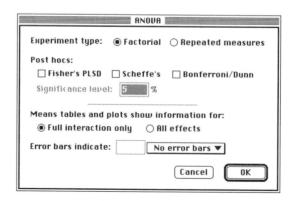

Experiment type

You must first choose the type of your ANOVA, either factorial or repeated measures. If you specify a repeated measures design, StatView automatically builds the correct ANOVA table for this type of model. Remember, if you select repeated measures, your dataset must contain a simple compact variable to identify the within factor. For more information on compact variables, see the preceding section, Data organization.

Post hoc tests

There are three post hoc tests to choose from, and a box in which to set the significance level used to interpret them. If your model is a repeated measures design, a table will be produced for each between factor in the model (the independent variables).

Means tables and interaction plots

The choices at the bottom of the dialog box control how many means tables and interaction plots are displayed (if you have selected these results from the analysis browser). If you choose "Full interaction only," StatView produces the means table and interaction plot for the full interaction effect only. If you choose "All effects," means tables and interaction plots appear for each effect in the model including the full interaction term. You can add error bars to your graphs with the pop-up menu at the bottom of the dialog box.

Once you choose the desired item from the pop-up menu, you enter a number in the text box, indicating the number of standard errors or standard deviations or the percent for the confidence interval.

Variables

Requirements

A factorial ANOVA requires one or more nominal variables (up to a maximum of 14) with one continuous variable. A repeated Measures ANOVA requires a single compact variable and zero or more nominal variables (up to a maximum of 13).

Variable browser buttons

Add   For factorial experiments, select one or more nominal grouping variables and one continuous variable and click the Add button. For repeated measures experiments, select zero or more nominal variables and a single compact variable and click Add.

Split By   When you assign one or more split-by variables to an ANOVA, results for each cell defined by the split-by variable(s) are displayed separately.

Additional variables

Add   Each additional nominal variable assigned is added to the analysis. Each additional continuous variable or compact variable assigned creates a new analysis using the previous nominal variable(s).

Results

For explanation of the results, please see the preceding discussion. The default output for this statistic is the ANOVA table.

ANOVA Table   Table containing the degrees of freedom, Sum of Squares, Mean Square, F-value and p-value for each effect in the ANOVA model.

Means Table   Table containing the count, mean, standard deviation, and standard error for each group or combination of groups in the nominal variable(s).

Interaction Bar Chart   Graph displaying the means of each group or combination of groups in the nominal variable(s) as bars. Error bars may be added using the dialog box.

Interaction Line Chart   Graph displaying the means of each group or combination of groups in the nominal variable(s) as points connected by lines. Error bars may be added using the dialog box.

Post Hoc Tables   Fisher's PLSD, Scheffé's F and Bonferroni/Dunn statistics can be created for any main effects. The tables show the mean difference, critical difference and p-value for the difference between all pairs of groups in the nominal variable(s). Cut-off levels for significance may be set in the dialog box.

Note that for interaction charts, StatView places groups of the first variable in the interaction (the first variable assigned to the model) in the legend. Cell plots, discussed in Chapter 22, offer additional control over creating interaction plots.

Templates

StatView offers many options for customizing all aspects of your statistical output, including which statistics are used and the appearance and location of tables and graphs. These customizations can be saved as templates and re-used.

Sample templates for both factorial and repeated measures ANOVA are included in the StatView Templates folder. You may wish to use these as is or create your own templates which contain the ANOVA statistics and graphs in the format that you commonly use. For more information on templates, see Chapter 7, Templates and Chapter 8, Building Analyses.

Exercises

Factorial experiment

In this exercise you perform a factorial ANOVA using data on weight and type for 116 cars from different countries. You will determine whether car weight is related to the type and country of origin of cars.

- Open Car Data in the Sample Data folder. The dataset appears on the screen. Scroll through the dataset to examine its contents.

- Choose New View from the Analyze menu. A blank view appears on the screen.

- In the analysis browser, click on the triangle next to ANOVA. The output appears in an indented list beneath the heading.

- Select ANOVA Table and click the Create Analysis button. The ANOVA dialog box appears for you to set parameters for the analysis.

- Because you are performing a factorial ANOVA, leave the setting Factorial and click OK. A table placeholder appears in the view until you assign variables.

- In the variable browser, select Type and click the Add button. It appears with a G usage markers indicating that it is a factor in the model. Select Country and click Add. It also appears with a G usage marker. Finally, select Weight and click Add. The analysis calculates and the ANOVA table appears in the view. Since Weight is the dependent variable in the analysis, a Y usage marker appears next to it.

ANOVA Table for Weight

	DF	Sum of Squares	Mean Square	F-Value	P-Value
Type	4	14307811.192	3576952.798	48.317	<.0001
Country	2	246287.238	123143.619	1.663	.1946
Type * Country	8	1404272.808	175534.101	2.371	.0221
Residual	101	7477200.453	74031.688		

From this ANOVA table, you can see that Type has a strong influence on the variable Weight, as indicated by the low p-value, <.0001. The interaction of Type and Country also seems to have a strong influence. The main effect of Country does not, however, as its much higher p-value shows. You will now examine the interaction of Type and Country more closely with an interaction plot.

- With the ANOVA table still selected, select Interaction Line Plot in the analysis browser and click the Create Analysis button. The plot appears in the view.

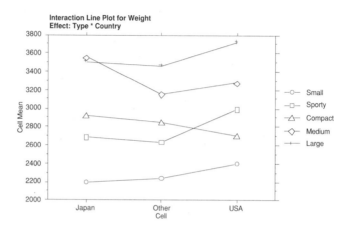

Because Type is the first variable in the interaction term, the different types appear in the legend. Notice that the lines for the different types of cars are spread out over the range of weights. This confirms that the type of car has a significant main effect. To understand the interaction between type and country, concentrate on the places in the graph where the lines are not parallel. For example, sporty cars made in the USA are heavier than other sporty cars, but USA compact cars are lighter than other compact cars. You might also like to produce an interaction chart which uses side-by-side bars to show this information. You are now finished with this exercise. You may save the view to any folder and open it with the same dataset to perform any further analyses you wish.

Repeated measures experiment

In this exercise, you perform a repeated measures ANOVA using data from a study involving industrial health. You will test the effectiveness of several teaching techniques for the use of a respirator mask. Subjects are divided randomly into three groups: a control group, which received no training in the use of the mask; a group which received a detailed instruction sheet on the use of the mask; and a third group which attended a 30 minute class discussing the use of the mask. The effectiveness of the mask, as measured by the amount of particulate matter that passed through the mask during a fixed task, was measured for each of the subjects before training, and then one and two weeks after training. (Lower scores mean increased effectiveness.)

You will find out if, averaged over time, there is any difference in effectiveness among the three teaching techniques. There are two hypotheses that concern the within-subjects factor (time): whether (averaged over treatments) the test scores change over time, and whether the pattern of change over time is the same for the different teaching techniques.

- Open the Teaching Effectiveness dataset in the Sample Data folder. The dataset appears on the screen. Scroll through the dataset to examine its contents.

The first column of the dataset contains the group labels for teaching technique—Control, Instructions and Lecture—in a category variable. The three remaining variables represent the measure of effectiveness for the mask at 0, 1 and 2 weeks. These have been made into a compact variable to analyze the repeated measures design (see Chapter 3, Datasets, for a discussion of compact variables). All repeated measures designs require the use of a compact variable.

By defining the three measurements over time as a compact variable and specifying a repeated measures analysis, you include the repeated measure (time) in the model. Since the three teaching techniques represent three different treatments, teaching technique is added as a factor. This automatically includes the time-by-teaching technique interaction in the model. Thus, by specifying the repeated measure as a compact variable and adding a between-subject factor (teaching technique) to the model, StatView includes the other terms necessary for the analysis.

- Choose New View from the Analyze menu. A blank view appears on the screen.

- In the analysis browser, click on the triangle next to ANOVA. The output appears in an indented list beneath the heading.

- Select ANOVA Table and click the Create Analysis button. The ANOVA dialog box appears for you to set parameters for the analysis.

- Next to Experiment Type, select Repeated Measures and click OK. A table placeholder appears in the view until you assign variables.

- In the variable browser, select Teaching and Effectiveness and click the Add button. (Note that the compact variable, Effectiveness is indicated by a triangle appearing next to the the variable name.) They appear highlighted with usage markers next to them indicating that Teaching is used as a grouping variable (G) and Effectiveness as the dependent variable (Y). The analysis calculates and this ANOVA table appears in the view.

ANOVA Table for Effectiveness

	DF	Sum of Squares	Mean Square	F-Value	P-Value
Teaching	2	26.751	13.376	2.154	.1370
Subject(Group)	25	155.225	6.209		
Time	2	18.926	9.463	8.783	.0005
Time * Teaching	4	18.171	4.543	4.216	.0051
Time * Subject(Group)	50	53.869	1.077		

Chapter 18: Analysis of Variance (ANOVA)

The between-group main effect for teaching technique is not significant. This means that averaged over the three times, there was no difference in the effectiveness of the three teaching methods as measured by the effectiveness scores. This test may be misleading, however, since it includes the initial (time 0) scores which you would expect to be the same for all the groups since they were taken before training began.

In many repeated measures experiments, the between-group main effect and interaction tests have this limitation, and are therefore not the main focus of the analysis. Keep in mind, however, that including these effects still reduces the estimate of residual error, making the tests more powerful, as well as providing an opportunity to study the between-subjects by within-subjects interactions, which are usually of great interest.

You can see that time after training had a very significant effect, not surprisingly. As the subjects became more familiar with the respirator masks, it is reasonable that they learned to use them more effectively. Of special interest is the significant teaching technique-by-time interaction, indicating that the patterns of changes in effectiveness of the masks over time differ depending on the teaching technique.

You will now use an interaction plot to display how the value of the dependent variable for the within factor varies for each level of the between factors.

• With the ANOVA table selected, choose Interaction Bar Plot in the analysis browser and click the Create Analysis button. This plot appears in the view.

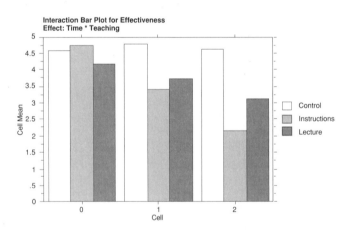

From the graph above, you see that the teaching technique-by-time interaction arose from the fact that the control group saw a very small change in effectiveness scores over time, while the two experimental groups saw considerable improvements, with the instruction group seeming to show greater reductions than the group which received the lectures. You are now finished with this exercise. You may save the view to any folder and open it with the same dataset to perform any further analyses you wish. You may want to learn more about other graphs in Chapter 22, Plots.

19

Contingency Tables

Contingency table analyses determine whether a relationship exists between two nominal variables. Other statistics (t-tests, regressions, means, correlation tests) apply to dependent variables that are continuous, that is, they are capable of taking on many different values with an obvious ordering to them like height, weight, income, chemical concentration, sales, etc. Tests applied to continuous variables lose their validity with nominal variables that do not have an ordered, continuous property. (See Chapter 3 for a discussion of nominal and continuous variable classes.)

Height is a continuous variable because an underlying meaning to the ordering of values applies to it-—sixty inches is clearly bigger than fifty inches—and this relationship holds through the range of the scale. But hair color and eye color, for example, cannot constitute continuous variables, for there is no natural ordering to brunette, blonde, red and black; nor to blue, gray, brown and green.

Thus, even if we recode a variable representing hair color as brunette = 1, black = 2, red= 3 and so forth, any tests performed on the transformed variable would be pointless. (It is possible for a nominal variable to be ordered, but StatView provides no special tests for this case.) For example, it is meaningless to say that brunette is only one third of red. In addition, if we study the relationship of hair color and eye color, we cannot calculate a mean for hair color because there is no numerical quantity we can assign to a particular hair color that helps describe it.

Discussion

When you collect data, it may be wise to think in terms of a two-way tabular arrangement in which you categorize each observation into one group for each of two nominal (grouping) variables. Such an arrangement is called a contingency table. The intersection of a row and column in the table is called a cell. If you study the cross-classification of eye color and hair color, for example, each cell would contain a count of observations for each possible combination of hair and eye color groups: blue eyes/brown hair, brown eyes/brown hair, blue eyes/blonde hair, brown eyes/blonde hair and so forth. It could look something like this:

	Brown hair	Blonde hair	Black hair	Red hair
Brown eyes	21	10	7	2
Blue eyes	9	17	2	3
Green eyes	1	3	1	3

Chi-square test

It may be of interest to study this contingency table to see which combinations of groups have more or less observations than would be expected if the two variables were independent. For this you can apply the chi-square test for independence. The hypothesis of independence states that the likelihood of an observation falling into one group for one variable is independent of the other group the observation falls into. To calculate this test, StatView finds the expected value for the number of observations for every combination of groups based on the hypothesis of independence and compares the expected with the observed values in each cell.

(The chi-square test is not valid when the minimum expected value is less than five. You may have cells in your contingency tables with observed values less than five without causing any problems. The key issue is whether or not the expected values are greater than five. You can print a table of expected values for your contingency table.)

A low chi-square value and high probability (p-value) would suggest accepting the null hypothesis. If the hypothesis of independence were not rejected for the example given, the chi-square test would indicate that people with blonde hair are no more likely to have blue eyes than any other color eyes, and that people with brown eyes are no more likely to have brown hair than any other color hair. If rejected—a large chi-square value and correspondingly low probability—the test would show that a relationship between certain variable groups exists. You would then study the contingency table to see which combinations of groups have more or fewer observations than would be expected if the two variables were independent. You can do this by comparing the contingency table (observed frequencies) to the expected values table, or by examining a tale of post hoc cell contributions to the overall chi-square statistic.

Tables produced

In addition to the contingency table itself, StatView offers a variety of displays with the groups of one variable in the cross classification displayed in the rows of a table and the groups of the other displayed in the columns of the table. One set of tables displays the percents of row or column totals. In a table displaying the Percents of Row Totals, for example, column percentages represent the proportion of data in the first variable that falls into each group of the second variable. Under the hypothesis of independence, the column percentages within each group of the first variable (each row of the table) should be the same. You can compare the values in a given row with the totals displayed at the bottom of the table and determine which cells are out of line. The cells that stand out indicate a larger or smaller proportion falling in a particular combination of groups than would be expected under the hypothesis of independence. A similar analysis holds for the Percents of Column Totals table, except that you compare the values in the rows with the totals on the right hand side of the table.

Post hoc cell contributions

An alternative to studying percents is to study the table of post hoc cell contributions. These numbers are a form of standardized residual that indicate what each cell in the table contributes to the chi-square statistic. Since they are calculated to follow a standard normal distribution, absolute values greater than, for example, 1.96 for a 0.05 probability level indicate that the cell in question provides significant information about the combinations of groups of the variables whose occurrence is different than would be expected under the hypothesis of independence. An example of the use of post hoc cell contributions is given at the end of this chapter.

Cell chi-squares

The chi-square statistic reported in the summary table is the sum of the values in the cell chi-squares table. By examining this table, you can tell which cells have observed frequencies that differ most from what is expected under the hypothesis of independence. This is the same information obtained from the post hoc cell contributions, except that the cell chi-squares are compared to the total chi-square whereas post hoc cell contributions are compared to the normal distribution.

Additional statistics: G-statistic and Cramer's V

An alternative statistic for testing the hypothesis of independence between two categorical variables is the G-statistic. The G-statistic is derived using a statistical principle known as the likelihood ratio principle.

Another statistic, the contingency coefficient, is offered by analogy to the correlation coefficient, which is used to test the association between two continuous variables. An attractive feature of the correlation coefficient is that it is always in the range of -1 to 1, so that several different relationships can be compared on an equivalent scale. The contingency coefficient is a transformation of the chi-square statistic so that the contingency coefficient is in the range of 0 and 1. Thus it can be useful for comparing associations between different pairs of variables. Closely related to the contingency coefficient, and testing the same hypothesis of no association between variables, is Cramer's V (pronounced kruh-merz´). High values of these statistics indicate that there is dependence between the variables. The range of V is from -1 to 1, so its interpretation is more in line with that of a correlation coefficient.

2 x 2 contingency tables: Fisher's exact test, Phi coefficient

Other statistics are available in the summary table for the special case of 2 x 2 tables (in which both variables studied have exactly two groups). Fisher's exact test is calculated by enumerating all possible rearrangements of the observations and comparing the number of unusual rearrangements to the observed counts under the assumption of no association between the two variables. The probability levels reported for this test are exact, not large sample approximations like the G-statistic and chi-square described earlier. The continuity correction for a 2x2 table, and its associated p-value is an alternative technique which is used to make the probability level of the 2x2 test for independence closer to the exact probability level. The phi coefficient is similar to the contingency coefficient in that it is bounded in the range from -1 to 1. It's interpretation is similar to that of the correlation coefficient and may be especially useful if the categories for each of the variables have a natural ordering.

Data organization

StatView offers three different data organization options as input to the contingency table analysis. The discussion below describes how you would enter the data using these options for the following experimental situation. If you use the contingency table analysis to determine whether a relationship exists between eye color and gender for eight athletes, the data could be entered as follows.

Coded raw data

In this situation, the dataset would contain two nominal columns: one indicating the eye color and the other the gender for each athlete. The dataset would contain eight rows, one for each athlete. A dataset organized in this manner would appear as:

	Eye Color	Gender
1	Brown	Male
2	Blue	Male
3	Blue	Female
4	Green	Male
5	Brown	Female
6	Blue	Male
7	Green	Female
8	Brown	Male

The nominal variables appear as separate columns in the dataset. Each row identifies the eye color group and the gender group for an athlete.

Coded summary data

In this situation, the dataset would contain two nominal grouping variables in columns and an additional column with the count in each combination of groups (cell). A dataset organized in this manner would appear as:

	Eye Color	Gender	Count
1	Blue	Female	1
2	Blue	Male	2
3	Brown	Female	1
4	Brown	Male	2
5	Green	Female	1
6	Green	Male	1

The dataset contains six rows, one for each possible combination of eye color and gender: blue eyes/female, blue eyes/male, brown eyes/female, and so on. Each combination is made up of entries in the nominal Eye Color and Gender columns. The count for each combination appears in the count column.

You are not required to have as many rows as there are combinations. If duplicate combinations appear in your data, StatView will sum the counts for that combination. Also, if a fractional value appears in a count column, the value will be rounded to the nearest integer.

Two way table

In this situation, you enter a contingency table of observed values directly into a dataset as input for the analysis. Each column is a column of the contingency table and each row a row of the table. The observed frequencies are entered as individual observations. There will be as many columns as groups in one nominal variable and as many rows as groups in the second nominal variable. A dataset organized in this manner would appear as:

	Column 1	Column 2
1	2	1
2	2	1
3	1	1

The two columns represent the two gender groups: male and female. The three rows the three eye color groups: blue, brown and green. The values in each cell are the counts for the particular combination.

Dialog box settings

When you create or edit a contingency table, you set the analysis parameters in this dialog box:

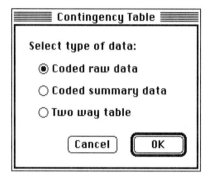

You use this dialog box to specify how your data is organized for the contingency table analysis. Please see the preceding section, Data organization, for more information and for examples of these types of data.

Variables

Requirements

Variable requirements differ depending on the type of data being analyzed. See preceding discussion for more information on data organization. Coded raw data requires two nominal variables. Coded summary data requires two nominal variables and one continuous variable. A two way table requires two or more continuous variables. (See the discussion of two way tables in the Data organization section earlier in this chapter). In the cases where continuous variables are required, those variables represent counts based on the levels of the nominal variables in your analysis.

Variable browser buttons

Add   For coded raw data, select two nominal variables and click Add. For coded summary data, select two nominal variables and one continuous variable and click Add. For a two way table, select two or more continuous variables, and click Add.

Split By   When you assign one or more split-by variables to a contingency table result, results for each cell in the split-by variable(s) are displayed in separate tables.

Additional variables

Add   For raw data, each additional nominal variable assigned creates a new analysis. For coded summary data, each additional nominal or continuous variable assigned creates a new analysis. For a two-way table, each additional variable you assign is added to the existing analysis.

Results

For explanation of the results, please see the preceding discussion. The Summary and Observed Frequencies tables are the default output for this analysis.

Summary Table   Table containing the degrees of freedom, the chi-square statistic and associated p-value, the G-squared statistic and its associated p-value, the contingency coefficient, and Cramer's V for the analysis. If 2x2 data is used, the Fisher's exact test, the continuity correction with its associated p-value are displayed, and the phi coefficient is displayed instead of Cramer's V.

Observed Frequencies   Table containing the number of observations in each cell (combination of groups) of the dataset with totals for each group in the grouping variables.

Percents of Row/Column Totals   Table containing the percentage of the observations in each group of one grouping variable that fall into each group of the second grouping variable.

Percents of Overall Total   Table containing the percent of total observations in the dataset that falls in each cell (combination of groups).

Expected Values   Table containing the expected values for the number of observations in each cell (combination of groups) if the variables were independent.

Post Hoc Cell
Contributions

Table containing the post hoc cell contributions for each cell (combination of groups).

Cell Chi
Squares

Table containing the chi-squares statistic for each cell (combination of groups).

Templates

StatView offers many options for customizing all aspects of your statistical output, including which statistics are used and the appearance and location of tables and graphs. These customizations can be saved as templates and re-used.

A sample template for contingency table analysis is included in the StatView Templates folder. You may wish to use this template as is or create your own templates customized for the contingency table data organization and results that you commonly use. For more information on templates, see chapters 7 and 8, Templates and Building Analyses.

Exercise

In this exercise you will perform a contingency table analysis of coded raw data. The dataset contains information on weight, gas tank size, turning circle, horsepower and engine displacement for 116 cars from different countries. You will determine whether some countries tend to produce larger or smaller cars than other countries.

- Open the Car Data in the Sample Data folder. The dataset appears on the screen. Scroll through the dataset to examine its contents.

- Choose New View from the Analyze menu. A blank view appears on the screen.

- In the analysis browser, click on the triangle next to Contingency Table. The results appear listed beneath it.

- Select Summary Table and Observed Frequencies and click the Create Analysis button. The Contingency Table dialog box appears for you to specify the format of your data.

- You are using raw data, so leave the default setting Coded raw data and click OK. Table placeholders appear in the view until you assign variables.

- In the variable browser, select Type and click the Add button. Next, click Country and click Add. (Note that the groups of the first variable added will appear as rows of the contingency table; the groups of the second variable will appear as the columns). The variables appear highlighted with G usage markers indicating grouping variables assigned to the analysis. The analysis calculates and tables appear in the view.

Summary Table for Type, Country

Num. Missing	0
DF	8
Chi Square	25.814
Chi Square P-Value	.0011
G-Squared	27.861
G-Squared P-Value	.0005
Contingency Coef.	.427
Cramer's V	.334

Observed Frequencies for Type, Country

	Japan	Other	USA	Totals
Small	7	12	3	22
Sporty	10	4	11	25
Compact	3	12	7	22
Medium	6	8	16	30
Large	4	1	12	17
Totals	30	37	49	116

From the high chi-square and low p-values in the summary table, there seems to be a relationship between country and car size. You will now determine which cells are contributing to the large chi-square values by examining post-hoc cell contributions.

- In the analysis browser, select Post Hoc Cell Contributions and click the Create Analysis button. This table appears in the view.

Post Hoc Cell Contributions for Type, Country

	Japan	Other	USA
Small	.709	2.532	-3.017
Sporty	1.823	-1.925	.201
Compact	-1.455	2.532	-1.100
Medium	-.852	-.714	1.428
Large	-.238	-2.491	2.561

You did not have to assign variables to the Post Hoc Cell Contributions table. The variables analyzed in the tables preceding it were used because those tables were selected when you created Post Hoc Cell Contributions.

Relative to what is expected if the distribution of car sizes were the same for each country, the Other group has more small cars than Japan, and more still than the USA. The USA, however, has many more cars categorized in the Large group. You may want to examine the table of expected values to verify that the discrepancies arise from the cells with large post hoc cell contributions.

Chapter

20

Nonparametrics

Nonparametric statistics test hypotheses about data for which the underlying distribution of the data is not assumed. Rather than estimate the parameters of a hypothesized distribution, then perform a computation on these estimates (parametric statistics), nonparametrics employ alternatives such as sequentially ranking observations from all groups or variables of interest or comparing two groups observation by observation to test hypotheses.

Discussion

Most of the hypothesis tests presented in other chapters require the data being studied to fulfill certain assumptions, usually regarding the nature of the underlying distribution from which the data arises. In order for the probability levels presented by a t-test to be valid, for example, the data being studied must come from a normal distribution. These assumptions are so important that many statisticians feel that a significant probability value associated with a test statistic needs to be interpreted as either evidence that the null hypothesis is false or evidence that the assumptions of the test have been violated.

Occasionally the assumptions required for a parametric test are not met because of the nature of the data. If you are measuring the amount of time it takes people to do a simple task, you might know that most responses will be around zero, with fewer and fewer responses corresponding to increasing time. This would not result in a normal distribution of data since normal distribution must be symmetric, with equal amounts of data on either side of the mean. In other cases, your examination of the data (or residuals from regression or analysis of variance) might indicate that the assumptions of the analysis are not being met. Under such circumstances, performing one of the nonparametric tests described in this chapter can be appropriate.

One sample sign test

The one sample sign test is the nonparametric equivalent of the one sample t-test. It tests whether the values of a variable are centered around a specified value. That is, it tests the hypothesis that the median of a distribution is equal to some hypothesized value by comparing the number of observations above and below that value.

Mann-Whitney U-test

The Mann-Whitney U test is useful in the same cases as an unpaired t-test. It is the nonparametric version of the two group unpaired t-test. Recall that a t-test tests the hypothesis that the means of the two groups are equal, assuming normality of the observations. The Mann-Whitney U tests the hypothesis that the distributions underlying the two groups are the same. The requirements for validity of the Mann-Whitney test are that the two groups of observations come from continuous distributions and are independent of each other, both within and between groups. Since the Mann-Whitney test does not look at the observations but instead considers their ranks, it is resistant to outliers in either of the groups being compared.

Kolmogorov-Smirnov test

The Kolmogorov-Smirnov test tests whether the distribution of a continuous variable is the same for two groups. That is, it tests the null hypothesis that two distributions are the same under the assumption that the observations from the two distribution are independent of each other. It is calculated by comparing the two distributions at a number of points and then considering the maximum difference between the two distributions. (The actual data points are not compared, but a function of the points is calculated and compared.) Since this test relies on the maximum value in a set of numbers, it may be heavily influenced by outliers and should be used with caution if outliers are suspected.

Wald-Wolfowitz runs test

The Wald-Wolfowitz runs test tests whether the distribution of a continuous variable is the same for two groups. This test compares two groups assumed to be independent of each other by combining the data for both groups, ranking the data and counting the number of runs present in the ranked data. A run is a sequence of consecutive observations in the ranked data coming from one or the other of the groups. (Only the number of runs is important, not their lengths.) If the two samples come from different distributions, we would expect many groups of small runs, while if observations from one group tend to be larger than those from the other group, we would see only a few runs in the data. Since the test is based on ranks, it is resistant to outliers.

The Wald-Wolfowitz test looks at the data across the entire range, whereas the Kolmogorov-Smirnov test looks at the maximum difference between the distributions. If there are only one or two outliers, the Kolmogorov-Smirnov may mistakenly state that the two distributions are different.

Wilcoxon signed rank test

The Wilcoxon signed rank test is appropriate in the same cases that a paired t-test would be used; it is the nonparametric version of the paired t-test (see the Paired Comparisons chapter). It is based on the rank of the differences between each pair of observations in the dataset, and tests the hypothesis that sum of the ranks is equal to zero under the assumption that the distribution of ranks is symmetric about 0.

Paired sign test

The paired sign test, or two sample sign test, is useful in the same situations that a paired t-test is used. It is another nonparametric version of the paired t-test. It tests the hypothesis that one of the paired variables is just as likely to be greater than the other variable as it is to be less than the other variable, without regard for the magnitude of the difference. Thus, it makes very few assumptions about the underlying distributions from which the data arise. If you feel that the differences between the two paired variables you are studying will be symmetric around some value, the Wilcoxon signed rank test is more powerful.

Spearman rank correlation coefficient

The Spearman rank correlation coefficient, sometimes referred to as Spearman's rho, is an alternative to the usual correlation coefficient. Since it is based on the ranks of the data and not the data itself, it is resistant to outliers. It calculates a correlation coefficient based on the ranks of the values of two variables. The null hypothesis tested by Spearman's rho is that the two variables are independent of each other, against an alternative hypothesis that the rank of a variable is correlated with the rank of another variable. Spearman's rho ranges in value from -1 (indicating high ranks of one variable occur with low ranks of the other variable) through 0 (indicating no correlation between the variables) to +1 (indicating high ranks of one variable occur with high ranks of the other variable).

Kendall's tau

Kendall's tau is an alternative to Spearman's rho and is useful in the same situations as Spearman's rho. In general, the interpretation of these two statistics results in similar conclusions about the data. Kendall's tau also ranges from -1 through 0 to +1.

Kruskal-Wallis test

The Kruskal-Wallis test is a nonparametric equivalent of a one-way analysis of variance by ranks, i.e., it tests the hypothesis that two or more groups all come from the same distribution against the alternative that at least one of the groups comes from a different distribution. It is basically calculated as a regular ANOVA, but it uses the ranks of the data and is resistant to outliers. Along with the test statistic, StatView displays a table including the mean rank for each of the groups to aid you in determining which group tends to have larger values than the others.

Friedman test

The Friedman test is a two-way analysis of variance by ranks for matched samples. It is a special case of a nonparametric two-way ANOVA in which, for each of several groups (usually called blocks), there are a number of observations, each representing the response for that group to a particular treatment. It tests the hypothesis that the effects of the treatments are the same against the hypothesis that at least one of the treatments has an effect different from the others. Like most of the other nonparametric tests, it is based on ranks and is therefore resistant to outliers.

Data organization

The nonparametric statistics are divided into five groups. Each group requires a different data organization as described below. For an introduction to dataset organization, see Chapter 3, Datasets.

One sample sign test

The one sample sign test analyzes a single sample (variable). All the observations for the sample must appear in a single column of the dataset.

Mann-Whitney, Kolmogorov-Smirnov, Wald-Wolfowitz tests

Each of these tests compares two unpaired groups. In order to compare two groups your data must be organized in a way that allows these tests to identify which group an observation belongs to. Data for these tests must be organized in the same manner as for the unpaired comparisons analysis.

Please see the Data organization section in Chapter 15, Unpaired Comparisons, for a complete discussion of the required data organization. In addition, there are exercises at the end of this chapter for both the Mann-Whitney U and Kolmogorov-Smirnov tests.

Wilcoxon, Paired Sign, Spearman, Kendall tests

Each of these tests compares two paired samples. The data for each sample of the paired comparison must be located in a single continuous variable (column). Each row entry for the two columns being analyzed must be a measure for the same subject or for observations that are naturally paired. There are exercises at the end of this chapter for both the Wilcoxon Signed Rank and Kendall Correlation tests.

Kruskal-Wallis test

The Kruskal-Wallis test is the nonparametric equivalent of a one-way analysis of variance by ranks. Data for this test must be organized in the same manner as for factorial analysis of variance experiments.

Please see the Data organization section in Chapter 18 for a complete discussion of the required data organization. In addition, there is an example at the end of this chapter for the Kruskal-Wallis test.

Friedman test

The Friedman test determines whether three or more matched samples are from the same population. The dataset must be entered so that each column contains information on a single sample (or treatment). Each row contains the response of a particular group for the treatment. The dataset will contains as many columns as there are different samples (or treatments) and as many rows as there are responses for the treatment. There is an example at the end of this chapter for the Friedman test.

Dialog box settings

When you create or edit nonparametric results, you set the analysis parameters in this dialog box:

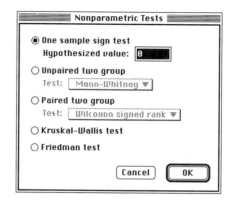

There are ten nonparametric tests to choose from in this dialog box. There are no further parameters for any of these tests except the One Sample Sign Test, for which you specify the hypothesized value around which you believe the values are centered. The pop-up menus of paired and unpaired two groups tests display:

Use these pop-ups to select the desired test. If you are editing nonparametric results by selecting a result and clicking Edit Analysis, you will not always be able to switch from one particular test to another. For example, you will not be able to switch to an unpaired two group test from a paired two group test if you have specified variables which the unpaired test cannot use (i.e., a second continuous variable).

Variables

Requirements

Nonparametric test	Requirements	Additional variables
One Sample Sign	one continuous variable	Each additional variable you assign creates a new analysis.
Mann-Whitney U, Kolmogorov-Smirnov, Wald-Wolfowitz Runs	one nominal variable with two levels only and one continuous variable	Each additional nominal and/or continuous variable you assign creates a new analysis for each nominal/continuous pair.

Wilcoxon Signed Rank, Paired Sign, Spearman Rank Correlation, Kendall Rank Correlation	two continuous variables	Each additional continuous variable you assign creates a new analysis for each pair.[*]
Kruskal-Wallis	one nominal variable with more than two levels and one continuous variable	Each additional nominal and/or continuous variable you assign creates a new analysis for each nominal/continuous pair.
Friedman	three or more continuous variables	Each additional variable you assign is added to the existing analysis.

Variable browser buttons

Add — To generate nonparametric statistics, select the variable(s) that you wish to analyze and click Add.

Split By — When you assign one or more split-by variable to a nonparametric analysis, results for each cell in the split-by variable(s) are displayed in separate tables or plots.

Results

For explanation of the results, please see the preceding discussion.

One Sample Sign

One Sample sign test — Table containing the number of observation above, below and equal to the hypothesized value, the p-value for the analysis.

Mann-Whitney U

Mann-Whitney U test — Table containing the U and U prime statistics, tied and untied Z-values and p-values, and the number of ties.

---

[*] Variables 1 and 2 are taken by analysis 1. Variable 3 clones analysis 1 to become analysis 2, which takes only Variable 3. Variable 4 is taken by analysis 2. Variable 5 clones analysis 2 to become analysis 3, which takes only Variable 5, and so on.

Chapter 20: Nonparametrics

Rank Info.   Table containing the count, sum and mean of the rankings for each group in the analysis.

Kolmogrov-Smirnov

Kolmogrov-Smirnov Test   Table containing the degrees of freedom, the number of observations in each group, the maximum difference between groups, and the Chi-square statistic and p-value for the analysis.

Wald-Wolfowitz

Wald-Wolfowitz Runs Test   Table containing the number of runs in the combined groups, the number of observations in each group, the mean and standard deviation used in the Z-value, and the Z-value and the p-value for the difference between groups.

Wilcoxon Signed Rank

Wilcoxon Signed Rank Test   Table containing the number of 0 differences between pairs, and tied and untied Z-values and p-values, and the number of ties.

Rank Info.   Table containing the count, sum and mean of the rankings for each group in the analysis.

Paired Sign

Paired Sign Test   Table containing the number of differences above, below and equal to 0 and the p-value for the analysis.

Spearman Rank Correlation

Spearman Rank Correlation   Table containing the sum of squared differences and the Rho (with and without correction for ties) for the groups, the tied and untied Z-values and p-values, and the number of ties in each group.

Kendall Rank Correlation

Kendall Rank Correlation   Table containing the sum of squared differences and the tau (with and without correction for ties) for the groups, the tied and untied Z-values and p-values, and the number of ties in each group.

Kruskal-Wallis

Kruskal-Wallis Test   Table containing the degrees of freedom, number of groups and ties, and the H and p-values, with and without correction for ties.

Rank Info.   Table containing the count, sum and mean of the rankings for each group in the analysis.

Friedman

Friedman Test   Table containing the degrees of freedom, number of groups and ties, and the chi-square and p-value, with and without correction for ties.

Rank Info.   Table containing the count, sum and mean of the rankings for each group in the analysis.

Note that some of the tests above show a correction for ties. Ties occur when two observations have the same value. Nonparametric tests assume that no two values are the same. In some tests, StatView is able to make a correction for the presence of ties; where it cannot, a warning message is produced if ties are present.

Templates

StatView offers many options for customizing all aspects of your statistical output, including which statistics are used and the appearance and location of tables and graphs. These customizations can be saved as templates and re-used.

A sample template for each nonparametric test is included in the StatView Templates folder. You may wish to use these templates as is or create your own templates containing the nonparametric tests that you commonly use. For more information on templates, see Chapters 7 and 8, Templates and Building Analyses.

Exercises

One sample sign test

In this exercise you will perform a one sample sign test using data from blood lipid screenings of medical students. You are concerned with one variable here: Cholesterol. You will find out if the cholesterol level of the students is significantly greater than 190, a point above which cholesterol levels may be unhealthy. You will test the null hypothesis that the value for cholesterol is 190. If you reject the null hypothesis, you can conclude that student cholesterol levels differ significantly from 190.

- Open Lipid Data in the Sample Data folder. The dataset appears on the screen. Scroll through and examine its contents.

- Select New View from the Analyze menu. A blank view appears on the screen.

- In the analysis browser, select Nonparametrics and click the Create Analysis button. The Nonparametric Tests dialog box appears.

- The test you want to perform, a one sample sign test, is the default. Enter "190" as hypothesized value and click OK. A table placeholder appears in the view until you assign a variable.

- In the variable browser, select Cholesterol and click the Add button. The variable name appears highlighted with an X usage marker next to it indicating you have assigned a continuous variable to the analysis. The analysis calculates and this table appears in the view.

One-Sample Sign Test for Cholesterol
Hypothesized Value: 190

# Obs. > Hyp. Value	48
# Obs. < Hyp. Value	43
# Obs. = Hyp. Value	4
P-Value	.6752

From these results, you see that you cannot reject the null hypothesis. The p-value is large, and there are roughly the same number of observations above and below the hypothesized value of 190, meaning that there are not enough students with elevated cholesterol levels to reject the null hypothesis.

Mann-Whitney U test

In this exercise you perform a Mann-Whitney U test using census data for 506 housing tracts in the Boston area. You will examine two groups of housing tracts, those near the Charles River and those farther away from it. You will find out whether median housing prices vary depending on how far houses are located from the river. This is the nonparametric equivalent of the unpaired t-test exercise in the Unpaired Comparisons chapter. You may wish to compare results between the two tests.

- Open Boston Housing Data in the Sample Data folder. The dataset appears on the screen. Scroll through the dataset to examine its contents.

- Choose New View from the Analyze menu. A blank view appears on the screen.

- In the analysis browser, select Nonparametrics and click the Create Analysis button. The Nonparametric Tests dialog box appears.

- Click the button next to "Unpaired two group" and leave Mann-Whitney U selected in the pop-up menu. Click OK. Two placeholders appear in the view until you assign variables.

- In the variable browser, select Median Value and click the Add button. The variable appears highlighted and an X usage marker appears next to it indicating you have assigned a continuous variable to the analysis.

- In the variable browser, select Charles and click the Add button. It appears highlighted with a G usage marker next to it indicating you assigned a grouping variable to the analysis. The analysis calculates and a table appears in the view.

Mann-Whitney U for Median Value
Grouping Variable: Charles

U	5605.500
U Prime	10879.500
Z-Value	-3.160
P-Value	.0016
Tied Z-Value	-3.160
Tied P-Value	.0016
# Ties	129

Mann-Whitney Rank Info for Median Value
Grouping Variable: Charles

	Count	Sum Ranks	Mean Rank
Near	35	11509.500	328.843
Far	471	116761.500	247.901

These results indicate a difference in price between houses near and far from the Charles River. The mean rank for housing near the river is much higher than that for housing far from it. Though the unpaired t-test performed in the Unpaired Comparisons chapter produced the same conclusion, it could have been fooled had there been significant outliers. The unpaired t-test, since it compares means, can be dramatically influenced by a few outliers. A nonparametric test, however, deals only with the rankings of the observations and cannot be affected by outliers.

Wilcoxon signed rank test

In this exercise you perform a Wilcoxon Signed Rank test using data from blood lipid screenings of medical students. You will determine whether initial triglyceride levels are different from those measured in the same subjects after three years. (This is the nonparametric equivalent of the paired t-test exercise in the Paired Comparisons chapter. You may wish to compare results between the two tests.)

- Open Lipid Data in the Sample Data folder. The dataset appears on the screen. Scroll through the dataset to examine its contents.

- Choose New View from the Analyze menu. A blank view appears on the screen.

- In the analysis browser, select Nonparametrics and click the Create Analysis button. The Nonparametric Tests dialog box appears.

- Click the button next to "Paired two group" and leave Wilcoxon Signed Rank selected in the pop-up menu (this is the default paired two group test). Click OK. Two table placeholders appear in the view until you assign variables.

- In the variable browser, select Triglycerides and Trig-3 yrs using the Command (⌘) key and click the Add button. The variables appear highlighted with X usage markers next to them indicating you have assigned continuous variables to the analysis. The analysis calculates and these tables appear in the view.

Wilcoxon Signed Rank Test for Triglycerides, Trig-3yrs

# 0 Differences	1
# Ties	7
Z-Value	-.013
P-Value	.9900
Tied Z-Value	-.013
Tied P-Value	.9900

52 cases were omitted due to missing values.

Wilcoxon Rank Info for Triglycerides, Trig-3yrs

	Count	Sum Ranks	Mean Rank
# Ranks < 0	22	450.500	20.477
# Ranks > 0	20	452.500	22.625

52 cases were omitted due to missing values.

From these results you can tell that there is no significant difference in triglyceride levels between the initial measurements and those made three years later because the p-values are very large and the mean ranks are quite close in value.

Kendall rank correlation

In this exercise you perform a Kendall rank correlation. The dataset consists of different western cities rated by nine criteria. You will discover whether there is a relationship between two of the variables, Climate&Terrain and Housing. For Climate&Terrain, the higher the score, the better. For Housing, the lower the score the better. The origin of the data and the components of the variables are described in Appendix C.

- Open the Western States Rated dataset in the Sample Data folder. The dataset appears on the screen. Scroll through the dataset to examine its contents.

- Choose New View from the Analyze menu. A blank view appears on the screen.

- In the analysis browser, select Nonparametrics and click the Create Analysis button. The Nonparametric Tests dialog box appears.

- Click the button next to "Paired two group" and select Kendall rank correlation from the pop-up menu. Click OK.

- In the variable browser, select Climate&Terrain and Housing and click the Add button. They appear highlighted with X usage markers next to them. The analysis calculates and this table appears in the view.

Kendall Rank Correlation for Climate&Terrain, Housing

Score	494.000
Tau	.373
Z-Value	3.898
P-Value	<.0001
Tau corrected for ties	.374
Tied Z-Value	3.913
Tied P-Value	<.0001
# Ties, Climate&Terrain	8
# Ties, Housing	0

The low Tau in these results shows a low correlation between Climate&Terrain and Housing.

Kruskal-Wallis test

In this exercise you perform a Kruskal-Wallis test using data on weight, gas tank size, turning circle, horsepower and engine displacement for 116 cars from different countries. You will determine whether some countries tend to produce larger or smaller cars than other countries.

- Open Car Data in the Sample Data folder. The dataset appears on the screen. Scroll through the dataset to examine its contents.

- Choose New View from the Analyze menu. A blank view appears on the screen.

- In the analysis browser, select Nonparametrics and click the Create Analysis button. The Nonparametric Tests dialog box appears.

- Select Kruskal-Wallis test and click OK. Two table placeholders appear in the view.

- In the variable browser, select Weight, hold down the Command (⌘) key and select Country, and then click the Add button. The X usage marker next to Weight indicates a continuous variable assigned to the analysis; the G usage marker next to Country indicates a nominal grouping variable assigned to the analysis. The analysis calculates and these two tables appear in the view.

Kruskal-Wallis Test for Weight
Grouping Variable: Country

DF	2
# Groups	3
# Ties	15
H	16.054
P-Value	.0003
H corrected for ties	16.056
Tied P-Value	.0003

Kruskal-Wallis Rank Info for Weight
Grouping Variable: Country

	Count	Sum Ranks	Mean Rank
Japan	30	1633.500	54.450
Other	37	1609.500	43.500
USA	49	3543.000	72.306

The small p-values in these results indicate that there is a difference in weight depending on the country of origin. The mean rank for the group Other is the lowest, and the rank for cars made in the USA appears to be the largest.

Friedman test

In this exercise you perform a Friedman test using data from a wine tasting in which fifteen people rated six red wines. Each wine was rated using criteria commonly used to judge wine quality. The totals for each judge and wine were calculated. You will determine whether there is a difference in the quality of the wines as determined by the judges. The judges are the blocks; the brand of wine is the treatment.

- Open the Wine Tasting dataset in the Sample Data folder. The dataset appears on the screen. Scroll through it to examine its contents.

- Choose New View from the Analyze menu. A blank view appears on the screen.

- In the analysis browser, select Nonparametrics and click the Create Analysis button. The Nonparametric Tests dialog box appears.

- Select Friedman test and click OK. Two table placeholders appear in the view until you assign variables.

- In the variable browser, select all the continuous variables and click the Add button. (Continuous variables have a ☺ symbol next to them.) They appear highlighted with X usage markers next to them. The analysis calculates and these two tables appear in the view.

Friedman Test for 6 Variables

DF	5
# Groups	6
# Ties	8
Chi Square	27.552
P-Value	<.0001
Chi Square corrected for ties	28.142
Tied P-Value	<.0001

Friedman Rank Info for 6 Variables

	Count	Sum Ranks	Mean Rank
Wine A	15	56.500	3.767
Wine B	15	57.500	3.833
Wine C	15	66.000	4.400
Wine D	15	27.500	1.833
Wine E	15	36.500	2.433
Wine F	15	71.000	4.733

The large chi-square value in these results indicates that the judges rated the wines differently. Examining the Rank Info table shows the order in which the wines were ranked.

21

Factor Analysis

Factor analysis reduces a large number of correlated variables to a smaller, more manageable number of factors. A factor is a linear combination of related variables that can take the place of the original variables in further analysis. The structure of the factors (the variables represented by each factor) is the most important information resulting from a factor analysis. The number of factors and sufficient dimensionality is also important from a theoretical standpoint, but StatView handles those for you.

Factor analysis is useful when you have many correlated measurements for each of your experimental units (subjects, plants, etc.) and you want to concentrate on a smaller number of values than the number of measurements at hand; or you want to learn about the interrelationships among the variables. This technique is known as dimensionality reduction. Consider a study of the anatomy of a species of bird, for which you record 100 measurements (beak length, beak width, weight, length of body, length of tail, etc.). It is reasonable to assume that the measurements will be correlated with each other. A factor analysis can help you understand which variables are related to each other, as well as provide a means for you to analyze fewer variables than the original 100.

Discussion

Data input

You can apply factor analysis to two types of data: raw data and a correlation matrix. Raw data occurs in standard row and column format (variables in columns, observations in rows). More observations than variables are required in the dataset. Correlation matrix data requires a Pearson correlation matrix, which has to be determined from a single pool of subjects rather than from different samples of subjects. You need to know the number of cases used to determine the matrix; StatView uses it for multivariate significance tests performed on the data. StatView uses only the values in the lower left of the correlation matrix. (The part of the correlation matrix below the diagonal is a mirror image of the part above the diagonal.) Thus, you may use either a square correlation matrix (such as one created using the Correlation analysis) or a lower left correlation matrix as input. Note that if your input is a correlation matrix, make sure that all rows in the dataset are included. If you have excluded any rows, make sure you do not add the corresponding column to the analysis.

 To calculate the factor scores, that is, the values of each of the factors for each of the observations in the data, you must perform the analysis using raw data.

Factor extraction methods

Four factor extraction methods are available in StatView: principal components analysis, Harris image analysis, Kaiser image analysis and iterated principal axis.

Principal components analysis

The principal components analysis performs a simple eigenvalue-eigenvector analysis of the correlation matrix in its original form. (Eigenvalues, sometimes called characteristic roots, latent roots or just roots, are a mathematical function of a matrix, and are used in many mathematical and statistical techniques.) Principal components analysis is a "classical" technique, often appropriate if your dataset represents a random sample of observations, and the variables you choose are a fairly complete collection of those that are of interest to you. If you are not sure which technique is most appropriate for your data, rely on principal components analysis.

Image analysis

Image analysis is focused more on the sampling of variables than the sampling of subjects. If you can think of the variables in your data as a sample of variables from a potentially large (possibly unmeasurable) universe of variables, an image analysis may be more suitable than principal components. Image analysis techniques tend to extract more factors than non-image analysis methods. They factor a modification of the original correlation matrix, the image variance covariance matrix. Due to the large number of factors that generally define an image factor solution, the final rotated solution usually has a large number of zero loadings. However, the non-zero loadings are not always as large as those of the more traditional factor analytic model. Two types of image analysis are available in StatView: Harris and Kaiser. The Harris technique appeared in the original literature of factor analysis. Kaiser's technique is a modification that produces a factor pattern whose interpretation can be carried out similar to the more traditional principal components technique.

Iterated principal axis

Iterated principal axis factor extraction is a modification of the principal components technique. It uses the information from the initial principal components extraction to improve the quality of the factor solution. It assumes that the initial number of factors determined by the principal components technique is the correct one, and finds a set of factors that most fully explain the original correlation matrix. To do this, it replaces the diagonal entries of the matrix (by definition equal to 1) with an estimate of the communality of each variable (a measure of how closely it relates to the estimated factor solution). It then recalculates the communalities, and continues to factor the adjusted matrix until the communalities no longer change. With this technique, you must choose between three methods for estimating the initial communalities.

Iterated principal axis choices

SMC uses the squared multiple correlation of the variable with all the other variables. Off-Diagonal uses the largest correlation between the variable and any other single variable. 1 simply starts the process with the original correlation matrix. The iterated principal axis method is appropriate if you are certain that your data can be very well explained with a small number of factors. Due to it's iterative nature, it requires more computing time than the other methods.

Factor loadings

The factor extraction method you choose depends on the nature of your data and the questions you want to answer. The results of a factor analysis are summarized by a primary pattern matrix. For each factor, the entries in this matrix represent the coefficients (often called loadings) of the linear combination of the original variables that define that factor. A rescaled version of this matrix, the oblique solution reference structure matrix, is displayed in StatView.

Rotations

The coefficients initially produced by a factor extraction method are difficult to interpret because their magnitude varies widely. To get around this, you transform the factor pattern matrix by one or more transformations or rotations. The rotation helps you see the structure of the matrix more clearly by transforming it so that, for a given factor, as many variables as possible have either large coefficients or coefficients near zero. You can identify which variables make up a large part of the factor (the large coefficients) and which variables are not very important in that factor. You can then use your knowledge of the dataset to assign meanings to the factors that were extracted. You can experiment with different rotations before deciding which one helps you see the underlying structure of your data best.

For many datasets, determining the number of factors and identifying the important variables in them will satisfy your needs. You may want to go further and incorporate into other analyses the insights into the structure of your data obtained through factor analysis. One easy way to do this is to save the factor scores and later plot or analyze them. For each factor extracted, every observation in your dataset has a factor score, provided that the raw data is available. This score is a measure of the magnitude of the variables underlying the factor in question for that observation. You can use the factor scores as you would use other variables to produce plots, compare groups, etc. Factor scores are artificially constructed from a number of different variables so assumptions underlying many statistical procedures may not be met for these scores. Therefore, probability levels reported for hypothesis tests using factor scores should be judged with caution.

Number of factors to extract

An important decision in the extraction stage of your analysis is the number of factors to retain for further study. This number is usually a function of the eigenvalues. Your options are: state the number of factors you wish to retain; choose the method default, which varies with each factor extraction technique; or specify the technique you want to use. The defaults for each extraction technique are described after the discussion of the available criteria. In all cases the number of factors extracted is at least two.

Extraction number choices

If you select a technique that depends on the data, there are three criteria used to determine the number of factors: roots greater than 1, root curve analysis and extraction of 75% of the variance.

Roots greater than 1

The roots greater than 1 criterion retains as many factors as there are eigenvalues greater than or equal to 1. Since the sum of the eigenvalues of the correlation matrix is equal to the number of variables, the average value of an eigenvalue is 1. This criteria essentially retains all factors whose eigenvalues are "above average," and tends to extract a larger number of factors than necessary.

Root curve

The root curve criterion is based on a plot of eigenvalues from largest to smallest. It looks for a point in this graph where there is a dramatic shift, i.e., one eigenvalue that is markedly smaller than the next largest one. The number of factors retained corresponds to the number of eigenvalues before this dramatic change. When you use this criterion, you also get a plot of the eigenvalues versus their ranks, called a scree plot, to help you assess the adequacy of the solution.

75% variance rule

The 75% variance criterion is determined by retaining factors until 75% of the original variance is explained by the factors retained. Since the eigenvalues are determined in order of decreasing magnitude, each eigenvalue accounts for less variance than the preceding one. When the sum of the proportionate contributions of the eigenvalues exceeds .75, factors are no longer retained in the final solution.

User specified

If you specify the number of factors to extract, your estimate must be at least two, and cannot exceed the number of variables. In practice, most useful factor solutions have a maximum number of factors less than half the number of variables.

Method default

The default method for principal components is the larger of the numbers determined by the 75% variance rule and the root curve analysis. The default method for the two image analysis models is Harris eigenvalues greater than 1. Harris eigenvalues are the eigenvalues of the image variance-covariance matrix. If you apply one of the three criteria discussed above in place of the default method, the criterion is applied to a modification of the Harris eigenvalues. If you enter a specified number of factors greater than that which might be determined by the image analysis default method, the number determined by the default will override. The default method for determining the number of factors with iterated principal axis method is to use the number of eigenvalues greater than 1.

Transformation method

You can consider the initial factor solution as your final solution matrix, but it is often difficult to interpret the results of a factor analysis without further transformation. You can choose one of three orthogonal transformations to define a final solution: varimax, equamax and quartimax. An orthogonal transformation is one that retains a basic property of the initial factor solution, namely that the factors extracted are uncorrelated with each other. While this property is attractive from a mathematical point of view, it can make it difficult to see the underlying structure of your data.

Transformation method choices

StatView automatically applies an additional transformation, the orthotran transformation, to the orthogonal transformation you choose in order to make the underlying structure clearer. It does this by relaxing the requirement that the factors remain uncorrelated. If this does not improve the solution, it retains the original orthogonally transformed structure. When the orthotran procedure does perform an additional transformation, the resulting factor pattern is said to be oblique, i.e., the factors are not uncorrelated with each other.

Factor scores

If you have a non-singular correlation matrix, you can compute regression estimate factor score weights. This option is available only if you input raw data, since the factor scores are a function of the variable values for each observation in the dataset. Your factor scores are unrotated if you did not choose a transformation method. You have a choice of saving a transformed solution as orthogonal or oblique factor scores. Orthogonal factor scores show zero intercorrelations; oblique scores are correlated. For more information on saving factors scores, see "Saving factor scores" below.

Dialog box settings

When you create or edit a factor analysis, you see this dialog box:

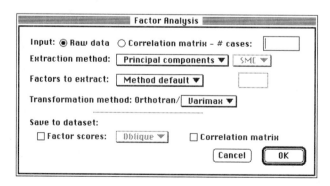

All the choices in the dialog box are discussed in greater detail throughout the preceding pages of this chapter. First you must specify the type of input data, raw data in row and column format, or a correlation matrix. If your input is a correlation matrix, the number of cases used to determine the correlation matrix must be entered.

You choose the factor extraction method from the pop-up menu. If you choose iterated principal axis extraction method, you must also specify the initial communality estimate as SMC (squared multiple correlations), off-diagonal, or 1 (see earlier discussion). You also choose the method for determining how many factors to extract, from the pop-up menu. More detail on these choices can be found in the earlier section entitled Number of factors to extract.

There are three transformation methods to choose from in addition to the automatic orthotran transformation. They are varimax, equamax, and quartimax. You may also choose no transformation. If your input data is raw data, the checkboxes at the bottom of the dialog box let you save either factor scores or a correlation matrix.

Saving a correlation matrix

If you check save correlation matrix, the computed correlation matrix is saved to a new dataset titled Factor Analysis Correlation Matrix. The dataset will have as many columns and rows as variables assigned to the factor analysis. The names of each column are Cor "Variable name" where "Variable name" is the name of one of the assigned variables for the factor analysis.

Note that the correlation matrix dataset is a very special dataset with many features. The dataset is linked to the factor analysis. If you change the parameters of the analysis or any of the input data, the dataset will *automatically* update to reflect the new correlation matrix. If you close the view that contains the factor analysis, this correlation dataset will close as well. When the view is reopened, the correlation matrix dataset will automatically be recreated. Please note that because this dataset is linked to your analysis, it is a "read only" dataset; you can not change any value in the dataset (except the formatting) until you break the link between the dataset and the analysis. In addition, the variables in this dataset can only be used in the view which contains the factor analysis that it is linked to.

To sever the link between the dataset and the factor analysis, you need to choose Save As from the File menu and save the dataset under a different name. This will save on the disk a copy of the correlation matrix as a normal dataset. You can then open this dataset as you would any other dataset. When you save a copy of the correlation matrix dataset to your disk, StatView automatically appends the letters "UE" to the beginning of the column names to indicate that these columns are now user entered.

Saving factor scores

This option is available only if you input raw data, as opposed to a correlation matrix, since the factor scores are a function of the variable values for each observation in the dataset. Your factor scores are unrotated if you did not choose a transformation method. You can save a transformed solution as orthogonal or oblique factor scores. Orthogonal factor scores show zero intercorrelations oblique scores are correlated.

The factor scores are appended to the end of the dataset to which the first specified variable belongs. They are assigned the names Obl 1, Obl 2, etc., or Orth 1, Orth 2, etc., depending on the type of scores saved. StatView identifies the source of these variables as *analysis generated*. They are dynamically linked to the factor analysis that created them. If you change the parameters of the analysis or any of the input data, the variables in the dataset automatically update. In addition, the variables are tied to the view that contains the analysis, not the dataset in which they appear. They will automatically be added to the dataset again when the view is reopened and the factor analysis recalculated. If you close the view that contains the factor analysis, the variables will be removed from the dataset. Note that one consequence of this is that if you plan to use an analysis generated factor scores in a formula, you need to open the view which contains the factor analysis in order for the formula to compute.

Since these variables are dynamic, if you generate a graph or statistic of these factor scores, these graphs or statistics will update when the analysis changes. If you plan to create new analyses or graphs from the factor scores, such as a histogram or descriptive statistics, these results must be contained in the same view as the factor analysis.

 To break the link between an analysis generated variable and the analysis, change its source to User Entered. This causes all ties to the analysis to be broken and the letters "UE" appended to the front of the variable name to indicate that it is now user entered. Any change to the factor analysis that created it will have no effect on the variable, and they will act just as any user-entered variable would.

Variables

Requirements

Factor analysis requires two or more continuous variables.

Variable browser buttons

Add   To generate a factor analysis, select two or more continuous variable(s) and click Add.

Split By
When you assign one or more split-by variable to a factor analysis, results for each cell in the split-by variable(s) are displayed in separate tables and plots.

Additional variables

Add
When you select a factor analysis result and assign additional variables, they are added to the existing analysis.

Results

The following results are available for factor analysis. For discussion of results, see preceding discussion. The Basic output is the default for this analysis.

Basic output
summary table, eigenvalues, unrotated factors, communality summary, oblique solution primary pattern matrix, and oblique solution reference structure

Supplemental output
correlation matrix, partial correlation matrix, eigenvectors, orthogonal transformation, primary intercorrelations, oblique factor score weights, orthogonal factor score weights

Advanced output
variable sampling, variable complexity, proportionate variance contributions

Plots
unrotated factor plot, orthogonal factor plot, oblique factor plot, scree plot

Templates

StatView offers many options for customizing all aspects of your statistical output, including which statistics are used and the appearance and location of tables and graphs. These customizations can be saved as templates and re-used.

A sample template for factor analysis is included in the StatView Templates folder. You may wish to use this template as is or create your own templates containing the factor analysis specifications and results that you commonly use. For more information on templates, see Chapter 7, Templates and Chapter 8, Building Analyses.

Exercise

In this exercise you perform a factor analysis to find the factors that best explain variability in a correlation matrix of eight physical measurements.

- Open the Eight Physical Variables dataset in the Sample Data folder. The dataset appears on the screen. Scroll through the dataset to examine its contents.

- Select New View from the Analyze menu. A blank view appears on the screen.

- Click the triangle next to Factor Analysis. The output appears in an indented list beneath the heading.

- Select Basic Output and click the Create Analysis button. The Factor Analysis dialog box appears for you to set parameters.

- Enter 305 in the box next to " # cases" and click OK to accept the default settings: Principal components, Method default and Varimax. Table placeholders appear in the view until you assign variables.

- In the variable browser, assign all the variables to the analysis by selecting them and clicking the Add button. The variables appear highlighted with X usage markers next to them. The analysis calculates and the results appear in the view.

Factor analysis summary

Factor Analysis Summary

Number of Variables	8
Est. Number of Factors	4
Number of Factors	2
Number of Cases	305
Number Missing	0
Degrees of Freedom	35
Bartlett's Chi Square	2116.975
P-Value	<.0001

Factor Extraction Method: Principal Components
Extraction Rule: Method Default
Transformation Method: Orthotran/Varimax

The summary table notes the number of variables used in the analysis, the factor procedure used to determine the number of factors, the transformation procedure and the number of factor scores defined. It also includes Bartlett's chi-square.

Eigenvalues

Eigenvalues

	Magnitude	Variance Prop.
Value 1	4.673	.584
Value 2	1.771	.221
Value 3	.481	.060
Value 4	.421	.053

The eigenvalues are presented in an order that corresponds to their size. Typically, there are as many eigenvalues as there are variables, and the sum of the eigenvalues equals the sum of the diagonal elements of the matrix from which they are determined. The variance proportion is an estimate of the proportion of variance that the eigenvalue and its eigenvector account for when they are used to define a factor.

Usually, StatView divides the number of variables by two to determine an initial estimate of the number of eigenvalues (also an initial estimate of the number of factors). The many rules for determining the number of final factors are then applied to the eigenvalues. You may override the number of eigenvalues determined initially by entering a number of factors in the dialog box. The eigenvalues displayed are of no great value in the interpretation of the factor solution. They are displayed for completeness and for those who wish to address subjectively the number-of-factors question.

Unrotated factors

Unrotated Factors

	Factor 1	Factor 2
height	.859	-.372
arm span	.842	-.441
forearm length	.813	-.459
lower leg length	.840	-.395
weight	.758	.525
bitrochanteric diameter	.674	.533
chest girth	.617	.580
chest width	.671	.418

Once the number of factors is determined, it is necessary to determine the correlation of each variable with each factor, a value typically referred to as a factor loading. Most modern-day factor analysts view this unrotated factor matrix as the initial step in determining a desirable factor solution matrix. The square of a loading represents the proportion of variance of the variable that can be predicted by the factor.

Communality summary

Communality Summary

	SMC	Final Estimate
height	.816	.877
arm span	.849	.903
forearm length	.801	.872
lower leg length	.788	.861
weight	.749	.850
bitrochanteric diameter	.604	.739
chest girth	.562	.717
chest width	.478	.625

Computing the sum of the squared loadings by row results in a proportion, the final communality estimate, that represents the total proportion of variance of the variable that can be predicted by the factors.

Prior to a factor analysis, the total proportion of variance of a variable is estimated by the squared multiple correlation (SMC) of the variable with all the other variables. The communality estimates and the SMC are reported in the communality summary table. Some analysts think of the SMC as the initial communality estimate, while others think of the largest off-diagonal entry associated with the variable as the initial communality estimate. When a singular (determinant equal to 0) correlation matrix is analyzed, the initial communality estimate is assumed to be 0.

You can see from this communality summary table that approximately 82 percent of the variation in height is predictable in a linear regression equation using the other seven variables. This conclusion is derived from the SMC of height with all the other variables. When two factors are used to predict height, approximately 88% of the variation is predictable, an improvement of approximately 6%.

Oblique solution primary pattern matrix

Oblique Solution Primary Pattern Matrix

	Factor 1	Factor 2
height	.919	.033
arm span	.973	-.047
forearm length	.971	-.080
lower leg length	.928	-4.821E-4
weight	-.001	.922
bitrochanteric diameter	-.064	.890
chest girth	-.146	.911
chest width	.043	.768

When determining an oblique solution, StatView uses an algorithm that simply takes a given orthogonal solution and releases the restriction of orthogonality. The algorithm, the orthotran solution, always defines a simple structure solution that is good as or better than the associated orthogonal simple structure solution.

There are two types of oblique solutions: a primary pattern solution and a reference structure solution. These two are quite similar; indeed, one is a column rescaling of the other. The pattern solution defines loadings that are regression coefficients for predicting the standard score of a variable in terms of the defined factors. The reference structure solution defines loadings that are correlations. Both solutions have good simple structure in that the high loadings are high, and the low loadings are near zero.

Oblique solution reference structure

Oblique Solution Reference Structure

	Factor 1	Factor 2
height	.795	.029
arm span	.841	-.041
forearm length	.839	-.069
lower leg length	.802	-4.167E-4
weight	-.001	.797
bitrochanteric diameter	-.056	.770
chest girth	-.127	.788
chest width	.037	.664

When comparing a primary pattern solution to a reference structure solution, it is immediately apparent that the large loadings are larger in the primary pattern solution. Sometimes these primary pattern values become larger than 1, simply because they are regression weights. Regardless of whether you use a primary pattern or reference structure solution, the conclusions should be the same. For this data, it is clear that the first four variables are associated with the first factor and not associated with the second factor. Using similar logic, it is apparent that the second four variables are associated with the second factor. To name the factors, you choose a name that represents the essence of the variables loading on it. The first factor could be named bone structure, the second factor could be named flesh factor.

For this data you would arrive at the same factor name if you used an orthogonal solution. Is it reasonable to assume that body weight or flesh is independent of bone structure? If you believe so, then you may be satisfied with an orthogonal solution. If, however, you assume that taller people are generally heavier and fleshier than shorter people, you will be satisfied with an oblique solution.

Plots

StatView provides several plots associated with factor analysis. In this part of the exercise, you create two: one associated with the unrotated factor solution, and one associated with the oblique solution. Within any particular set of plots, all pairwise factor plots are presented.

Unrotated solution

• Make sure one of the previous results is selected.

• In the analysis browser, select Unrotated Factor Plot and click the Create Analysis button. An unrotated factor plot is added to the results.

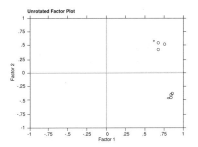

The plot of the unrotated solution allows you to make a quick judgment regarding the potential simple structure of the factor solution. For this data, two distinct clusters of points are apparent in the unrotated plot. An ideal factor solution for the variables would have one axis passing through the cluster of variables 1 through 4 in the upper right quadrant, and the other axis passing through the other cluster. If the data were under-factored (which is not possible with the eight physical variables), you might see points scattered through all four quadrants with no definitive clusters of points. If the data were over-factored, you would see many points near the point of intersection of the two axes, and perhaps one or two points defining a cluster.

Oblique solution

• In the analysis browser, select Oblique Factor Plot and click the Create Analysis button. A oblique factor plot is added to the results.

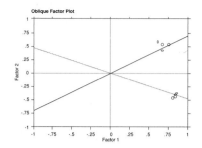

The plot of the oblique solution shows the oblique axes, primary axes, passing through the clusters of points as they do for the eight physical variables. The plotted primary axes are not at right angles because they are correlated. In this example, the simple structure of the oblique solution is quite good; the primary axes pass directly through the clusters. When the orthogonal solution passes axes through the clusters, the oblique solution and the orthogonal solution are identical and the factor intercorrelations are zero.

Chapter

22

Plots

Plots offer a powerful way of looking at data to complement a numerical analysis. They allow you to see patterns and relationships among variables, spot outliers, examine and compare distributions, distinguish information concerning different groups of your data and help you validate assumptions about your data. Plots also offer a graphic presentation of your analysis results which aids you in communicating information about your data to others. This chapter discusses: univariate plots, bivariate plots, cell plots, box plots, percentile plots, and comparison percentile plots. Each offers a distinct method of graphically analyzing your data and serve to complement the other analyses. The plots depicting the results of a certain analysis—regression plots, interaction plots, histogram, pie charts—are discussed in the preceding chapters that deal with those analyses.

Univariate plots

Univariate plots show the distribution of a variable in an essentially one-dimensional plot with a single numeric axis, the Y axis. Each observation is plotted along the horizontal axis in the sequence the data appears in the dataset. You can display the observations as points in a scattergram, as points connected by lines in a line chart, or as bars in a bar chart. You can plot multiple variables in a single univariate plot and use split-by variables to distinguish different groups within the variables. You can also add reference lines to show the variable's mean plus or minus one or more standard errors or standard deviations as well as a specified confidence interval. Univariate charts showing these reference lines are a type of quality control chart.

If you are using split-by variables you can specify whether to display a separate line for each group or a single line for all groups. This choice is in the Univariate Plot dialog box (described below), accessible through the Create Analysis button, or by clicking Edit Analysis when the entire graph is selected. If a univariate plot displays information on several groups, the plot will show separate lines for each group or one line for all groups. To change this setting, click on one of the points to select just the plot, and click the Edit Display button. You see this dialog box:

By default there are no values displayed on the horizontal axis, but you can optionally choose to display observation numbers on this axis. The observation number ranges from one to n, where n is the number of non-missing, non-excluded values in the variable. The first such value has observation number 1, the second observation number 2, etc. There are many other modifications you can make to this graph. All are described in Chapter 9, Customizing Graphs and Tables.

Dialog box settings

When you create a univariate plot or edit it using the Edit Analysis button, you see the dialog box below. You can add lines for the mean, standard deviations, standard error and confidence intervals.

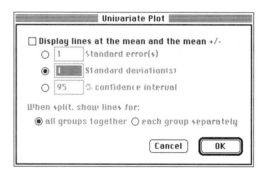

If you choose to display lines at the mean, you must also display lines around the mean at a specified standard error, standard deviation, or confidence interval. The option at the bottom of the dialog box determines how these lines appear when you assign a split-by variable.

There is an additional setting for univariate plots, found in a separate dialog box. By default, the horizontal axis has no ticks or values displayed on the axis. You choose to add an axis whose value ranges from 0 to the count of values for the variable displayed.

Select the horizontal axis by clicking on it. Click the Edit Display button and the Ordinal Axis dialog box appears:

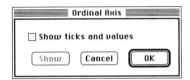

Click in the checkbox to show ticks and values, and click OK. To preview the change first, click the Show button. You cannot modify any aspects of this axis, unlike other axes.

Variables

Requirements

Univariate plots can be generated for one or more continuous or nominal variables.

Variable browser buttons

Add   To generate a univariate plot, select one or more variables and click Add.

Split By   The cells of any nominal variable(s) assigned using the Split By button appear in the legend.

Additional variables

Add   Each additional variable assigned is added to the same plot.

By holding down the Command (⌘) and Shift keys simultaneously and then clicking Add, you create a new plot for additional variables rather than adding to the selected plot. Any split-by variables will automatically be assigned to the new plot(s). By holding down the Command and Shift keys and then clicking Split By, you create a new plot containing the Added variables split by the new variable.

Results

For explanation of the plots, please see the preceding discussion. The default univariate plot is a scattergram.

Scattergram   shows observations as points. Lines indicating the mean, standard deviations, standard error and confidence intervals can be added to the plot using the dialog box.

Line Chart   shows observations as points connected by lines. Lines indicating the mean, standard deviations, standard error and confidence intervals can be added to the plot using the dialog box.

 Bar Chart   shows observations as bars. Lines indicating the mean, standard deviations, standard error and confidence intervals can be added to the plot using the dialog box.

Templates

 StatView offers many options for customizing all aspects of your plots, including their appearance and location and which statistics, if any, are used with them. These customizations can be saved as templates and re-used.

A sample template for each plot is included in the StatView Templates folder. You may wish to use these templates as is or create your own templates which contain the plots you commonly use, formatted to your specifications. For more information on templates, see Chapter 7, Templates and Chapter 8, Building Analyses.

Exercise

 In this exercise you create a univariate scattergram to examine the distribution of car weights. The dataset you will use has measurements of weight, gas tank size, turning circle, horsepower and engine displacement for 116 cars from different countries.

• Open Car Data in the Sample Data folder. The dataset appears on the screen.

• Choose New View from the Analyze menu. A blank view appears on the screen.

• In the analysis browser, click on the triangle next to Univariate Plots. The three available plots appear indented below.

• Select Scattergram and click the Create Analysis button. The Univariate Plot dialog box appears.

If you did not wish to display additional information you would click OK without checking any other options. For this example you will add a line at the mean as well as at one standard deviation above and below the mean.

• Click the Display lines checkbox. Leave the default at one standard deviation. Click OK. A graph placeholder appears in the view until you assign variables.

• In the variable browser, select Weight and click the Add button.

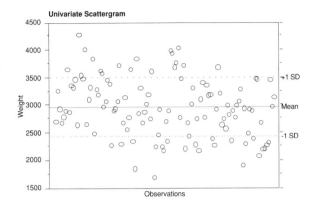

The graph displays the individual observations of each car's weight along with lines indicating the variable mean and values at +/- one standard deviation. Visual inspection shows that approximately 50 cars fall outside plus or minus one standard deviation of the mean.

This dataset also includes a nominal variable identifying the manufacturing country for each car. We can use this variable to split the observations into different groups.

• With the graph still selected, click on Country in the variable browser and click the Split By button.

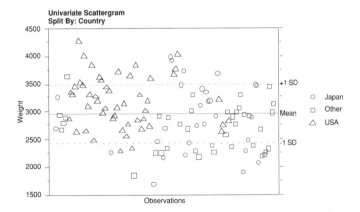

The three different origin countries: Japan, Other and USA are distinguished by different plotting symbols. You can see that most of the heaviest cars are manufactured in the USA, and the lightest cars are manufactured in Japan and Other countries.

You can display this information as a line chart or bar chart by choosing the appropriate graph from the analysis browser. You can also draw different mean and standard deviation lines for each group rather than for the entire variable by clicking the Edit Analysis button and changing that parameter in the dialog box.

Bivariate plots

A bivariate plot graphs the relationship between at least one dependent and one independent variable. They can display the observations as scattergram points with or without connecting lines.

Bivariate plots display the relationship between two variables, X and Y. In a bivariate plot each individual observation Y_i is plotted against X_i for i = 1 to the number of observations of X and Y. You can plot multiple variable pairs in a bivariate plot and use split-by variables to distinguish different groups. You can also use nominal variables in a bivariate plot to construct a point graph that distinguishes the measurements of the groups of a nominal variable.

You can add a simple regression line to the bivariate plot as well as confidence bands around the mean and slope of the regression line. Regression lines can be calculated and displayed for each X-Y pair, and the equation for the line and R^2 are noted at the bottom of the graph. The bivariate plot with a regression line is an excellent graph to use in conjunction with the regression analysis to see how the model fits your data. The regression analysis also offers a regression plot, but it is limited to plotting a single X-Y variable pair in each plot.

A bivariate plot offers more flexibility than a regression plot. You can identify different subgroups of your data by adding a split-by variable. With a split-by variable you can display the simple regression line for the entire X-Y pair or display a separate line for each group of the X-Y pair. And you can plot multiple X-Y pairs on a single graph and display the simple regression line for each.

Regression lines with scattergrams

Regression lines are a type of fitted line you can add to a bivariate scattergram. If you choose Regression Plot from the analysis browser, you can plot a regression line for a scattergram using only one independent and one dependent variable. With a bivariate scattergram, however, you can show regression lines for more than one independent (X) and dependent (Y) variable.

If you want to plot two independent variables against a dependent variable and have a regression line for each variable combination, you create a bivariate scattergram and add regression lines with the dialog box described in this section. You cannot do this with a regression analysis since it accepts only one independent and dependent variable.

Another thing you can do only with a bivariate scattergram is plot an independent and dependent continuous variable split by a nominal variable (cholesterol levels for males and females, for instance) and create a *single* regression line for both variable combinations. Again, you create this scattergram with regression line settings in the Bivariate Plot dialog box.

Keep in mind that a scattergram with regression lines is just a scattergram with fitted lines. If you need to see summary information, the ANOVA table, residuals or other such information you must perform a regression analysis.

Dialog box settings

When you create a bivariate plot or edit it using the Edit Analysis button, you see the dialog box below. You can add regression lines and confidence bands.

If you display regression lines, you can also specify a confidence level and show confidence bands for the mean of Y as predicted by the regression for a given value of X. You can also show confidence bands for the slope of the regression line. The checkbox at the bottom of the dialog box determines how these lines are shown when you use a split-by variable.

Variables

Requirements

Bivariate plots can be generated for one or more continuous or nominal X variables vs. one or more continuous or nominal Y variables.

If there is a single X variable and more than one Y variable, each Y variable is plotted against the X variable. The same rule applies if there is a single Y variable and more than one X variable. If multiple X and Y variables are plotted, the first X assigned is plotted against the first Y, the second X against the second Y, and so on.

Variable browser buttons

X Variable	Select one or more variables and click X Variable.
Y Variable	Select one or more variables and click Y Variable.
Split By	The groups of any nominal variable(s) assigned using the Split By button appear in the legend.

Additional variables

X and Y Variables	Additional X and Y variables are added to the same plot.

By holding down the Command (⌘) and Shift keys simultaneously and then clicking Add, you create a new plot for additional variables rather than adding to the selected plot. Any split-by variables will automatically be assigned to the new plot(s). By holding down the Command and Shift keys and then clicking Split By, you create a new plot containing the Added variables split by the new variable.

Results

For explanation of the plots, please see the preceding discussion. The default plot is a scattergram.

Scattergram	shows one point for each X-Y pair. Regression lines, confidence bands, and equations may be added for the entire plot or for each group of a split-by variable using the dialog box.

Line Chart	shows one point for each X-Y pair. The points are connected by lines. Regression lines, confidence bands, and equations may be added using the dialog box.

Templates

StatView offers many options for customizing all aspects of your plots, including their appearance and location and which statistics, if any, are used with them. These customizations can be saved as templates and re-used.

A sample template for each plot is included in the StatView Templates folder. You may wish to use these templates as is or create your own templates which contain the plots you commonly use, formatted to your specifications. For more information on templates, see Chapter 7, Templates and Chapter 8, Building Analyses.

Exercises

The data used in the following exercises comes from medical students. Blood lipid levels and other cardiovascular risk factors are evaluated in students as freshman and later as seniors. In the following exercises you examine the relation between initial cholesterol count and cholesterol count three years after students received instruction on reducing cholesterol through dieting. You will also examine whether this relationship appears the same for male and female students.

Bivariate scattergram

- Open Lipid Data in the Sample Data folder. The dataset appears on the screen.

- Choose New View from the Analyze menu. A blank view appears on the screen.

- In the analysis browser, click on the triangle next to Bivariate Plots. The two available plots appear indented below.

- Select Scattergram and click the Create Analysis button. The Bivariate Plot dialog box appears.

- We will not add simple regression lines in this exercise, so leave the default setting and click OK. A graph placeholder appears in the view until you assign variables.

- In the variable browser, select Cholesterol and click the X Variable button, then select Chol-3yrs and click the Y Variable button.

The dataset includes a nominal variable which identifies the gender of the student. We can use this variable to split the observations into the different groups.

- In the variable browser, select Gender and click the Split By button. The following scattergram appears in the view:

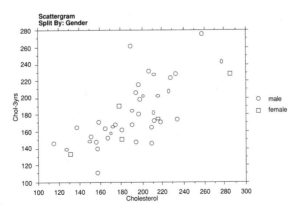

The male and female observations are distinguished by different plotting symbols. To determine whether a different relationship exists between the cholesterol levels for males and females we can calculate a simple regression and add the fitted line to the graph.

•   Click the Edit Analysis button. The Bivariate Plot dialog box appears.

We have the option of displaying a single line for all observations or calculating a different regression for each group.

•   Click the checkbox labelled Display regression lines. Since we are comparing males and females, click the "each group separately" radio button. The following scattergram appears.

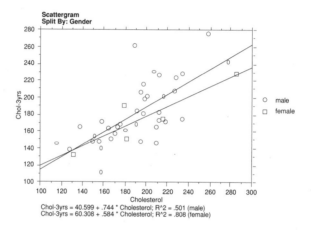

Chol-3yrs = 40.599 + .744 * Cholesterol; R^2 = .501 (male)
Chol-3yrs = 60.308 + .584 * Cholesterol; R^2 = .808 (female)

Notice that the equation for each line as well as the R^2 values are added to the bottom of the graph. You can see there is a slight difference between males and females. The difference is not significant, which you can see if you add confidence bands for the mean (Click Edit Analysis to see the dialog box). If we showed the regression line for all groups together there would be only a single regression line and the simple regression would be calculated using all the data.

Bivariate plots with nominal data

Bivariate plots can have nominal as well as continuous variables assigned to the X or Y axis. When assigning a nominal variable, you can construct a graph to compare the different distributions of the data in each of the nominal variable's groups. The previous example showed a difference between the cholesterol reduction in male and female students. We can use the bivariate plot to examine the differences between the weights of the male and female students.

•   Make sure that Lipid Data is still open. Choose New View from the Analyze menu.

- In the analysis browser, click on the triangle next to Bivariate Plots. The two different available plots appear indented below.

- Select Scattergram, hold down the control key and click the Create Analysis button. This bypasses the Bivariate Plot dialog box, since you do not wish to add regression lines. A graph placeholder appears in the view until you assign variables.

- In the variable browser, select Gender and click the X Variable button, then select Weight and click the Y Variable button. A scattergram appears in the view.

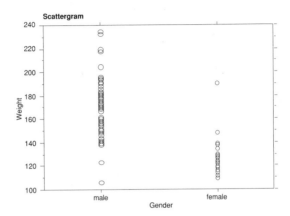

As you might expect, the female students' weights are less than the male students'.

Cell plots

Cell plots graph means or sums of variables and can show the variability around means. They are useful for showing the side by side comparison of continuous variables measured for each of several nominal groups.

When your data falls into groups, it is common to question whether some factor affects the groups in the same way or affects each group differently. You may know that the means of the two groups are different, but you also want to know the effect of one or more additional factors on the relationship. Cell plots present a set of lines, bars or points so you can visually compare variable to variable and group to group. This is extremely useful in conjunction with any statistic that tests differences between groups, such as ANOVA and t-tests.

As an example, suppose you have two nominal variables A and B, and a continuous variable Y. You may know that the mean of Y is different for different levels of A or of B, but the question remains whether there is any interaction effect, i.e., whether the relationship among the means for the different levels of A is affected by the level of B and vice versa. In a cell line plot with A on the axis and B in the legend, the lines will show you whether this interaction is present or not: if not, the lines will have the same pattern for each level of B; if so, the lines will show different patterns depending on the levels of B.

Cell plots can depict data as bar charts (often referred to as side-by-side bar charts), line charts, or point charts. You can choose which graphing variable appears on the horizontal axis and which appears in the legend. If you are examining means, you have the option of adding error bars. The Edit Display button described in Chapter 8 lets you modify the structural appearance of cell line plots.

Dialog box settings

When you create a cell plot or edit it using the Edit Analysis button, you see the dialog box below. Cell plots have two simple statistics associated with them—sums and means. You choose which to graph for the variables you select. If you select means, you can also specify whether to display error bars. These choices are found in the Cell Plot dialog box:

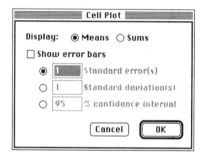

If you want to show error bars, you must choose Means at the top of the dialog box; you cannot use error bars with Sums. If you show error bars, they can represent a specified number of standard errors, a specified number of standard deviations, or confidence intervals at a specified level. When you display error bars but they do not show in a particular cell, it is because there is only one observation in that cell.

There is an additional setting for cell line charts, found in a separate dialog box. Normally, variables are connected by lines, but you can eliminate the lines. Select only the plot (not the entire graph) by clicking on a point or line. Click the Edit Display button and the Cell Line Plot dialog box appears:

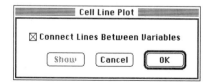

Click in the checkbox to deselect this option, and click OK. To preview the change first, click the Show button.

Variables

Requirements

Cell plots can be generated for one or more continuous variables. Nominal grouping variables are optional.

Variable browser buttons

Add
To generate a cell plot, select one or more continuous variables and click Add. The groups of any nominal variable assigned using the Add button appear on the horizontal axis.

Split By
The cells of any nominal variable(s) assigned using the Split By button appear in the legend.

Additional variables

Add
Each additional continuous variable assigned is added to the same plot. Each additional nominal variable assigned creates new cells which are shown on the horizontal axis.

 By holding down the Command (⌘) and Shift keys simultaneously and then clicking Add, you create a new plot for additional variables rather than adding to the selected plot. Any split-by variables will automatically be assigned to the new plot(s). By holding down the Command and Shift keys and then clicking Split By, you create a new plot containing the Added variables split by the new variable.

Results

For explanation of the plots, please see the preceding discussion. The default plot is a line chart.

 Point Chart
shows the means or sums of the cells or variables as points. Error bars can be displayed for means.

 Line Chart
shows the means or sums of the cells or variables as points connected by lines. Error bars can be displayed for means.

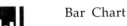 Bar Chart
shows the means or sums of the cells or variables as bars. Error bars can be displayed for means.

Templates

StatView offers many options for customizing all aspects of your plots, including their appearance and location and which statistics, if any, are used with them. These customizations can be saved as templates and re-used.

A sample template for each plot is included in the StatView Templates folder. You may wish to use these templates as is or create your own templates which contain the plots you commonly use, formatted to your specifications. For more information on templates, see Chapter 7, Templates and Chapter 8, Building Analyses.

Exercises

The data you will use in this exercise contains measurements of gas tank size for 116 cars of various types from different countries. You will compare the average size of gas tanks for each country of manufacture as well as see whether the type of car affects gas tank size.

- Open Car Data in the Sample Data folder. The dataset appears on the screen.

- Choose New View from the Analyze menu. A blank view appears on the screen.

- In the analysis browser, click on the triangle next to Cell Plots. The three available plots appear indented beneath it.

- Select Bar chart and click the Create Analysis button. The Cell Plot dialog box appears.

- Select Means as the display option. Since you are displaying means you could also add error bars, but we will not in this example.

- Click OK. A graph placeholder appears in the view until you assign variables.

- In the variable browser, select Gas Tank Size and click the Add button. A single bar is drawn in the graph.

The bar represents the mean size of all 116 gas tanks. We are interested in comparing the size for both the country of origin (Japan, Other and USA) and type of car (Small, Sporty, Compact, Medium and Large). The groups of any nominal variable assigned to the cell plot using the Add button appear on the horizontal axis. The groups of any nominal variable assigned to the cell plot using the Split By button appear in the legend, and appear side-by-side within the other groups in the bar chart. Whether to add a nominal variable or split by a nominal variable depends on which factor you wish to emphasize in the graph. In this exercise, we are primarily interested in how the type of car affects the size of the gas tank in a particular country.

- Select Country in the variable browser and click the Add button. The horizontal axis has three different tick marks, one for each group. A single bar represents the means of the gas tanks sizes for the cars in that country.

- Select Type in the variable browser and click the Split By button. A bar appears for each type of car.

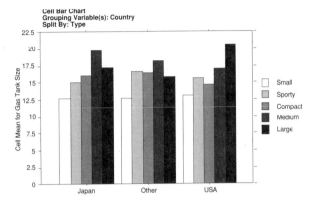

Now you can see for each country of manufacture how the type of car affects the gas tank size. You can also see how the pattern of the effect of type on gas tank size varies from country to country. Large size cars have smaller gas tanks except in the USA. If you were interested in examining gas tank size with the roles of country and type reversed, you would construct the cell bar chart differently.

- Remove Type and Country from the plot by selecting each in the variable browser and clicking Remove. You will now assign these variables in a different order.

- Select Type in the variable browser and click the Add button. The horizontal axis has five different tick marks, one for each group, with a single bar representing the means of the gas tanks sizes for each type of car.

- Select Country in the variable browser and click the Split By button. A bar appears for each country.

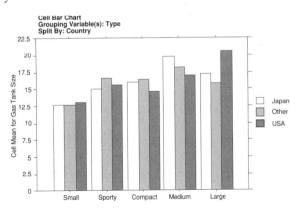

Now you can see for each type of car how the country of manufacture affects gas tank size. You can also see how the pattern of the effect of country on gas tank size varies from type to type.

By choosing a line chart you can display the different groups as lines with different symbols as opposed to side-by-side bars.

- With the last bar chart selected, select Line Chart in the analysis browser and click the Create Analysis button.

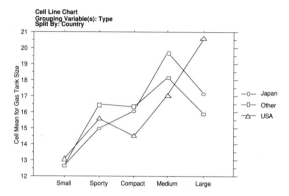

Point charts are similar to line charts except they display the value of the mean as a single point as opposed to a line. Points are not connected with lines and points for a split cell are displayed side-by-side instead of stacked. They are most useful when you are displaying error bars as well.

- Click in the empty space in the view to deselect all results.

- Choose Point Chart in the analysis browser and click the Create Analysis button.

- Check the Show error bars box, select standard deviation, and enter one in the text box. Click OK. A graph placeholder appears in the view until you assign variables.

- In the variable browser, select both Weight and Type and click the Add button.

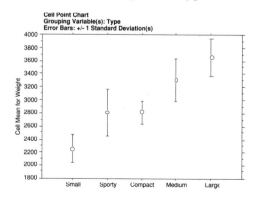

These examples have compared different groups, but you can also use cell plots to compare the means or sums of different variables. To do that you would use the Add button to assign the continuous variables to the cell plot. A bar or point appears for each assigned variable.

Box plots

A box plot is a graph for displaying the 10th, 25th, 50th, 75th and 90th percentiles of a variable. You can use box plots to compare variable distributions, or to see the distribution of a single variable. Each box plot is composed of five horizontal lines that display the 10th, 25th, 50th, 75th and 90th percentiles of a variable. All values for the variable above the 90th percentile and below the 10th percentile are plotted separately, so box plots are especially useful for displaying outliers.

The box plot allows you a great deal of flexibility, comparing not only the distribution of an entire variable or variables but also comparing the distributions of groups defined by nominal variables. In addition, you can plot the outliers and display notched box plots that represent a 95% confidence interval around the median in addition to the percentiles. The Edit Display button described in Chapter 8 lets you modify the structural appearance of box plots.

Dialog box settings

Box plots have no analysis parameters, but you can choose whether to display notches representing a 95% confidence interval for the median. Select the interior of the plot and click the Edit Display button to display the Box Plot dialog box.

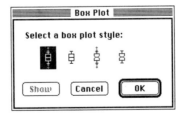

Variables

Requirements

Box plots can be generated for one or more continuous variables. Nominal grouping variables are optional.

Variable browser buttons

Add   To generate a box plot, select one or more continuous variables and click Add. The groups of any nominal variable assigned using the Add button appear on the horizontal axis.

Split By   The cells of any nominal variable(s) assigned using the Split By button appear in the legend.

Additional variables

Add   Each additional continuous variable assigned is added to the same plot. Each additional nominal variable assigned creates new cells which are shown on the horizontal axis.

By holding down the Command (⌘) and Shift keys simultaneously and then clicking Add, you create a new plot for additional variables rather than adding to the selected plot. Any split-by variables will automatically be assigned to the new plot(s). By holding down the Command and Shift keys and then clicking Split By, you create a new plot containing the Added variables split by the new variable.

Results

For explanation of the plots, please see the preceding discussion.

Box Plot   shows the 10th, 25th, 50th (median), 75th and 90th percentiles of a variable. Values above the 90th and below the 10th percentile are plotted as points.

Notched Box Plot   shows the same information as a Box Plot with the addition of a notch showing the 95% confidence interval around the median.

Templates

StatView offers many options for customizing all aspects of your plots, including their appearance and location and which statistics, if any, are used with them. These customizations can be saved as templates and re-used.

A sample template for each plot is included in the StatView Templates folder. You may wish to use these templates as is or create your own templates which contain the plots you commonly use, formatted to your specifications. For more information on templates, see Chapter 7, Templates and Chapter 8, Building Analyses.

Exercises

The data used in the following exercises comes from medical students. Blood lipid levels and other cardiovascular risk factors are evaluated in students as freshmen and later as seniors. In these exercises you examine the distribution of several of the lipid measurements. You will also see if there are any differences between the distributions for males and females.

- Open Lipid Data in the Sample Data folder. The dataset appears on the screen.

- Choose New View from the Analyze menu. A blank view appears on the screen.

- In the analysis browser, select Box Plot and click the Create Analysis button. A graph placeholder appears in the view until you assign variables.

- In the variable browser, assign Cholesterol, Triglycerides, HDL and LDL to the graph by selecting them and clicking the Add button.

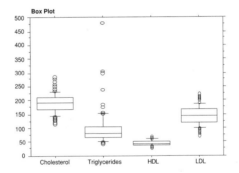

The box plot allows you to compare the distributions of these variables. Box plots work similarly to cell plots discussed above. You can group boxes along the horizontal axis as well as using the legend to distinguish groups. To examine whether the distributions compare for males and females:

- In the variables browser, select Gender and click the Split By button.

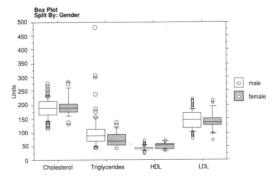

The male and female groups appear next to each other so you can compare their distributions. You could just as easily add nominal variables which would break the groups out along the horizontal axis by using the Add rather than the Split By button.

Percentiles

A percentile plot graphs observed values of a variable against its percentile. It allows you to see the percentage of the data that is less than or equal to an observation. Percentile plots are useful in comparing the distribution of different groups or variables. You can plot multiple variables in a single percentile plot and use split-by variables to distinguish different groups. In addition, you can add reference lines to show the 10th, 25th, 50th, 75th, and 90th percentiles as well as display a table listing these values.

Dialog box settings

When you create or edit a percentiles plot, you see this dialog box. You can place lines at various percentiles by checking the box:

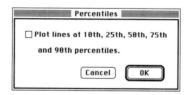

Variables

Requirements

Percentile tables and plots can be generated for one or more continuous variables.

Variable browser buttons

Add   To generate a percentiles table or plot, select one or more continuous variables and click Add.

Split By   The groups of any nominal variable(s) assigned using the Split By button appear in the same table or plot.

Additional variables

Add   Each additional variable assigned is added to the analysis.

By holding down the command and shift keys simultaneously and then clicking Add, you create a new plot for additional variables rather than adding to the selected plot. Any split-by variables will automatically be assigned to the new plot(s). By holding down the command and shift keys and then clicking Split By, you create a new plot containing the Added variables split by the new variable.

Results

For explanation of the plots, please see the preceding discussion. The default output for this analysis is both the Summary Table and the Percentiles Plot.

Percentiles Summary Table   shows the values of the 10th, 25th, 50th (median), 75th and 90th percentiles.

Percentiles Plot   shows the values in each variable plotted against their percentiles. Lines indicating the 10th, 25th, 50th (median), 75th and 90th percentiles can be added to the plot using the dialog box.

Templates

StatView offers many options for customizing all aspects of your plots, including their appearance and location and which statistics, if any, are used with them. These customizations can be saved as templates and reused.

A sample template for each plot is included in the StatView Templates folder. You may wish to use these templates as is or create your own templates which contain the plots you commonly use, formatted to your specifications. For more information on templates, see Chapter 7, Templates and Chapter 8, Building Analyses.

Exercise

This example uses data containing measurements of weight, gas tank size, turning circle, horsepower and engine displacement for 116 cars from different countries. You will see whether there is a difference between the weights of cars from different countries.

- Open Car Data in the Sample Data folder. The dataset appears on the screen.

- Choose New View from the Analyze menu. A blank view appears on the screen.

- In the analysis browser, click on the triangle next to Percentiles. Select Percentile Plot and click the Create Analysis button. The Percentiles dialog box appears:

- You can choose to add summary reference lines that show five percentiles, but you will not do that in this example so simply click OK. A graph placeholder appears in the view until you assign variables.

- In the variable browser, select Weight and click the Add button. The graph plots the percentiles for the weights of all the cars.

- To compare the distributions of the weights by country, select Country and click the Split By button. The graph updates to show the percentiles for each group of cars.

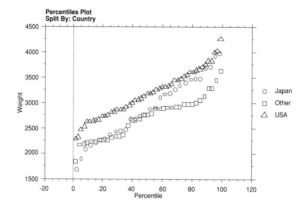

This graph shows how weights differ by country of manufacture. You can see that the 50th percentile, or median, of Japan and other countries is significantly lower than that of the U.S.

Compare percentile plots

A compare percentiles plot allows you to compare the distributions of two groups of one or more continuous variables. It graphs 19 corresponding percentiles of one group set against another group. The percentiles graphed are the 1, 2, 3, 4, 5, 10, 20, 30, 40, 50, 60, 70, 80, 90, 95, 96, 97, 98, and 99 percentiles. If either group has less than fifty values, not all percentiles can be calculated, so the plot displays as many percentiles as can be computed. The plot is designed to compare two groups only, so the assigned nominal variable can contain only two groups.

Dialog box options

When you create a compare percentiles plot or edit it using the Edit Analysis button, you see the dialog box below. The two options in the Compare Percentiles dialog box are both selected by default:

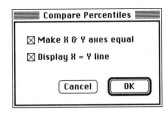

The first setting makes the axis lengths equal. The second displays a diagonal line to makes it easier to see if the percentiles for the two groups are similar. If identical, they would lie exactly on this line.

Variables

Requirements

Compare percentile plots are generated using one nominal variable with two groups only and one or more continuous variables.

Variable browser buttons

Add   To generate a compare percentiles plot, select a nominal variable with two groups only and one or more continuous variables and click Add.

Split By   The cells of any nominal variable(s) assigned using the Split By button appear in the legend.

Additional variables

Add   Each additional variable assigned is added to the same plot.

By holding down the Command (⌘) and Shift keys simultaneously and then clicking Add, you create a new plot for additional variables rather than adding to the selected plot. Any split-by variables will automatically be assigned to the new plot(s). By holding down the Command and Shift keys and then clicking Split By, you create a new plot containing the Added variables split by the new variable.

Templates

StatView offers many options for customizing all aspects of your plots, including their appearance and location and which statistics, if any, are used with them. These customizations can be saved as templates and re-used.

A sample template for each plot is included in the StatView Templates folder. You may wish to use these templates as is or create your own templates which contain the plots you commonly use, formatted to your specifications. For more information on templates, see Chapter 7, Templates and Chapter 8, Building Analyses.

Exercise

The data used in the following exercise comes from medical students. Blood lipid levels and other cardiovascular risk factors are evaluated in students as freshmen and later as seniors. In the following exercises you will compare the distribution of cholesterol values for male and female freshmen.

• Open Lipid Data in the Sample Data folder. The dataset appears on the screen.

• Choose New View from the Analyze menu. A blank view appears on the screen.

• In the analysis browser, select Compare Percentiles and click the Create Analysis button. The Compare Percentiles dialog box appears.

You have two options which help you analyze the information displayed in the graph. You can make axes the same size in order to produce a square graph. You can also display a reference line which fits the line X = Y. If the distributions of both variables is equal, all points fall on this X =Y line.

• Leave both options selected and click OK. A graph placeholder appears in the view until you assign variables.

• In the variable browser, select Gender and Cholesterol using the Command (⌘) key and click the Add button.

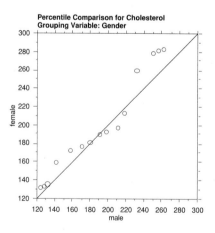

The 1st, 2nd, 98th and 99th percentiles are missing in this chart because there are less than fifty cholesterol values for females. (See the first paragraph of this section.) The point in the lower left hand corner of the graph is the 3rd percentile of females plotted against the third percentile of males. The point at the upper right hand corner is the 97th percentile of females plotted against the 97th percentile of males. At the 50th percentile the cholesterol values are almost exactly equal—the value lies almost directly on the $X = Y$ line. Below the 50th percentile, the female cholesterol count is higher than the male at every percentile. However, between the 50th and 80th percentiles the male cholesterol count is higher than the female count. At the upper extreme, the 90th to the 97th percentiles, the females once again exceed the males.

23

Troubleshooting

This chapter contains tips and troubleshooting information to help you use StatView more efficiently and solve problems you may have with the application. It also contains information about using our free technical support line. Abacus Concepts is happy to assist you with any difficulty you have using its products. However, the answers to many questions can be found in the Hints window and this manual. Please use these resources first before calling us with a question.

Eligibility for technical support

 Please fill out and mail the registration card that comes with this product, if you have not done so already. Only registered owners are entitled to the following benefits:

- Free maintenance upgrades of the software

- Free subscription to the Abacus News, our semiannual newsletter containing the latest information and tips about our software

- Free technical support by mail, phone, fax and AppleLink

- Special offers of other Abacus Concepts products

If you are not registered, we cannot verify that you own StatView and therefore cannot provide you with any of the services listed. The serial number on the back of this manual is your key to the perks we provide to our customers. Please insure your eligibility by registering this copy of StatView.

Hints window

The Hints window is a floating window that contains helpful information about every item on the screen. It is hidden when you first start the program, and you can make it visible any time by choosing Hints from the Window menu.[*] The Hints window appears automatically in some situations, but does not close automatically. You can hide it by clicking in its close box. You can resize it, move it anywhere on your screen, and hide it by clicking the close box. You can also use the Hints Preferences dialog box (discussed below) to control when the window automatically appears. An empty Hints window looks like:

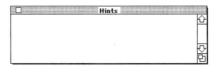

The Hints window displays two different types of information:

> 1. helpful information (hints) that tell you how to use the program

> 2. error messages that note when an incorrect program operation occurs

When you are first learning StatView, it may be helpful to keep the Hints window visible so you get instant feedback on how to use the program. It is also a valuable tool to use any time you are uncertain about a particular part of the program.

Helpful information

The Hints window displays two different levels of helpful information: balloon hints and informational hints. These types of hints appear in the Hints window when you click on an item of interest in the dataset, a view or a dialog box. When the Hints window is visible, the information changes as you click on different buttons, commands or features of the program. Using the Hints Preferences dialog box (described below) you can set the hints window to appear automatically when these messages are available.

---

[*] If you have an extended keyboard, the Help key toggles the state of the Hints window, making it visible if it is hidden and hiding it if it is visible.

Balloon hints

Balloon hints explain almost all program features: the choices in dialog boxes, buttons in the view and dataset windows and all browsers, all the parts of the dataset and views. These hints are called Balloon hints because they contain the same information that appears when you turn on Balloon Help if you are running System 7.

Even if you are running System 7, you can use the Hints window to show balloon hints (as opposed to System 7 balloons). The only items for which System 7 Balloons are available but not StatView's balloon hints are menu items.

Informational hints

Informational hints offer more detailed information than balloon hints. They explain the following features:

- definitions of the functions in the Formula, Recode, Series, Random Numbers and Criteria dialog boxes
- variable usage for template slots in the Assign Variables dialog box
- dimmed options in analysis dialog boxes when you edit an analysis

Error messages

When an error occurs, StatView generates an error message. The Hints window automatically appears to display the error message, often an explanation of why the requested action cannot be completed. In the Hints Preferences dialog box, you can set an option to have the program beep as well when it displays an error message.

Alert messages

An alert message warns you of potentially dangerous situation or advises you of the consequences of an action you requested. Alert messages sometimes appear in a box with a single OK button. You can set a preference to have these appear in the Hints window instead, which automatically opens when there is an alert message to display. The advantage to this setting is that your work is not interrupted by an alert box, yet you still see the alert message.

Hints preferences

The settings in the Hints Preferences dialog box determine when the Hints window appears and some aspects of what it contains:

- whether the Hints window automatically opens when there is either a balloon hint or informational hint to display

- the font and size of the text in the Hints window

- whether StatView beeps when displaying an error message

- whether alert messages appear in the Hints window instead of in a box with a single OK button

To set Hints preferences:

- Choose Preferences from the Manage menu. The Choose Preferences dialog box appears.

- Choose Hints from the scrolling list and click Modify. The Hints Preferences dialog box appears.

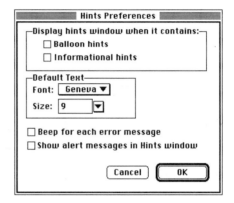

- Click the desired check boxes and click OK. You return to the Choose Preferences dialog box.

- Click Done to execute the preference settings. New preferences go into effect immediately.

Data organization

As mentioned in the Datasets chapter, data organization is a crucial first step in creating your dataset. If you are having trouble with data organization, refer to the analysis chapter that pertains to the analysis you are using. Data organization for each type of statistical analysis is discussed in these chapters (11 through 22). In particular, the following analyses require specific formats of data organization:

Repeated measures ANOVA

Unpaired comparisons

Paired comparisons

Cell plots

Contingency tables

StatView Library and temp files

StatView stores information in a file called the StatView Library that is kept in the same folder as StatView. The Library contains all preference settings and information the program needs keeps to speed up certain operations (for example, application preferences and category definitions). It also keeps information about where the StatView Templates and StatView Tools folders are located. If the Library file is thrown out or missing, StatView creates a new one with default preference settings, etc., restored. A new Library will not contain the previous Library's preference settings. You will have to specify these settings again in the Preference dialog boxes.

The Library can be corrupted anytime StatView (or potentially any other program) crashes. StatView attempts to reconstruct the information in the Library if it finds it out of date or corrupted.

In addition to the StatView Library, StatView uses temp files which are kept either in the System Folder in a folder called StatView 4.0 Temp Files or within the Temporary File folder under System 7. These temp files provide a place for StatView to store information for an undo operation when there is not enough RAM for that information to be stored in memory. These files, under normal circumstances, are deleted when they are no longer needed. If you delete them while StatView is running, then you confuse the program (any information that was needed in that file will be lost). If you delete them when StatView is not running, there is no problem.

Importing

It is important to identify the correct separator characters to make the importing process simple and trouble-free. A separator character is a character that occurs between data points and tells StatView where a data point in one column ends and the next begins. Separator characters also define the end of rows in the dataset.

If you are not certain what separator characters are used in a text file you are importing, open the file in a word processing application and choose the setting that enables you to see formatting characters within the document. Formatting characters are non-textual characters that indicate tabs, spaces, paragraphs and so forth. Each word processing application represents these characters a little differently, so check the user manual for your application to see how they appear.

If a separator character other than a Tab is used, such as a comma, StatView needs to know. Problems can arise if an improper separator is used in the source file, or if you tell

StatView to use a separator character that does not match the one used in the source application.

Spaces as separators

If you choose *spaces* and the text file contains strings with spaces within an individual entry, StatView expects the spaces to indicate separate data points. For example, it would be a mistake to import this text file with spaces as a separator:

Employee Age

Kate Bishop 46

David Wong 19

In this data, spaces appear not only between data points but also inside them. StatView would import this text file as the following three-variable dataset:

	Column 1	Column 2	Column 3	Input Colum
1	Employee	Age	•	
2	Kate	Bishop	46.000	
3	David	Wong	19.000	

Incorrect Spaces Import — Compact Expand Criteria: No Criteria

As you can see, StatView split the employee names in two. To remedy this, you could either separate data points with some other character besides spaces (such as Tabs), or place double quotation marks around distinct data points having spaces within them.

The text file should look like this:

Employee Age	Employee Age
John Frank 34	"John Frank" "34"
Eric Jones 45	"Eric Jones" "45"

or this

Commas as separators

Another example of an incorrect choice would be to import the following file without specifying commas as a separator:

Name,Age

Yukito,32

Setsuko,35

Armita,30

Choosing Tab, for example, tells StatView to import the file as a one-variable dataset:

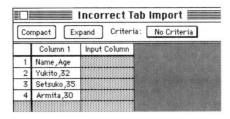

Remedies for common errors

- If some values in certain rows are shifted to the right, see if the source text file contains groups of the separator character you used (two commas, for instance). If it does, edit out the extra separator characters from the source text file and import the file into StatView again.

- If some values are shifted to the left in a file imported with space separators, you used a space separator to indicate a missing value. Remember that two or more spaces are condensed into one. If two or more spaces are grouped together, edit those out of the source text file. Type a period with a space on either side into the source file where the missing value belongs and import the file again.

- If you have an empty data cell (without a missing value symbol), you probably chose the return character to separate values on a line. Since duplicate returns are not compressed into a single missing value (•), your data will be imported improperly. Check the text file to see if there are any duplicate return characters and remove them.

- If you want to import a variable of mixed data type (real, integer and string, for instance) or one with errors, choose "Make columns with errors have type string" in the Import dialog box. This setting turns a variable of mixed data type or a variable with field errors into a variable with a String data type. You can import the dataset and examine the variable to see what caused the errors. Correct the errors and change the variable to the appropriate data type (through the attribute pane).

- If you have an inordinately large number of missing values in your dataset, check to see if the source text file has formatting characters in it such as dollar signs, percent signs, etc. This is more likely to occur if you import a text file from a spreadsheet application such as Excel.

Printing

If you are having problems related to printing, following these guidelines may remedy the situation.

- Try printing from another application to determine if it is indeed a printing problem or if the problem lies only in the use of StatView.

- Make sure the printer driver for the printer you are using shows in the Chooser and is selected.

- Make sure the name of the printer appears in the Chooser. If it does not, check your cable connection.

- Some printers require you to install their own screen fonts that ship with the printer, otherwise you may get misaligned print or odd spacing.

- If you are using background printing, turn background printing off (in the Chooser) or turn print spooler off under the Apple menu.

Formulae

Some important guidelines to follow in creating formulas: always use Date/Time operators for calculations involving Date/Time values; never use category variables in arithmetic formulas (use them with if/then/else statements only).

StatView warns you of an error in creating formulas, such as entering an invalid argument (i.e., a constant rather than a variable, or vice versa, the wrong number of arguments, unknown variable names, etc.). StatView highlights the problem area, shows an Error Hint telling you what to do about it and does not compute the function. When you satisfy the requirements of the formula and click Calculate, the formula calculates. The Hints window contains useful information about functions and the arguments they require.

Opening SuperANOVA files with formulae

If you open a SuperANOVA dataset that contains a formula with a function StatView cannot recognize (ExcludeRow, IncludeRow and SelectRow), StatView will not be able to calculate the formula. When the dataset opens, StatView will show the Formula dialog box with the unreadable function highlighted. You can then enter a new function or click Cancel. If you cancel the dialog box, no new column will appear.

Problem-solving techniques

If you encounter a problem using StatView or do not understand something about the program, we recommend that you follow these steps:

1. If you get an Error Hint when trying to do something, follow the instructions in the Hints window to solve the problem. In the Formula dialog box, Hints give information about functions that may prove helpful. There are instructions on how to use the Hints window earlier in this chapter.

2. Read this book, using the table of contents or index to locate information.

3. See if your question is addressed in the appropriate section of this chapter.

4. If your question involves setting up an experiment, see if one of the sample datasets provided with the program mirrors your situation.

5. If you believe a bug in StatView is the cause of your problem, please follow the Troubleshooting steps later in this chapter and send us a bug report, if necessary.

6. If your attempts at finding a solution fail, contact us.

Technical support

Please provide your serial number (from the back of this manual) whenever you contact Abacus Concepts for technical support. Only registered users are eligible for technical support, and we provide support only to the person on record as the registered owner.

Mail: Abacus Concepts, Inc.
Technical Support
1984 Bonita Avenue
Berkeley, CA 97404-1038

Phone: (510) 540-1949
8:30 am to 4:00 pm PST
Monday through Friday

Fax: (510) 540-0260

On-line: AppleLink: ABACUS

Problems and solutions

Here are some common dilemmas, followed by suggestions or explanations.

Results appear incorrect

- Results may seem incorrect if you have too few significant digits displayed in your tables. Change the number of decimal places displayed with the Preferences command in the Manage menu. Choose Table, click Modify, and change the default number of decimal places.

- All statistical routines in StatView have been validated using standard datasets and compared to results obtained with other commercially available software packages. If you feel that there is an error, please send us information about what you feel is incorrect and why. If you have compared the result to that of another application, please send us the output from that package as well.

- StatView's calculations depend on Apple's numerics package (SANE). If you use software with an INIT that bypasses SANE and uses its own numerics package you may get different results. Remove the INIT from your system folder to get StatView's actual results.

Running out of memory

If StatView does not have enough memory to perform an operation, it alerts you with a dialog box. If this happens, you need to increase the amount of memory that StatView sets aside for itself. Regardless of the amount of RAM in your Macintosh, StatView uses only the amount of memory you allocate for it. To increase this amount of memory:

- Quit the program and select the StatView icon.

- Choose Get Info from the File menu.

- If you are running System 6, type a larger amount in the Application Size text box. If you are running System 7, type a larger amount in the Current Size text box.

The next time you start StatView, it will use the new amount of memory you allocated.

Your Macintosh may not have enough memory to give StatView an increased amount of memory. If that occurs, you can try the following steps to free up additional memory.

- Check the RAM cache (in the control panel). Turn it off, or set it to a low number (32K).

- Turn MultiFinder off and run StatView under the Finder (if you are using System 6.0.x).

- If you are running System 7, turn on virtual memory.

- If all else fails, you may need to buy additional memory for your computer.

Unexpected results

StatView's behavior in the view is largely dependent on what results are selected. If StatView creates several tables and graphs when you expect only one, it is probably using variables or analyses from results that are selected in a part of the view not visible in the window. Open the Results browser from the Window menu to see which results are selected, and look at the Results Selected note in the upper right corner of the window to see the number of results currently selected. The "Create an Analysis" section in the Analysis Skills chapter explains the interactions between the analysis browser, variable browser and view selections.

Grouped objects can account for unexpected numbers of results appearing. You may intend to add a variable to a single result, but effectively assign it to several. If you used the Group command in the Layout menu to group graphs and tables, selecting one of the objects effectively selects them all. The next action you take in the view then applies to all objects in the group.

Random crashes

If the program appears to crash somewhat randomly, try throwing away the StatView Library file contained in the same folder as StatView. (See earlier section on Library and Temp files.) StatView will rebuild the file when you reopen it. Take note that doing this restores all default preference settings. If throwing away the Library file does not help, try booting with a "clean" system. This will reveal whether the difficulty is simply an incompatibility between StatView and an INIT or cdev in your system. To reboot from a clean System 7, hold down the Shift key and choose Restart from the Special menu. The startup screen will say "Extensions off."

To reboot from a clean System 6:

1. Turn off your machine.
2. Insert the System Tools disk that came with your Macintosh and restart.
3. Check that the topmost icon on the desktop is the System Tools disk.
4. Drag the System document out of the system folder on your hard disk onto the desktop.
5. Run the application using the "clean" system and see if the problem recurs.
6. Before you restart, drag the System document back into the system folder on your hard disk.

Repeatable problems

When you have a problem with StatView, first try to duplicate the problem. Come up with a series of steps that reliably reproduce the problem. When you can reproduce it, boot from a clean system (see above) and try again. Answer the following questions:

Can you repeat the problem using the clean system?

No. Then the problem is in the system. You can do a binary search through your system to isolate the culprit. Remove half of the INITs and cdevs and try to recreate the problem. Repeat this process until you narrow it down to the cause of the problem. If you discover an incompatibility between StatView and another product, we would like to hear about it.

Yes. Then try to recreate it using one of the sample datasets that came with StatView.

Can you repeat the problem using sample data?

No. Then the problem lies in the structure of your data. If you imported your data, try importing it again, and examine the data carefully for importing errors. Read the "Importing" section earlier in this chapter for more help.

Yes. Then reinstall StatView from your master diskettes.

Can you repeat the problem with a new copy of StatView?

No. Then your application had been corrupted somehow.

Yes. Then remove additional hardware or try to reproduce it on a different hardware set-up.

Can you repeat the problem without added hardware or on a different machine?

No. Then the problem is hardware-related. If you can isolate the cause, we would like to hear about it, and the hardware manufacturer probably would, too.

Yes. Then send us a report, using the Report Form on your StatView disk. We will respond promptly and keep you informed of our findings.

If you think you've found a bug…

 We would like to hear about it, but first please run through the steps above to eliminate possible causes other than StatView. We do our best to insure the quality and consistency of StatView, but no software is bug-free. We are very appreciative of the help we get from StatView owners who tell us about any problems that our testing did not uncover. If you want to tell us about a suspected bug, please print a copy of the Report Form on your StatView disk, fill it in and send it to us at this address:

> Abacus Concepts, Inc.
>
> Technical Support
>
> 1984 Bonita Avenue
>
> Berkeley, CA 94704-1038

We strongly prefer that you send us your dataset and analyses on diskette. We ask this for several reasons: it increases the likelihood that we can duplicate your problem and diagnose the cause, reduces processing time and eliminates the need for us to call you and ask for more information. We respect necessary confidentiality guidelines with all information sent to us and will send it all back at your request. We use the information you send *only* for the purpose of isolating and solving the problem you reported. If it is not possible to send us your data and analyses on disk, please send printouts.

Shortcuts

This appendix summarizes the shortcuts you can use with the keyboard and mouse.

Assign variables dialog box

Mouse/keyboard action	Command
Double-click on variable	Assign variable to selected slot and move selection to next slot (if present)
Command double-click	Assign variable to selected slot and keep selection in current slot
Tab	Select next slot
Shift-Tab	Select previous slot
Delete	Remove selected variable from slot

Analysis browser

Mouse/keyboard action	Command
Double-click on analysis	Same as selecting an analysis or result and clicking Create button
Double-click on analysis header	Creates the default output for the analysis

| Control double-click or Control Create button | Bypass dialog box for analysis |
| Double-click on pane control (∑ if open, ⊞ if closed) | Show/hide analysis browser |

Variable browser

Mouse/keyboard action	Command
Double-click on variable	Same as selecting variable and clicking top browser button (Show or Add)
Control double-click	Makes selected variable a dependent or Y variable
Option double-click	Makes selected variable a split-by variable
Control-option double-click	Removes selected variable
Command-Shift-double-click	Creates a new result using added variable
Command-Shift-Control double-click	Creates a new result using added variable as a dependent
Command-Shift-Option double-click	Creates a new result using added variable as a split-by variable

View

Mouse/keyboard action	Command
Double-click on table or graph	Brings up Edit Display or Edit Analysis dialog box depending on preference
Option double-click on table or graph	Brings up Edit Analysis or Edit Display dialog box depending on preference
Command-click empty Recalculate box	Forces recalculation of all analyses in view, rather than just those that need updating
Double-click on imported picture	Returns picture to original size (only imported PICTs)
Double-click on the empty space in top bar of view	Brings dataset to front if only one dataset is associated with the view
Shift-click	Select multiple objects
Hold down control key	Toggles cursor to reshape mode
In Draw menu, double-click on arrow	Toggles cursor to reshape mode
In Draw menu, command-foreground or fill color	Changes both foreground and fill attributes simultaneously
Arrow keys	Move selected object one unit in direction of arrow

Page up, page down keys	Scroll view one page up or down
Home, end keys	Position view to top left corner (home) or bottom right corner (end)
Help key	Show or hide hints window

Dataset

Mouse/keyboard action	Command
Double-click on attribute pane control ($\overline{x}$ if closed, $\overline{x}$ if open)	Opens attribute pane if it is closed. Closes attribute pane if only first five lines are showing or else closes to show only first five lines.
Double-click on split pane control	Open or close vertical split window pane
Click in blank space above row numbers	Deselect all rows, columns and cells in dataset
Double-click in blank space above row numbers	Create a new view
Control-click on a criteria in Criteria pop-up menu	Select all rows in the dataset that meet the criteria
Double-click on row number	Include or exclude row
Double-click on empty space at top	Bring view to front, if only one view is associated with dataset
Arrow keys	Move selection one cell, column or row in direction of arrow
Page up, page down keys	Scroll dataset one page up or down
Home, end keys	Position dataset to top left corner (home) or bottom right corner (end)
In compact variable More choices dialog box: Command-click on New	Creates category with group names using column names of selected variables
Click on Source pop-up menu in attribute pane for Formula variables	Opens Formula dialog box containing formula definition for the variable

Dialog boxes and alerts

Mouse/keyboard action	Effect
Command-Period, Escape	Cancels any dialog box that has a Cancel button
Enter	Executes dialog box settings (the same as clicking OK, Done, or other button)

Return	Executes dialog box settings if there are no text fields in the dialog box. With text fields, acts as a normal Return key.
Tab	Moves cursor from one text field or scrolling list to the next
Shift-Tab	Moves cursor to the previous text field or scrolling list
Up and Down arrow keys	Moves the selection from one item to another in scrolling lists
Type first letter	In dialog boxes without scrolling lists or text fields, selects the button or checkbox which begins with this letter

Formula, Random, Series, Criteria

Mouse/keyboard action	Command
Double-click on lines in variable or function browser	Adds variable or function to the definition area
Double-click on browser control triangle	Open or close browser split pane
Double-click above definition area	Brings dataset to the front

Scrolling lists in dialog boxes and browsers

Mouse/keyboard action	Command
Command-click	Select multiple discontinuous entries in browser or dialog box scrolling lists (if applicable)
Shift-click	Select multiple continuous entries in browser or dialog box scrolling lists (if applicable)
Command-click on triangle	Open or close all headings
Type first letter	Selects entry in scrolling list which begins with that letter (dialog boxes only)

Results browser

Mouse/keyboard action	Command
Double-click on result	Select and scroll to result
Double-click on result heading	Select all results in heading and scroll to first result

B

Algorithms, Formulas and Functions

Computational considerations

All calculations are performed in 80 bit extended arithmetic which ensures approximately 18 decimal places of accuracy.

Sum of Squares calculations

Several statistics require calculation of the sum of squared deviations (sum of squares):

$$\sum (X-\bar{x})^2$$

StatView uses an algorithm which provides more accurate results for the sum of squared deviations than the Monroe Calculator variance formula:

$$\sum X^2 - \frac{(\sum X)^2}{n}$$

StatView uses the following algorithm for the sum of squared deviations:

$$\sum(X-k)^2 - n(k-\bar{x})^2$$

where k is the first non-missing, non-excluded value for the variable, and $\bar{x}$ is the calculated variable mean.

In addition, several statistics require that the sum of deviation cross products be calculated:

$$\sum(X-\bar{x})(Y-\bar{y})$$

StatView uses the following algorithm for the sum of deviation cross products:

$$\sum(X-a)(Y-b) -n(a-\bar{x})(b-\bar{y})$$

where (a,b) is the first non-missing, non-excluded X, Y pair, $\bar{x}$ is the X variable mean, and $\bar{y}$ is the Y variable mean.

Matrix inversions

Several statistics require matrix inversions. StatView uses the Sweep Operator procedure to invert matrices.

Descriptive Statistics

Formulas for continuous variables

n = number of non-missing, non-excluded values

Count = n

Mean = $\dfrac{\sum X}{n}$ (referred to below as $\bar{x}$ or $\bar{y}$)

Variance (s^2) = $\dfrac{\sum(X-\bar{x})^2}{n-1}$

Standard Deviation $(s) = \sqrt{s^2}$

Standard Error of the Mean $(s_{\bar{x}}) = \dfrac{s}{\sqrt{n}}$

Coefficient of Variation $= \dfrac{s}{\bar{x}}$

Minimum = smallest value among X

Maximum = largest values among X

Range = Maximum - Minimum

Sum $= \sum X$

Sum of squares $= \sum X^2$

missing = Count of the missing values

Geometric Mean $= \sqrt[n]{\prod X}$

Harmonic Mean $= \left(\dfrac{\sum \frac{1}{X}}{n} \right)^{-1}$

Kurtosis $= \left(\dfrac{m_4}{m_2^2} \right) - 3$

Skewness $= \dfrac{m_3}{m_2 \sqrt{m_2}}$

where: $\quad m_2 = \dfrac{\sum (X - \bar{x})^2}{n}, \quad m_3 = \dfrac{\sum (X - \bar{x})^3}{n}, \quad m_4 = \dfrac{\sum (X - \bar{x})^4}{n}$

Mode = unique most commonly occurring value among X

Median = 50th percentile (see below for percentile calculation)

Interquartile Range (IQR) = 75th percentile - 25th percentile (see below for percentile calculation)

Median Absolute Deviation from the Median (MAD) = Median(D), where $D = |X -$ Median(X) $|$

$p\%$ Trimmed Mean $= (X_{k+1} + \cdots + X_{n-k})/(n-2k)$, where the X's are sorted from smallest to largest & k is chosen so that k observations represent p % of the data

Formulas for nominal variables

Count, # missing and mode are as above

levels = number of uniquely occurring values among X

Percentiles

The pth percentile using linear interpolation is: $(1-f)\,x_k + f^*x_{k+1}$

where x_k and x_{k+1} are the kth and $k+1$th non-missing, non-excluded values in the variable, after sorting the X's from smallest to largest.

k and f are determined from the value v shown below. k is the integer part of v and f is the fractional part:
$$v = \frac{np}{100} + 0.5$$
where n is the count, p is the desired percentile.

One Sample Analysis

N = number of observations

$DF = N - 1$

SE = standard error of $\bar{x} = \dfrac{s}{\sqrt{N}}$

One Sample t-Test

U = hypothesized mean, entered by user

$$t = \frac{\bar{x} - U}{SE}$$

Confidence interval for the mean

t_a is the (two-tailed) critical value of the t distribution at level a & degrees of freedom

lower $= \bar{x} - t_a * SE$

upper $= \bar{x} + t_a * SE$

Chi-Square Test for Variance

σ^2 = hypothesized variance, entered by user

$X^2 = DF * s^2 / S^2$

Confidence Interval for the Variance

x_l = lower chi-square critical value, level a, DF degrees of freedom

x_u = upper chi-square critical value, level a, DF degrees of freedom

lower $= DF * s^2 / x_u$

upper $= DF * s^2 / x_l$

Paired Comparisons

N = number of paired observations

$D = X_1 - X_2$

$DF = N - 1$

$\bar{D}$ = mean of D

s_d = standard deviation of D

SE = standard error of $\bar{D} = \dfrac{s_d}{\sqrt{N}}$

Paired t-Test

Δ = hypothesized mean difference, entered by user

$$t = \frac{\overline{D} - \Delta}{SE}$$

Confidence interval for the paired mean difference

t_a is the (two-tailed) critical value of the t distribution at level a & degrees of freedom

$$\text{lower} = \overline{D} - t_a * SE$$

$$\text{upper} = \overline{D} + t_a * SE$$

Z Test and confidence interval for the correlation coefficient

These are calculated using the r to z transformation discussed under Correlation/Covariance, below.

Unpaired Comparisons

N_1 = number of observations in group 1

N_2 = number of observations in group 2

$DF = N_1 + N_2 - 2$

$\overline{x}_1$ is the mean of the group 1 observations

$\overline{x}_2$ is the mean of the group 2 observations

$D = \overline{x}_1 - \overline{x}_2$

s_1 is the standard deviation of the group 1 observations

s_2 is the standard deviation of the group 2 observations

$$SE = \sqrt{\frac{N_1 * s_1^2 + N_2 * s_2^2}{DF} * \frac{N_1 + N_2}{N_1 * N_2}}$$

Unpaired t-Test

Δ = hypothesized mean difference, entered by user

$$t = \frac{D - \Delta}{SE}$$

Confidence interval for the unpaired mean difference

t_a is the (two-tailed) critical value of the t distribution at level a & degrees of freedom

lower $= D - t_a * SE$

upper $= D + t_a * SE$

F Test for Variance Ratio

VR = hypothesized variance ratio, entered by user

$$F = \frac{s_1^2}{s_2^2} * VR$$

$df = N_1 - 1, N_2 - 1$

Confidence Interval for the variance ratio

lower $= F\left(N_1 - 1, N_2 - 1, a\right)$

upper $= F\left(N_2 - 1, N_1 - 1, a\right)$

where $F(n, m, a)$ is the critical value of the F distribution with n and m degrees of freedom at level a

Correlation/Covariance

Covariances and correlations are computed in StatView using provisional means.

Partial Correlations

$$PC_{ij} = -IC_{ij} / \sqrt{IC_{ii} * IC_{jj}} ,$$

where PC is the partial correlation matrix & IC is the inverse of the correlation matrix

Bartlett's Test of Sphericity

$$X^2 = -N \ln\left(\det(C)\right)$$

$$df = [n * (n + 1) / 2] - 1$$

N = # observations

n = # variables

$\det(C)$ = determinant of the correlation matrix

P-values and confidence intervals

These are computed using the transformation

$$z = \frac{1}{2} \ln\left(\frac{1+r}{1-r}\right)$$

which has an approximately normal distribution with

$$\text{mean} = \frac{1}{2} \ln\left(\frac{1+R}{1-R}\right) \text{ and}$$

$$\text{variance} = \frac{1}{N-3}$$

when the data are a random sample of N observations from a bivariate normal population with correlation R.

Regression

StatView applies the Sweep Operator to the XX' matrix of cross product deviations in order to calculate regression coefficients. Sweeping operations are discussed in Draper and Smith (1981), Hocking (1985) and Goodnight (1979). The sweeping operation is used to add and delete variables from the regression equation. Beta coefficients, partial correlations, multiple correlation, partial Fs and residual sum of squares are computed as each variable enters (or leaves) the regression equation. The calculation of confidence bands for the mean and confidence intervals for the slope of a simple regression is discussed in Draper and Smith (1981) and Sokal and Rohlf (1981).

ANOVA

Single factor Factorial model

For a single factor factorial model StatView uses the procedures outlined by Winer (1971) in Chapter 3. The Model II estimate of between component variance is discussed both by Winer and Afifi and Azen (1979). The formula is as follows:

$$\frac{\left(\text{Mean Square}_{\text{between groups}} - \text{Mean Square}_{\text{within groups}}\right)\left(k - 1\right)}{\sum\limits_i J_i - \dfrac{\sum\limits_i J_i^2}{\sum\limits_i J_i}} \qquad i = 1 \cdots k$$

where J_i is the count of non-missing non-excluded values for the ith group.

Single factor Repeated Measures model

For a single factor repeated measures model StatView uses the procedures outlined by Winer (1971) in Chapter 4. For a single factor model reliability estimates are computed (Winer, p. 283). Reliability estimates are given for the mean of all treatments and for a single treatments. The formulas are provided below:

$$\widehat{\Theta} = \frac{\left(MS_{\text{between groups}} - MS_{\text{within groups}}\right)}{k * MS_{\text{within groups}}}$$

$$\text{mean of all treatments} = \frac{k\,\widehat{\Theta}}{1 + k\,\widehat{\Theta}}$$

$$\text{mean of single treatment} = \frac{\widehat{\Theta}}{1 + \widehat{\Theta}}$$

k = number of treatments

Two- and more-factor factorial and repeated measures models

The technique used for calculating the sums of squares for the various tests reported by StatView is the reduction technique as described by Searle (1971, pp. 246 - 248). The basic idea of the reduction technique is as follows. First a model is fit with all possible main effects and interactions (the full model), and the residual sum of squares, RSS_{full} is calculated. Then for each main effect or interaction to be tested, another model is fit, containing all the terms in the model except the one currently being considered. Once again, the residual sum of squares is calculated. Let the residual sum of squares for the model excluding only effect X (where X is any main effect or interaction in the model) be denoted RSS_x. Then the sum of squares for testing the hypothesis that effect X has no influence on the dependent variable is calculated as: $SS_x = RSS_x - SS_{full}$. This calculation is carried out for each term in the model.

The reduction sums of squares are calculated using a method described in detail by Hocking (1985, pp. 146 - 148). First, the matrix X^TX is calculated, using a full rank parameterization for the design matrix X. In this parameterization, the first element of each row of the design matrix is a 1 (for the intercept), and for a main effect with k levels, there are $k-1$ columns in the design matrix. For all but the last level of the factor, a 1 is placed in the column corresponding to the level of that factor for a given observation (row), while for observations with the last level of the factor, all $k-1$ columns are filled with -1s. The columns corresponding to interaction terms for a particular row are formed as the Kronecker product of the columns corresponding to all main effects contained in the interaction. Finally, the value of the dependent variable is stored as the last column in the design matrix.

The residual sum of squares for the full model, (SS_{full}) can be found in the lower right hand corner of the matrix X^TX after it has been swept on all of its columns except the last one, i.e. the one corresponding to the dependent variable. (See Goodnight (1979), for a description of the sweep operator). Due to the reversibility of the sweep operator, RSS_x for any effect X can be calculated by re-sweeping the columns corresponding to the effect in question in the fully swept matrix, and extracting the lower right hand element. The sums of squares for each effect are then calculated as described above.

For factorial models with no missing cells, this technique produces sums of squares which generally agree with such programs as BMDP4V or SAS GLM (Type III SS), even for models in which the cell sizes are not equal (unbalanced data). If missing cells are present, then at some point in the sweeping described above, a pivot element will become too small to allow the sweeping process to continue. By recording the point at which the algorithm fails and then attempting to successfully sweep those columns in the course of resweeping the matrix to calculate the sums of squares for each of the effects, the algorithm described here produces what Hocking (1985) terms *effective hypotheses*. These hypotheses often have fewer degrees of freedom than would otherwise be expected, because they only consider those parts of the hypothesis for which there is sufficient data to calculate the necessary contrasts. For example, in a 2-way analysis with factors A and B each having two levels, if there are no observations for the cell (A=2,B=1), then each of the effects A, B and the A*B interaction will lose one degree of freedom, since, for example, the sum of squares for factor A will be calculated without considering level 2 of A. Essentially, the algorithm described here is attempting to test "as much as possible" of the usual hypotheses which would be tested if there were no missing cells, and ignores those levels of the factors for which any values are missing. Thus, this algorithm may report zero degrees of freedom for some of the effects in the model, whereas other programs may still produce a sum of squares with non-zero degrees of freedom. Programs which do produce sums of squares in these cases are generally testing hypotheses involving weighted averages of the cell means involved in the effect. These hypotheses may or may not be of interest for any particular dataset.

Multiple Comparisons

Multiple comparisons are discussed in Winer (1971) and Milliken and Johnson (1984). The formulas used are listed below.

For all tests:

k is the number of groups

a is the user entered significance level

$r = \dfrac{1}{N_1} + \dfrac{1}{N_2}$, where N_1 is the count of group 1 and N_2 is the count of group 2

MSE is the error mean square

DF is the error degrees of freedom

MD is the mean difference between the group means

a difference is declared significant if $|\ MD\ | > D$, where D is the test specific critical difference defined below

Fisher's Protected Least Significant Difference (PLSD)

$D = t * \sqrt{r * MSE}$ where t is the (two-tailed) critical value of the t distribution at level a & degrees of freedom

DF Scheffé F test

$D = \sqrt{F * MSE * DF * r}$ where F is the critical value of the F distribution at level a & degrees of freedom k-1.

DF Bonferroni/Dunn

$D = t * \sqrt{r * MSE}$ where t is the (two-tailed) critical value of the t distribution at level $a\ /m$ & degrees of freedom DF & m is the number of comparisons ($= k * (k - 1) / 2$)

Contingency Table Analysis

Two way tables

N = number of observations

r = # rows of contingency table

c = # columns of contingency table

$DF = (r-1)(c-1)$

$$\chi^2 = \sum \frac{(O-E)^2}{E} \quad \text{where:}$$

$E = CR/N$, the expected values

C = column total

R = row total

O = observed value

N = grand total

$$G \text{ Statistic} = 2\left[\left[\sum O \ln O\right] - \left[\sum R \ln R\right] - \left[\sum C \ln C\right] + N \ln N\right]$$

$$\text{Contingency Coefficient} = \sqrt{\frac{\chi^2}{\chi^2 + N}}$$

$$\text{Phi} = \sqrt{\frac{\chi^2}{N}}$$

$$\text{Cramer's } V = \sqrt{\frac{\chi^2}{N(q-1)}}$$

Note: when $r = c = 2$, V is the same as Phi where $q = \min(r,c)$.

Chi-Square with continuity correction ($r = c = 2$ only)

$$\chi^2 = \frac{N\left[\,|AD - BC| - \frac{N}{2}\right]^2}{(A+B)(C+D)(A+C)(B+D)} \quad \text{where:}$$

A=observed value in row1 column1

B=observed value in row1 column2

C=observed value in row2 column1

D=observed value in row2 column2

Fisher's Exact Test ($r = c = 2$ only)

Post-hoc cell contribution $= \dfrac{O - E}{\sqrt{E\left(1 - \dfrac{R}{N}\right)\left(1 - \dfrac{C}{N}\right)}}$

Cell chi-square $= \dfrac{\left(O - E\right)^2}{E}$

Nonparametrics

One Sample Sign Test

U = user specified hypothesized value

N_+ = # observations $> U$

N_- = # observations $< U$

$N = N_+ + N_-$

Exact P-Value: Binomial $(N, 1/2)$

Approximate P-Value:

Mean $= N / 2$

$SD = \sqrt{N} / 2$

$Z = (N_+ - \text{Mean}) / SD$

Mann-Whitney U

N = number of observations

Appendix B: Algorithms, Formulas and Functions

n_1 = number of observations in group 1

n_2 = number of observations in group 2

$N = n_1 + n_2$

$R_1 = \sum$ Rank of first group

$R_2 = \sum$ Rank of second group

$$U_1 = n_1 n_2 + \frac{n_2 (n_2 + 1)}{2} - R_2$$

$$U_2 = n_1 n_2 + \frac{n_1 (n_1 + 1)}{2} - R_1$$

$U = \min(U_1, U_2)$

$U' = n_1 n_2 - U$

$$\text{Mean} = \frac{n_1 n_2}{2}$$

$$\text{Standard Deviation} = \sqrt{\frac{n_1 n_2 (n_1 + n_2 + 1)}{12}}$$

$$Z = \frac{U - \text{Mean}}{\text{Standard Deviation}}$$

Correction for Ties:

$$\text{Standard Deviation becomes} = \sqrt{\left[\frac{n_1 n_2}{N (N - 1)} \right] \left[\frac{N^3 - N}{12} - \sum T \right]}$$

where $T = \frac{t^3 - t}{12}$ and t is the number of observations tied for a given rank.

Kolmogorov-Smirnov

See Siegel, pp. 127-136, and Hollander.

Wald-Wolfowitz Runs Test

N_1 = number of group 1 observations.
N_2 = number of group 2 observations.
R = # of Runs. A run is any sequence of scores from the same group.

$$\text{Mean} = \frac{2\,n_1 n_2}{n_1 + n_2} + 1$$

$$\text{Std. Deviation} = \sqrt{\frac{2\,n_1 n_2 \left(2\,n_1 n_2 - n_1 - n_2 \right)}{\left(n_1 + n_2 \right)^2 \left(n_1 + n_2 - 1 \right)}}$$

$$Z = \frac{\left| R - \text{Mean} \right| - 0.5}{\text{Std. Deviation}}$$

Note that there are no correction for ties. Ties may invalidate the results.

Wilcoxon Signed-Rank

$D = X - Y$ for each matched pair

N = number of matched pairs excluding those with a D of zero

R = Rank of $|D|$

$R+ = \Sigma R$ with $D > 0$

$R- = \Sigma R$ with $D < 0$

$T = R^+$ if $R^+ \leq R^-$ else R^-

$$\text{Mean} = \frac{N\left(N+1\right)}{4}$$

$$\text{Standard Deviation} = \sqrt{\frac{N\left(N+1\right)\left(2N+1\right)}{24}}$$

$$Z = \frac{T - \text{Mean}}{\text{Std. Deviation}}$$

Correction for Ties:

$$\text{Standard Deviation} = \sqrt{\frac{N(N+1)(2N+1)-\frac{\sum T}{2}}{24}}$$

Where $T = t^3 - t$ and t is the number of observations tied for a given rank.

Paired Sign Test

$N_+ = \#$ pairs with $X_1 > X_2$

$N_- = \#$ pairs with $X_1 < X_2$

$N = N_+ + N_-$

Exact P-Value: Binomial$(N, 1/2)$

Approximate P-Value:

$\quad$ Mean $= N/2$

$\quad$ $SD = \sqrt{N} / 2$

$\quad$ $Z = (N_+ - \text{Mean}) / SD$

Spearman Rank Correlation Coefficient

N = number of matched pairs

R_x = Rank of X_i

R_y = Rank of Y_i

$D = R_x - R_y$ for each matched pair

Rho $(\rho) = 1 - \dfrac{6 \sum D^2}{N(N^2 - 1)}$

$Z = \rho \sqrt{N - 1}$

Correction for Ties:

Rho (ρ) becomes $= \dfrac{\sum x^2 + \sum y^2 - \sum D^2}{2\sqrt{(\sum x^2)(\sum y^2)}}$

$$\sum x^2 = \frac{N^3 - N}{12} - \sum T_x$$

$$\sum y^2 = \frac{N^3 - N}{12} - \sum T_y$$

$$T_x = \frac{t^3 - t}{12}$$ where t is the number of X observations tied for a given rank.

$$T_y = \frac{t^3 - t}{12}$$ where t is the number of Y observations tied for a given rank.

Kendall Correlation Coefficient

N = number of matched pairs

C = Kendall Statistic determined as follows:

Rank the observations on the X variable from 1 to N. Rank the observations on the Y variable from 1 to N. Arrange the list of N subjects so that the X ranks of the subjects are in their natural order, i.e. 1, 2, 3,...N. For each Y rank, count the number of ranks below it which are larger. Then subtract the number of ranks below it which are smaller. The sum of this for each Y is C.

$$t = \frac{C}{\frac{1}{2} N (N - 1)}$$

$$\text{Standard Deviation} = \sqrt{\frac{2(2N + 5)}{9N(N - 1)}}$$

$$z = \frac{t}{\text{Standard Deviation}}$$

Correction for Ties:

$$t \text{ becomes} = \frac{C}{\sqrt{\left[\frac{1}{2} N (N - 1) - \sum T_x \right]\left[\frac{1}{2} N (N - 1) - \sum T_y \right]}}$$

$$T_x = \frac{t^2 - t}{2}$$ where t is the number of X observations tied for a given rank

$$T_y = \frac{t^2 - t}{2}$$ where t is the number of Y observations tied for a given rank

Kruskal-Wallis Test

k = number of groups

n_j = number of cases in jth group

$N = \sum n_j$, the number of cases in all groups combined

R_j = sum of ranks in the jth group

$$H = \frac{12}{N(N+1)} \sum_{j=1}^{k} \frac{R_j^2}{n_j} - 3(N+1)$$

Correction for Ties:

$$H \text{ becomes} = \frac{\dfrac{12}{N(N+1)} \displaystyle\sum_{j=1}^{k} \dfrac{R_j^2}{n_j} - 3(N+1)}{1 - \dfrac{\sum T}{N^3 - N}}$$

where $T = t^3 - t$ (where t is the number of tied observations in a tied group of scores) and $\sum T$ directs one to sum over all groups of ties.

Friedman Test

k = number of variables

N = number of rows

$R_i = \sum R$ for each column where R is the score ranked by row, $i = 1 \ldots k$

$$X_r^2 = \left[\frac{12}{N k (k+1)} \left[\sum R_i^2 \right] \right] - 3N(k+1)$$

Correction for Ties:

$$X_r^2 = \frac{12 \sum \left(R_i - N \left(\frac{k+1}{2} \right) \right)^2}{N k (k+1)} - \frac{\sum T}{k-1}$$

Functions and Operators

The following table lists all the functions and operators available in StatView. All of the functions are available when creating or editing a formula using the Formula dialog box. Some are also available in the Random Numbers and Series dialog boxes and when creating or editing a criteria. A complete definition for each function is available in the Hints window. To see a specific definition, select the function in the appropriate dialog box and display the Hints window.

Appendix B: Algorithms, Formulae and Functions

ArcCos(?)

ArcCosh(?)

ArcCot(?)

ArcCsc(?)

ArcSec(?)

ArcSin(?)

ArcSinh(?)

ArcTan(?)

ArcTanh(?)

Average(?, ...)

AverageIgnoreMissing,(?,...)

BinomialCoeffs

BoxCox(?, ?)

Ceil(?)

CoeffOfVariation(?, AllRows)

Combinations(?, ?)

Correlation(?, ?, AllRows)

Cos(?)

Cosh(?)

Cot(?)

Count(?, AllRows)

Covariance(?, ?, AllRows)

Csc(?)

CubicSeries(1, 0, 0, 1)

CumProduct(?)

CumSum(?)

CumSumSquares(?)

Date(?, ?, ?)

DateDifference(?, ?, ?)

Day(?)

DegToRad(?)

Difference(?,1,1)

Div(?, ?)

DotProduct(?, ?)

e

Erf(?)

ExponentialSeries(1)

Factorial(?)

false

FibonacciSeries

Floor(?)

GeometricMean(?, AllRows)

GeometricSeries(1, 2)

Groups(?, ...)

HarmonicMean(?, AllRows)

Hour(?)

if ? then ? else ?

IsMissing(?)

IsRowExcluded

IsRowIncluded

Lag(?,1)

LinearSeries(1, 1)

Ln(?)

Log(?)

LogB(?, ?)

LogOdds(?)

MAD(?, AllRows)

Maximum(?, AllRows)

Mean(?, AllRows)

Median(?, AllRows)

Minimum(?, AllRows)

Minute(?)

Mod(?, ?)

Mode(?, AllRows)

Month(?)

MovingAverage(?, ?)

Norm(?, AllRows)

NOT(?) or ¬(?)

NumberMissing(?, AllRows)

NumberOfRows

OneGroupChiSquare(?, ?, ?)

Percentages(?, AllRows)

Percentile(?, ?, AllRows)

Permutations(?, ?)

ProbBinomial(?, ?, ?)

ProbChiSquare(?, 1)

ProbF(?, 1, 1)

ProbNormal(?, 0, 1)

Probt(?, 1)

QuadraticSeries(1, 0, 1)

QuarticSeries(1, 0, 0, 0, 1)

RadToDeg(?)

RandomBeta(1, 1)

RandomBinomial(?, ?)

RandomChiSquare(1)

RandomExponential(1)

RandomF(1, 1)

RandomGamma(1)

RandomGaussian(0, 1)

RandomInclusion(?)

RandomNormal(0, 1)

RandomPoisson(1)

RandomT(1)

RandomUniform(0, 1)

RandomUniformInteger (?, ?)

Range(?, AllRows)

Rank(?, AllRows)

Remainder(?, ?)

ReturnF(?, 1, 1)

ReturnNormal(?, 0, 1)

ReturnT(?, 1)

Round(?)

RowNumber

Sec(?)

Second(?)

Sin(?)

Sinh(?)

Sqrt(?)

StandardDeviation(?, AllRows)

StandardError(?, AllRows)

StandardScores(?, AllRows)

Sum(?, …)

SumIgnoreMissing(?,…)

SumOfColumn(?, AllRows)

SumOfSquares(?, AllRows)

Tan(?)

Tanh(?)

Time(?, ?, ?)

TrimmedMean(?, ?, AllRows)

true

Trunc(?)

Variance(?, AllRows)

Weekday(?)

Year(?)

{..}

| ? |

≤? or <=? or =<?

≥? or >=? or =>?

π or ∏ or pi

(?)

(?:?)

(?:?]

+?

-?

<?

>?

? ^ ? or ? ** ?

? * ?

? + ?

? - ?

? / ? or ? ÷ ?

? < ?

? = ?

? > ?

? AND ?

? & ?

? ElementOf ?

? IS ?

? IS NOT ?

? OR ? or ? | ?

? XOR ?

? ≠ ? or ? <> ?

? ≤ ? or ? =< ? or ? <= ?

? ≥ ? or ? => ? or ? >= ?

[?:?)

[?:?]

Appendix

C

References and Sample Data

References

Afifi, A. and Azen, S. 1979. *Statistical Analysis: A Computer Oriented Approach.* Academic Press, New York.

Andrews, D.F., and Herzberg, A.M. (eds.). 1985. *Data: A collection of Problems from Many Fields for the Student and Research Worker.* Springer-Verlag, New York.

Bishop, Yvonne, M.M., Fienberg, Stephen E., and Holland, Paul W. 1975. *Discrete Multivariate Analysis: Theory and Practice.* M.I.T. Press, Cambridge, Mass., London.

Chambers, John M. Cleveland, William S. Kleiner, Beat Tukey, Paul A. 1983. *Graphical Methods for Data Analysis.* Wadsworth Statistics/Probability Series, Belmont, California.

Cleveland, William S. 1985. *The Elements of Graphing Data.* Wadsworth Advanced Book Program, Monterey, California.

Draper, N. and Smith, H. 1981. *Applied Regression Analysis.* 2nd ed. John Wiley & Sons, New York.

Everitt, B.S. 1977. *The Analysis of Contingency Tables.* Chapman and Hall Ltd., London.

Goodnight, J. H. 1979. "A Tutorial on the SWEEP Operator, " *The American Statistician*. 33. 149 - 158.

Hocking, R. R. 1985. *The Analysis of Linear Models*. Brooks/Cole, Monterey, California.

Hollander, M. and Wolfe, D. 1973. *Nonparametric Statistical Methods*. John Wiley & Sons, New York.

Kendall, M. and Stuart, A. 1977. *Volume 1: Advanced Theory of Statistics*. Charles Griffin & Company, London.

Kleinbaum, D.G. & Kupper, L.L. 1978. *Applied Regression Analysis and Other Multivariate Methods*. Duxbury Press, Wadsworth Publishing Company, Belmont, California.

Milliken, G. A. and Johnson, D. E. 1984. *Analysis of Messy Data Volume 1: Designed Experiments*. Lifetime Learning Publications, Belmont, California.

Montgomery, D. & Peck, E. 1982. *Introduction to Linear Regression Analysis*. John Wiley & Sons, New York.

Searle, S.R. 1971. *Linear Models*. John Wiley & Sons, New York.

Siegel, S. 1956. *Nonparametric Statistics for the Behavioral Sciences*. McGraw-Hill, New York.

Simpson, G.G., Roe, A. and Lewontin, R.C. 1960. *Quantitative Zoology*. revised ed. Harcourt, Brace & Co., New York.

Snedecor, G. and Cochran, W. 1980. *Statistical Methods*. Iowa State University Press, Ames, Iowa.

Sokal, Robert R. and Rohlf, F. James. 1981. *Biometry*. W. H. Freeman and Company, New York.

Winer, B. J. 1971. *Statistical Principles in Experimental Design*. McGraw-Hill, New York.

Factor Analysis

Armstrong, J.S. and Soelberg, P. 1968. *"On the Interpretation of Factor Analysis."* Psychological Bulletin. 70(5):361.

Bartlett, M.S. 1951. "A Further Note on Tests of Significance in Factor Analysis." *British Journal of Psychology*: 4(1):1.

Carroll, J.B. 1953. *"Approximating Simple Structure in Factor Analysis."* Psychometrika. 18:23.

Cattell, R.B. and Jaspers, J.A. 1967. "A General Plasmode (No. 30-10-5-2) for Factor Analytic Exercises and Research." *Multivariate Behavioral Research Monographs*. 67(3): 211.

Cattell, R.B. 1966. "The Scree Test for the Number of Factors." *Multivariate Behavioral Research*. 1(2):245.

Gorsuch, R. 1983. *Factor Analysis*. Lawrence Erlbaum Publishers, Hillsdale,N.J.

Guttman, L. 1954. "Some Necessary Conditions for Factor Analysis." *Psychometrika*. 19:149.

Harman, H. 1976. *Modern Factor Analysis*. 3rd ed. University of Chicago Press, Chicago.

Harris, C.W. 1962. "Some Rao-Guttman Relationships." *Psychometrika*. 27:247.

Harris,C.W. 1967. "On Factors and Factor Scores." *Psychometrika*. 32:363.

Hofmann, R.J. 1975. "Brief Report: On the Proportionate Contributions of Transformed Factors to Common Variance." *Multivariate Behavioral Research*. 10(4):507.

Hofmann, R.J. 1978. "Complexity and Simplicity as Objective Indices Descriptive of Factor Solutions." *Multivariate Behavioral Research*. 13(1):247.

Hofmann, R.J. "Indices Descriptive of Factor Complexity." *The Journal of Psychology*. 96:103, 107.

Hofmann, R.J. 1978. "The Orthotran Solution." *Multivariate Behavioral Research*. 13(1):99.

Hotelling, H. 1933. "Analysis of a Complex of Statistical Variables into Principal Components." *Journal of Educational Psychology*. 24: 417 and 498.

Kaiser, H.F. 1970. "A Second Generation Little Jiffy." *Psychometrika*. 35:401.

Kaiser, H.F. 1965. "Psychometric Approaches to Factor Analysis." *Proceedings of the 1964 Invitational Conference on Testing Problems*. Educational Testing Service, 37, Princeton, N.J.

Kaiser, H.F. 1958. "The Varimax Criterion for Varimax Rotation in Factor Analysis." *Psychometrika*. 23: 187.

Mulaik, S. 1972. *The Foundations of Factor Analysis*. McGraw Hill, New York.

Saunders, D.R. 1962. "Trans-Varimax." *American Psychologist*. 17:395.

Thurstone, L.L. 1947. *Multiple Factor Analysis*. University of Chicago Press, Chicago.

Timm, N. 1975. *Multivariate Analysis with Applications in Education and Psychology*. Brooks/Cole, New York.

Wilkenson, J.H. 1965. *The Algebraic Eigenvalue Problem*. Oxford University Press, London.

Sample Data

The following datasets are included in the Sample Data folder and used in this manual to illustrate the practical application of statistical concepts and demonstrate some of the features of StatView.

Boston Housing Data

The Boston Housing Data consists of 506 U.S. Census Housing Tracts in the Boston area, with measurements taken of the following variables:

Median Val.	Median Value of owner-occupied homes (in thousands)
Crime	Crime rate by town
Zone	% of residential land zoned for lots greater than 25,000 sq. ft.
Industry	Percent of non-retail business acres by town
Charles	Near if the tract is on Charles River; Far if it is not
NOX	Nitrogen oxide concentration, parts per billion
Rooms	Average number of rooms in owner units
Bef. 1940	Percent of owner units built before 1940
Dist. Empl.	Weighted distance to five employment centers
Highways	Index of accessibility to radial highways
Tax Rate	Full property tax rate ($ per $10,000)
Pupil/Teacher	Pupil/Teacher ratio by town school district
Low status	Percent of lower status population

The data comes from *Regression Diagnostics* by Belsley, Kuh & Welch, published by John Wiley & Sons. They cite the following paper as a source: Harrison, D. and D.L.

Rubinfeld(1978),"Hedonic Prices and the Demand for Clean Air," *Journal of Environmental Economics and Management*, 5, 81-102.

Car Data

Car Data was developed from a variety of sources by Abacus Concepts, Inc. The information includes measurements of weight, gas tank size, turning circle, horsepower and engine displacement for cars from Europe, the United States and Japan.

Eight Physical Variables Data

The Eight Physical Variables dataset is a correlation matrix derived from data in Harmon, *Modern Factor Analysis*, © 1967, University of Chicago Press, Chicago, Illinois. Measurements were taken of eight different physical parameters: height, arm span, forearm length, lower leg length, weight, bitrochanteric diameter, chest girth and chest width.

Lipid Data

Lipid Data was provided by Dr. Terence T. Kuske, Professor of Medicine and Associate Dean for Curriculum, Medical College of Georgia, Augusta, GA. The data is blood lipid screenings of medical students at the college. Blood lipid levels and cardiovascular risk factors (cigarette smoking, hypertension, family history of coronary heart disease) are evaluated in students as freshman and later when they are seniors.

Lipids include cholesterol and triglycerides and their lipoprotein carriers in blood, very low, low and high density lipoproteins (VLDL, LDL and HDL). Cardiovascular risk is increased proportional to all these parameters except for an inverse relationship to HDL cholesterol. This study measures cholesterol, triglycerides and HDL cholesterol. A factor allows an estimate of VLDL cholesterol from the triglycerides Value. Subtraction of VLDL and HDL cholesterol from total cholesterol yields a calculated LDL cholesterol value.

Healthy values for adults are:

< 200 mg/dl	Total cholesterol
< 130 mg/dl	LDL cholesterol
> 50 mg/dl	HDL cholesterol
< 150 mg	Triglycerides

Opera Data

The Opera Data was invented for the purpose of illustrating functional aspects of this program. The simulated data is as follows: The weight of eighty opera singers was measured. The eighty singers represents ten right-handed and ten left-handed singers for each of four parts (soprano, alto, tenor and bass). The eight variables in the resulting dataset are:

LHS	left-handed sopranos	RHS	right-handed sopranos
LHA	left-handed altos	RHA	right-handed altos
LHT	left-handed tenors	RHT	right-handed tenors
LHB	left-handed basses	RHB	right-handed basses

Teaching Effectiveness Data

This data was invented for purposes of illustrating functional aspects of this program. The simulated experiment is as follows: A study involving industrial health tests the effectiveness of two teaching techniques for the use of a respirator mask. Subjects are divided randomly into three groups: a control group, which receives no training in the use of the mask; a group which receives a detailed instruction sheet on the use of the mask; and a third group which attends a 30 minute class discussing the use of the mask. The effectiveness of the mask, as measured by the amount of particulate matter which passed through the filter mask during a fixed task, is measured for each of the subjects before training, and then one and two weeks after training. (Lower scores indicate increased effectiveness.) The first column of the dataset represents the categories of teaching technique: the control, instructions and lecture. The three remaining variables represent the measure of effectiveness for the mask at 0, 1 and 2 weeks.

Tree Data

This data is a fragment of data published in *Data: A Collection of Problems from Many Fields for the Student and Research Worker*, edited by D.F. Andrews and A.M. Herzberg, published in New York by Springer-Verlag, 1985. The data was published with the permission of the director of the East Malling Research Station, contributed by S.C. Pearce at the University of Kent at Canterbury.

This data was collected to determine whether apple trees propagated asexually were smaller than those that reproduced by seed. Nine kinds of asexually reproduced root-stocks from all over Europe were collected in 1913 and labeled I to IX. Later, seven root-stocks raised from seed in Germany were added and numbered X to XVI. A clone was raised from each of these sixteen sources. Trees of the scion, the upper part of the plant that determines the main characteristics of the fruit and leaves, were grafted on root-stocks from these clones.

In the winter of 1933-34 a number of these trees were removed to make more room. The data presented came from 104 trees, eight on each of thirteen kinds of root-stock. At that stage, no trees on root-stocks VIII, XI and XIV were removed; therefore no data are available for them. Measurements included weight and trunk girth.

Western States Rated Data

This dataset is taken from the *Places Rated Almanac*, by Richard Boyer and David Savageau, copyrighted and published by Rand McNally. The data are reproduced by permission of the publisher, with the request that the copyright notice of Rand McNally, and the names of the authors appear in any paper or presentation using these data.

Fifty-two western cities were rated on nine criteria to determine the most desirable place to live. For all but two of the variables, the higher the score, the better. For Housing and Crime, a lower score is better. The scores are computed taking into account a variety of component statistics for each variable.

Wine Tasting Data

This data was collect from a wine tasting conducted at Abacus Concepts, Inc. in which fifteen staff members rated six different California Zinfandel wines. Each wine was rated using several criteria commonly used in the wine trade to judge wine quality. The totals for each judge and wine were calculated. The first column contains the judges' names. The remaining six columns contain the total scores for each wine. The wines are named by the color of their labels to preserve objectivity.

Suggested Reading

Belsey, David A., Kuh, Edwin, Welsch, Roy E. 1980. *Regression Diagnostics: Identifying Influential Data and Sources of Collinearity*. Wiley, New York.

Bock, Richard Darrell. 1975. *Multivariate Statistical Methods in Behavioral Research*. McGraw-Hill, New York.

Freedman, D., Pisani, R., and Purves, R. 1978. *Statistics*. W. W. Norton & Company, New York.

Johnston, John. 1984. *Econometric Methods*. 3rd ed. McGraw-Hill, New York.

Lehmann, E.L. 1975. *Nonparametrics: Statistical Methods Based on Ranks*. Holden-Day, San Francisco; McGraw-Hill, New York.

Appendix C: References and Sample Data

Snedecor, George W. and Cochran, William G. 1989. *Statistical Methods*. Iowa State University Press, Ames. Iowa.

Steel, Robert G. D. and Torrie, James H. 1980. *Principles and Procedures of Statistics: a Biometrical Approach*. McGraw-Hill, New York .

Glossary

alphanumeric data: Data which contains both letters and numerals; a mixture of words and numbers. This data is handled differently during importing.

argument: A value on which a function operates. The arguments to a function can be constants, column names or formulas.

attribute pane: The pull-down pane in a dataset in which you set and change variable attributes (type, source, class, format, decimal places). This pane also displays twelve descriptive and summary statistics on the data.

bivariate graph: A graph which plots the relationship between an X and Y variable. Can be displayed as a scattergram or line chart. (See also univariate graph.)

browser: An index pane from which you select and use variables, analyses, or results. The variables browser lists all the variables in a dataset, the analysis browser lists all analyses in a group, the results browser lists all results in a view.

category: An association between the values of a nominal variable and a set of group labels. A category differs from a set of group labels in that it must be predefined, it can be applied to more than one variable and its values are limited to its group labels. A category can be used with variables, for recoding, and for defining a compact variable, and stored in the StatView library for use with other datasets.

category variable: A nominal variable which can only have the values defined by the groups of its associated category. (See also category and data class).

cell: A subset of your data. Specifically, the intersection of the groups in your data when several nominal variables are considered. A cell is defined by the group labels of the nominal variables. Multiply the number of distinct group labels in all nominal variables to get the maximum number of cells in the resulting analysis.

cell plot: A plot which compares the means or sums of related variables or groups. You can depict data as bar charts (often referred to as side-by-side bar charts), line charts, or point charts to visually compare variable to variable and group to group.

class: A setting in the attribute pane. See data class.

collinearity: A strong relationship between independent variables in a regression that makes it impossible to discern their individual effect on a dependent variable.

compact variable: An alternative to entering each observation's group label in a column, a compact variable is a way to use individual columns to identify the groups of a nominal variable. Created by selecting the columns and clicking the Compact button in the dataset or the variable browser. In a compact variable, all the data in a column must belong to the same group. This structure is required to define the within factor of a repeated measures model. (See also nominal variable).

confidence interval: A range of values such that there is a known probability that the true value of some quantity lies within that range. This probability is known as the confidence level, and must be stated before the confidence interval is calculated. For example, the 95% confidence interval for a mean represents a range of values within which we expect to find the true value of the mean 95% of the time.

continuous selection: Selection (using the mouse) of cells, rows, columns or elements that are next to each other. Selected by clicking the first item and then dragging the mouse to the last item.

continuous (data): One of three possible classes of data in StatView. Continuous data can assume any numerical value over a given interval. For example data that describes a person's weight or height is continuous (See also nominal data).

continuous variable: Data that assumes any numerical value over a given interval. An analysis determines that a variable is continuous by looking at its data class.

criteria: Rules for selective inclusion or exclusion of subsets of data from analysis. Criteria are defined by choosing Create Criteria from the Manage menu.

data class: A characteristic assigned to a variable to indicates whether an analysis uses its data as continuous, nominal or informative. Data class is set in the attribute pane of the dataset.

data format: A setting in the attribute pane, governing the display options for real, date/time and currency data.

data type: A setting in the attribute pane, governing the data that can be entered in a column. The types are: integer, long integer, real, date/time, currency, string and category.

dataset: A file window containing a row and column arrangement of data. Variables are in vertical columns and individual cases are in horizontal rows.

degrees of freedom: When you are dealing with a model, the total number of degrees of freedom is determined by the number of observations in your data. As your model becomes more complicated (as you specify more parameters), you allocate more degrees of freedom to the model, leaving fewer degrees of freedom with which to estimate the variability in the data. (Each parameter you specify for your model shifts one degree of freedom from error to model.) The more degrees of freedom you have to estimate the variability, the more powerful the statistical test is, ie., the more able it is to detect differences when they are present. When you are dealing with a distribution, the number of degrees of freedom differentiate between different members of a family of distributions.

directory dialog box: A standard Macintosh dialog box that allows you to open and save a file or otherwise gain access to the hierarchy of files and folders on your disk.

dynamic formula: A characteristic of a variable (visible in the attribute pane as "source") created using the Formula or Recode commands. The variable automatically updates when any variable on which it is based changes.

eigenvalue: A value of lambda (λ) for which $Ax = \lambda^* x$, for $x \neq 0$; where A is a square matrix and x is a vector. Each eigenvalue is associated with a corresponding eigenvector. The eigenvectors corresponding to large eigenvalues are usually the most useful.

eigenvector: A vector $x \neq 0$ for which $Ax = \lambda^* x$, where A is a square matrix & lambda is an eigenvalue of A. The eigenvectors of a correlation matrix are useful in determining which variables explain the variability seen in a dataset.

error bar: The extension of a single point on a graph to reflect the confidence interval of the quantity being estimated.

excluded row: A row of a dataset that has been selectively removed or excluded from an analysis. When a row is excluded, its row number appears dimmed and its values are not used in calculations. (See also included row.)

fitted value: The values of the dependent variable generated by a regression equation when you calculate it using the values of the independent variables in your data. (See also predicted values.)

frequency plots: Graphical displays of the frequency distribution of a variable. the frequency plots produced by StatView are histograms (regular and z-score) and pie charts.

grid lines: Lines that run across a graph perpendicular to an axis and mark the major and minor intervals along the axis. Grid lines correspond to tick marks. (See also tick marks.)

group: A subdivision of a dataset based on the related but distinct values of a nominal variable. All observations with the same value for the nominal variable are said to be

Glossary

in the same group. For example, a nominal variable describing a person's gender divides the data into two groups: male and female.

group label: A name that identifies the distinct groups of a nominal variable. A label is also used to identify the groups of a category.

grouping variable: A nominal variable which has a distinct value for each group in the dataset and thereby identifies the different groups in the data when the variable is used in an analysis.

histogram: A bar chart that plots the distribution of a variable.

hypothesized value: A value you suspect a particular statistic to have in the population you are studying. You can construct a hypothesis test to see if your hypothesized value is reasonable considering the data you collected.

included row: A row in a dataset included in an analysis. All rows are included by default; any row(s) can be selectively excluded and included again. If a row is included, its values are used in calculations. (See also excluded row).

informative (data): One of three possible classes of data in StatView. Only string variables can be informative. An informative variable is used for identification purposes only and is not available for analysis. A column containing the names of patients in a study is an example of informative data.

input column: An empty column which always appears (dimmed) at the right end of a dataset. As soon as you enter data or change the attribute pane for the input column it becomes a part of the dataset and a new input column is added to its right.

input row: An empty row at the bottom of a dataset for entering additional data. As soon as you enter data in the input row it becomes a part of the dataset and a new input row is added below it.

library: See **StatView library**.

missing cell: An intersection of the groups in combined nominal variables for which there is no data. You get missing cells in your data when one of the combinations of groups among the nominal variables does not exist in the data.

missing values: Squares in the grid of the dataset which contain no data, either because no data was entered, or due to StatView's translation of data during importing. A missing value is represented by either a • (option - 8) or a . (period).

nominal (data): One of three possible classes of data in StatView. Nominal data is used to identify which group an observation belongs to. For example, data that describes a person's gender is nominal and identifies each observation as belonging to one of two groups: male or female (see also continuous data).

nominal variable: A nominal variable divides data into groups, in contrast to a continuous variable which identifies a range of values. Analyses treat data differently depending on whether a variable is nominal or continuous. (See also data class).

nonparametric: Statistical procedures which make less restrictive assumptions about the population(s) from which the data were sampled.

null hypothesis: A statement that a quantity has a particular value, or that several quantities are equal. The null hypothesis is the statement you are evaluating through your analysis of the data. It provides a basis for hypothesizing a known distribution for a statistic. You compare an observed value to the hypothesized value to see if the data supports the null hypothesis. If the test statistic seems unreasonable under the assumption of the null hypothesis, you can reject the null hypothesis in favor of some alternative, usually a statement which is the opposite of the null hypothesis. For example, the null hypothesis for an unpaired t-test is that there is no difference between the means of the two groups you are comparing. So, a rejection of the null hypothesis means that these two groups are different; the means of the measurements are different.

old StatView format: The file format for StatView files created by all versions of StatView II, StatView SE+ Graphics and StatView 512+. StatView 4.x can read and write files in this format to maintain compatibility between StatView applications.

one-sided test: A statistical test which considers the possibility of change or difference in only one direction. For example, a test of the hypothesis that one mean is equal to another mean versus an alternative hypothesis that the first mean is greater than the other mean. This is in opposition to the two-sided test which has an alternative hypothesis that the means are simply not equal. One-sided tests should only be performed when you have secure knowledge that a change in the other direction is physically impossible. The option to perform a one-sided test is available in the one sample inference, paired comparison and unpaired comparison.

p-value: A value indicating the likelihood that the data used to carry out a statistical test would occur under a specified hypothesis. A p-value represents the probability that a statistic would have a value at least as extreme as the one observed, assuming the hypothesis in question is true. Thus, with a low p-value (less than 0.05, for example) it is unlikely that the hypothesis is reasonable; similarly a high p-value indicates that the data does not contradict the null hypothesis. A low p-value leads you to reject the null hypothesis. (See also unpaired t-test.)

paired comparison: A comparison of two variables, both measured on each of several subjects.

pica: A unit of approximately 1/6 of an inch used in measuring typographical material.

population: The collection of all possible units similar to the ones you are studying. The population is usually the group to which you extend your results after your analysis is performed. A sample is a subset of a population.

predicted values: The values of the dependent variable predicted by a regression equation using independent variable values not contained in the original data.

raw data: Raw data consists of the information originally obtained from a test, experiment or survey, before it has been summarized or condensed by any method.

recode: To describe any change in the representation of a variable's values by recoding continuous values to levels of a category or substituting computed values to replace missing values.

regression line: The graphic depiction of a regression equation, with the independent variable plotted on the vertical axis and the dependent variable plotted on the horizontal axis.

residual: The difference between the predicted value of the dependent variable in a regression and its actual value. (See also predicted value.)

sample: The specific collection of units from which a dataset is derived. The units of a sample are usually a subset of the population.

scattergram: A graph that represents data points as unconnected marks or dots.

significance level: A preset value, expressed as a probability between zero and one (p-value), used as a cutoff value in determining whether to reject a null hypothesis. Essentially, the significance level is an estimate of how often you will err by rejecting a hypothesis which is in fact true. A common significance level is 0.05, which means you are willing to be wrong one out of twenty times (1/20 = 0.05) when you reject the null hypothesis.

sort: A command in the Manage menu which reorders rows in a dataset by arranging the values in one or more columns in ascending or descending order.

split-by: The process of analyzing different subgroups of your data.

split-by variable: A nominal variable which causes the analysis to be performed for each group of the nominal variable. If an analysis has been assigned more than one split-by variable, the analysis is performed for each cell defined by the combination of the groups of the nominal variables.

static formula: A characteristic of a variable (visible in the attribute pane as "source") created using the Formula, Series or Recode commands. The variable retains the formula definition but does not update when any variable on which it is based changes. Changing a column from dynamic formula to static formula is the suggested way to control recalculation of computed columns.

StatView 4.x: Notation referring to all versions of StatView which begin with the numeral four. Thus, 4.0, 4.01, 4.2, etc. are all included in the term 4.x.

StatView library: A file created by StatView which contains category definitions as well as preference settings for the program.

string: A data type consisting of alphanumeric data.

tail: The extreme region of a distribution curve for a particular variable or statistic. If there are extreme values spread out over a large range, the distribution has long tails. The upper tail of a distribution refers to extremely large values; the lower tail refers to extremely small values.

template: A view window blueprint which specifies all analysis parameters, the structure of data required for the analyses and any formatting characteristics of graphs, tables and drawn objects. A template can be applied to any dataset and used by itself or as a part of an existing view.

tick marks: Short lines perpendicular to the axis of a graph, overlapping the axis and marking major and minor intervals. Tick marks correspond to grid lines. (See also grid lines.)

type: A setting in the attribute pane. See data type.

univariate graph: A graph that presents one-dimensional data, with only a Y axis. Each individual observation is plotted. (See also bivariate graph.)

unpaired comparison: A comparison of the measurements of two distinct groups of equal or unequal size.

user-entered (column): A variable created by entering data into a dataset. Changing a dynamic or static formula variable to user-entered retains the data, but causes all formula information to be lost.

variable browser: A floating panel visible in both the dataset and the view that displays all the variables in any dataset, one dataset at a time. This is the list from which variables are chosen and assigned to analyses.

view: One of the two windows in StatView. The view contains lists of analyses and variables, and is the document in which all results and graphics are displayed. (See also template.)

Index

Index

Index

Index